Retail Merchandising

Second Edition

Ernest H. Risch

Marian College of Fond du Lac

Macmillan Publishing Company
New York

Collier Macmillan Canada, Inc.
Toronto

Maxwell Macmillan International Publishing Group
New York   Oxford   Singapore   Sydney

Editor-in-Chief: David Boelio
Production Editor: Constantina Geldis
Cover Designer: Brian Deep

This book was set in Garamond.

Copyright © 1991 by Macmillan Publishing Company,
a division of Macmillan, Inc.

Previous edition copyrighted 1987 by Merrill Publishing
Company.

Printed in the United States of America

Macmillan Publishing Company
866 Third Avenue, New York, New York 10022

Collier Macmillan Canada, Inc.

Library of Congress Cataloguing-in-Publication Data
Risch, Ernest H.
    Retail merchandising / Ernest H. Risch.—2nd ed.
        p.   cm.
    Includes index.
    ISBN 0-675-21277-4
    1. Retail trade.   2. Merchandising.   I. Title.
HF5429.R55   1991
    658.8'7—dc20   90-42696
                                                     CIP

Printing: 1 2 3 4 5 6 7 8 9   Year: 1 2 3 4

Macmillan Series in College Marketing

Bagozzi
PRINCIPLES OF MARKETING MANAGEMENT

Beisel
CONTEMPORARY RETAILING

Berman and Evans
RETAIL MANAGEMENT, Fourth Edition

Bowersox, Closs, and Helferich
LOGISTICAL MANAGEMENT, Third Edition

Chapman and Bradley
DYNAMIC RETAILING, Second Edition

Cohen
THE PRACTICE OF MARKETING MANAGEMENT, Second Edition

Douglas
WRITING FOR PUBLIC RELATIONS

Etzel and Woodside
CASES IN RETAILING STRATEGY

Evans and Berman
MARKETING, Fourth Edition

Evans and Berman
PRINCIPLES OF MARKETING, Second Edition

Galloway, Evans, and Berman
PAINTCO III: A COMPUTERIZED MARKETING SIMULATION

Greer
CASES IN MARKETING, Fifth Edition

Hair, Anderson, and Tatham
MULTIVARIATE DATA ANALYSIS, Second Edition

Hartley
SALES MANAGEMENT

Hise and McDaniel
CASES IN MARKETING STRATEGY

Hisrich and Peters
MARKETING DECISIONS FOR NEW AND MATURE PRODUCTS, Second Edition

Horton
BUYER BEHAVIOR

Johnson and Wood
CONTEMPORARY LOGISTICS, Fourth Edition

Katzenstein and Sachs
DIRECT MARKETING

Kincaid
PROMOTION: PRODUCTS, SERVICES, AND IDEAS, Second Edition

Lewison
RETAILING, Fourth Edition

Lewison
ESSENTIALS OF RETAILING

Lewison and Hawes
CASES IN RETAIL MANAGEMENT

Lill
SELLING: THE PROFESSION

Morris
INDUSTRIAL AND ORGANIZATIONAL MARKETING

Mowen
CONSUMER BEHAVIOR, Second Edition

O'Connor
PERSONAL SELLING

Olszewski
PRODUCT PURSUIT

Onkvisit and Shaw
INTERNATIONAL MARKETING

Risch
RETAIL MERCHANDISING, Second Edition

Runyon
ADVERTISING, Second Edition

Runyon and Stewart
CONSUMER BEHAVIOR, Third Edition

Scheuing
NEW PRODUCT MANAGEMENT

Seitel
PRACTICE OF PUBLIC RELATIONS, Fourth Edition

Soldow and Thomas
PROFESSIONAL SELLING: AN INTERPERSONAL PERSPECTIVE

Tull and Hawkins
MARKETING RESEARCH, Fifth Edition

Tull and Kahle
MARKETING MANAGEMENT

Weeks, Perenchio, Miller, and Metcalf
MERCHANDISING MATHEMATICS

Weilbacher
CASES IN ADVERTISING

Weilbacher
MARKETING MANAGEMENT CASES, Fourth Edition

Wood and Johnson
CONTEMPORARY TRANSPORTATION, Third Edition

Preface

In a very real sense, *Retail Merchandising* represents a genuine departure from the standard merchandising texts currently available. It acknowledges that the activities of retail merchandising are essentially a product of a series of philosophical concepts, all directed toward the ultimate marketing objective: the *profitable* satisfaction of customers' requirements. It also recognizes the fact that the economic progress of the human race has historically depended upon the expansion of trade and commerce, always with the objective of realizing a profit in the *retail* marketplace. Thus, the philosophical concepts inherent in the dynamics of retail merchandising represent the pillars that support the entire capitalistic system of a free-market economy. The success of this system is entirely dependent upon the ability of the retail merchant to earn a fair return on capital investment and, at the same time, satisfy the constantly changing requirements of the marketplace.

A fair profit is the only justification for the existence of any retail system, yet this profit must never be an end unto itself. Profit must be viewed as a by-product of efficient planning and the application of sound merchandising tactics and strategies. This, in turn, implies a thorough grounding in merchandising theory. The traditional talent for having a keen "nose" for merchandising will no longer suffice in the dynamics of the modern retail marketplace. Thus, one of the prime requisites of large-scale retailing is a well-educated, skillful buyer who understands and implements the accepted techniques of using capital to the best advantage, so as to build balanced stocks and to contribute departmental profit consistent with the investment of space, time, and money.

Because retail merchandising is the only business activity that deals directly with the ultimate consumer, it stands unique and apart from other commercial and industrial establishments. The retail industry exhibits the following qualities that govern the formation of merchandising theory and its manifestation in terms of strategic planning and tactical control:

1. The volatile nature of the retail inventory, the merchant's single largest asset:
   a. Seasonal dollar value can fluctuate as much as 30% from the average dollar value.

b. The heterogeneous composition of retail merchandising is constantly changing as new items are added and other items are dropped in response to consumer demand.

c. The composition of consumer-oriented products lends itself to both internal and external theft.

d. The effective functioning of the retail system necessitates the transfer of inventory custody, or control, into the hands of many individuals, all of whom are subject to the universal propensities of the human psyche. Human nature functions irrespective of defining titles; consider, for example, the effect of merchandise managers, buyers, salespersons, stock clerks, and delivery and housekeeping personnel on the integrity of retail inventories.

2. The relatively low dollar sales volume per retail transaction.

3. The service features of the business as demanded by the consumer.

4. The lack of a homogeneous inventory, which precludes the use of historical data as a guide for detailed planning.

5. The seasonal nature of the business dictates the profitability of merchandise, while the cost of the merchandise remains a constant liability.

6. The problem of establishing a retail price that will achieve a corporate-mandated gross margin across a diversity of classifications and selling departments.

7. The consumer's routine contact with the store and the resulting "retail image" are largely a product of rank-and-file employee activity, rather than the management authority and initiative behind those employees.

8. The merchandising function occurs simultaneously over a variety of different geographic locations, thus inherently posing a dilemma regarding the extent of centralized control versus decentralized autonomy.

9. Departmental margins of profits must be defined efficiently so as to absorb direct and overhead expense and yet provide net operating profit.

10. The extended hours of store operation economically dictate an increasing percentage of part-time employees.

11. Because of the labor-intensive nature of the retail industry and its obvious consumer orientation, government legislation in the areas of pricing, consumer protection, employment, and taxation particularly affect the merchandising strategies of any retail store.

These and other distinctive characteristics of the retail industry have necessitated unique operating procedures centering on the management and control of the merchant's single largest asset: retail inventory. Thus, this text is concerned with the theories and applications of merchandise planning and control, particularly as they relate to inventory management objectives and the enhancement of specific ratios of merchandising profitability.

While it is virtually impossible to separate merchandising theory from the mathematical application of that theory, the intent of this book is not meant to be an exercise in mathematical computation so much as to be an explanation of theory in the language of the retail merchant, that is, merchandising ratios. Retail merchandising is essentially an integrated series of theoretical concepts, of necessity expressed in terms of numbers, including dollars, turns, units, and percentages. Therefore, an understanding of the concepts is necessary to comprehend the mathematical data.

Retail Merchandising is designed as an upper-level text, and its use is predicated upon the assumption that the student is well versed in the basic principles of retailing and marketing. It is intended for those aspiring to entry-level management positions in the retail industry, to executive trainees, and to those practitioners of retail merchandising who wish to enhance their comprehension of the art and techniques of practical merchandising application. Therefore, the text is detail oriented, exposing serious students to an in-depth understanding of merchandising concepts, normally lightly treated or totally ignored. Also, while some concepts may not be relevant to a given merchandising situation—such as the cost method of inventory—they are presented as part of the general body of merchandising knowledge. Obviously, teachers and students alike are free to select only those topics that best fit a curriculum or the learning needs of individual students.

The major objective of this text is to equip the reader with the fundamentals of sound merchandising theory and the ability to mathematically translate that theory into the planning factors that govern the daily operations of a profitable retail enterprise.

To achieve that end, *Retail Merchandising* takes a realistic and pragmatic approach to the presentation of the subject matter.

First, it presents a new rationale for a deeper understanding of retail merchandising and its relationship to consumer behavior. This rationale, in turn, supports an innovative model of the retail merchandising concept. Second, the student is lead step by step through a hierarchy of merchandising concepts that culminate in the six-month merchandise plan and the resultant crux of the entire retail merchandising process: the planning and control of staple and model stocks. The final chapter takes the student outside the realm of the retail store into the area of vendor relations, where the "terms of the sale"—i.e., dating, discounts, and transportation arrangements—are analytically discussed and quantitatively defined. Third, the theoretical aspects of all merchandising concepts subject to mathematical expression are discussed in depth, including a specific quantitative explanation, so that theory is related to practical application. Each mathematical explanation is in turn followed by a series of application exercises designed to reinforce the students' comprehension of the concept at hand. Solutions to all problems are provided in the Instructor's Manual.

Fourth, each chapter ends with a sequence of open-ended, analytical discussion questions. Each inquiry is designed to elicit an original, management-type response, predicated upon the text material but augmented by the reader's rational and original thought processes. The intention of the questions is not to seek rote solutions but to stimulate alternative answers.

Finally, each chapter begins with definitions of key merchandising terms and specific learning objectives, all relevant to the subject matter of the chapter. It is anticipated that a general understanding of the terms discussed in each chapter will facilitate the integration of new concepts into the reader's progressively growing body of knowledge.

I wish to thank several reviewers for their helpful comments and suggestions: Holly Bastow-Shoop of North Dakota State University, Maryann Bohlinger of the Community College of Philadelphia, Leslie Davis of Utah State University, Susan Fiorito of the University of Iowa, and Kathryn Greenwood of Oklahoma State University.

Contents

Chapter 1
Introduction: The Nature of Retail Merchandising

Learning Objectives

- Define retail merchandising.

- Explain the relationship between retail merchandising objectives and corporate profitability.

- Explain the concept of matched parallelism.

- Explain the concept of the retail image.

- Define and explain the model of retail merchandising.

- Discuss the role of the retail merchant in the modification of social structure, including the retail merchant as an agent of change, as a societal gatekeeper, as an opinion leader, and as an innovator.

- Identify the function of retail merchandising in a free-market economic system.

Key Terms

Change Agent: One who influences others to conform with his or her patterns of activity.

Convenience: The minimal level of the financial, physical, and mental expenditure required to overcome the frictions of time, space, and pecuniary loss inherent in any retail transaction.

Cultural Symbols: The products of a society: the goods, services, ideas, knowledge, and institutions that social orders produce, consume, and utilize.

Environmental Influences: Consumer demographics, economic factors, ecological considerations, technological advances, political attitudes, and cultural values, all of which impinge upon and influence the activities of the retail merchant.

Five Rights of Retail Merchandising: The merchant's obligation to have the *right* merchandise in the *right* place, at the *right* time, in the *right* quantities, and at the *right* price.

Innovation: That which is perceived to be new and different.

Matched Parallelism: A matching of the merchant's offering of goods and services with the consumer's wants and expectations.

Merchandising: The profitable planning, acquisition, and distribution of an inventory.

Opinion Leader: One who influences the attitudes and actions of others.

Retail: The sale of commodities in small quantities to the consumer. Derived from a French verb, meaning to "cut up."

Retail Image: The consumer's perception of a retail store.

Retail Merchandising: The profitable planning, acquisition, and unit distribution of a retail inventory to the consumer.

Satisfaction of Effort: A sensation of pleasure derived from the satisfaction of a want: for the merchant, profit; for the consumer, the acquisition of cultural symbols.

Societal Gatekeeper: One who has the ability and power to influence the transfer of innovations from an external source into the social system.

1.1
Retail Merchandising Defined

Because the concept of retail merchandising has historically been defined in so many ways, it is not surprising to find a great deal of confusion as to its exact meaning. Therefore, before we discuss retail merchandising any further, we must establish what that term means.

The term *retail* means the sale of small quantities of commodities to the ultimate consumer, and it is derived from the old French verb *retailer,* meaning "to cut up." Within the context of retail merchandising, then, the adjective *retail,* refers to the acquisition and division of a large quantity of merchandise into smaller assortments, with the objective of profitable sale to the ultimate consumer. *How* this is accomplished is the function of retail merchandising, which now may be operationally defined as:

a management system of strategic planning and tactical control, directed toward the financial enhancement of an inventory and the profitable distribution of that inventory to the retail consumer.

The Goal and Objectives of Retail Merchandising

The primary goal of any retail merchandising system is to influence potential consumers to buy a particular merchandise assortment at a particular retail store. Retail merchandising aims, then, to influence not only what merchandise the consumer will purchase, but also where that transaction will take place.

In order to achieve this ultimate goal of a retail transaction, the merchant must meet these more immediate objectives:

1. Forecasting accurately what the store's customers will want and when they will want it and estimating how much they will need, in kinds of goods, qualities, styles, and prices.

2. Purchasing goods as economically as possible.

3. Conserving and manipulating capital by buying only those goods likely to sell well.

4. Using effective sales promotion, including advertising, display, and sales techniques that will induce customers to come to the store and purchase the available goods.

5. Building a permanent clientele and community goodwill.

Implicit within these five basic objectives is the merchant's obligation to have the right goods, in the right place, at the right time, in the right quantities, and at a price that will both stimulate the consumer to buy and compensate the merchant for the efforts in the planning, buying, and controlling process.

Merchandising Objectives and Corporate Profitability

The retail merchant must meet the above objectives in his or her effort to complete retail transactions. These objectives should not be confused with the retail merchant's effort to make a profit. The survival and growth of a retail store or corporation does depend on a sound return on the merchant's investment in inventory, but profit must be viewed as a long-term objective, as the by-product of the successful implementation of sound merchandising strategy and tactics. Profit should never be an end in itself. Indeed, the merchant must at times employ strategies and tactics that are not immediately profitable but in the long run serve to increase profit ratios and to strengthen the corporate retail structure.

For example, in order to enhance the image and increase the market share of the retail store, the merchant might aim for a substantial increase in sales volume, stimulated by a lower markon (the difference between the price the merchant paid and the price the consumer pays for the same item). The reduced gross margin and the probable increase in operating expenses due to higher stock turnovers could well produce profits substantially less than those that could have been achieved with a lesser sales volume. Consider also the retail store that attempts to modify its image by adding merchandise classifications; profits may be reduced considerably over the time span that the new lines take to reach their full potential. In each of the above cases, the retail merchant directed merchandising objectives toward the growth and establishment of the retail store, not immediate profitability; successful retail merchants hope that long-term profitability evolves from their current merchandising objectives.

1.2
The Concept of Retail Merchandising

Matched Parallelism

In its most elementary form, retail merchandising may be considered as a management system of organized group behavior. Young offers a comprehensive definition of a management system:

> A management system can be defined as the subsystem of the organization whose components consist of a subset of individuals (man to man) whose duties are to receive certain organizational problems (inputs) and thereupon to execute a set of activities (process) which will produce organizational solutions (output) for either increasing the value of return of the total organizational activity (satisfying) or for optimizing some function of the total organizational inputs and outputs.[1]

The typical large retail organization consists of some arrangement of six major subsystems, or divisions, each specifically charged with solving problems in the areas of merchandising, financial control, publicity, human resource management, branch stores, and operations.[2] Merchandising is the primary subsystem of the retail store; the other five divisions comprise the support services necessary not only to maintain the merchandising division but also to make the merchandise assortments seem even more convenient for the consumer by providing merchandise information, retail services, and store atmospherics.

---

[1]Stanley Young, *Management: A Systems Approach* (Glenview, Ill.: Scott, Foresman, 1966), 15.
[2]See Delbert J. Duncan, Stanley C. Hollander, and Ronald Savitt. *Modern Retailing Management: Basic Concepts and Practices* (Homewood, Ill.: Richard D. Irwin, 1983), 142–77.

As the major subdivision of the total retail system, the merchandising division is responsible for interpreting and processing incoming information so that it can formulate, explain, predict, and control the primary outputs of the retail corporation. This incoming information consists of the continual flow of the consumer's insatiable wants. These wants justify the existence of the entire system of retailing; however, it is the immediate function of the merchandising division to receive and analyze these "problems" and to execute a plan of action that will satisfy these wants. The problems are signals to the merchandising executive that some type of action is required; the merchant's response is to search the market and acquire and present a package of expectations that will satisfy the wants of the consumer. To the extent that the merchant's offering reduces wants and satisfies the consumer, the merchandising division has achieved its goal of matched parallelism.

Matched parallelism—the aligning of merchandise assortments and services with the wants of a defined group of consumers—is, therefore, the primary objective of all merchandising strategy and ensuing tactics.

Satisfaction of Effort

The ultimate goal of both the retail merchant and the consumer is "satisfaction of effort," a sensation of pleasure arising from the reduction of a want. The merchant's satisfaction of effort is the achievement of an immediate objective that will result in higher profit; the consumer's satisfaction of effort is the security and the reinforcement of self-image derived from acquiring additional goods and services. However, since these satisfactions are always perceptual in nature and thus short-lived, greed soon manifests itself as the insatiable want for "more;" merchants want more corporate profits, and consumers want more goods and services.

The role of convenience in the satisfaction of effort

Within the dynamics of retail merchandising, a transaction will take place only when the consumer perceives that the exchange of personal time, effort, and money for the merchant's offering of goods and services, is "convenient." In other words, if the merchant cannot create the perception of a convenient environment, a transaction will not occur. There are two reasons for this phenomenon. First, from a merchandising perspective, the customer is inherently lazy; the customer will tend to resist an expenditure of time, effort, and money unless the outlay is perceived to be self-enhancing. Second, in any affluent society, consumer behavior is motivated by "wants" rather than "needs." Needs are those requirements essential to the sustenance of life; if needs are not soon satisfied, the consumer will die! Wants, on the other hand, are any unnecessary requirements, the deprivation of which are not life threatening. Unlike true needs, wants are pleasure- and future-oriented and do not require immediate satisfaction. Thus, in any affluent society, the retail merchant generally caters to a lazy consumer with many wants and very few, if any, needs. There is a relationship between the consumer's awareness of a want and the amount of merchant-supplied convenience necessary to satisfy that want; as the consumer's awareness of a want increases, the demand for convenience necessarily decreases. Thus, the consummation of a retail transaction is entirely dependent upon the proper relationship between the intensity of the consumer's want and the degree of convenience offered by the retail merchant.

Figure 1.1 illustrates the transactional pattern produced by the inverse relationship of the customers' wants and their perception of convenience. As the intensity of want increases, the level of convenience necessary to consummate a transaction, T_1 through T_4, must decrease; conversely, as want intensity decreases, the role of convenience as a transaction facilitator must correspondingly increase.

The consumer psyche must perceive some level of convenience before a transaction can be consummated, particularly when shopping behavior is motivated by wants rather than needs. Thus, convenience is defined as the catalyst that unites and transforms merchandise, services, and consumer wants into matched parallelism. As a general principle, consumers will behave in whatever manner is most convenient for them.

A Model of Matched Parallelism

Figure 1.2 illustrates the model of matched parallelism. Consumer wants activate the system, and awareness of these wants prompts merchants to select from all available goods and services an assortment that they feel is theoretically compat-

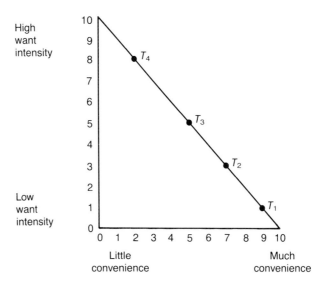

Figure 1.1 Convenience-want relationship

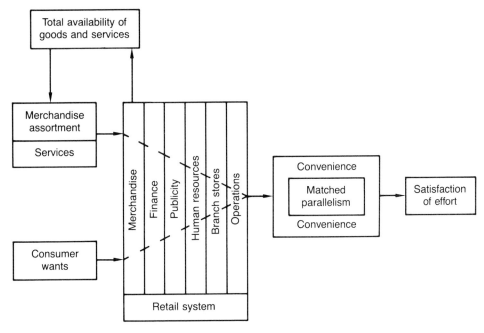

Figure 1.2 A model of matched parallelism

ible with those wants. Consumer wants and merchants' proposed solutions—the second set of inputs—are processed simultaneously by the various components of the retail system and hopefully synthesized, through the catalyst of convenience, into matched parallelism. This parallel alignment of consumer wants with an assortment of merchandise and services realizes the mutual goal of both merchant and consumer: satisfaction of effort.

The Retail Image

Consumers' perception of what is or is not convenient relies on their accumulated attitudes toward particular retail stores. Consumers would be hard pressed to explain why they prefer one store to another, but there is no doubt that they do. Their attitudes are based on emotion, not on logic or reason.

In essence, every retail store has its own atmosphere because of stimuli that its management chooses to present. The consumer will interpret these stimuli within an emotional framework. Such interpretation is imprinted upon the consumer psyche as an understanding of a retail store or, for lack of a better term, as the retail image. The retail image is the way a store is defined in the mind of the consumer, in terms of what the consumer sees as its function and how it makes the consumer feel. Since this retail image is perceived uniquely by each consumer, it cannot be defined more precisely.

The concept of image may be viewed from either the merchant's or the consumer's perspective. The merchant would define the retail image as the summation of the store's projected characteristics, while the consumer's response to those projected characteristics is learned through experience and is thus perceptually grounded and emotionally defined. Because the single most valuable asset that the retail merchant possesses is a clear, sharp image, this dichotomy implies two concepts of vital importance to the retail merchant:

1. A store has no image, and thus perceptually does not exist, until it communicates with the consumer by means of its promotional strategy.

2. The projection of the store's characteristics may not be perceived by the consumer as the merchant originally intended, thus creating a distorted or fuzzy image that could lead to financial disaster.

The Model of Retail Merchandising

Figure 1.3 depicts retail merchandising as an operating system composed of image, convenience, matched parallelism, and satisfaction of effort, all interacting, interrelated, and interdependent elements. This system functions within a larger macroenvironment that forms opportunities for, as well as threats to, the successful operation of the retail store.

Environmental Influences

Six major forces interact to form the macroenvironment of the retail store. These forces, while consistent in their presence, are inconsistent in nature; individually, they represent the collective manifestations of the human psyche, as it interacts with the perceptions of its physical environment. As a result, these forces are dynamic, constantly changing, and essentially without a rational definition of their genesis. Nevertheless, they exist as the primary determinants of merchandising strategy and the tactics that strategy dictates. Briefly, these environmental influences consist of customer demographics, economic factors, ecological considerations, technological advances, political attitudes, and cultural values.

Because these forces essentially represent the innate tendencies of the human psyche to strive constantly toward security, comfort, pleasure, and self-enhancement, new trends, as evidence of these goals, constantly loom on the horizon. For example, consider the major emerging trends that are expected to affect retail merchandising well into the twenty-first century.[3]

---

[3]Jagdish N. Seth, "Emerging Trends for the Retailing Industry," *Journal of Retailing* 59 (Fall 1983): 6–17; Rodger D. Blackwell and W. Wayne Talarzyk, "Lifestyle Retailing: Competitive Strategies for the 1980's," *Journal of Retailing* 59 (Winter 1983): 7–27.

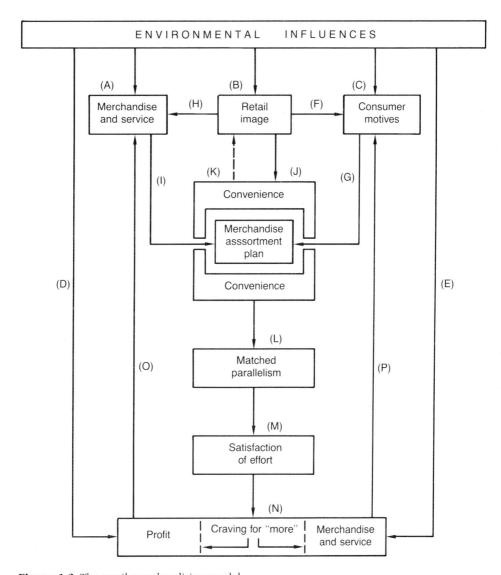

Figure 1.3 The retail merchandising model

1. The consumer's desire for premium products instead of value-oriented goods.

2. The predominance of want satisfaction over need requirements.

3. The nontraditional, dual-income household, whose individuals buy separately, not as a family.

4. The blending of home, workplace, and marketplace, with people shopping and working at home.

5. The expansion of the national specialty chains outstripping that of conventional department stores.[4]

6. The consumer's recognition of time scarcity—the short amount of time available for shopping—and the resulting need to prioritize shopping time.

Because these social and economic trends are evolutionary rather than revolutionary, they may go unnoticed by retail merchants, who are, too often, so busy "running the store" that they never fully plan long-term strategy. The day-to-day mechanics of merchandising operations are obviously important, but no more so than the awareness and comprehension of the changing environment in which the retail store must function.

Linkages A, B, C, D, and E in Figure 1.3 indicate that these environmental influences affect all the basic constructs of the retail merchandising model.

The Retail Image and System Inputs

A salient feature of the retail merchandising model is the position of the retail image; it is the intervening variable between merchandise and service (strategy) and consumer motives (patronage). The consumer's wants and the merchant's proposed fulfillment of those wants are the system's inputs. Their admission is determined by the retail image, because the image attracts only that sector of the consumer market interested in its characteristics (Linkage F): fashion level, price, quality, breadth and depth of the merchandise assortment, and other factors interpreted by the consumer psyche.[5] Thus, it screens out consumers who perceive from the image that that store is unable to satisfy their wants. Linkage G depicts those chosen consumer motives as the first inputs of the retail merchandise system. Linkage H represents the impact of the retail image on merchandise and service. The image, in effect, selects from a larger offering the merchandise and service that seem most profitable for the system and most appropriate for the consumer motives. Linkage I represents the second input of the system: those unique offerings of merchandise and services that manifest themselves as the tangible realities of the perceptual retail image (Linkage J), that is, the merchandise assortment plan within the framework of convenience. The broken Linkage K indicates that the merchandise assortment plan and its attendant elements of convenience, as perceived by the consumer, will either reinforce the intended image or modify it.

---

[4]David P. Schulz, "Planning for Expansion: Slower Growth," *Stores* (August 1984): 43–45.
[5]Robert F. Hartley, *Retailing: Challenge and Opportunity* (Boston: Houghton Mifflin, 1984), 107–8.

Matched Parallelism and Satisfaction of Effort

Merchandise and service, with convenience as the catalyst, unite with consumer motives to form matched parallelism (Linkage L) and its ensuing satisfaction of effort (Linkage M). However, because in our society satisfaction is of short duration, it is soon replaced by feelings of inadequacy, discontent, and a craving for more: more profit for the merchant and more goods and services for the consumer. This transition is indicated by Linkage N.

Linkages O and P represent the successful merchant and consumer, influenced by the same motive structure, striving for ever higher levels of achievement. Linkages D and E illustrate that although our craving for more may be innate, it is certainly enhanced by external environmental influences, especially those produced by a complex and highly varied socioeconomic environment.

The Essence of the Model

The essence of the model is that it is a mechanistic system, fundamentally driven by people's insatiable craving for more. The merchant is constantly striving for higher profit ratios and expanded profit dollars, while the consumer persistently seeks increased levels of self-enhancement and an ever higher standard of living.

This craving for more is simply a manifestation of greed—a rapacious desire for more goods, services, and money than one needs. However, from a marketing perspective, greed is not to be perceived in a negative light. Greed, obviously within controllable limits, is the driving force behind the success of any democratic, free-market economy, particularly those in North America and Western Europe.[6] Greed, again within limits, translates into consumption, and it is consumption that fuels the fires of industry and determines the success or failure of any retail store.

The concept of greed as a basic human drive is certainly not new. Over a quarter of a century ago, Maslow observed that

> The single holistic principle that binds together the multiplicity of human motives is the tendency for a new and higher need to emerge as the lower need fulfills itself by being sufficiently gratified. The child who is fortunate enough to grow normally . . . gets satiated and bored, . . . and eagerly . . . goes on to higher, more complex delights. . . . He wants to go on, to move, to grow.[7]

---

[6]William Safire, "In Defense of 'Greed': The Best Way to Help the Needy," *The Providence Journal Bulletin,* January 7, 1986, A-11.
[7]Abraham H. Maslow, *Toward a Psychology of Being* (Princeton: D. Van Nostrand, 1962), 178–79.

More recently, in a discussion of consumer behavior, Blum agreed, stating that

> After the period of happiness, excitement, and fulfillment comes the inevitable taking it all for granted and becoming restless for more! This statement is basic to understanding ourselves and others, whether we are consumers, retailers, or makers. In other words, asking the question, 'Why aren't they satisfied?' is futile most of the time. The answer is more. At the core of motivation is drive, fulfillment, and then more.[8]

Thus, while the concept of human greed may be readily apparent, its application to a model of retail merchandising is unique, in that it adds a new and human dimension to our understanding of merchandising tactics. From the perspective of retail management, we merchandise to a customer with insatiable wants, always seeking that which is new, different, and contributes something to the perception of unlimited self-enhancement. Why Jane bought her twenty-third pair of shoes, when she only has two feet, is a moot question; it is enough for us to know that she did—and more importantly, that she will soon add another pair to her already extensive collection. Of more immediate concern is this question, "How can the retail merchant assist Jane in her acquisition of more pairs of shoes and at the same time enhance the profit ratios derived from the sale of those shoes?" This is the essential question that the ensuing chapters will attempt to answer. But first, we must consider the social implications of retail merchandising.

1.3
The Societal Impact of Retail Merchandising

To consider retail merchandising solely at its most basic level, as a "planning and control function," is to oversimplify it and to ignore its complex supporting structures and its profound impact upon the socioeconomic fabric of our present-day culture. The activities of the retail merchant influence every facet of the consumer's daily living. Indeed, to a large extent, no consumer's cherished individuality of personality and life-style is unique; all are mere reflections of the set of cultural symbols that is in fashion at the time and that is transmitted by the retail merchandising system. In other words, consumers en masse are essentially whatever the retail merchant leads them to be and thus they are conformers rather than innovators.

As our society becomes more and more materialistic, demanding an ever higher standard of living and level of personal comfort, the role of the merchant is proportionately enhanced; none of the material symbols of this "good life" are

---

[8]Milton L. Blum, *Psychology and Consumer Affairs* (New York: Harper and Row, 1977), 37.

available to consumers unless retail merchants provide access to them. As Engel points out:

> Retailing is the final link in the process of moving goods from producer to consumer. It is for this reason that retailing places such heavy reliance on correct analysis of consumer behavior and is emphasized as a reason for consumer analysis. Regardless of how much value the manufacturer has built into the product, how well this value is communicated to the consumer, and how smoothly the production and physical distribution may be functioning, it is the retailer who either consummates or obstructs the sale.[9]

Because retail merchandising promotes fashion by providing styles consumers see as fashionable and serves as the single link between producers and consumers, it is a crucial factor in the distribution of cultural symbols and in the resulting changes in society.[10]

> Expressive (cultural) symbols are, in essence, the product of a society; they are the goods, services, ideas, knowledge, and institutions that are produced, consumed, and utilized within a given societal setting. In the present United States society, the vast majority of expressive symbols that are produced to be consumed by 'ultimate' (as opposed to 'industrial') consumers are distributed through and by retail organizations. Hence, retailers are the purveyors of expressive symbols, the manifestations of a material culture.[11]

The Role of the Retail Merchant in the Modification of Social Structure

The retail merchant diffuses popular culture in four ways:[12] as an agent of change, as a societal gatekeeper, as an opinion leader, and as an innovator.

The Retail Merchant as an Agent of Change

The primary objective of all merchandising strategy is to motivate a targeted segment of consumers to simultaneously adopt a particular merchandise assortment within the confines of a unique retail image. Thus, the retail merchant may be defined as an agent of change, as "a professional who purposefully and directly influences the innovation decision of others in a way that the change agent deems

---

[9]James F. Engel, Rodger D. Blackwell, and David T. Kollat, *Consumer Behavior,* 3rd ed. (Hinsdale, Ill.: Dryden Press, 1978), 11.
[10]Elizabeth C. Hirschman and Ronald W. Stampel, "Rules of Retailing in the Diffusion of Popular Culture: Microperspectives," *Journal of Retailing* (Spring 1980): 16–36.
[11]Ibid., 18.
[12]Ibid., 16–17.

desirable."[13] Since every change implies that the consumer has abandoned one thing and adopted another, the retail store must, in its self-interest, promote its own superiority and denigrate its competitors, which include not only other retail stores but also the now outdated fashions currently being promoted in them. Thus, the retail store can irresistibly attract the hedonistic nature of the human psyche, offering the consumer anticipated pleasure through the process of exchanging something old for something new, different, and exciting.

As an agent of change, the retail merchant is fundamentally charged with the responsibility of modifying consumer behavior to be consistent with the retail store's goals and objectives. However, because change is difficult for consumers to accept, the retail merchant, as the instigator of change, must through various tactics make it easier for the consumer to accept new cultural symbols. Therefore, the primary role of the retail merchant as an agent of change is to facilitate or assist the desire for change by intensifying the consumer's awareness of currently recognized wants or by creating an awareness of latent wants previously unrecognized by the consumer. The retail merchant contrasts what the consumer perceives as the ideal state of affairs with what the consumer sees as the actual—and deficient—state of affairs. The resulting discrepancy manifests itself in varying degrees of tension, and the consumer naturally tends to avoid the pain of tension. Seeking the path of least resistance and gravitating away from pain toward pleasure, the consumer, sooner or later, accepts the new cultural symbol, if for no other reason than to relieve this tension.

So the merchant, by creating pain through tension, facilitates the consumer's transition from the "old" to the "new," thus breaking down the inertia of tradition, experience, habit, and the status quo and making a unique contribution to the growth of materialism and hedonism in any given social order.

The Retail Merchant as a Societal Gatekeeper

Implicit within the concept of change is the notion of modification, or a small alteration, adjustment, or limitation. For the retail merchant, a "small alteration, adjustment, or limitation" applies to the selective distribution of cultural symbols throughout a materialistic and wanting society. The one who has the ability and the power to influence the transfer of innovations from an external source into the social system is referred to as a gatekeeper.

> True innovations or products that produce highly desirable social outcomes but only indirect individual benefit are not likely to be offered, since they would be of high risk when analyzed from a profit and gross margin point of view.[14]

---

[13]Ibid., 21.
[14]Hirschman and Stampel, "Roles of Retailing in the Diffusion of Popular Culture: Microprospectives," 35.

The merchandising division within the retail organization and its primary agent, the retail store buyer, perform this gatekeeping function. In essence, it is the retail buyer, working within corporate and creative limitations, who preselects for the consumer a limited offering of merchandise distilled from all the goods potentially available to that consumer. The buying agents of the retail merchandising system, by restricting the flow of innovations into the social system, are thus primarily responsible for the modification of societal mores and cultural values. Thus, the consumer's choice is limited to those items of merchandise and service that the retail buyer, in the guise of the consumer's official purchasing agent, allows to pass through the retail gate. And the only criterion for that passage is the enhancement of corporate profitability; the buyer's endorsement of any other standard would be absurdly stupid.

The Retail Merchant as an Opinion Leader

Opinion leadership is the process by which one person (the opinion leader) informally influences the actions or attitudes of others, who may be opinion seekers or merely opinion recipients; opinion leaders act not only as channels of information but also as a source of social pressure toward a particular choice and as the social support to reinforce that choice once it has been made.

Opinion leadership is, then, almost entirely the influence of interpersonal relationships on the individual's consumption behavior, but it can sometimes refer to the retail merchandising system's ability to modify consumer purchase decisions. In this sense, the retail organization exerts opinion leadership in two ways. First, as an active agent of change, it aggressively and deliberately attempts to influence the consumer's decision process. Second, the retail store passively influences the consumer's choices by disseminating product information through point-of-purchase advertising, visual merchandising, and sales personnel. The retail organization facilitates consumers' decisions by providing alternative products; these perceived options reduce the consumer's perception of risk.

The retail merchant serves as an opinion leader primarily by establishing criteria for evaluating products and services and their appropriate social usage. Because the consumer's perception of self-image and attendant life-style manifests itself in the need to shop for and acquire merchandise that is representative and supportive of that self-image, the consumer, as an opinion seeker, examines merchandise assortments in retail stores in order to learn about fashion trends and the product innovations that support them. A study conducted by Rich and Portis found that 30% of department- and discount-store shoppers said that one reason for their shopping trip was "seeking new items and getting new ideas." By exposing the consumer to a preselected assortment of product innovations, with all their implications for social adaptation and cultural modification, the retail merchant acts as an opinion leader for the consumer.

The Retail Merchant as an Innovator

An innovation may be defined as any concept, practice, or product that the targeted individual or group perceives to be new. The innovators of any one innovation are those members of society prepared to adopt the new product early in its diffusion and therefore without the personal or social support gained from discussions with prior users.

In the role of opinion leader, the retail merchant may also be an innovator, providing other retailers and potential consumers with information and at least tacit advice about products, concepts, and practices perceived to be new. Hirschman and Stampel state:

> One of the most fundamental roles, we believe, that may be performed by a retail organization in the diffusion of popular culture is that of innovator. . . . It is evident that retail organizations may function as innovators, to the extent that they purchase (adopt) products before these products have been adopted by other retail organizations. They may also innovate the creation of new institutional types that alter the popular cultural environment of a society at a point in time. . . . The product offering and institutional innovativeness of retailers, then, can be thought of as contributing, in a major way, to the operation of popular culture in a given society.[15]

Although we do not yet know how profoundly retail merchandising affects our social structures and cultural values, we do know that retail institutions play a more than casual role in reinforcing or modifying the cultural mores of the society in which they operate. By directly and purposefully influencing the innovative decisions of manufacturers and consumers, retail merchandising, in effect, defines the parameters of our social existence. For the most part, the cultural symbols through which we express our self-image and perceptually define our individuality are symbols accepted by all members of society. The retail merchant defines, provides, and encourages the acquisition of these symbols.

1.4
The Function of Retail Merchandising in a Free-Market Economic System

Figure 1.4 illustrates that a free-market system has four basic functional components: extraction, production, distribution, and consumption.

The extraction component is composed of the resource suppliers: the farmers, forestry workers, miners, fishermen, and others who "extract" raw materials from the earth. These materials are bought by manufacturers who give them form

---

[15]Hirschman and Stampel, "Roles of Retailing in the Diffusion of Popular Culture: Microprospectives," 33.

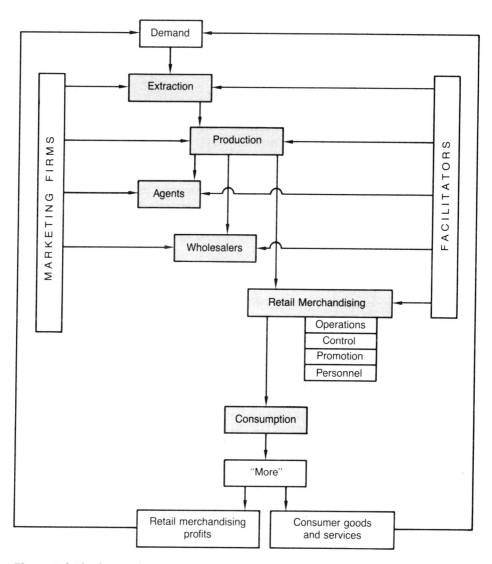

Figure 1.4 The free-market economic system

utility, converting them into the potential cultural symbols that have been de-signed to satisfy latent wants of the ultimate consumer. Distributors—buying agents, wholesalers, and retailers—purchase, ship, and store the goods. The key component of the system is consumption, the manifestation of the fundamental human craving for more, whether interpreted as corporate profit or as merchan-dise and services; thus, consumption only fuels the fires of greed and becomes the incessant demand that drives the system. Facilitators assist in the logistical and financial activities of the economic system and consist of such businesses as banks, transportation systems, insurance companies, and real estate companies. Marketing firms contribute to extraction, production, and distribution by identifying and promoting the seller's products to the proper markets; essentially advisors, they consist primarily of consulting firms, advertising agencies, and marketing research companies.

The Role of the Retail Merchant in the Marketing Channel

In effect, what Figure 1.4 illustrates is a marketing channel for consumer goods: a set of independent functions or organizations involved in the process of making a product or service available to the ultimate consumer.[16]

Note that the thrust of the model is forward, toward the retailer and the consumer, thus implying that the manufacturer is more concerned with the selling of goods than the merchant or consumer is with the buying of those goods. Normally, the vendor courts the retail buyer, just as the merchant attempts to gain the favor of the consumer. This is simply because the vendor's marketing mix does not align with the merchant's—ultimately the consumer's—buying mix: the vendor sells from a relatively homogeneous product line, whereas the merchant purchases an eclectic assortment of merchandise in order to maintain a heterogeneous inventory. Thus, the vendor's gain from a sale to the merchant tends to be relatively large; whereas, because of spatial limitations, the merchant's gain from selling that product to a consumer may be only the difference in profit between brand "X" and brand "Y." Also, the merchant is generally under no real constraint to purchase from one particular vendor because retail stores can easily substitute one product and brand for another, with little or no loss in operating profit.

Because of the structure of the retail store, its role in society, and its position in the marketing channel, the retail merchant is able to draw upon unique power sources to enhance its role as leader, relative to the other channel members. These sources of power are as follows:

> *Market proximity.* Because the retail merchant, not the manufacturer or the vendor, deals face to face with the consumer, suppliers must ask the merchant for primary market information. Thus, the merchant is the channel's gatekeeper of marketing information and is, as a result, the final arbiter of what passes through the channel to the ultimate consumer.

> *Local monopoly.* Within any given retail market area, the vendor's options are limited to the amount of available retail selling space, and it is the merchant who decides what products and brands will occupy that space.

---

[16]Paul S. Bush and Michael J. Houston, *Marketing: Strategic Foundations* (Homewood, Ill.: Richard D. Irwin, 1985), 454.

Thus, the merchant generally dominates the channel by simply filtering out those products that will be least likely to enhance profitability. The merchant can minimize loss by substituting products and brands, but the vendor's lost sale to the merchant represents revenue lost forever.

The retail image. Because consumers do not buy solely on the merits of the merchandise offering, but consider the whole retail image, the retail merchant, rather than the vendor, is the purveyor of cultural symbols. Major retail institutions with large and strong consumer franchises are a critical channel link to any vendor. And in the final analysis, the retail merchant still stands as the "societal gatekeeper."

Private labels. More and more frequently, retail merchants who want to carve out their own niche in the national-brands marketplace are developing private-label merchandise.[17] These private-label programs guarantee exclusivity in the merchandise offering, reinforce and differentiate the store image, and project and enhance profit margins. However, from the vendor's perspective, private labels further restrict the amount of available retail selling space and thus contribute to the competition for that space. This competition in turn provides the merchant with increasing power to dominate in the distribution channel by obtaining from the vendor such concessions as advertising allowances, favorable shipping terms, faster delivery schedules, increased cash discounts, and lower prices.

These sources of power will not always allow the retail merchant to dominate the marketing channel, however. To the extent that the vendor or manufacturer has developed a strong consumer franchise, grounded in long-term product acceptance and national advertising, the merchant's control over that vendor may be reduced or even negated. Consider, for example, the preeminent roles of Heinz ketchup, Reebok high-tops, and Kodak film in the marketing channel.

Topics for Discussion and Review

1. Discuss the essence of retail merchandising.
2. Why is the retail merchant defined as an "agent of change"?
3. Why might retail institutions be defined as "giant cultural sieves"?
4. How would you explain the role of the retail merchant as a contributing factor to the growth of materialism and hedonism in the social order?
5. In what sense is the retail merchant to be considered as an opinion leader?

---

[17]Penny Gill, "Private Label: Home Stores' Growing Tactic," *Stores* (September, 1985): 52–53, 55.

6. Discuss the concept of matched parallelism as it relates to consumption behavior and merchandising strategy.

7. What is meant by a "convenience-want" relationship?

8. Define the concept of the "retail image."

9. How would you generally explain the model of retail merchandising and specifically define the concepts inherent in the model?

10. If the retail merchant could truly satisfy the requirements of the consumer, what effect would this have on the theory of consumer behavior and the resulting model of retail merchandising?

11. Discuss the relationship between merchandising objectives and long-term profitability in the retail store.

12. Why is convenience an important concept in retail merchandising?

13. Why is the thrust of the marketing channel for consumer goods generally forward, toward the merchant and the consumer?

14. Why is the retail image just as important to the vendor as it is to the merchant? What effect does this image have upon the vendor?

15. Discuss each of the power sources available to the retail merchant. How do they tend to enhance the merchant's leadership capacity in the marketing channel?

16. What are two assumptions that support the concept of convenience?

17. Distinguish between the consumers "wants" and "needs."

18. Discuss why convenience must increase as the intensity of a want decreases.

19. Explain the concept of retailing.

20. In your own words, explain the concept of retail merchandising.

21. What does satisfaction of effort mean, and to whom does it apply?

22. Discuss the impact of environmental chance on merchandising strategy and tactics.

23. How does the retail image function to "screen" a store's clientele?

24. Why is the concept of greed so important to the success of a free-market economy?

25. Discuss the role of the retail merchant in the modification of social structure.

Chapter 2
The Components of Profit

Learning Objectives

- Discuss the nature of profit.

- Identify the components of profit.

- Explain the operating statement.

- Identify and explain the component parts of the operating statement in detail.

- Construct an operating statement down through operating profit.

Key Terms

Consignment Merchandise: Merchandise possessed by the merchant but owned by the vendor. Title to the merchandise transfers from the vendor to the merchant at the point of retail sale; any unsold merchandise is returned to the vendor and is treated as a credit to gross purchases.

Cost of Merchandise Sold: All costs involved in the sale of merchandise; determined by adding the billed cost of the merchandise, transportation costs, and alteration costs, less the amount of cash discounts earned.

Cost of Sales: The beginning inventory at cost plus net purchases, less the closing inventory at cost, minus cash discounts, plus alteration costs.

Earned Discounts: A percentage reduction in the billed cost of the merchandise granted by the vendor as a concession to the merchant for the payment of the invoice within a specified period of time.

Employee and Special Discounts: Discount privileges granted to store employees and specific social institutions, such as schools, churches, and civic and charitable organizations. Also referred to as sales discounts.

Gross Cost of Merchandise Sold: The difference between the total merchandise handled and the ending inventory.

Gross Margin: The difference between net sales and the total cost of merchandise sold.

Gross Sales: The summed total of merchandise and services sold over a particular period of time.

Inventory Shortage: Exists when the dollar value of the physical inventory is less than the book inventory.

List Price: The retail price listed by the vendor in a catalog, subject to trade and cash discounts.

Markdown: A reduction in the retail price of merchandise, expressed as a percentage. Markdowns include allowances and sales discounts, but not inventory shortages.

Markon: The difference between the billed cost price (before deductions of cash discounts) of the merchandise plus transportation costs and the first retail price at which it is offered for sale.

Net Alteration and Workroom Costs: The net cost of altering merchandise for customers and stock repairs.

Net Cost of Merchandise Sold: The gross cost of the merchandise sold less the cash discounts earned.

Net Other Income: That net income derived from nonretail sources which does not enter into the determination of operating income, such as investment income, and revenue derived from pay telephones, sale of waste materials, and the rental of unused real estate.

Net Profit: The operating profit plus net other income less income tax liabilities; the net income available for distribution, or surplus.

Net Sales: The initial basis for the calculation of all merchandising ratios except returns and allowances; determined by deducting returns, allowances, and sales discounts from the gross sales. The dollar amount of sales volume retained by the store.

Operating Expenses: All those expenses incurred in the normal buying, selling, and administrative functions of the retail store other than merchandise costs, or those costs incurred below gross margin.

Operating Profit: That profit derived from the primary function of the retail store, that is, the sale of merchandise; determined by the deduction of all operating expenses from gross margin.

Operating Statement: An analytical statement of profit or loss as the determinant of income and expenses applying to a specific accounting period, normally a year, season, or month.

Profit: Income after all merchandise costs, operating expenses, and taxes have been deducted from net sales.

Profit Mix: The emphasis placed upon the components of profit before taxes, that is, sales volume, the cost of sales, operating expenses, and net other income.

Profit Ratio: A dollar amount of profit expressed as percent of net sales.

Quantity Discount: A reduction in the cost of merchandise based on the size of the order.

Returns and Allowances: The sum of the merchandise returned to the store plus price concessions granted to the customer for some merchandising deficiency.

Sales Volume: The retail price times the number of units sold.

Total Cost of Merchandise Sold: The net cost of merchandise sold plus the net alteration and workroom costs.

Total Merchandise Handled: The sum of the beginning inventory and net purchases to date, including transportation.

Trade Discount: The discount allowed on a list or retail price before the consideration of credit terms; applies to any allowance granted without reference to the date of payment.

Transportation Inward: All freight charges paid by the store and not chargeable to the vendor.

2.1

The Nature of Profit

Retail merchandising is a service function in that it attempts to provide a merchandise offering of the right type, at the right time, at the right price, in the right quantities, and in the right place. In this sense, merchandising profits are simply the charges for the risk-bearing services rendered to the ultimate consumer; the merchant has an implied right to expect fair compensation for the marketing efforts expended in the buying, transportation, storage, financing, and promotion of the retail inventory. The survival and growth of the retail firm entirely depends upon profit; thus, profit is a socially desirable goal as long as our economic system of production and distribution is to continue as the prime satisfier of consumer needs and wants.

Profit, then, is simply the economic gain that the retail firm realizes over a measured period of time or the difference between net sales and the total expenditures required to produce those sales. Profit is a dollar figure, normally expressed as a percentage to, or a ratio of, net sales—that is, profit dollars divided by net sales. For example, a profit of $3,000 derived from a net sales of $60,000 is equivalent to 5% of that sales volume, or

$$\frac{\$3,000}{\$60,000} = .05 \times 100 = 5\%$$

Sales volume is the natural basis for the expression of all profit ratios, because sales, in the final analysis, is the ultimate determinant of all income and profit is simply the residue of sales, or the excess of retail sales over whatever expenses were incurred to produce those sales. Thus, the derivatives of sales volume, whether they are defined as expenses or some degree of profit, are normally expressed as a relationship to their point of origin. A profit of $3,000 on a sales volume of $60,000 is incidental to the fact that profit represents 5% of sales. While dollars of profit are obviously important to the merchant, profit expressed as a ratio to sales is more meaningful, in that it provides a statistical basis for comparative analysis with other retail operation, provides an immediate basis for analysis and management decision making, and serves as a vehicle for the projection of future merchandising plans.

However, while recognizing the utilitarian value of percentages, a word of caution must be exercised: A percentage is simply a relationship between two numbers or the explanation of one number as a function of another. In this sense, percentages may be misleading in their connotation of profitability. For example, Store A can generate a 5% net profit while Store B can only show a 4% net profit. Based on percentages, Store A is obviously more profitable, until that profit is defined in dollars, as illustrated:

	Store A			*Store B*	
Profit =	$\frac{\$7,500}{\$150,000}$	= 5%	Profit =	$\frac{\$32,000}{\$800,000}$	= 4%
Sales =			Sales =		

It may be said than Store A is more efficient that Store B, but certainly in terms of profit dollars generated Store B is the more productive. The point to be made is that percentages are only indicators of profitability and not profitability itself; the merchant, in the final analysis, covers expenses and the cost of merchandise with dollars, not the relative considerations inherent in profit ratios. Thus, profit represents an absolute amount of dollars, and that which is defined as "profitability" is simply a ratio of profit to some measure of the investment. Store A made a profit of $7,500; that $7,500 expressed as a measure of sales defines the merchandising and operational efficiency, or the profitability, of Store A to be 5% of net sales.

2.2

The Components of Profit

Essentially, profit consists of the interaction of its four constituent parts, sometimes referred to as the elements of the *profit mix*. These elements consist of

1. Sales volume.

2. Cost of sales.

3. Operating expenses.

4. Net other income.

All of these concepts will be discussed in more detail in later chapters. For the immediate purpose of discussing profit, a limited explanation will be given here.

Sales Volume

A retail sale is an exchange of property between one person and another for an agreed-upon consideration. Implicit within the concept of a retail sale is at least one unit of merchandise and a specific dollar value mutually perceived to be acceptable. Thus *sales volume* is the product of the number of units sold times the retail price.

Cost of Sales

The *cost of sales,* or the cost of goods sold, defines not only what the merchant paid for the merchandise that was sold but the attendant transportation costs and alterations, less any cash discounts received from the vendor. Thus, in this instance, we speak of the cost of merchandise sold in terms of its total cost. The total cost of merchandise sold is derived from the gross cost and the net cost of the merchandise sold. The difference between the net sales and the total cost of the merchandise that produced those sales is defined as gross margin, or the profit derived solely from the sale of the merchandise.

Operating Expenses

Operating expenses refer to all the nonmerchandise costs incurred in the sale of the merchandise. The term *operating* generally applies to all those sales support functions necessary for the efficient operation of the retail system, including general and administrative expenses in such areas as store maintenance, delivery systems, warehousing, and personnel. Such expenses, when deducted from the gross margin, produce the operating profit, the final figure in the departmental or divisional analysis of the retail store. However, operating profit is not the final, or net, profit upon which the store incurs a tax liability. Other income must also be taken into consideration.

Net Other Income

Net other income is monies derived from sources other than the sale of merchandise. Such sources, among others, include interest and dividends received, carrying charges collected from installment accounts, and profits from the redemption of securities. The sum of the operating profit plus the net other income equals net profit on which the retail store must pay income taxes.

From the foregoing discussion, it becomes clear that for the retail merchant any consideration of profit must be viewed from four distinct aspects:

1. *Gross margin:* the profit attributable to the sale of merchandise, or the excess of sales over the cost of sales.

2. *Operating profit:* the income derived from the primary function of the retail store, that is, the gratification of consumer needs and wants.

3. *Net profit prior to corporate income taxes:* profit as a function of operating profit plus the addition of net other income.

4. *Net profit after the deduction of income tax liability:* the net income available for dividend distribution and reinvestment in the company.

2.3

The Abbreviated Operating Statement

The relationship among the four elements of the profit mix can best be illustrated in the highly simplified corporate operating statement shown in Table 2.1. The important consideration to note is that the gross margin, the profit derived from the sale of merchandise, is the pivotal factor in the determination of operating profit and the resulting net profit, however modified by other income and taxes. Gross margin is the key factor in the overall determination of the profitability of any retail store, in that it provides the necessary income to pay for the expenses incurred in operating the store and compensates the merchant for efforts in terms of profit. Thus, we see that gross margin is essentially a derivative of

Sales   − Cost of sales = Gross margin
$100,000 − $60,000   = $40,000

or

Operating expenses + Operating profit = Gross margin
     $35,000   + $5,000   = $40,000

It is also important to note that retail sales constitute the apex of the merchant's efforts and are thus mathematically defined as 100%; all expenses, whether the product of merchandising activities or retail operations, are expressed as a percentage of net sales, as Table 2.1 indicates. Thus, when working with percentages, as is often the case, the merchant need not know the dollar volume of net sales; it will always be 100%.

Table 2.1

The abbreviated operating statement

	Dollars	% of Sales
Sales (4,000 units × $25)	$100,000	100.0%
Less the cost of sales	60,000	60.0
Gross margin	40,000	40.0
Less operating expenses	35,000	35.0
Operating profit	5,000	5.0
Other income*	1,000	1.0
Net profit before taxes	6,000	6.0
Less taxes	1,500	1.5
Net profit after taxes	$ 4,500	4.5%

*Other income and net profit before and after taxes would not normally appear on the departmental operating, or profit and loss, statement. They are shown here for illustrative purposes only.

■ Study Problem

Given: A menswear store had an annual sales volume of $250,000. The cost of sales was $137,500, operating expenses were $104,500, and other income amounted to $2,500.

Find: In dollars and percentages, the gross margin, operating profit, and net profit.

Solution:

	Dollars	% of Sales
Sales	$250,000	100.0%
Less cost of sales	137,500	55.0
Gross margin	112,500	45.0
Less operating expenses	104,500	41.8
Operating profit	8,000	3.2
Other income	2,500	1.0
Net profit	$ 10,500	4.2%

▪ Application Exercise

1. A hardware store had sales of $300,000 with a gross margin of $125,000 and operating expenses of $113,000. Find the cost of sales and the operating profit in dollars and percentages.

2. The operating profit of a ski shop was 3%, derived from operating expenses of 43.5%. Find the gross margin and the cost of sales.

3. The "Hi-wheeler" bicycle shop shows a net profit of $3,500, $1,000 of which consists of other income. Operating expenses are $36,500, and sales are $60,000. Find the gross margin and the cost of sales in both dollars and percentages.

4. Sales for the fall season are planned at $860,000 for a men's department. The gross margin objective is 46%, and operating profit is targeted at 4.8%. What is the dollar limitation on operating expenses?

Manipulation of the Elements of the Profit Mix

While retail merchandising is the subject of this text, the merchandising process must of necessity function within the parameters dictated by any normal business venture; in this instance, we speak of the retail store and its ultimate objective of net profit. While net profit is generally synonymous with the concept of operating profit, specifically it is derived from the impingement of other income and corporate taxes upon that operating profit. Thus, operating profit, for those retail executives who buy, manage, and control inventory, assumes primacy over those other factors that ultimately dictate net profit. The merchant's immediate concern is, progressively, with net sales, the cost of those sales, gross margin, operating expenses, and operating profit. Our concern, therefore, lies with the manipulation of the three major components of the profit mix—sales volume, the cost of merchandise sold, and the operating expenses—and their interactive effect upon the operating profit.

Sales Volume

Although sales volume, as previously discussed, is a function of many variables besides the retail price, for the sake of this illustration retail price is defined as the economic determinant of retail sales. Consider, for example, a sales volume for mattresses in the furniture department of a large department store. The average retail price of a mattress is $129, the buyer's cost is $71, the normal rate of sale for a particular period of time is 500 units, and operating expenses constitute 40% of sales. The resulting situation is illustrated as follows:

Sales (500 × $129)	$64,500	100.0%
Less cost of sales (500 × $71)	35,500	55.0
Gross margin	29,000	45.0
Less operating expenses	25,800	40.0
Operating profit	$ 3,200	5.0%

Now, assume that competition forces the buyer to reduce the retail price by $4, or approximately 3%. Further assume that the new unit price only meets the competition, thus the number of units sold, the buyer's cost, and the operating expenses will remain constant. The following situation would then exist:

Sales (500 units × $125)	$62,500	100.0%
Less cost of sales (500 × $71)	35,500	56.8
Gross margin	27,000	43.2
Less operating expenses	25,800	41.3
Operating profit	$ 1,200	1.9%

Note the dramatic impact of a relatively small 3% decrease in the unit price and the corresponding decline in sales volume:

- Gross margin will decline by 6.9%[1]

- Operating profit will decline by 62.5%.

- While the cost of sales and operating expenses remain constant, as a ratio of sales volume they increase, respectively, by 1.8% and 1.3%.

Thus, it can readily be shown that even though a sales volume remains constant in the number of units sold, even a slight drop in the retail price can have a dramatic effect on the dollar volume, which in turn geometrically affects the operating profit.

---

[1]The percentage decrease, or increase, is always the product of the previous figure as the base. For example, the decrease in profit equals

$$\frac{\$29,000 - \$27,000}{\$29,000} = 6.9\%$$

Dismayed by the disaster of the attempts to meet competition, the mattress buyer seeks a solution by means of an increase in the department's unit sales volume. Assuming that the quantity of units sold is a function of the retail price, the buyer reasons that by undercutting the competition in terms of price, more units will be sold. Therefore, if operating expenses and gross margin dollars can be held in line, operating profits can be enhanced. Experimentation with a $110 retail price produced an increase of 50% in the number of pieces sold; market share rose to 750 mattresses. The results of the price reduction yielded the following data:

Sales (750 units × $110)	$82,500	100.0%
Less cost of sales (750 × 71)	53,250	64.5
Gross margin	29,250	35.5
Less operating expenses	25,800	31.3
Operating profit	$ 3,450	4.2%

It is evident that, from a dollar perspective, the merchant was eminently successful in combating the competition on the second attempt. Note the following accomplishments achieved compared to the initial "normal" situation:

▪ A 14.7% reduction in the original unit price (from $129 to $110) increased the "normal" unit volume by 50%, resulting in a dollar volume increase of 27.9%.

▪ The cost of sales increased by 50% as a result of the increase in unit volume. However, the resulting gross margin also increased by a slight 0.9%. The main point to be made here is that the gross margin did not register any decrease that would have eroded operating profit.

▪ By whatever means employed, the merchant was able to hold down operating expenses in their normal level of $25,800.[2]

▪ As a result, operating profit was enhanced by 7.8%, from $3,200 to $3,450.

However, one must also look at the other side of the coin, or the elements of profit as they are defined as ratios, or percentages, of retail sales. It is understood that the merchant's liabilities are discharged by means of dollars, not percentages; nevertheless, it is the relationship existing between sales and the profit variables that is vital to the planning process and the ultimate success of the retail merchant. It is not enough to know that gross margin is currently $29,250; what is important

---

[2]Although such an accomplishment is possible, in the real world it is highly improbable. The sheer weight of increased sales volume imposes heavy burdens upon such operating functions as receiving, checking, marking, storage, and physical distribution. However, in this illustrative case we are employing the talents of an unusually brilliant merchant!

to know is that the margin of profit on the merchandise sold is 35.5% of sales. Thus, if an increase in sales is planned, one may expect the dollars of margin to increase; realistically, the increase will not depart too far from 35.5% of those sales. Ratios also aid in the explanation as to how and why a current dollar position came into existence, especially when considered in relationship to previous performance. Consider, for example, the ratio comparison between the initial position of the mattress buyer and that which currently exists:

	Intial Position	Current Position	% Changes In
Sales	100.0%	100.0%	0.0%
Less cost of sales	55.0	64.5	+9.5%
Gross margin	45.0	35.5	-9.5%
Less operating expenses	40.0	31.3	-8.7%
Operating profit	5.0%	4.2%	-0.8%

Predicated upon a comparison of profit ratios alone, the performance of the mattress buyer leaves a great deal to be desired; while the decrease in operating expenses of 8.7% is commendable, it is insufficient to offset a 9.5% increase in merchandise costs (or a 9.5% decrease in gross margin). As a result, operating profit as a percentage of sales has declined by 0.8%. In effect, what the ratios tell us is that in spite of a dollar increase in sales volume and operating profit, the percentage of sales remaining as a profit base is declining. These ratios by themselves could be viewed as a dangerous trend; on the other hand, when considered with the increased sales volume, they could logically be explained as the predictable and planned outcome of a tactical maneuver to enhance long-term profitability through deeper market penetration.

The Cost of Merchandise Sold

Gross margin is always the complement ratio of the cost of merchandise sold, or the cost of sales. Taken together in dollars, they always must equal the dollar volume of sales; or added together as ratios, they will always equal 100%. Obviously, then, the cost of sales has a direct bearing on the gross margin and the resulting operating profit. Let us consider the effect of manipulating the cost of sales on the 4.2% operating profit in the previous example.

Suppose that the bedding buyer is indeed unhappy with the declining profit ratio and seeks as a solution a reduction in the unit cost of the average mattress. As a result of astute vendor negotiations, the buyer is able to reduce the cost of a mattress by $1, to $70. While $1, or a 1.4% reduction in merchandise costs, may appear trivial, notice the consequence on operating profit, assuming that the other variables are held constant:

Sales (750 units × $110)	$82,500	100.0%
Less cost of sales (750 units × $70)	52,500	63.6
Gross margin	30,000	36.4
Less operating expenses	25,800	31.3
Operating profit	$ 4,200	5.1%

By reducing the cost of the merchandise sold by 1.4%, the buyer increased the operating profit by $750, or 21.7% over the previous figure of $3,450. As a result, operating profit, as a percentage to sales, climbed 0.9%, slightly exceeding the normally anticipated 5%.

Operating Expenses

Although not considered as part of the merchandising function, the expenses generated in operating the retail store are crucial to the success of the merchandising effort. The skillful execution of all of the five rights of merchandising (see page 23) does not necessarily ensure the profitability of the department or the retail store; operating expenses must be kept sufficiently below gross margin to ensure an adequate operating profit. Consider, for example, the distinct possibility of escalating operational costs as a product of increased sales volume in the previous illustration. Assume that operating expenses rise by a slight 2%; the following situation will then exist:

Sales (750 units × $110)	$82,500	100.0%
Less cost of sales (750 units × $70)	52,500	63.6
Gross margin	30,000	36.4
Less operating expenses	26,316	31.9
Operating profit	$ 3,684	4.5%

Notice that the operating expenses have increased by $516 over the previous example, thus decreasing current profits by an equal amount to $3,684, or 4.5% of sales. What is of far greater significance is the fact that a "slight" 2% increase in operating expenses over the previous example generates a 12.3% decline in the current profit dollars.

Theoretical Conclusions

Four tentative conclusions may be derived from the foregoing observations, assuming the consistency of the profit variables:

1. Gross margin and operating profit will be enhanced through an increase in sales volume. Increased sales volume may be accomplished by means of
   a. Increasing price and maintaining the current unit sales.
   b. Decreasing price and increasing the current unit sales.
   c. Increasing price and increasing the current rate of sale.

2. Conversely, profit will deteriorate as sales volume declines, regardless of whether that decline is a product of price erosion or a decrease in unit volume.

3. A decrease in the cost of sales will contribute to an increase in both gross margin and operating profit, while a reduction in operating expenses alone will enhance only the operating profit.

4. In contrast, an increase in the cost of sales will negatively affect both gross margin and operating profit, whereas increased operating expenses can only reduce operating profit.

While theoretically these relationships will always hold true, in the real world of human experience it is impossible to always maintain strict control over all of the variables of the profit mix; we tend to be able to control some of the variables all of the time and all of the variables some of the time! Sales volume may suffer due to price increases; a higher volume of sales may so increase operating expenses that all profit is eliminated; and a reduction in operating expenses could modify the service image of the store to the extent that sales volume is adversely affected; it is even conceivable that a price decrease could be perceived as a negative rather than a positive factor in the maintenance of sales volume.

All of the above phenomena exist as probable impediments to merchandising strategy, due almost entirely to the perceptual nature of the consumer psyche, and that psyche as it moves in a world of emotional reality, or relative "absolutes." Thus, the merchant must be constantly aware of such movement or modes of endeavor and adjust the elements of the profit mix to the current standards of what is defined as "reality."

▪ Study Problem

Given: A bicycle shop sold 500 bicycles this year at an average retail price of $175. The cost of the average bike was $91, and the operating expenses amounted to 42% of sales. For the coming year, sales are planned to increase by 9%, with the average unit price remaining the same. It is expected that the cost of the average bicycle will decrease by $5 due to a new line of French bicycles and that operating expenses, as a result of the increase in sales, will rise by 11.2% over this year.

Find: The percentage that planned operating profit will increase or decrease over what was achieved this year.

Solution:

1. The operating profit for this year:

Sales = (500 units × $175)	$87,500	100.0%
Less cost of sales (500 units × $91)	45,500	52.0
Gross margin	42,000	48.0
Less operating expenses (42% × $87,500)	36,750	42.0
Operating profit	$ 5,250	6.0%

2. The planned operating profit:

Sales = $87,500 + (9% × $87,500)	$95,375[3]	100.0%

Planned units = $95,375 ÷ $175 = 545
or 500 × 1.09 = 545

Less cost of sales = (545 units × $86)	46,870	49.2
Gross margin	48,505	50.8
Less operating expenses	40,866	42.8
Operating profit	$ 7,639	8.0%

3. Percentage increase in operating profit:

Planned operating profit	$7,639
Less operating profit this year	5,250
Dollar difference	$2,389
Percentage increase = ($2,389 ÷ $5,250)	45.5%

▪ Application Exercise

1. A toy department had an annual sales volume of $320,000. The buyer was unhappy with an achieved gross margin of 32% and plans to increase it to 35% through a reduction in merchandise cost. In terms of dollars and percentage, by how much must the cost of sales be reduced to achieve the desired results?

2. A market study indicates that a 10% reduction in the average unit price will increase sales volume by 18%. With a current sales volume of $30,000 predicated upon 300 units, how many additional units must be sold at the reduced price to achieve the sales increase?

---

[3]The easier method of computing the planned figure on a percentage basis is to assume that the previous figure is 100%, and that the planned percentage figure is either above or below that 100%. Thus, a 9% increase over the previous figure is defined as 109% (1.09); a 9% decrease becomes 91% (.91). By multiplying $87,500 × 1.09, the planned sales of $95,375 is directly obtained, thereby eliminating one mathematical step.

3. A jewelry store sold 735 units last January at an average retail price of $50. The average cost of the units sold was 52%, and operating expenses amounted to $15,435. Management feels that sales for next January can be increased by 10% with an advertising expenditure that would increase operating expenses by only 3% of sales, cost-of-sales and gross-margin ratios are expected to remain constant. Should the store advertise or not? Justify your opinion with mathematical calculations.

4. A handbag buyer plans to increase the planned sales for the fall season by 12%. Operating expenses are expected to rise to 40%, and the cost of sales is anticipated to remain constant at 54%. What is the ratio of operating profit expected for the coming fall season?

2.4

The Amplified Operating Statement

The operating statement provides the merchant with a detailed account of the individual components of profitability over a specific period of time. The normal time frame is a fiscal year; however, the concept is applicable to any period of time during which the merchant desires to exercise a more detailed control over the various determinants of profitability. Thus, the operating statement may reflect the merchant's activities for a month, a quarter, or a season. Because the operating statement is an analytical account of the sum of the merchant's operations, defined in terms of income, expenses, and resulting profit, it is often referred to as the income, or profit-and-loss, statement. Regardless of the title used, the operating statement performs at least three specific functions for the retail merchant:

1. It permits an accurate determination of investment in the retail business in relation to derived profits and therefore is an indication of the degree of success or failure in the achievement of overall profit objectives.

2. It serves as an explanation as to why more profits and sales volume were not achieved and offers suggestions to guide the management decision-making process in the direction of enhanced profitability.

3. When prepared in a standardized format, the operating statement invites a point-by-point comparison of individual strengths and weaknesses with those of similar retail operations.

The operating statement is the final product, or a dollar summarization, of the strategies and tactics employed by the retail merchant over a specific period of time. It is a by-product of merchandising concepts, operating profit standing as the final arbiter of the comprehension and skill with which those concepts were applied. As such, the operating statement, when thoroughly understood, serves as a point of departure for the further study of the merchandising tactics from which it ultimately derives its form.

In the previous section of this chapter, the key items of the operating statement and their interdependent relationship were discussed; it is now appropriate to amplify those concepts so as to provide the fundamental basis for successful merchandise management. Table 2.2 presents the retail operating statement in its most comprehensive standardized format. Note that it is a departmental statement and thus does not show final, or net, profit. Our concern does not lie with taxes, net other income, or arbitrarily apportioned indirect expenses such as general management salaries, institutional promotion, or fixed policy expenses incurred by the corporation. For our purposes, the "bottom line" is defined as operating profit, or the departmental contribution to corporate profitability. The following explanation of the component items of the operating statement will serve to enhance the concept of profit and provide a basis and the justification for the further study of merchandising strategy.

Gross Sales

Gross sales are the total sales, prior to any adjustments made for customers' returns of merchandise or any retail allowances granted by the selling unit. Gross sales consist of both the revenue derived from the distribution of tangible merchandise and the income produced from a profit-oriented service offering. The sale of such services that simply accommodate the customer, such as shopping bags, are not considered to be a part of gross sales.

Gross sales include

1. The full retail value of layaways.
2. Federal and state excise taxes levied on the manufacturing and wholesale levels of distribution, such as the taxes imposed upon tires, cigarettes, alcoholic beverages, and gasoline.

Gross sales do not include

1. State and local sales taxes levied upon the consumer but collected by the merchant.
2. Employee and special sales discounts; all sales are recorded net of markdowns and sales discounts (after markdowns and discounts have been taken).
3. The sale of gift certificates.
4. Interstore or interdepartmental merchandise transfers.
5. Service or interest charges on credit accounts.
6. Revenue generated from employee-only services, such as cafeterias.

Table 2.2

The amplified operating statement

Department			
		Fiscal Year Ending	
Item	Cost $	Retail $	% of Sales
Gross sales		83,400	
Less returns and allowances		7,089	8.5
Net sales		76,311	100.0
Cost of sales			
Inventory, beginning of period	25,000		32.8
Net purchases (billed costs less returns and allowances)	55,518		72.8
Transportation inward	800		1.0
Total merchandise handled	81,318		106.6
Less inventory, end of period	35,000		45.9
Gross cost of merchandise sold	46,318		60.7
Less earned discounts	2,289		3.0
Net cost of merchandise sold	44,029		57.7
Net alteration and workroom costs	305		0.4
Total merchandise cost		44,334	58.1
Gross margin (net sales less total merchandise cost)		31,977	41.9
Less operating expenses		28,543	37.4
Operating profit (department contribution)		3,434	4.5

7. Income received as a product of merchandise alterations; that is, revenue derived from the operation of workrooms.[4]

Returns, Allowances, and Sales Discounts

As Table 2.2 indicates, net sales, the basis for the calculation of all merchandising ratios, are derived from gross sales by deducting *customer returns* and *allowances* and *sales discounts* (discounts to employees and special customers). The normal accounting procedure would be to treat the discounts as markdowns at the point of sale; all sales initially enter the retail system net of markdowns as well as sales and customer discounts. Thus, for accounting purposes, returns and allowances constitute the difference between gross and net sales and are considered to be a portion of the gross sales of business transacted, but not a part of the sales volume retained by the retail store. As a result, the ratio of returns and

[4]R. Patrick, ed., *The Buyers Manual* (New York: National Retail Merchants Association, 1979), 173–74.

allowances is always calculated as a percentage of gross rather than net sales. Table 2.2 illustrates this point by showing returns and allowances to be 8.5% of $83,400 rather than 9.3% of $76,311.

Returns from Customers

Merchandise returned by customers and reentered into the merchant's inventory voids the initial transaction and reduces gross sales by the amount of the original retail price of the returned merchandise. If the resale price of the return is less than the original price, the difference is treated as a markdown.

When the return takes the form of an exchange of merchandise for goods of dissimilar retail value, the merchandise brought back is treated as a normal return, and the new selection is credited to gross sales. However, an even exchange, whereby a customer returns an item of merchandise in exchange for a similar item of like price, is not normally included in either category of gross sales or returns.

Allowances to Customers

An allowance to customers is a reduction in the original retail price paid by the customer in lieu of the return of unsatisfactory merchandise. In other words, the customer is compensated for some minor defect in merchandise discovered after the transaction has occurred. This compensation amounts to an allowance that must be deducted from gross sales and also must be recorded as a markdown. Not only are the gross sales reduced by the amount of the allowance, but the retail value of the book inventory[5] must also be reduced by an equal amount to avoid an overstated position and an eventual inventory shortage. As a result, allowances require two accounting entries: (1) a deduction from gross sales and (2) an equivalent addition to the markdown record.

Assume that a customer is granted a $5 allowance on a sweater as a result of a post-purchase discovery of some minor defect. Table 2.3 illustrates the compounding effect of the allowance upon gross sales and the corresponding book inventory.

The beginning inventory consists of one sweater with a retail value of $25, confirmed by the physical inventory. An additional sweater is purchased to retail at $30, thus bringing the total merchandise handled up to two units and $55. One unit is sold for $25, resulting in a simultaneous reduction in both the book and physical inventory to one sweater and $30. At some point after the sale, a $5 allowance is granted to the customer to compensate for some minor defect. Gross sales are automatically reduced by the $5 allowance, to net sales of $20. At this

---

[5]The dollar amount of retail inventory that is shown to be available for resale as a product of the retail method of accounting.

Table 2.3

Allowances

	Sales	Physical Inventory	Book Inventory $
Beginning inventory		1 at $25	$25
Purchases		1 at $30	$30
Total merchandise handled		2 at $55	$55 ──►$55
Less gross sales	$25	1 at $25	$25
Inventory to date		1 at $30	$30
Less allowances	$ 5	Less markdown	$ 5
Net sales	$20		$25 ──►$25
Ending inventory		1 at $30	$30

point, a markdown equivalent to the allowance is required in order to maintain the book inventory as an accurate reflection of the sales activity. Note that, in effect, the markdown reduces the value of the remaining inventory by $5, thus effectively compensating for the allowance by increasing the total reduction from $20 to $25. By subtracting the true value ($20 + $5) of the sweater removed from inventory from the total merchandise handled, the ending inventory accurately reflects the one remaining $30 sweater. In actual practice, had the markdown not been taken, the book inventory would have been inflated by $5, thus resulting in a future inventory shortage. Table 2.4 illustrates this concept:

Table 2.4

Inventory shortage

	Sales	Physical Inventory	Book Inventory $
Beginning inventory		1 at $25	$25
Purchases		1 at $30	$30
Total merchandise handled		2 at $55	$55 ──► $55
Less gross sales	$25	1 at $25	$25
Inventory to date		1 at $30	$30
Less allowances	$ 5		
Net sales	$20		──► $20
Ending inventory		1 at $30	$35

Cost of Sales

The *cost of sales* refers to the total cost of the merchandise that was sold. Thus, it is the cost equivalent of net sales—the cost of the merchandise that produced the sales—and is the product of the beginning inventory at cost plus net cost purchases (including transportation) less the ending inventory at cost.

Beginning Inventory

The beginning, or opening, inventory is the cost of the merchandise on hand at the start of a specified period of time. Depending upon the application, the opening inventory may be defined either in terms of cost dollars or retail dollars. Generally speaking, the beginning inventory for one period is the ending inventory for the previous period. For example, the end of the month inventory for December is the beginning of the month inventory for January; the inventory that the merchant closes the doors upon on December 31 is the same inventory that is found when the store is opened on January 1.

Gross Purchases (Billed Cost)

Billed cost refers to the price stated on the vendor's invoice prior to deducting the cash discounts, but after the deduction of trade and quantity discounts from the list price. For example, merchandise purchased for $3,000 with a trade discount of 40% and a cash discount of 3% is received into the retail system at $1,800 ($3,000 × .60); the cash discounts ($1,800 × .03 = $54) are deducted later in the accounting process, assuming certain conditions are met.

Gross purchases represent the total dollar amount of merchandise purchased prior to the deduction of returns to vendors. As such, they include

1. The billed cost of domestic purchases and the landed costs of imported merchandise.

2. Inward-bound transportation from the manufacturer or wholesaler to the store or warehouse. Freight charges, including insurance in transit, are normally indicated apart from purchases on the operating statement to emphasize their impact on operating income.

3. Consignment merchandise[6]

4. When the operating statement pertains to a department or a store unit within a chain, transfers in from other units are considered to be a part of purchases; transfers out are treated as returns, and the difference is categorized on the operating statement as net transfers.

---

[6]Title to the merchandise remains with the vendor until such time as the goods are resold by the merchant; any unsold portion may be returned to the vendor without penalty. Returns to the vendor are treated as deductions from gross purchases.

5. Repossessed merchandise.

6. Vendor charges for special handling, such as the prepacking or prepricing of merchandise.

Purchase returns and allowances

While purchase returns and vendor allowances, or price concessions, obviously reduce gross purchases, two particular types of vendor allowances are worthy of mention at this point:

1. Quantity discounts: allowances granted by the vendor to the merchant based upon the size of the order. Such discounts are immediately credited to gross purchases and should be recorded as reductions of purchases at cost. Quantity discounts may be based upon the size of an individual order or may be the product of purchases over a period of time. In the latter case, they are defined as "cumulative quantity discounts" and are credited to purchases in one lump sum.

2. Advertising allowances: financial concessions granted by the vendor to the merchant, usually under contract, to offset the cost of advertising that vendors merchandise. However, it is to be noted that while such allowances are the product of gross purchases, they are not a credit to gross purchases; advertising allowances serve to reduce advertising expenditures and thus are a credit to operating expenses.

Transportation Inward

Most merchandise is purchased F.O.B. origin, meaning that the vendor is to place the merchandise "Free on Board" the carrier at the point of shipment, with the merchant responsible for the payment of freight charges and transit insurance. Freight and insurance are considered to be an integral part of the cost of merchandise because the true cost of the goods is in the store, not at the point of origin. *Transportation inward* is an important consideration in the cost of merchandise, usually contributing approximately 1.5% to 2% to the net purchase figure, thus seriously affecting gross margin and the resulting operating profit.

Consider the effect of the $800 transportation cost on operating profit in Table 2.2 (page 37). By hypothetically eliminating the transportation inward, the following results could be achieved.

1. Total merchandise cost would be reduced by 1.8% ($800 ÷ $44,334) to $43,534.

2. Gross margin would be increased by $800 to $32,777 or 2.5% ($800 ÷ $31,977).

3. Operating profit would be increased by $800, or a whopping 23.3% over the previous period ($800 ÷ $3,434).

While obviously not all transportation charges can be eliminated, it is undoubtedly true that in many instances operating profit can be dramatically increased by a careful scrutiny of these merchandise costs.

Total Merchandise Handled

The *total merchandise handled* (or, theoretically, the dollar value of the sum of the merchandise available for resale to the customer) is simply a compilation of the beginning inventory, net purchases, and the transportation costs up through a particular point in time.

Inventory, End of Period

The *ending inventory* is the cost value of the merchandise on hand at the end of the accounting period. Under the retail method of inventory, this figure is mathematically derived from the retail value of the ending inventory by the complement of the cumulative markon. This is discussed in greater detail in the chapters on gross margin (Chapter 8) and methods of inventory valuation (Chapter 11).

Gross Cost of Merchandise Sold

The *gross cost of merchandise sold* represents the difference existing between the total merchandise handled at cost and the closing inventory at cost.

Earned Discounts and the Net Cost of Merchandise Sold

Earned discounts, often referred to as cash discounts, are a percentage reduction in the billed cost price of the merchandise; they are "earned" by the merchant for the prompt payment of the invoice on or before the expiration of the cash discount period indicated on the invoice. For example, a $500 invoice may contain the purchase terms "2/10, net 30," which means the merchant will "earn" a 2% cash discount, or a $10 reduction, in the billed cost of the merchandise, if the invoice is paid within ten days or less from the issued date of the invoice. Because markon and the resulting retail price structure is predicated upon the gross cost of the merchandise, the subsequent cash discount serves as a contribution to the merchant's profit in the sense that the cost reduction has never been passed on to the customer. In effect, the cost of the merchandise sold has been overstated, and at this point the operating statement must be adjusted to reflect the reality of the situation.

Table 2.2 shows that the total merchandise handled is $81,318, the closing inventory is $35,000, and the gross cost of merchandise sold is $46,318. Since the cash discounts have not been deducted at this point from either the total merchandise handled ($81,318) or the closing inventory ($35,000), it becomes evident that the cost of merchandise sold ($46,318) is overstated by the amount of cash discount earned ($2,289). Thus, by subtraction, the *net cost of merchandise sold* equals $44,029, or 57.7%, of net sales, rather than the 60.7% as might be generally anticipated. Because the cash discounts are not passed on to the customer, they are absorbed by the merchant as a direct contribution, through gross margin, to operating profit or some other extraneous account. In a very real sense, then, earned cash discounts serve as a profit cushion for the merchandising function by providing additional income as the result of efficient management of cash, rather than the control of merchandise inventories per se.

Net Alteration and Workroom Costs

Net alteration and workroom costs consist of labor, materials, supplies, and overhead, plus any expenses incurred from the purchase of like services from outside sources, less the income derived from customers. The resulting net alteration costs are applied to the retail selling department served by the workroom. Note that the sales, or the customer charges generated by the workroom, are not considered to be part of the total store sales as they have already been used to partially offset the workroom costs.

While proper retail accounting procedure identifies four categories of *workroom costs*,[7] our concern lies with the merchandise service workroom, that nonretail operation maintained as a subsidiary function of a primary selling department. Examples of such workrooms might be the women's apparel alteration department, the men's busheling room, the curtain and drapery workroom, furniture and major appliance workrooms, silver engraving, and so forth. The major functions of the workroom are to alter or repair merchandise sold or in stock and to prepare goods for delivery to the customer. Essentially, the service workroom provides some type of form utility to enhance the sale of merchandise already sold. As an illustration, a pair of men's trousers may not be salable to the individual customer until they are altered to specifications in terms of waist size, length, crotch, and cuff style. The alterations provide the form utility to complete the garment to the customer's satisfaction; only then can the transaction be completed.

As the name implies, the primary function of the service workroom is to provide service to the selling department and the customer, rather than to generate income. As a result, the expenses of operating workrooms, especially in a major department store, can be expected to exceed any income that they do generate by 0.3% to 0.5% of net sales.

---

[7]Specifically, merchandise service workrooms, cost selling departments, indirect manufacturing departments, and expense service departments. See Louis C. Moscarello, Francis C. Grau, Roy C. Chapman, *Retail Accounting and Financial Control* (New York: Ronald Press, 1976), 298–310.

Total Merchandise Cost

With the addition of the net alteration costs to the net cost of the merchandise sold, we arrive at the *total merchandise cost,* or the cost of goods sold, $44,334, as illustrated in Table 2.2.

Total merchandise cost may now be stated as:

> Beginning inventory + Net purchases + Transportation − Ending inventory − Earned discounts + Net alteration costs

Gross Margin

As previously discussed, *gross margin* is the difference between net sales and the total cost of merchandise sold, in this instance $31,977. Thus, gross margin, within this context, may be defined as the gross profit realized on the sale of merchandise, or simply what is left over from sales after the merchandise costs have been deducted. However, this is not to suggest a sense of corporate profitability; most of this "profit," anywhere from approximately 94% to 99%, will be consumed in the payment of operating expenses.

Note the pivotal position of gross margin on the operating statement, as shown in Table 2.2; it is both net sales less the total merchandise cost ($76,311 − $44,334 = $31,977) and operating profit plus operating expenses ($28,543 + $3,434 = $31,977). Remembering this concept will greatly help you understand the concept of markon discussed in Chapter 3.

Operating Expenses and Operating Profit

For the sake of illustration, operating expenses are arbitrarily expressed in Table 2.2 as $28,543, thus resulting in an operating profit of $3,434, or 4.5%.

Operating expenses—such as selling services, advertising, security, housekeeping, display, and credit, to name but a few—consist of all those nonmerchandise costs incurred in the sale of the retail inventory.[8] They provide the support structure for the merchandising function, and this must be paid for out of gross margin. What is left over after operating expenses are paid is *operating profit*—the profit derived from the sale of merchandise. Thus, operating profit may be more specifically defined as the excess of gross margin over operating expenses and thus exists as a measure of merchandising efficiency; it provides the only criterion for the evaluation of the ultimate mission of the retail store: the profitable distribution of goods and services to the consumer.[9]

---

[8]For an in-depth analysis of operating expenses, see *Financial and Operating Results of Department and Specialty Stores* (New York: Financial Executives Division, National Retail Association) (published yearly), and the *Retail Accounting Manual* (New York: Financial Executive Division, National Retail Merchants Association, 1983).

[9]Ernest H. Risch, "Operating Profit in the Conventional Department Store: A Statistical Prognosis," *Retail Control* 8 (January 1986): 37.

▪ Study Problem

Given:

Gross sales = $95,000
Customer returns = $3,800
Customer allowances = $2,300
Beginning inventory = $28,000
Ending inventory = $36,500
Freight = $1,100
Earned discounts = 3.3%
Net purchases = $59,500
Alteration costs = $3,200
Customer-paid alterations = $1,700
Operating expenses = 38.5%

Find: Net sales and the percentage of returns and allowances, total merchandise handled, gross cost of merchandise sold, total merchandise cost, and operating profit in dollars and percentage.

Solution:

1. Net sales and the percentage of returns and allowances:

Returns	$3,800	Gross sales	$95,000
Allowances	2,300	Less returns and allowances	6,100
	$6,100	Net sales	$88,900

$$\text{Percentage of returns and allowances} = \frac{\$6,100}{\$95,000} = 6.4\%$$

2. Total merchandise handled:

Beginning inventory	$28,000
Net purchases	59,500
Transportation	1,100
Total merchandise handled	$88,600

3. Gross cost of merchandise sold:

Total merchandise handled	$88.600
Less ending inventory	36,500
Gross cost of merchandise sold	$52,100

4. Total merchandise cost:

Gross cost of merchandise sold	$52,100
Less earned discounts ($88,900 × 3.3%)	2,934
Net alteration costs ($3,200 − $1,700)	1,500
Total merchandise cost	$50,666

5. Operating profit in dollars and percentage:

Net sales	$88,900
Less total merchandise cost	50,666
Gross margin	$38,234
Less operating expenses (88,900 × 38.5%)	34,227
Operating profit	$ 4,007

$$\frac{\$4,007}{\$88,900} = 4.5\%$$

By rearranging the given data into the proper sequence of the operating statement, the solutions to the previous problem can be illustrated as follows:

Item	Cost $	Retail $	% of Sales
Gross sales		95,000	
Less returns and allowances		6,100	6.4
Net sales		88,900	100.0
Cost of sales			
Inventory, beginning of period	28,000		31.6
Net purchases	59,500		66.9
Transportation inward	1,100		1.2
Total merchandise handled	88,600		99.7
Inventory, end of period	36,500		41.1
Gross cost of merchandise sold	52,100		58.6
Less earned discounts	2,934		3.3
Net cost of merchandise sold	49,166		55.3
Net alteration and workroom costs	1,500		1.7
Total merchandise cost		50,666	
Gross margin (net sales less total merchandise cost)		38,234	43.0
Less operating expenses		34,227	38.5
Operating profit		4,007	4.5

▪ Application Exercises

1. Returns and allowances are expected to amount to 5.8% of April's total receipts. What are the anticipated net sales for April in percentage terms?

2. Rearrange the following data into the proper accounting format:

Operating expenses	41.1%
Inventory, beginning of period	39.8%
Inventory, end of period	36.5%
Gross sales	$104,000
Transportation inward	1.3%
Earned discounts	2.9%
Returns and allowances	5.6%
Net alteration and workroom costs	1.5%
Net purchases	51.9%

Find, in dollars and percentages:

a. Net sales
b. Total merchandise handled
c. Gross cost of merchandise sold
d. Net cost of merchandise sold
e. Total merchandise cost
f. Gross margin
g. Operating profit

▪ Solutions to the Application Exercises

Abbreviated Operating Statement (pp. 26–27)

1. Cost of sales = $300,000 − $125,000 = $175,000
   $175,000 ÷ $300,000 = 58.3%
   Operating profit = $125,000 − $113,000 = $12,000
   $12,000 ÷ $300,000 = 4%

3. Gross margin = $3,500 − $1,000 + $36,500 = $39,000
   $39,000 ÷ $60,000 = 65%
   Cost of sales = $60,000 − $39,000 = $21,000
   $21,000 ÷ $60,000 = 35%

Manipulation of the Elements of the Profit Mix (p. 28)

Current Position

1. Sales = $320,000   100%

Sales =			$320,000	100%
Less cost of sales =	($320,000 − $102,400)	=	217,600	68
Gross margin =	($320,000 × 32%)	=	$102,400	32%

Planned Position

Sales =			$320,000	100%
Less cost of sales =	($320,000 − $112,000)	=	208,000	65
Gross margin =	($320,000 × 35%)	=	$112,000	35%

Reduction in cost of sales = $217,600 − $208,000 = $9,600

$$\frac{\$9,600}{\$217,600} = 4.41\%$$

Last January

3. Sales = (735 units × $50) =	$36,750	100%
Less cost of sales = ($36,750 × 52%)	19,110	52
Gross margin	17,640	48
Operating expenses	15,435	42
Operating profit	$ 2,205	6%

Planned January

Sales = ($36,750 × 110%)	$40,425	100%
Less cost of sales = ($40,425 × 52%)	21,021	52
Gross margin	19,404	48
Less operating expenses = ($40,425 × 45%)	18,191	45
Operating profit	$ 1,213	3%

The store should not advertise because:

a. In spite of a 10% sales increase, operating expenses will increase by 17.9% over last January, or by 3% of sales:

$$\frac{\$18,191 - \$15,435}{\$15,435} = 17.9\%$$

b. While gross margin dollars will increase, the ratio to sales will remain the same, 48% of sales. Thus, operating profit will be depressed by 3% of sales to $1,213, which represents a 45% decline over the previous January,

$$\frac{\$2,205 - \$1,213}{\$2,205} = 45\%$$

The Amplified Operating Statement (p. 35)

1. 100%. Regardless of the percentage of returns and allowances, net sales are always 100%.

Topics for Discussion and Review

1. Distinguish between the concepts of profit and profitability. Why is profitability the more appropriate means of expressing profit?

2. How does gross margin relate to the total cost of goods sold and net sales?

3. Explain the difference between the two elements of expenses in the merchant's profit mix.

4. Mathematically illustrate how net profit is derived from the four components of the profit mix, and indicate the key derivative of the profit mix.

5. Is it realistic to suspect that if sales volume increases, the percentage of gross margin and operating profit will also increase?

6. How can an increase in sales volume result in a decrease in gross margin?

7. What would be the effect on operating profit if sales increased, gross margin decreased, and operating expenses increased?

8. Discuss three methods of increasing sales volume.

9. Explain what an operating statement is and the functions it performs for the retail merchant.

10. What constitutes gross sales? Speculate why the revenue derived from gift certificates would not be included.

11. While all other merchandising ratios are predicated on net sales, the return and allowance ratio is based upon gross sales. Why?

12. Explain why a markdown must be taken when an allowance is granted to the customer by the merchant.

13. Why is the beginning inventory for April the same as the ending inventory for March?

14. Define net purchases.

15. What are included in gross purchases?

16. Why are advertising allowances a credit to operating expenses?

17. Explain the impact of transportation charges on operating profit.

18. How does the earned cash discount contribute to the retail merchant's profit structure?

Chapter 3
Individual and Cumulative Markon

Learning Objectives

- Discuss the concept of retail price.

- Explain the items that the markon must cover.

- Explain the expression of the markon in terms of retail and cost.

- Calculate the markon as a percentage of retail and cost, and explain the difference.

- Derive the cost price from the retail price.

- Derive the retail price from the cost price.

- Derive the cost and retail prices from a known markon in dollars and percent.

- Explain the concept of the cumulative markon.

- Identify and explain the components of the cumulative markon.

- Explain the formula for the cumulative markon percent.

- Calculate the cumulative markon from known inventory totals.

- Derive the cumulative markon from previously unknown inventory totals.

Key Terms

Alteration or Workroom Charges: The net expenditures incurred in altering goods for customers and/or inventory repair.

Cost Complement of the Markon Percentage: The percentage value of the cost price when the retail price is valued at 100%. This figure indicates the average relationship existing between the cost and retail value of merchandise handled in a specific accounting period. For example,

100%	Retail price	$100
− 40	Markon	− 40
60%	Cost complement	$ 60

Cumulative Markon: The total markon on a beginning inventory plus the aggregate purchase markon achieved during a specific accounting period, including additional markups but excluding any markdowns; the difference between the total cost and the total original retail value of all merchandise handled to date, commonly expressed as a percentage of the cumulative original retail.

Expression of Markon: Markon may be expressed as either a percentage of the retail price,

$$\frac{\text{Retail} - \text{Cost}}{\text{Retail}} = \text{Markon percentage}$$

or a percentage of the cost price,

$$\frac{\text{Retail} - \text{Cost}}{\text{Cost}} = \text{Markon percentage}$$

Individual Markon: The markon achieved on one item, as compared to the average markon derived from multiple items.

Markon: The difference between the billed cost price (before deductions of cash discounts) of the merchandise plus transportation costs and the first retail price at which it is offered for sale.

Markup: An upward revision of the original, or initial, markon, resulting in a higher retail selling price. The markup is not to be confused with the concept of markon.

Markup Cancellation: A reduction in the retail price from the markup down to the original markon, not chargeable against the buyer's markdown sales allowance.

National Retail Federation: Considered by most merchants to be the major trade association for all retailing. Concentrates its efforts on the department store and specialty store aspects of the industry. Among its many publications are the MOR (Merchandising and Operating Results) and the FOR (Financial and Operating Results), two widely quoted sources of secondary data in retail merchandising.

Net Purchases: As used in the cumulative markon shown on the operating statement, the value of the merchant's gross purchases during a specific accounting period less returns to and allowances from vendors.

Retail Method of Inventory: The taking of a physical inventory at its retail price and then reducing it to cost value by means of the appropriate departmental or classification markon.

Retail Reductions: The sum total of markdowns, sales discounts to employees and special customers, and estimated inventory shortages.

Transfers: The movement of merchandise between selling departments or store locations.

3.1

The Retail Price

The retail price is only one stimulus, and not necessarily the most important one, among many stimuli that bear upon the consumer's purchase decision. However, from the merchant's perspective, the retail price assumes a unique position among the tactics of merchandising strategy designed to influence the consumer's perception of choice alternatives:

1. It provides the consumer with the only realistic, or practical, means of alternative evaluation in a marketplace of relatively homogeneous merchandise offerings.

2. Its tactical manipulation remains the prerogative of the retail merchant up to and even through the point of sale.

Thus, the retail price defines the merchant's most potent tactic; it is the merchant's manipulation of the retail price that provides the consumer with the only tangible evidence of a realistic basis for appraising perceived value. The components of the retail price consist of the cost of the merchandise and the markon; the *markon* is herein defined as the amount added to the cost to produce the original retail price plus any future markups added to enhance that selling price. The markup is to be distinguished from the markon, even though it is common practice throughout the industry to use the two terms interchangeably. Whereas the markon is the first addition to cost so as to establish the initial price, the *markup* is the subsequent addition to the current selling price to revise it upward. For example, an item purchased at a cost of $8 is priced to sell at retail for $12; the $4 difference between the cost and retail price is defined as the markon. If, however, the retail price is revised upward to $13, that $1 addition is known as a markup. Thus, the retail price is the sum of the original-cost price and the markon (including any additional markup) and may be expressed as the basic retail formula

Retail = Markon + Cost

$100 = $40   + 60

It is important to note at this point that the percentage value of the retail price is always 100%. Thus, the percentage of cost is always the complement of the markon, and conversely, the percentage of markon must always be the complement of cost. Thus the following percentage relationship exists:

Retail = Markon + Cost

100% = 40%　　+ 60%

3.2

The Individual Markon: Single-Item Pricing

The Determinants of Markon

Assuming the acceptance of the markon as the gap existing between the cost of the merchandise and the retail price, that gap requires further definition. Because it is not possible, or even desirable, for the merchant to obtain the same markon for all merchandise items, the concept of markon must generally be viewed as an average of many markons that in the aggregate must be redefined as "income" sufficient to cover the following items:

1. All operating expenses incurred in the normal functions of the retail store. Here we speak of payroll, rent, utilities, advertising, and other costs of conducting business, often referred to as "expenses," "overhead," "the burden," or "the big nut."

2. The anticipated "reductions," or those factors that over a period of time diminish the retail value of the merchant's inventory: markdowns, estimated stock shortages, and discounts to employees and special customers.

3. Alteration or workroom charges.

4. A reasonable amount of profit.

The Expression of Markon

By transposition of the terms in the basic retail formula, we may state that

$Markon = $Retail − $Cost

However, the value of the markon as a tactical tool of retail merchandising stands not so much as the dollar difference existing between the cost and retail price, but that markon as expressed in a percentage relationship to either the cost or the retail price of the merchandise. Consider, for example, the following two examples:

1. An article retails for $12 and costs $7. What is the markon?

Since	Markon = Retail − Cost
Then	Markon = $12 − $7
Therefore	Markon = $5

2. An article retails for $15 and costs $10. What is the markon? Following the above procedure we find that the markon is again $5, retail price minus cost.

   The dollar amount of markon is the same in both examples, suggesting that both articles are equally profitable: however, such is not the case. When the $5 markon is expressed as a percentage of either its cost or retail price, we find that substantial differences exist between the profitability, or dollar return, on each article sold. The following expressions indicate those various differences as found in the preceding examples of dollar markon calculation:

1. $12 (Retail) − $7 (Cost) = $5 (Markon)

   $$\frac{\$5\,(\text{Markon})}{\$12\,(\text{Retail})} - 41.7\%\ (\text{Markon percentage})$$

   The 41.7% is a product of the formula

   $$\frac{\text{Retail} - \text{Cost}}{\text{Retail}}$$

   and it tells us that the $5 markon is equivalent to, or represents a profit margin of, 41.7% of the retail price.

2. Consider, for comparison purposes, the $15 item that costs $10:

   $15 (Retail) − $10 (Cost) = $5 (Markon)

   $$\frac{\$\,5\,(\text{Markon})}{\$15\,(\text{Retail})} = 33.3\%\ (\text{Markon percentage})$$

   In this instance, the profit margin of 33.3% of the retail price is far less desirable than that derived from the $12 retail/$7 cost relationship. This is so because in the latter case it requires only $12 at retail to generate a $5 markon, whereas in the former instance $15 at retail is required; in essence, we have produced the identical dollar profit margin with a $3 ($15 − $12), or 20% ($3 ÷ $15), reduction in sales volume.

   Now consider the same relationship between the two examples when the markon is expressed as a percentage of the cost price. Note that while the markon percentages respectively increase, the higher percentage of profitability prevails with the $12 retail/$7 cost item.

1. $12 (Retail) − $7 (Cost) = $5 (Markon)

$$\frac{\$\ 5\ (\text{Markon})}{\$\ 7\ (\text{Cost})} = 71.4\%\ (\text{Markon percentage})$$

In this instance, the markon is 71.4% of the cost price, or 71.4% of the invest-ment required to produce the $5 markon. Compare this percentage to that derived from the $15 retail/$10 cost item:

2. $15 (Retail) − $10 (Cost) = $5 (Markon)

$$\frac{\$\ 5\ (\text{Markon})}{\$10\ (\text{Cost})} = 50\%\ (\text{Markon percentage})$$

Obviously, this 50% markon is less desirable because it requires a higher proportionate cost, or investment in merchandise, and thus reduces the per-centage return on that investment.

The point to be made is that while the markon in dollars may remain the same, the percentage of markon is a far better indicator of profitability than those dollars themselves. This presents a most important point in the consideration of merchandising tactics: Markon is most useful and valuable when expressed as a percentage of a commonly accepted and definable base, because it may then be applied as a common standard of comparison for the dollar returns on many items, regardless of the individual cost or retail price.

Two immediate questions obviously follow:

1. Should the markon be based upon the cost price or the retail price of the merchandise?

2. How is the markon percentage calculated?

The Retail Expression of Markon

While some merchants, particularly the smaller and less sophisticated ones, still continue to employ the cost of the merchandise as the basis for the derivation of the markon, the retail base has been generally accepted as the more desirable of the two.

There are several reasons for basing the markon on the retail price rather than the cost price:

1. Since sales determine profit, it is only reasonable to assume that the markon should be based on the retail price.

2. The percentage of markon based upon retail price is always less than that based upon cost price, obviously because the retail price must necessarily be greater than cost. That is, retail equals cost plus markon, whereas cost is derived from retail minus the markon. In this sense, the markon based upon retail can never exceed 100%, whereas there are no limitations on the percentage of markon derived from cost. Witness the following extremes as a case in point:

$$\text{Retail} = \$1,000$$
$$\text{Cost} = \underline{\hspace{1.5em} 1}$$
$$\text{Markon} = \$ \ 999$$

$$\text{Cost-based markon} = \frac{\$999}{\$1} = 999\%$$

$$\text{Retail-based markon} = \frac{\$999}{\$1,000} = 99.9\%$$

Note that no matter how ridiculous the relationship between retail and cost, the markon dollars are always less than those at retail by the amount of the cost dollars. Thus, the markon as a percentage of retail can never go beyond 100%; this is not true for the cost-based markon, as the previous example dramatically points out. The main point to be made is that to the casual observer a markon of 40% on retail appears far more reasonable than a markon of 66.7% of cost.

3. The exchange of data, such as profit and operating ratios, among retail establishments provides invaluable opportunities for comparison and analyses only if all communicants adhere to the same base. Since this information is gathered, synthesized, and disseminated by the various retail trade associations, such as the National Retail Federation, on a sales or retail basis, it is advisable that all merchants do likewise.

4. The retail method of inventory, the more prevalent technique for maintaining the accounting value of an inventory, is possible only when the markon is predicated on the retail price of the merchandise. This concept is discussed in detail in Chapter 11.

5. The use of the retail percentage of markon forces the merchant to properly think in terms of retail dollars rather than cost dollars. Because customer demand is predicted upon a perception of retail values (not cost), the merchant must plan and control inventory assortments in harmony with that demand. Also, because operating expenses and profits must of necessity be expressed as percentages of income or retail sales, it follows logically that for the sake of compatibility in the operating statement the percentage of markon must be derived from the same base.

Application of the Markon Percentage

Throughout the remainder of this text, the markon will be defined as a percentage of the retail price, simply because this is the practice common to current merchandising philosophy. The cost basis will be ignored, not because it lacks feasibility, but because it lacks practical application in the current definition of retail merchandising.[1] Thus, the basic formula for the markon percentage may be stated

$$\frac{\$\,\text{Retail} - \$\,\text{Cost}}{\$\,\text{Retail}} = \text{Markon \%}$$

Calculation of the Markon Percentage When the Cost and Retail Prices Are Known

In order to maximize profit, the merchant must be able to evaluate a product in terms of its cost, retail price, and resultant markon. This is the merchant's first responsibility: to ensure that what is purchased will sell at a particular retail price and yield the required percentage of markon.

■ Study Problem

Given: An item of merchandise retails for $300. It costs the merchant $180.

Find: The achieved markon percentage.

Solution:

Step 1. In order to better visualize the relationship existing between the dollars and their proportionate percentages, construct a simple matrix[2] and fill in the known quantities:

---

[1]The reader who desires to study the cost method of pricing in greater depth is referred to Murphy Krieger, *Practical Merchandising Math for Everyday Use* (New York: Merchandising Division, National Retail Merchants Association, 1980), 144–174.

[2]R = Retail; C = Cost; M = Markon

	$	%
R	300	
– C	– 180	
M		

Step 2. We are immediately able to add two additional figures: the markon dollars ($300 − $180 = $120) and the retail percentage. Note that here, as in every instance, the retail price is always 100%. Let *X* and *Y* stand for unknown percentages of markon and cost. The matrix now looks like this:

	$	%
R	300	100
– C	– 180	– X
M	120	Y

Step 3. Now solve for *X* (% of cost) by establishing a proportional relationship between the dollars and percentage of the retail price and the dollars and percentage of cost. Thus, we have the following proportional equation:

$$\frac{\$300}{100\%} = \frac{\$180}{X}$$

By cross multiplication, we have $\$300X = \$180$, and $X = 60\%$ (Cost).

Step 4. Retail − Cost = Markon. Therefore, 100% (R) − 60% (C) = 40% (M). The matrix is now complete, illustrating the relationship existing between the dollar and percentage components of the markon:

	$	%
R	300	100
− C	− 180	− 60
M	120	40

Alternate Solution: While using the matrix is obviously the more difficult method of solving a relatively simple problem, its value lies in its explicit nature. The quickest and easiest method is to use the formula

$$\frac{\text{Retail} - \text{Cost}}{\text{Retail}} = \text{Markon \%}$$

wherein

$$\frac{\$300 \ (R) - \$180 \ (C)}{\$300 \ (R)} = 40\%$$

▪ Application Exercises

1. A dress retails for $65. It cost the buyer $32. What is the markon percentage?

2. Christmas decorations cost the merchant $5.76 per dozen. The planned retail price is $1 apiece. What is the individual markon percentage?

3. A lamp is purchased at a cost of $30, with an anticipated retail price of $50. What is the planned markon percentage?

4. A candy bar costs thirteen cents and carries a retail price of twenty-five cents. What is the markon percentage?

5. A gross of neckties cost the buyer $864. Assuming that each will retail for $13, what markon percentage does the buyer anticipate on the gross of ties?

Derivation of the Cost Price from the Known Retail Price and Markon Percentage

The essence of this markon situation is the ability of the merchant to convert the known retail price to its cost equivalent by means of the application of the cost complement of the markon percentage. This concept has fundamental application throughout the entire retail accounting process, because the very nature of that process is predicated upon the derivation of an unknown cost from an established retail price, whether stated in percentages or quantitative dollars. This concept will be further developed as we progress through the text.

▪ Study Problem

Given: A man's dress shirt retails for $25, with a 48% markon.

Find: The cost of the shirt.

Solution: While the practical solution to the problem is relatively quite simple, it precludes the basic understanding of the principles at work. Thus, at the risk of appearing too academic, four solutions to the problem are offered.

First Solution: The retail markon formula:

$$\frac{\$\,\text{Retail} - \$\,\text{Cost}}{\$\,\text{Retail}} = \text{Markon \%}$$

Through substitution, we find that

$$\frac{\$25 - \text{C}}{\$25} = 48\%$$

Thus, by cross multiplication, $25 − C = $12, or C = $25 − $12, C = $13.

Second Solution: Use of the dollar/percentage matrix:

Step 1. Construct the matrix with the known information, as defined in the previous study problem. Thus, we have the following situation:

	$	%
R	25	100
– C	– X	– 52
M	Y	48

Step 2. Set up the following proportional equation:

$$\frac{\$25}{100\%} = \frac{X\,(\text{Cost})}{52\%}$$

Through cross multiplication, we find that 100% X = $13. Thus cost (X) = $13, or 52% of the $25 retail price. The completed matrix illustrates the percentage and dollar relationships existing between the components of the retail price:

	$	%
R	25	100
– C	– 13	– 52
M	12	48

Third Solution:

Step 1. Notice that in the above matrix the retail price of $25 is equal to 100%. Therefore, if 100% = $25, then

$$1\% = \frac{\$25}{100}, \text{ or } \$.25$$

Step 2. Because 1% of the retail price = $.25 and cost = 52% (or 52 × the value of 1%), then

$.25 × 52 = $13

Fourth Solution: The theme common to all three solutions is the reduction of the retail price to cost by means of the reciprocal of the markon. Thus, the following rule is offered as a simplified solution to the determination of cost:

> *Subtract the markon percentage from 100% and multiply the resulting cost complement times the retail price.*

Stated quantitatively:

> The cost of the merchandise = The retail price × (100% − The markon percentage)

Thus;

Cost = $25 (100% − 48%)

Cost = $25 × 52%

Cost = $13

■ Application Exercises

1. The retail price of a bicycle is $150. The markon is 42%. What was the cost?

2. A buyer plans to purchase a sofa to retail for $420. The planned markon is 38%. How much should the buyer plan to spend for the sofa?

3. A small merchant needs to replenish a $650 retail inventory. A markon of 38% is anticipated. What will the cost of the new inventory be?

4. A men's furnishings department achieved a net sales volume of $750,000 with a markon of 48.5%. What was the cost of sales?

5. A dozen pairs of socks retailed for $3.50 per pair with a 46.8% markon. What did the buyer pay for the dozen pairs of socks?

Derivation of the Retail Price from the Known Cost Price and Markon Percentage

Essentially, this is a pricing situation in which the merchant is confronted with a known cost price, for example in the wholesale market, and must translate that cost via the markon into a retail price. Merchandise buying decisions are predicated not so much on the wholesale cost itself, but upon that cost as the complement of the markon in the predetermined and relatively inflexible framework of the retail price. In other words, the merchant must constantly think in terms of retail while negotiating at cost in the vendor's environment.

▪ Study Problem

Given: A buyer was shopping for women's blouses and selected a group priced at $155.50 per dozen. Merchandising considerations dictated a markon of 52%.

Find: The retail price of the individual blouses.

Solution: Again, for the sake of the understanding of basic principles, multiple solutions are offered to a relatively simple problem.

First Solution:

Step 1. Dividing the cost per dozen by 12, construct the price/percentage matrix and insert all known information, substituting X and Y for the unknown retail and markon dollars.

	$	%
R	X	100
– C	– 12.96	– 48
M	Y	52

Step 2. Establish the following proportional equation,

$$\frac{X}{100\%} = \frac{\$12.96}{48\%}$$

and solve for X (retail price).

$$48\%X = \$12.96, \ X = \frac{\$12.96}{48\%}, \ X = \$27$$

Step 3. Verify the retail price by reducing it to its original cost: (100% – 52%) × $27 = $12.96.

Second Solution:

Step 1. From the above matrix we see that the cost of $12.96 represents 48% of the retail price.

Step 2. Then 1% of cost = $\dfrac{\$12.96}{48}$ = $.27.

Therefore, if 1% = $.27, 100% (retail price) = $.27.

Third Solution: At this point, it should be fairly obvious that the retail price, when the cost and markon are known, is the result of dividing that cost price by the cost complement of the markon. Thus, the following is offered as a simplified solution to the determination of retail:

*Subtract the markon percentage from 100% and divide the cost price by that percentage.**

Stated quantitatively:

The retail price = The cost price ÷ (100% – The markon percentage)

Thus,

Unit cost = $155.50 ÷ 12 = $12.96

Unit retail = $12.96 ÷ (100% – 52%)

Unit retail = $12.96 ÷ 48%

Unit retail = $27

■ Application Exercises

1. If a buyer purchases a man's suit for $65 and plans a markon of 44.5%, what will the retail price be?

2. At what price would an item retail for if it had a 43% markon and cost $23.50?

3. A box of two dozen candy bars cost the merchant $3.50. What should he plan to retail each one for if the achieved markon on the entire box is to be 57.5%?

4. What is the retail price of a TV set that costs $199.80 and carries a markon of 26%?

*Note: When going from retail to cost, "subtract and multiply;" when going from cost to retail, "subtract and divide."

5. What is the retail price required to support a 32% markon on an item that costs $3.80?

Calculation of the Cost and Retail Prices When the Markon in Dollars and Percentage Is Known

From time to time, the merchant will be required to determine the cost and retail price when only the markon in dollars and percentage is known. Consider the following situation:

▪ Study Problem

Given: A buyer is committed to a markon of 42% on a particular item, or $18, to cover handling costs and provide a reasonable amount of profit.

Find: The cost of the item and the required retail price.

Solution: Three solutions are offered to this problem, all of which should now be familiar.

First Solution:

Step 1. In order to understand the relationship existing between the two given variables, we again construct the dollar/percentage matrix and enter the knowns; because the markon is 42%, and we know that retail price is always 100%, cost must be 58%. Thus, the matrix appears like this:

	$	%
R	X	100
– C	– Y	– 58
M	18	42

Step 2. Establish the relationship between retail price and cost:

$$\frac{X}{\$18} = \frac{100\%}{42\%}$$

Step 3. Solve for X (Retail):

$$42\% \, X = \$18 \quad X \, (\text{Retail}) = \$42.86$$

Step 4. Find the cost price:

$$\text{Retail} - \text{Cost} = \text{Markon}$$

$$\$42.86 - Y = \$18$$

$$Y \, (\text{Cost}) = \$42.86 - \$18$$

$$Y \, (\text{Cost}) = \$24.86$$

Proof: $\dfrac{\text{Retail} - \text{Cost}}{\text{Retail}} = \text{Markon \%}$

$$\frac{\$42.86 - \$24.86}{\$42.86} = 42\%$$

Note: The required $18 markon is not the result of the difference existing between any casual set of cost and retail prices—for example, $50 and $68—but a unique cost/retail relationship defined in terms of a specific 42% markon. Observe the markon percentage obtained from the $18 markon when taken as a percentage of the $68 retail price:

$$\frac{\$68 - \$50}{\$68} = \frac{\$18}{\$68} = 26.5\%$$

It therefore becomes obvious that while the $18 markon was achieved, in terms of retail sales or price it is insufficient to cover the handling costs and profit, thus precipitating a merchandising disaster!

Second Solution: Use the retail percentage formula:

Step 1. $\dfrac{\$\text{Retail} - \$\text{Cost}}{\$\text{Retail}} = \text{Markon \%}$

Step 2. $\dfrac{\$18 \, (\$\text{Retail} - \$\text{Cost})}{X \, (\text{Retail})} = 42\%$

Step 3. Cross multiplication provides:

$$42\% \, X = \$18$$

$$X \, (\text{Retail}) = \$42.86$$

Step 4. $\$\text{Retail} - \$\text{Markon} = \$\text{Cost}$

$$\$42.86 - \$18 = \$24.86$$

Third Solution: Divide the markon dollars by the markon percent to obtain retail dollars; cost equals retail dollars less the markon dollars. Thus,

$$\text{Retail} = \frac{\text{Markon}}{\text{Markon\%}} = \frac{\$18}{42\%} = \$42.86$$

$\$\text{Cost} = \$\text{Retail less }\$\text{Markon}$

$\$\text{Cost} = \$42.86 - \$18 = \$24.86$

▪ Application Exercises

1. A buyer places an $86 markon on a chair in order to achieve a 34% markon. What will the cost of the chair be, and at what price must it be retailed?

2. A shoe department requires a 52% markon to cover $6,000 in operating expenses and profit. What must the planned sales be? What should the buyer pay for the merchandise?

3. A buyer requires a 42.5% markon, or $18, to cover the expenses and profit required to carry a particular item of merchandise. An item is selected with a cost of $34 and a planned retail price of $52. Was this a wise choice? Justify your answer with numbers.

4. A dozen shirts are purchased anticipating a total markon of $108, or 45% of retail. What is the cost per shirt?

5. Define the cost and retail prices of an item that carries a markon of $0.24, or 33.3%.

3.3
The Cumulative Markon

Thus far, we have been discussing the markon achieved on individual items. While of obvious importance, the merchant's ultimate interest lies not so much with the individual markon as it does with the markon achieved on accumulated groups, or classifications, of merchandise. Such a markon is known as the *cumulative markon*. More specifically, the cumulative markon is defined to be the average percentage of markon achieved over a given period of time, derived from the beginning inventory plus all merchandise received and recorded to date. In dollars, the cumulative markon is the difference between the delivered cost of the merchandise and the cumulative retail prices previously established, without any regard for retail reductions, that is, markdowns, anticipated shortages, without any regard for retail reductions, that is, markdowns, anticipated shortages, and sales discounts. The delivered cost of the merchandise refers to the beginning inventory at cost plus the gross cost of the additional merchandise subsequently purchased, adjusted for vendor returns and interdepartmental transfers, including the addition of all transportation charges.

In this sense, the cumulative markon is synonymous with the initial markon, discussed in Chapter 5. Conceptually, the cumulative markon percentage is arrived at through the following calculations:

1. The beginning inventory at retail plus additions at retail $=$ Cumulative (total) merchandise available at retail

2. The beginning inventory at cost plus net additions at cost $=$ Cumulative (total) merchandise available at cost

3. The cumulative retail dollars minus the cumulative cost dollars $=$ The cumulative markon dollars

4. The cumulative markon dollars divided by the cumulative merchandise available at retail $=$ The cumulative markon percentage

Net Additions

The term *cumulative* implies an increase in quantity or to accumulate by successive additions. Those additions are defined as net purchases, net transfers-in, net markups, and transportation. *Net* defines what remains after all necessary deductions have been made.

Net Purchases

Net purchases represent the remaining dollar amount of purchases after allowing for vendor reductions. Such reductions normally consist of

1. The return of purchased merchandise to the vendor for full credit.

2. Vendor rebates, or deductions. These represent a refund of a portion of the cost price paid for merchandise, generally because of the large quantity of goods purchased.

3. Allowances received from a vendor to compensate the merchant for damaged merchandise, late delivery, price competition, or for any other reason defined as "allowances from vendors."

Note that the returns to the vendor reduce both the cost and retail value of the inventory, while the rebates and allowances affect only the cost value of the merchandise. For example,

	Cost	Retail
Gross purchases	$10,000	$20,000
Less returns to vendor	2,000	4,000
Less allowances	1,200	
Less rebates	800	
Net purchases	$ 6,000	$16,000

Net Transfers-in

Transfers refer to an intrafirm transaction accounting for the movement of merchandise from one selling department or location to another; for the receiving unit, that transaction is a transfer-in; for the sending unit, it is a transfer-out. In short, transfers either increase or decrease the cumulative inventory at both cost and retail price. If the transfers-in are greater than the tranfers-out, the difference becomes an addition to the existing inventory defined as net transfers-in.

Net Markups

As previously discussed, a markup is the upward revision of an initial markon, resulting in a higher-than-original selling price. For example,

New retail price	$16
Less original retail price	13
Additional markup	$ 3

A markup may be taken to

1. Compensate for pricing errors.

2. Meet competition.

3. Adjust the retail price to the vendor's increased replacement cost.

4. Distort the customer's perception of value.

In the previous example, if the buyer decides to reduce the new retail price of $16 to its original $13, the $3 markup is considered to be cancelled. Thus, this form of price reduction is defined as a cancellation of markup or a markup cancellation.

Net additional markups refer to the difference between the gross additional markups and the dollar amount of cancellations taken to reduce that markup. Note that the net markup is an addition to the retail price only, as markup has no effect on cost.

Cumulative Markon Derived from Known Inventory Totals

The basic formula for the expression of the cumulative markon percentage, with all of the foregoing explanations, appears below:

		Cost	Retail	Markon %
Opening inventory		$80,000	$150,000	46.7%
Gross purchases	$12,000			
Less purchase reductions	2,000			
Net purchases		10,000	19,000	47.4
Transfers-in	6,000			
Less transfers-out	2,000			
Net transfers-in		4,000	8,000	50.0
Gross markups	1,500			
Less markup cancellations	500			
Net markups			1,000	
Total merchandise handled and percentage of cumulative markon		$94,000	$178,000	47.2%

$$\frac{\$178,000 - \$94,000}{\$178,000} = \frac{\$84,000}{\$178,000} = 47.2\%$$

Note that the cumulative markon dollars, $84,000, is the difference between the total cost and retail dollars and is expressed as a percentage of the total retail dollars. Essentially, we have the basic formula for the definition of markon percentage,

$$\frac{\text{Retail} - \text{Cost}}{\text{Retail}} = \text{Markon \%}$$

expanded to include the following concepts:

$$\frac{\begin{array}{c}\text{Beginning inventory} \\ \text{at retail + Additions}\end{array} - \begin{array}{c}\text{Beginning inventory} \\ \text{at cost + Additions}\end{array}}{\begin{array}{c}\text{Beginning inventory} \\ \text{at retail + Additions}\end{array}}$$

In essence, the cumulative markon is the average markon achieved to date, and it is indicative of the merchant's ability to achieve the initial, or planned, markon percentage. Because retail reductions (markdowns, estimated shortages, and customer discounts) are not included in the computation of the cumulative markon percentage, the final determinant of an acceptable cumulative markon is the merchant's awareness of the cost and retail value inherent in market transactions.

Also, because the cumulative markon percentage is the average markon achieved to date, it allows the merchant at any time to calculate the closing cost value of the inventory, as we shall see shortly.

▪ Study Problem

Given:

	Cost	Retail
Beginning inventory, 9/1	$6,000	$9,000
Additions, 9/1–9/30		
Purchases	2,000	4,000
Transfers-in	500	900
Transfers-out	250	500
Returns to vendor	300	600
Vendor allowances	200	-0-
Markup	-0-	300
Markup cancellations	-0-	150

Find: The cumulative markon percentage as of 9/30.

Solution:

Step 1. Calculate the net additions to the beginning inventory:

	Cost	Retail	Cost	Retail
Transfers-in	$ 500	$ 900		
Less transfers-out	250	500		
Net transfers-in			$ 250	$ 400
Purchases	2,000	4,000		
Less returns to vendors	300	600		
Less vendor allowances	200	-0-		
Net purchases			1,500	3,400
Markup	-0-	300		
Markup cancellations	-0-	150		
Net markup			-0-	150
Net additions			$1,750	$3,950

Step 2. Add the net additions at cost and retail to the beginning inventory at cost and retail:

	Cost	Retail
Beginning inventory, 9/1	$6,000	$9,000
Additions, 9/1–9/30	1,750	3,950
Total merchandise handled	$7,750	$12,950

Step 3. Calculate the cumulative markon dollars:

Total merchandise handled at retail	$12,950
Less total merchandise handled at cost	7,750
Cumulative markon dollars	$ 5,200

Step 4. Calculate the cumulative markon percentage:

$$\frac{\$\text{Cumulative markon}}{\$\text{Total merchandise handled at retail}} = \frac{\$\ 5,200}{\$12,950} = 40.2\%$$

Note again that vendor allowances do not affect the retail price and markups do not alter the cost price.

▪ Application Exercise

1. Find the resulting markon percentage on the accumulated totals:

	Cost	Retail
5/1 Beginning inventory	$8,000	$12,000
5/1–31 Net purchases	2,000	4,000

2. Stock on hand at the beginning of the month was $7,000 at cost and $13,500 at retail. Additional purchases were $3,000 at cost and $5,500 at retail. However, one order of merchandise was partially defective, resulting in a vendor allowance of $300 and vendor returns of $500 at cost and $800 at retail. What was the achieved cumulative markon percentage?

3. Inventory as of 6/1 was $14,000 at cost and $25,000 at retail. During the period 6/1 through 6/30, net transfers-in amounted to $3,300 at cost and $5,000 at retail. Net markup for the month was $800. What was the cumulative markon percentage?

4. On 1/1, there was an inventory in the women's shoe department of $67,000 at retail and $33,000 at cost. Transfers-in amounted to $4,000 at cost and $9,500 at retail, while transfers-out were $3,500 at cost and $7,000 at retail. What was the resulting percentage of markon?

5. A buyer received a quantity discount of 3% on gross purchases of $1,200 with a retail value of $2,200. Additional markup achieved was $135. Defective mer-

chandise valued at $100 at cost and $175 at retail was returned to the vendor. Net transfers-in were $800 at cost and $1,300 at retail. All of these activities transpired during the month of May, which began with an inventory of $7,500 at cost, worth $14,000 at retail. What was the cumulative markon for May?

Cumulative Markon Derived from Previously Unknown Inventory Totals

As is often the case, the cost value of the cumulative inventory is not always immediately available. On the other hand, the merchant may be well aware of planned purchases at cost without the knowledge of the retail valuation. However, as previously discussed in the "application of the markon percentage," retail and cost dollars can always be determined if the markons on the inventory and purchases are known. Consider the following study problem.

∎ Study Problem

Calculate the cumulative markon when the markons on the beginning inventory and purchases are known, but either cost or retail value is unknown.

Given:

	Cost	Retail	Markon
Beginning inventory 6/1		$15,000	43.0%
Purchases 6/1–6/30	$17,000		48.0%

Find: The cumulative markon percentage for the month of June.

Solution:

Step 1. Set up the problem as follows:

	Cost	Retail	Markon
Beginning inventory	X	$15,000	43.0%
Purchases	$17,000	Y	48.0%
Total merchandise handled			

Step 2. Solve for X (Cost):

$$X = (100\% - 43\%) \times \$15,000$$

$$X = 57\% \times \$15,000$$

$$X = \$8,550$$

Step 3. Solve for Y (Retail):

$$Y = \$17,000 \div (100\% - 48\%)$$

$$Y = \$17,000 \div 52\%$$

$$Y = \$32,692$$

Step 4. Fill in the cost and retail:

	Cost	Retail	Markon
Beginning inventory	$ 8,550	$15,000	43.0%
Purchases	17,000	32,692	48.0%
Total merchandise handled	$25,550	$47,692	46.4%

Add up total cost and total retail.

Step 5. Calculate the cumulative markon percentage for the month of June, using the formula

$$\frac{R - C}{R} = MO \%$$

$$\frac{\$47,692 - \$25,550}{\$47,692} = 46.4\%$$

▪ Application Exercise

1. Calculate the cumulative markon to date for a department with the following available data:

	Cost	Retail	Markon
Beginning inventory		$85,000	38%
Additions	$12,000		40%

2. The inventory on hand in a blouse department was $35,000 at retail with a 48.3% markon. Subsequent purchases amount to $18,000 at cost with an anticipated markon of 43.5%. What is the departmental cumulative markon for the period?

3. A small boutique began the month of July with an inventory at cost of $23,000 and a markon of 51.1%. During the month, additional purchases totaled $14,500 at cost and $23,000 at retail. What was the markon for the purchases and the cumulative markon for the month?

4. A Christmas shop began the season with a planned markon of 53% on a retail inventory of $27,000. No additional purchases were made; however, mark-ups

were $4,500 and markup cancellations totaled $2,000. What was the cumulative markon at the end of the season?

5. The stock on hand in a women's hosiery department was $12,000 at cost and $22,500 at retail. Subsequent purchases totaled $8,000 at retail and carried a markon of 47.5%. During the period, the buyer was offered a 10% rebate to meet competition. What was the cumulative markon for the period?

■ Solutions to the Application Exercises

Calculation of the Markon Percentage When the Cost and Retail Price Are Known (p. 60)

1. $\dfrac{\$65 - \$32}{\$65} = 50.8\%$

3. $\dfrac{\$50 - \$30}{\$50} = 40\%$

5. $\$864 \div 144 = \$6$ cost per tie

$\dfrac{\$13 - \$6}{\$13} = 53.8\%$

or, $\$13 \times 144 = \$1,872$ (Retail on gross)

$\dfrac{\$1,872 - \$864}{\$1,872} = 53.8\%$

Derivation of the Cost Price from the Known Retail Price and Markon Percentage (p. 63)

1. $100\% - 42\% = 58\%$

$\$150 \times 58\% = \$87$

3. $100\% - 38\% = 62\%$

$62\% \times \$650 = \$403$

5. $100\% - 46.8\% = 53.2\%$

$53.2\% \times \$3.50 = \$1.86$

$\$1.86 \times 12 = \$22.32$

Derivation of the Retail Price from the Known Cost Price and Markon Percentage (p. 65)

1. $100\% - 44.5\% = 55.5\%$

    $\$65 \div 55.5\% = \$117.12$

3. $100\% - 57.5\% = 42.5\%$

    $\$3.50 \div 42.5\% = \$8.24$

    $\$8.24 \div 24 = \$.34$

5. $100\% - 32\% = 68\%$

    $\$3.80 \div 68\% = \$5.59$

Calculation of the Cost and Retail Prices When the Markon in Dollars and Percentage is Known (p. 68)

1. Retail $= \$86 \div 34\% = \$252.94$

    Cost $= \$252.95 - \$86 = \$166.94$

    Proof:

    $$\frac{\$252.94 - \$166.94}{\$252.94} = 34\%$$

3. This reflects poor judgment on the part of the buyer. While the $18 markon was achieved, as a percentage of sales it represents only 34.6%.

    $$\frac{\$52 - \$34}{\$52} = \frac{\$18}{\$52} = 34.6\%$$

    The correct retail and cost are derived as follows:

    $\$18.00 \div 42.5\% = \$42.35$ (Retail)

    $\$42.35 - \$18.00 = \$24.35$ (Cost)

    Proof:

    $$\frac{\$42.35 - \$24.35}{\$42.35} = \frac{\$18.00}{\$42.35} = 42.5\%$$

5. $\$.24 \div 33.3\% = \$.72$ Retail

    $\$.72 - \$.24 = \$.48$ Cost

    Proof:

    $$\frac{\$.72 - \$.48}{\$.72} = \frac{\$.24}{\$.72} = 33.3\%$$

Cumulative Markon Derived from Known Inventory Totals (p. 73)

1. Total retail $16,000
   Less total cost   10,000
   Markon $ 6,000

   $$\frac{\$6,000}{\$16,000} = 37.5\%$$

	Cost	Retail
3. Beginning inventory	$14,000	$25,000
Net transfers-in	3,300	5,000
Net markup	-0-	800
Total merchandise handled	$17,300	$30,800

Cumulative markon $ = $30,800 − $17,300 = $13,500

Cumulative markon % = $\dfrac{\$13,500}{\$30,800}$ = 43.8%

	Cost	Retail	Cost	Retail
5. Inventory 5/1			$7,500	$14,000
Gross purchases	$1,200	$2,200		
Less returns	100	175		
Less discounts (3% × $1,200)	36	-0-		
Net purchases			1,064	2,025
Markup			-0-	135
Net transfers-in			800	1,300
Total merchandise handled			$9,364	$17,460

Cumulative markon $ = $17,460 − $9,364 = $8,096

Cumulative markon % = $\dfrac{\$8,096}{\$17,460}$ = 46.4%

Cumulative Markon Derived from Previously Unknown Inventory Totals (p. 76)

1. Cost of the beginning inventory = (100% − 38%) × $85,000 = $52,700
   Retail price of the additions = $12,000 ÷ (100% − 40%) = $20,000
   Therefore,

	Cost	Retail	Markon
Beginning inventory	$52,700	$85,000	38.0%
Additions	12,000	20,000	40.0%
Total merchandise handled	$64,700	$105,000	38.4%

$$\frac{\$105,000 - \$64,700}{\$105,000} = 38.4\%$$

3. Retail price of the beginning inventory = $23,000 ÷ (100% − 51.1%) = $47,035

   Markon for purchases = $\dfrac{\$23,000 - \$14,500}{\$23,000}$ = 36.9%

   Therefore:

	Cost	Retail	Markon
Inventory 7/1	$23,000	$47,035	51.1%
Inventory 7/1–7/31	14,500	23,000	36.9%
Total merchandise handled	$37,500	$70,035	46.5%

   $$\dfrac{\$70,035 - \$37,500}{\$70,035} = 46.5\%$$

	Cost	Retail	Markon
5. Beginning inventory	$12,000	$22,500	46.7%
Gross purchases	4,200	8,000	47.5%
Less rebate ($4,200 × 10%)	420	-0-	-0-
Total merchandise handled	$15,780	$30,500	▪ 48.3%

   $$\dfrac{\$30,500 - \$15,780}{\$30,500} = 48.3\%$$

Topics for Discussion and Review

1. What makes the retail price unique among the merchant's tactics?

2. What does the retail price consist of?

3. Explain the difference between a markon and a markup. Why are the two concepts not interchangeable?

4. Markon may be considered as the merchant's income for the purpose of covering various expenses. What are these expenses, and why is the cost of the merchandise not included?

5. Why is the percentage of markon a better indicator of profitability than the dollar markon?

6. Why is it that a markon based upon the retail price can never exceed 100%, regardless of the amount of the markon?

7. Discuss the reasons why the markon percentage should be derived from a retail base rather than a cost base.

8. Explain the easiest method of converting the retail price to its equivalent cost value.

9. What is the most efficient method of converting a known cost price to its unknown retail value?

10. Explain the concept of the cumulative markon. How is the cumulative markon percentage calculated?

11. What constitute the "additions" to the beginning-of-the-month inventory? Discuss each one in detail.

12. What functions does the markup serve?

13. Explain the method of deriving the retail and cost dollars from a given markon in dollars and percent.

14. While the matrix method for obtaining cost and retail values is rather cumbersome to use, it does have its value in explaining "relationships." What are these relationships?

15. What is the effect of returns to vendor on the cumulative markon percent?

16. How do allowances and rebates affect the cumulative markon percent?

17. What effect does a markup have on the cumulative markon percent?

18. What is the effect of a markup cancellation on gross markups?

19. Explain the derivation of the cumulative markon from unknown inventory totals.

20. Explain the concept of net transfers in.

21. What is the relationship of the initial markon to the cumulative markon?

22. What is the function of a markup?

23. What constitutes retail reductions?

24. What does the term *gross purchases* mean?

25. How do you determine the cost value of a retail inventory?

Chapter 4
The Average Markon

Learning Objectives

- Explain the concept of the average markon.

- Explain the concept of price lining.

- Identify the advantages and disadvantages of price lining.

- Determine the average unit cost so as to achieve the planned markon percentage.

- Calculate the average unit retail price so as to achieve the planned markon percentage.

- Determine the markon required on the remaining purchases at retail, in order to achieve a predetermined average markon.

- Calculate the markon required on a purchase when the retail value of that purchase and the average markon for the period have been planned.

- Determine the markon required on a purchase when the cost value of the purchase and the average markon for the period have been planned.

- Maintain the average markon when there is one cost and two retail prices.

- Maintain the average markon when there is one cost and three or more retail prices.

- Maintain the average markon when there are two costs, and one retail price.

- Explain why one retail price may represent two or more wholesale prices.

- Maintain the average markon when there are three or more costs, and one retail price.

Key Terms

Average Markon: The dollar or percentage difference between the total retail and total cost of a particular assortment of merchandise.

Balanced Inventory: The proper assortment (in size and color) of merchandise within style or classification lines to meet customer demand.

Closeout: Merchandise offered by the vendor at reduced prices in order to clear slow-moving or incomplete inventories.

Job Lot: A promotional grouping of merchandise in which a vendor disposes of end-of-season surplus and broken or incomplete assortments.

Loss Leader: Merchandise sold at or below cost, generally to attract customers.

Markdown: A reduction in the retail price of merchandise.

Open-to-Buy: The amount of merchandise that the merchant may order during the balance of a month or an accounting period.

Prestige Price Zone: The highest price of merchandise.

Price Line: A series of preestablished retail prices within a classification or department set by store policy to facilitate customer choice. For example, a man's shirt classification might carry three price lines: $12.95, $16.95, and $19.95.

Price Point: A price line established within a range of retail prices.

Price Range: The number of price points existing between the highest and lowest price point.

Price Zone: A tactical range of retail prices used to build a price structure.

Promotional Price Zone: The lower price ranges appealing to customers through a "big bargain" connotation.

Stock Turnover: The number of times within a year that an average inventory is sold and replaced.

Volume Price Zone: Those retail price lines that produce the largest sales volume.

4.1

Average Markon and Effective Merchandising

The *average markon* is the dollar or percentage difference between the cost and retail totals of a group of items or for an inventory of merchandise. However, as the name implies, it is not one markon for many items but the medium markon achieved as the result of many markons applied across a wide variety of merchandise offerings. While the individual markon is obviously important, it is the average markon obtained on the entire inventory that establishes the effectiveness of merchandising tactics. The cumulative markon, as we have seen, is an example of an average markon, in the sense that it represents the difference between the total cost and total retail price of the combined opening inventory and accumulated additions.

In the pricing of merchandise, it is virtually impossible and tactically undesirable to achieve the same markon for all items in a department or even in a particular merchandise classification. For example, wholesale prices fluctuate far more rapidly than does the retail price, and this varying differential between cost and retail will result in different markons. Also, consider that the operational expenses—such as advertising, handling, storage, and alteration costs—have a direct bearing on the amount of markon required for the profitable merchandising of certain retail classifications. Furthermore, fashion dictates various retail *price points* for particular styles, depending upon their position in the fashion curve.

It is important to note that the average markon is never the sum of the markons but is the result of the total cost and retail dollars applied to the markon percentage formula. For example,

	Cost	Retail	Markon	Markon
Item A	$8	$12	$4	33.3%
Item B	7	14	7	50.0%
Total	$15	$26	$11	42.3%

The average markon is 42.3%, or

$$\frac{\$26.00 - \$15.00}{\$26.00} = 42.3\%$$

not the average of the markons achieved on Items A and B:

$$\frac{33.3\% + 50.0\%}{2} = 41.7\%$$

While the 0.6% differential (42.3% − 41.7%) may not appear significant, it represents a $6,000 profit or loss in gross margin on net sales of a modest $1,000,000.

4.2

Price Lining

One of the most effective tactics of retail merchandising is the manipulation of the customer's perception of a merchandise offering through the profitable averaging of the retail price into *price ranges, price zones,* and *price lines.* This is referred to as *price lining,* or the establishment of a limited number of predetermined price points at which goods will be offered for sale.

The price range defines a series of prices appealing to customers in a specific demographic group—for example, men's ties retailing between $5 and $15. The price zone is a grouping of prices at a particular place within the price range; and the price point is the unique retail price within the price zone. Most large stores have three price zones: *volume, promotion,* and *prestige.* The volume, or middle, zone is the most important because that is where most stores do their volume business. The promotion zone normally represents the lower price points, or "low-end" merchandise, while the prestige zone usually defines higher prices and "high" fashion. The percentage of total store volume done in each price zone is obviously dependent upon the projected retail image. Figure 4.1 illustrates the concept of price lining for an assortment of men's ties.

The Advantages of Price Lining

In spite of some limitations, for example, adjusting the price line in proportion to a rising or falling wholesale market, this strategy has many advantages:

1. It increases sales because:
   a. Larger assortments in each price line are made possible by the elimination of in-between prices.

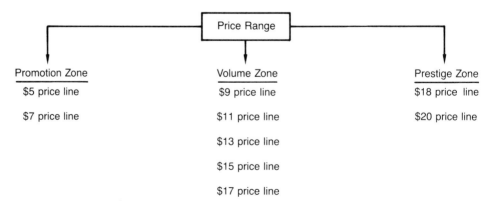

Figure 4.1 Price lining

b. It facilitates the customer's decision-making process by limiting selection to specific price points and by defining the perception of price-value relationships at each point.

c. It contributes to more-effective advertising and promotion, because the merchant can concentrate customer interest at a few price points. Promotional activities consistent with these price points will over time tend to reinforce and enhance the retail image.

2. It facilitates the balancing of inventories to customer demand; the merchant's attention can be concentrated on a relatively small assortment of prices, rather than diluted across a larger but less productive assortment.

3. It reduces the required amount of inventory to produce a specific amount of sales; thus, profitability is enhanced through a higher stock turnover and reduced markdowns.

4. It facilitates the coordination of price lines between complementary merchandise classifications, for example, between men's shirts and ties.

5. It facilitates the buying process because the preestablished retail price points automatically dictate the merchant's cost price; a man's tie that retails for $9 with a 48% markon must theoretically cost $4.68.

The major point to be made is that while price lining is a most effective merchandising strategy, its successful implementation depends on the tactics of averaging the markon, or pricing the merchandise considerably above or below the desired markon, and at the same time achieving that markon as a predetermined average ratio of profitability.

Determination of the Average Unit Cost so as to Achieve the Planned Markon Percentage

It is not unusual for the merchant to offer price lines that consist of merchandise with different costs. Thus, costs must be averaged to achieve the planned retail and markon percentages.

▪ Study Problem

Given: A merchant has an established price line of $15 shirts consisting of 250 units with a planned markon of 49.5%. In order to enhance the customer's perception of the overall quality of the line, 60 shirts have been purchased at a cost of $8.50, in spite of the fact that the planned markon cannot be achieved. The merchant is now faced with an immediate problem.

Find: At what cost should the remaining units of the price line be purchased in order to achieve the planned 49.5% markon?

Solution:

Step 1. Set up the problem as follows, and fill in the blanks as we progress:

	Cost	*Retail*	*Markon*	*Units*
Merchandise needed	$1,894 (Step 3)	$3,750 (Step 2)	49.5%	250
Less merchandise purchased	510 (Step 4)			60
Remaining purchases	$1,384 (Step 5)			190 (Step 6)

Step 2. Find the total retail value of the merchandise needed:

$15 × 250 units = $3,750

Step 3. Find the total cost value of the merchandise needed:

$3,750 × (100% − 49.5%) = Cost value

$3,750 × 50.5% = $1,894

Step 4. Determine the cost value of the merchandise purchased:

$8.50 × 60 units = $510

Step 5. Calculate the remaining purchases at cost:

Merchandise needed	$1,894
Less merchandise purchased	510
Remaining purchases	$1,384

Step 6. Calculate the remaining units to be purchased:

Units needed	250
Less units purchased	60
Units remaining	190

Step 7. Determine the average cost of the remaining units to be purchased:

$$\frac{\text{Remaining purchases at cost}}{\text{Remaining units to be purchased}} = \frac{\$1,384}{190} = \$7.28$$

The implications should be clear. The remaining units to be purchased must carry a higher than planned markon in order to compensate for the markon lost on the 60 units already purchased. Compare the two markons:

$$\frac{\$15 - \$8.50}{\$15} = 43.3\%$$

$$\frac{\$15 - \$7.28}{\$15} = 51.4\%$$

It is only through the averaging of these two markons that we are able to obtain the planned markon of 49.5%.

	Units	Cost	Retail	Markon
Merchandise purchased	60	$ 510	$ 900	43.3%
Merchandise to be purchased	190	1,384	2,850	51.4
Total merchandise needed	250	$1,894	$3,750	49.5%

▪ Application Exercise

1. Calculate the average cost per unit on the remaining purchases, given the following data:

Planned markon	38.5%
Price point	$16.95
Total merchandise units required	350
Units purchased to date	84
Cost per unit purchased to date	$12.00

2. A line of television sets consists of 75 units, with a cumulative markon of 25.5% and a retail price of $145. Twenty-five sets were purchased at a cost of $90. What should the merchant pay for the balance of the line in order to maintain the 25.5% cumulative markon?

3. A buyer manages a $30 price line of 450 women's blouses. The cumulative markon is established at 51%. Purchase plans for the coming season dictate three vendors as sources of merchandise. 150 blouses will be purchased from Vendor A at a cost of $13 per unit. 200 units will be acquired from Vendor B at $15.50 apiece. How many units must be bought from Vendor C and at what cost price to ensure the maintenance of the price line and its 51% markon?

Determination of the Average Unit Retail Price so as to Achieve the Planned Markon Percentage

This situation is conceptually the same as the previous example; in this instance, however, we are moving from a known cost to an unknown retail price. In essence, the merchant is presented with multiple cost prices that must be translated into a retail price structure in harmony with a predetermined cumulative markon percentage.

▪ Study Problem

Given: A merchant begins the season with 386 ties that cost $7.50 apiece and retail for $14 each. Another 144 ties are purchased at a cost of $6 each.

Find: At what unit price must the 144 ties be retailed if the planned cumulative markon of 53.5% is to be achieved?

Solution: *Step 1.* Set up the problem with the known information and fill in the blanks progressively:

	Cost	Retail	Markon	Units
Beginning inventory	$2,895 (2)	$5,404 (2)	46.4% (2)	386
Purchases	864 (3)	2,680 (6)	67.8% (7)	144
Total merchandise handled	$3,759 (4)	$8,084 (5)	53.5%	530

Step 2. Find the beginning inventory at cost and retail and the markon percentage achieved:

$$386 \times \$14.00 = \$5,404 \quad \text{Retail}$$
$$386 \times \$7.50 = \underline{\$2,895} \quad \text{Cost}$$
$$\$2,509 \quad \text{Markon}$$

Markon % = $2,509 ÷ $5,404 = 46.4%

Step 3. Calculate the total purchases at cost:

144 × $6 = $864

Step 4. Find the total merchandise handled at cost:

$2,895 + $864 = $3,759

Step 5. Calculate the total merchandise handled at retail:

$3,759 ÷ (100% − 53.5%) = Retail

$3,759 ÷ 46.5% = $8,084

Step 6. Determine the purchase dollars at retail:

$8,084 − $5,404 = $2,680

Step 7. Find the unit price at retail and the markon percentage for the 144 ties to be purchased:

$2,680 ÷ 144 = $18.61 Retail per unit

$2,680 − $864 = $1,816

$1,816 ÷ $2,680 = 67.8%

▪ Application Exercise

1. A buyer is offered a closeout on two groups of blouses. Group A consists of 300 units at a cost of $8.50 per unit; the buyer is certain that these can be retailed at $16 each. Group B is composed of 250 blouses at a unit cost of $7. At what unit price should the group B blouses be retailed if the planned cumulative markon of 51% is to be achieved?

2. An opening inventory consists of 80 units, with a cost value of $200 each and a markon of 33.3%. Planned additional purchases are 30 units at a cost of $225 each. The planned cumulative markon is 34.5%. Find the required unit retail price on the planned purchases necessary to achieve the desired cumulative markon.

3. The opening inventory for a particular classification of men's shoes consists of 36 pairs that cost $19 and retail for $37.50. The buyer desires to increase the unit inventory by purchasing an additional 24 pairs of shoes costing $25 per pair. Assuming a required average markon of 50%, what is the required markon on the additional purchase? What is the unit retail price for the 24 pairs of shoes?

4.3
The Average Markon Achieved on Two or More Purchases

The essence of this particular situation is the determination of cumulative markon over a specific period of time and the derivation of markon for planned purchases during that period so as to maintain the desired average markon and prevent the erosion of profitability. Specifically,

▪ An average markon must be obtained on the total merchandise handled by a store or department over a span of time.

▪ The markon on purchases within a period must be planned so as to obtain the required average markon.

▪ It may be necessary to determine the markon required on a purchase when either the retail value or cost value of that purchase and the average markon for the period have been planned.

Calculation of the Markon Required on Remaining Purchases at Retail in Order to Achieve a Predetermined Average Markon within a Particular Time Frame

In this situation, the merchant is required to achieve an average markon over a specific period of time. Thus, it becomes necessary to determine the markon on purchases required during the period in order to obtain the desired average markon.

▪ Study Problem

Given:

	Cost	Retail
Beginning inventory 1/1	$ 8,000	$15,000
Purchases 1/1–1/31	13,000	25,000
Planned purchases 2/1–2/28		20,000

The average markon for the period 1/1 through 2/28 is planned at 45%.

Find: The markon required on planned purchases 2/1 through 2/28 in order to achieve the 45% markon for the entire period 1/1 through 2/28.

Solution:

Step 1. Determine the retail value of the total merchandise handled:

	Cost	Retail	Markon
Beginning inventory 1/1	$ 8,000	$15,000	46.7%
Purchases 1/1–1/31	13,000	25,000	48.0%
Planned purchases 2/1–2/28	?	20,000	?
Total merchandise handled	?	$60,000	45.0%

Step 2. Find the cost of the total merchandise handled:

$60,000 × (100% − 45%) = Cost

Cost = $60,000 × 55%

Cost = $33,000

Thus:

	Cost	Retail	Markon
Beginning inventory 1/1	$ 8,000	$15,000	46.7%
Purchases 1/1–1/31	13,000	25,000	48.0%
Planned purchases 2/1–2/28	?	20,000	?
Total merchandise handled	$33,000	$60,000	45.0%

Step 3. Find the cost of the planned purchases:

	Cost
Beginning inventory 1/1	$ 8,000
Purchases 1/1–1/31	13,000
Total merchandise handled 1/1–1/31	$21,000

	Cost
Total merchandise handled 1/1–2/28	$33,000
Less total merchandise handled 1/1–1/31	21,000
Planned purchases 2/1–2/28	$12,000

Step 4. Find the required markon percentage for the planned purchases 2/1–2/28:

$$\frac{\text{Retail} - \text{Cost}}{\text{Retail}} = \text{Markon \%}$$

$$\frac{\$20,000 - \$12,000}{\$20,000} = 40\%$$

The completed problem appears as follows:

	Cost	Retail	Markon
Beginning inventory 1/1	$ 8,000	$15,000	46.7%
Purchases 1/1–1/31	13,000	25,000	48.0%
Planned purchases 2/1–2/28	12,000	20,000	40.0%
Total merchandise handled	$33,000	$60,000	45.0%

▪ Application Exercise

1. Determine the markon required on the remaining month's purchases in order to achieve a planned average markon of 43%.

	Cost	Retail
Inventory 6/1	$3,500	$5,000
Purchases through 6/15	1,500	3,000
Planned purchases 6/16–6/30		2,000

2. A shoe buyer had a beginning inventory of $25,000 at cost and $48,000 at retail. Additional merchandise was purchased at a cost of $12,000 with a planned retail of $24,000. In order to obtain an average markon of 49%, more shoes were ordered to retail at $18,000. What must the markon be to achieve the desired average markon?

3. The housewares department began the season with an inventory of $35,000 at cost and $62,300 at retail. Total purchases to date amount to $23,000 at retail and $13,000 at cost. For the balance of the period, retail purchases are planned at $9,000. What should be the markon on these planned purchases if an average markon for the season is to be 42.5%?

Determination of the Markon Required on a Purchase When the Retail Value of That Purchase and the Average Markon for the Period Have Been Planned

Here the merchant is required to determine the markon required on a purchase when the retail value of that purchase and the average markon for the period are known.

■ Study Problem

Given: A hosiery buyer is expected to realize an average markon of 48.5%. The cumulative inventory has a retail value of $23,000 and a markon of 47%.

Find: If additional purchases at retail are planned at $10,000, what is the markon required to achieve the 48.5% average markon?

Solution:

Step 1. Set up the problem and define the retail value of the total merchandise to be handled:

	Cost	Retail	Markon
Cumulative inventory	?	$23,000	47.0%
Planned purchases	?	10,000	?
Total merchandise handled	?	$33,000	48.5%

Step 2. Determine the cost of the total merchandise handled:

Cost = $33,000 × (100% − 48.5%)

Cost = $33,000 × 51.5% = $16,995

Step 3. Determine the cost of the cumulative inventory:

Cost = $23,000 × (100% − 47%)

Cost = $23,000 × 53% = $12,190

Step 4. Find the planned purchases at cost:

Total merchandise handled at cost	$16,995
Less cost of the cumulative inventory	− 12,190
Planned purchases at cost	$ 4,805

Step 5. Determine the markon on planned purchases:

$$\frac{\text{Retail} - \text{Cost}}{\text{Retail}} = \text{Markon \%}$$

$$\frac{\$10,000 - \$4,805}{\$10,000} = 52\%$$

Thus:

	Cost,	*Retail*	*Markon*
Cumulative inventory	$12,190	$23,000	47.0%
Planned purchases	4,805	10,000	52.0%
Total merchandise handled	$16,995	$33,000	48.5%

■ Application Exercise

1. A costume jewelry buyer is committed to a 53.5% cumulative markon. The beginning inventory plus purchases to date are $36,000 at retail, with an achieved average markon of only 51.3%. The remaining open-to-buy at retail is $18,000. What percentage of markon must be obtained on purchases in order to acquire the 53.5% cumulative markon?

2. Your store requires a 48.3% average markon in order to support operating commitments. Sales to date have been $600,000 with an achieved markon of 51%. Total sales are planned at $900,000. What is the minimum markon required on remaining purchases in order to meet the required 48.3% average markon?

3. The budget linen department has an average markon goal of 37.3%. There is an inventory on hand of $11,250 at retail, which achieves this markon. The planned total merchandise handled for the period is $18,500 at retail. What

should the markon be on planned purchases if the average markon goal is to be increased by one percentage point?

Determination of the Markon Required on a Purchase When the Cost Value of That Purchase and the Average Markon for the Period Have Been Planned

Here, the merchant is in the position of having to replenish inventory at some time during a season and must determine the required markon when one cost value of that purchase and the average markon for the season are known.

■ Study Problem

Given: A towel buyer has a seasonal budget of $56,000 at cost. Purchases for February and March cost $18,500 and had a markon of 46.5%.

Find: What markon must be obtained on the remaining purchases at cost in order to achieve an average markon of 48.5%?

Solution: As in the previous study problem, in order to find the markon on remaining purchases, we must first define the cost and retail price of those purchases.

Step 1. Set up the problem and establish the cost of the remaining purchases:

	Cost	Retail	Markon
Purchases	$18,500	?	46.5%
Remaining purchases	37,500	?	?
Total merchandise handled	$56,000	?	48.5%

Step 2. Find the retail price of the February–March purchases:

$18,500 ÷ (100% − 46.5%) = The retail price of the purchase

$18,500 ÷ 53.5% = $34,579

Step 3. Determine the retail price of the total merchandise handled:

$56,000 ÷ (100% − 48.5%) = The retail price of the total merchandise handled

$56,000 ÷ 51.5% = $108,738

Step 4. Calculate the retail price of the remaining purchases:

Total merchandise handled at retail	$108,738
Less February–March purchases at retail	34,579
Retail price of remaining purchases	$ 74,159

Step 5. Find the required markon percentage for the remaining purchases:

$$\frac{\text{Retail} - \text{Cost}}{\text{Retail}} = \text{Markon \%}$$

$$\frac{\$74,159 - \$37,500}{\$74,159} = 49.4\%$$

Thus:

	Cost	Retail	Markon
Purchases	$18,500	$ 34,579	46.5%
Remaining purchases	37,500	74,159	49.4%
Total merchandise handled	$56,000	$108,738	48.5%

■ Application Exercise

1. A merchant has an open-to-buy at cost of $15,000; to date, $9,000 has been spent, with an achieved markon of only 35.5%. Determine the markon for the remaining purchases if the cumulative markon goal of 38% is to be met.

2. A buyer of women's sportswear purchased merchandise for $10,500 at cost, upon which was placed a 48% markon. The merchandise immediately sold out, and an $8,000 reorder was placed with the vendor. Determine the markon on this reorder, if the average markon is to be increased to 51.5%.

3. On the first trip to the market, a toy buyer spent $4,800, with a planned markon of 38.5%; on the second trip, $6,300 was spent, with an anticipated markon of 45.7%. What should the markon percentage be on the third and final purchase of $5,300, if the planned cumulative markon of 43% is to be achieved?

Maintaining the Average Markon When There Is One Cost and Two Retail Prices

There are many occasions when the merchant has the opportunity to purchase groups of merchandise, defined as job lots or manufacturers' closeouts, which consist of miscellaneous assortments in terms of size, color, pattern, style, fashion level, and so forth of similar goods. In effect, the attractive price of the vendor's offering forces the merchant to think in terms of one initial cost and at least two retail prices. This necessitates the numerical division of the merchandise into an unequal assortment of retail price points and thus in turn dictates the averaging of at least two different markons into one required markon.

In the process of averaging, fractional units of merchandise and dollars will occur, necessitating their rounding into whole units and dollars. As a result, exact totals are not always obtainable; these small discrepancies will not affect the desired results.

▪ Study Problem

Given: A buyer purchased a quantity of women's blouses at $6.72 each, knowing that some will retail for $15 and that the rest will sell at the $10.50 price point.

Find: In what proportion must these blouses be priced so as to obtain an average markon of 52%?

Solution:

Step 1. Determine the average retail price:

$6.72 ÷ (100% − 52%) = Average retail

$6.72 ÷ 48% = $14

Step 2. Establish the ratio, or relationship, existing between the average retail price and the established retail price points:

Established retail price points	$15.00	$10.50
Less average retail price	14.00	14.00
Gain or (loss) on average price	$1.00	($3.50)

On every blouse that retails for $15, the buyer will gain $1 above the average retail price, which would provide the required 52% markon. On the other hand, at the $10.50 price point, the buyer falls short of the average required retail price by $3.50. Therefore, in order to break even and obtain the average retail price of $14, the buyer must sell one blouse at $10.50 for every 3.5 blouses retailed at $15. This is so because for every one blouse retailed at $10.50 the buyer will lose $3.50:

$$1 × (\$3.50) = (\$3.50)$$

For every 3.5 blouses retailed at $15 the buyer will gain $3.50:

$$3.5 × \$1.00 = \$3.50$$

Schematically, we observe:

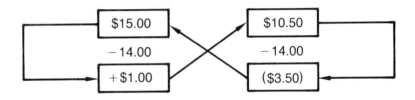

or

$$1 \times (\$3.50) = (\$3.50)$$
$$\left.\frac{3.5 \times \ \$1.00}{} = \frac{\$3.50}{\$0.00}\right\} \text{ Breakeven Point}$$

Therefore, the ratio of retail price points to be established is 1:3.5; for every one blouse retailed at $10.50, 3.5 must be retailed at $15 in order to break even, or achieve the average retail price of $14 and obtain the 52% markon.

Step 3. Obviously 3.5 blouses cannot be retailed; therefore it becomes necessary to convert the numbers in the ratio to whole numbers, reduced by their lowest common denominator. Thus, multiplying the ratio 1:3.5 times 10 will remove the decimal point and create the ratio of 10:35. That ratio divided by its lowest common denominator, 5, will result in the ratio of 2:7.

$$1:3.5(10) = 10:35$$

$$\frac{10:35}{5} = 2:7$$

Step 4. However, our concern is not with 9 blouses (2 + 7) but with the proportional relationship existing between the price points for any given quantity of blouses. Thus, we need to convert the 2:7 ratio to a percentage relationship.

2 blouses (at $10.50)
7 blouses (at $15.00)
9 blouses (at the average retail of $14.00)

or

$$\frac{2}{9} = 22\% \text{ (at \$10.50)}$$

and

$$\frac{7}{9} = 78\% \text{ (at \$15.00)}$$

Thus, for any quantity of blouses purchased, 22% must be retailed at $10.50 and 78% must be retailed at $15 in order to achieve the average retail price of $14 and the average markon of 52%.

■ Application Exercise

1. A buyer purchases a quantity of jackets at $10 each, knowing that some will retail at $18 and the rest at $22 apiece. In what proportion must these jackets be priced so as to obtain an average markon of 48%?

2. The cost for a certain line of shirts is $4 each. The established retail price for similar quality shirts is $5.50 and $7. In what proportion must these shirts be retailed if a 37.5% average markon is to be achieved?

3. A buyer purchased 144 ties at $5 each. The more colorful ones are placed in the $9.50 price line and the rest in the $5.50 price line. How many ties should be placed in each price line in order to obtain an average markon of 37.5%?

4. A candy buyer purchases 300 chocolate Easter bunnies for the Easter and post-Easter season for a cost of $4.94 each. For the Easter season, the markon will be 55%; a one-half price "clearance" sale is planned for the post-Easter season. How should the buyer apportion the candy to obtain an average markon of 45%?

Maintaining the Average Markon When There Is One Cost and Three or More Retail Prices

It is not always possible or even desirable to distribute a job lot of merchandise across only two retail price points. As is often the case, a job lot may consist of many items of quite different qualities, all of which have to be worked into an existing inventory. Consider the following problem.

■ Study Problem

Given: A men's furnishings buyer is offered 500 fancy bow ties at a cost of $2 each. Inspection of the merchandise indicates that the ties would fit very nicely into a promotional offering of four different price lines, $1.95, $2.95, $3.95, and $4.95. The quality range of the offering is such that the buyer is confident that 150 ties will sell at $1.95 and another 100 can be retailed at $4.95.

Find: How is the balance of the merchandise to be distributed between the remaining $2.95 and $3.95 price points so that a 40% average markon is achieved?

Solution:

Step 1. Determine the retail value of the 500 ties:

Total cost = 500 ties × $2 = $1,000

Total retail = $1,000 ÷ 60% = $1,667

Step 2. Calculate the number of ties allocated to the $1.95 and $2.95 price points and their total retail value:

150 ties	×	$1.95	=	$292.50 Retail
100 ties	×	$4.95	=	$495.00 Retail
250 ties				$787.50 Total retail

Step 3. Find the number of ties remaining and their total retail value:

	Units	Retail
Total offered	500	$1,667.00
Less total allocated	250	787.50
Total remaining	250	$ 879.50

Step 4. Determine the average retail price per unit of the remaining total:

$879.50 ÷ 250 = $3.52

Step 5. Allocate the 250 remaining ties to the $2.95 and $3.95 price points:

Established price points	$2.95	$3.95
Average price point	3.52	3.52
Gain or (loss)	($ .57)	$ .43
Reduced to lowest terms	(57)	43

Thus the ratio is 57 ($3.95 ties):43 ($2.95 ties) or proportionally, 57/100, or 57%, of the remaining ties must be retailed at $3.95, and 43/100, or 43%, must be retailed at $2.95. Or,

250	(Remaining)		250	(Remaining)
× 57%	($3.95)		× 43%	($2.95)
142	(at $3.95)		108	(at $2.95)

Proof:

Unit Retail		Units	Total Retail	Total Cost	Markon
$1.95	×	150	$ 292.50	$ 300.00	(2.6%)
2.95	×	108	318.60	216.00	32.2%
3.95	×	142	560.90	284.00	49.4%
4.95	×	100	495.00	200.00	59.6%
		500	$1,667.00	$1,000.00	40.0%

$$\frac{\$1,667 - \$1,000}{\$1,667} = 40\%$$

■ **Application Exercise**

1. A buyer is offered a closeout of 500 designer dresses at $46.83 each. The buyer decides that 100 can be retailed at $99 and 150 at $69. How many must be retailed at $79 and at $89 if the average markon is to be 42%?

2. A misses' coat buyer purchased 300 spring raincoats at a manufacturer's close-out price of $15,600 for the lot. One hundred were selected to be loss leaders and were priced at cost. The balance was to be worked into a $109 and a $129 price line. How many must be retailed at each of these prices in order to obtain a 49% average markon?

3. A sportswear buyer is considering the purchase of an end-of-the-season, man-ufacturer's closeout of 500 bathing suits in assorted styles and colors. The unit cost is $8. The buyer feels that they can be retailed accordingly:

   150 at $17
   100 at $14
   200 at $12
    50 at $20

   Should the purchase be made if the average markon desired is 52%?

Maintaining the Average Markon When There Are Two Costs and One Retail Price

It is relatively impossible and totally impractical for the merchant to attempt to carry as many retail prices as there are wholesale prices. In short, the one retail price will in all likelihood represent at least two, and probably more, wholesale prices because of the following:

■ The wholesale price may fluctuate between the periods of purchase.

■ Different styles created by one manufacturer may have different costs.

■ Similar merchandise offered by different manufacturers will have different costs.

■ The impact of fashion will at times dictate markdowns and thus force the movement of previously high-priced merchandise into relatively cheaper price lines, which nevertheless must also maintain an average markon.

   Despite these factors resulting in cost variation, the merchant must maintain the previously determined average markon. This is accomplished through the grouping of merchandise into retail price categories, so that low-cost, high-markon merchandise will counterbalance the high-cost, low-markon merchandise. It is through this balancing process that the required average markon is achieved.

▪ Study Problem

Given: A men's furnishings buyer has a $20 price line of oxford shirts. Some may be purchased from Vendor A at a cost of $9, but to complete a full price line, the balance must be obtained from Vendor B at a unit cost of $10.50.

Find: In what proportion should these shirts be purchased so as to obtain an average markon of 50%?

Solution:

Step 1. Determine the average cost price which will provide the desired average markon of 50%:

$20 × (100% − 50%) = Cost

$20 × 50% = $10

Step 2. Compare the average cost price of $10 to the established costs of $9 and $10.50:

Established cost	$ 9.00	$10.50
Less average cost	(10.00)	(10.00)
Gain or (loss)	($ 1.00)	$ .50
Lowest terms	(2)	1

Thus, the ratio is 2:1, or for every two $10.50 shirts purchased, the buyer is over the average cost by $1 (2 × $.50), and for every $9 shirt acquired, the buyer is under the average cost by $1 (1 × $1).

$$2 × \$ .50 = \$1.00$$
$$1 × (\$1.00) = (\$1.00)$$ } Breakeven point

Step 3. The proportion in which to purchase the $9 and $10.50 shirts is:

$$\frac{2\ (\$10.50)}{3\ (2\ +\ 1)} = 67\%\ at\ \$10.50$$

$$\frac{1\ (\$9)}{3\ (2\ +\ 1)} = 33\%\ at\ \$9$$

Proof: Assume that 12-dozen shirts are to be purchased under the above conditions:

67% × 144 = 96 shirts × $10.50 = $1,008

33% × 144 = 48 shirts × $9 = $432

Total cost = $1,008 + $432 = $1,440

Total retail = $20 × 144 = $2,880

$$\frac{\$2,880 - \$1,440}{\$2,880} = 50\%$$

■ Application Exercise

1. A buyer offers a price line of men's socks retailing at $4.50 a pair. The normal wholesale cost from Vendor A is $2.25 for these socks. However, Vendor A cannot currently supply a sufficient quantity, and the buyer is forced to purchase additional similar merchandise from Vendor B at a cost of $2.64 per pair. In what proportion should the purchases be distributed in order to achieve an average markon of 48%?

2. A buyer wishes to replenish an inventory of $15 wallets by purchasing another 300. It is found that one vendor will furnish some at a cost of $8 each; however, it is unable to supply the required 300 units. Another vendor is located that has comparable merchandise, but at a cost of $11 each. What percentage should be purchased at each cost so as to achieve a planned average markon of 40%?

3. In what proportion must the merchant purchase sweaters to retail at $50, when the costs are $23.50 and $28.95 and the required markon is 49.5%?

Maintaining the Average Markon When There Are Three or More Costs and One Retail Price

It is rare that the merchant will be limited to only two vendors when selecting goods for resale. Merchandise buying is a selection process spread across many different vendors; thus, a variety of costs may have to be taken into account. Consider the following buying situation.

■ Study Problem

Given: An accessories buyer carries a price line of handbags retailing at $45. A stock count indicates that an additional 350 units are required to bring the inventory level up to its optimum point. Following a trip to the market, the buyer selects merchandise from three different manufacturers, costing $18, $22, and $26. Because the required average markon is 52%, the buyer allocates only 20% of the 350 handbags to the $26 cost price.

Find: How many units should be purchased at all three costs so as to achieve the 52% markon?

Solution:

Step 1. Given the retail price and the markon percentage, determine the average cost price of the handbags to be purchased:

$45 × (100% − 52%) = Average cost price

$45 × 48% = $21.60

Step 2. Find the total cost for the 350 units to be purchased:

$21.60 × 350 = $7,560

Step 3. Calculate the dollar amount and the number of units allocated to the $26 cost price:

350 units × 20% = 70 units

70 units × $26 = $1,820

Step 4. Determine the balance remaining to be distributed between the $18 and $22 cost price:

	Units	*Dollars*
Total to be purchased	350	$7,560
Less allocated to $26 cost	70	1,820
Balance	280	$5,740

Step 5. Calculate the average cost of the remaining 280 units:

$5,740 ÷ 280 = $20.50

Step 6. Find the ratio to determine the proportion in which the balance is to be distributed:

Established cost	$18.00	$22.00
Less average cost	20.50	20.50
Gain or (loss)	($2.50)	$ 1.50
Lowest terms	(5)	3

The ratio is 5 (at $22):3 (at $18) The percentage distribution is:

3/8 ($18) = 37.5% ($18)

5/8 ($22) = 62.5% ($22)

The actual distribution is:

280 × 37.5% = 105 handbags at $18

280 × 62.5% = 175 handbags at $22

or

105 units at $18	$1,890	
175 units at $22	3,850	
70 units at $26	1,820	
350	$7,560	

Proof:

Unit Cost		Units	Total Cost	Total Retail	Markon
$18	×	105	$1,890	$ 4,725	60.0%
$22	×	175	$3,850	$ 7,875	51.1%
$26	×	70	$1,820	$ 3,150	42.2%
		350	$7,560	$15,750	52.0%

$$\frac{\text{Retail} - \text{Cost}}{\text{Retail}} = \text{Markon \%}$$

$$\frac{\$15,750 - \$7,560}{\$15,750} = 52\%$$

■ Application Exercise

1. A gift shop buyer decides to stock 300 Christmas candles to retail at $6 each, with a 50% average markon. Twenty percent of the inventory is to be purchased from Vendor A at a unit cost of $4. The balance will be supplied by Vendors B and C at a cost of $2.50 and $3.50, respectively. How many candles should be purchased at each cost to ensure the average markon?

2. A retail florist decides to purchase 100 Easter lilies to supplement the 200 previously grown for the approaching Easter season. It is estimated that those 200 plants cost $3.50 apiece to grow. Two outside resources are available with costs of $4 and $4.50. How many should be purchased at each cost to ensure an average markon of 53% and a retail price of $8 per lily?

3. An assistant buyer is offered an assortment of men's belts for the annual assistant buyers' day sale. The belts are available at a cost of $4.84, $5.90, $6.50, and $7.92. If the sale price of 250 belts is to be $12.88, with 30% of the assortment at the $4.84 cost and 20% at the $7.92 cost, how many belts should be purchased at the $5.90 and $6.50 costs to maintain an average markon of 52.5%?

▪ Solutions to the Application Exercises

Determination of the Average Unit Cost so as to Achieve the Planned Markon Percentage (p. 87)

1. Find the retail value of the total merchandise required:

   $16.95 × 350 = $5,933

   Find the cost value of the total merchandise required:

   $5,933 × (100% − 38.5%) = Cost

   $5,933 × 61.5% = $3,649

   Determine the cost value of the merchandise purchased to date:

   $12 × 84 = $1,008

   Calculate the remaining purchases at cost:

   $3,649 − $1,008 = $2,641

   Find the remaining units to be purchased:

   350 − 84 = 266

   Determine the average cost per unit in the remaining purchases:

   $2,641 ÷ 266 = $9.93

   Thus:

	Units	Cost	Retail	Markon
Merchandise purchased to date	84	$1,008	$1,424	29.2%
Merchandise to be purchased	266	2,641	4,509	41.4%
Total merchandise needed	350	$3,649	$5,933	38.5%

3. Determine the retail value of the price line:

   $30 × 450 − $13,500

   Convert the retail value to cost:

   $13,500 × 49% = $6,615

   Set up the problem:

	Units	Cost
Price line	450	$6,615
Less Vendor A	150	1,950
Balance	300	$4,665

| Less Vendor B | 200 | 3,100 |
| Balance | 100 | $1,565 |

Determine the cost per blouse from Vendor C:

$1,565 ÷ 100 = $15.65

Thus:

	Units	Cost	Retail	Markon
Vendor A	150	$1,950	$ 4,500	56.7%
Vendor B	200	3,100	6,000	48.3%
Vendor C	100	1,565	3,000	47.8%
Total line	450	$6,615	$13,500	51.0%

Determination of the Average Unit Retail Price so as to Achieve the Planned Markon Percentage (p. 89)

	Cost	Retail	Markon	Units
1. Group A	$2,550 (Step 1)	$4,800	46.9% (Step 1)	300
Group B	1,750 (Step 2)	3,976 (Step 4)	56.0% (Step 4)	250
Total merchandise handled	$4,300 (Step 3)	$8,776 (Step 3)	51.0%	550

Step 1. Determine the total cost, total retail price, and markon percentage for Group A:

$ 8.50 × 300 units = $2,550 (Cost)

$16.00 × 300 units = $4,800 (Retail)

$$\frac{\$4,800 - \$2,550}{\$4,800} = 46.9\% \text{ (Markon)}$$

Step 2. Find the total cost of Group B:

$7 × 250 = $1,750 (Cost)

Step 3. Calculate cost and retail of total merchandise handled:

$2,550 + $1,750 = $4,300 (Cost)

$4,300 ÷ (100% − 51%) = Retail

$4,300 ÷ 49% = $8,776

Step 4. Find the retail value and markon percentage for Group B.

$8,776 − $4,800 = $3,976 (Retail value)

$$\frac{\$3,976 - \$1,750}{\$3,976} = 56\%$$

Step 5. The retail price per unit of Group B blouses is:

$3,976 ÷ 250 = $15.90

	Cost	Retail	Markon	Units
3. Existing inventory	$ 684 (1)	$1,350 (1)	49.3% (1)	36
Additions	600 (2)	1,218 (4)	50.7% (4)	24
Total merchandise handled	$1,284 (3)	$2,568 (3)	50.0%	60

Step 1. Determine the total cost, retail, and markon of the existing inventory:

```
36 × $37.50 = $1,350    Retail
36 × $19.00 =    684    Cost
              $ 666    Markon
```

$666 ÷ $1,350 = 49.3%

Step 2. Calculate cost of the additions:

24 × $25 = $600

Step 3. Determine the cost and retail value of the total merchandise handled:

Existing inventory	$684
Additions	600
Total cost	$1,284

$1,284 ÷ (100% − 50%) = Retail

$1,284 ÷ 50% = $2,568

Step 4. Determine the retail value of the additions and the markon percentage:

Total merchandise handled	$2,568
Less existing inventory	1,350
Retail value of additions	$1,218

The required markon percentage is:

$$\frac{\$1,218 - \$600}{\$1,218} = 50.7\%$$

Step 5. The average unit retail for the additions is:

$1,218 ÷ 24 = $50.75

Calculation of the Markon Required on Remaining Purchases at Retail in Order to Achieve a Predetermined Average Markon within a Particular Time Frame (p. 91)

	Cost	Retail	Markon
1. Inventory 6/1	$3,500	$ 5,000	30.0%
Purchases 6/1–6/15	1,500	3,000	50.0%
Planned purchases 6/16–6/30	?	2,000	?
Total merchandise handled	?	$10,000	43.0%

Total merchandise handled at cost:

$10,000 × (100% − 43%)

$10,000 × 57% = $5,700

Planned purchases at cost:

$5,700 − ($3,500 + $1,500) = $5,700 − $5,000 = $700

$$\frac{Retail - Cost}{Retail} = Markon\ \%$$

$$\frac{\$2,000 - \$700}{\$2,000} = 65\%$$

Thus:

	Cost	Retail	Markon
Inventory 6/1	$3,500	$ 5,000	30.0%
Purchases 6/1–6/15	1,500	3,000	50.0%
Planned purchases 6/16–6/30	700	2,000	65.0%
Total merchandise handled	$5,700	$10,000	43.0%

	Cost	Retail	Markon
3. Opening inventory	$35,000	$62,300	43.8%
Purchases to date	13,000	23,000	43.5%
Planned purchases	?	9,000	?
Total merchandise handled	?	$94,300	42.5%

Total merchandise handled at cost:

$94,300 × (100% − 42.5%) = $94,300 × 57.5% = $54,223

Planned purchases at cost:

$54,223 – ($35,000 + $13,000) = $54,223 – $48,000 = $6,223

$$\frac{\text{Retail} - \text{Cost}}{\text{Retail}} = \text{Markon \%}$$

$$\frac{\$9,000 - \$6,223}{\$9,000} = 30.9\%$$

Thus,

	Cost	Retail	Markon
Opening inventory	$35,000	$62,300	43.8%
Purchases to date	13,000	23,000	43.5%
Planned purchases	6,223	9,000	30.9%
Total merchandise handled	$54,223	$94,300	42.5%

Determination of the Markon Required on a Purchase When the Retail Value of That Purchase and the Average Markon for the Period Have Been Planned (p. 93)

	Cost	Retail	Markon
1. Cumulative inventory	?	$36,000	51.3%
Remaining open-to-buy	?	18,000	?
Total merchandise handled	?	$54,000	53.5%

Determine the cost of the cumulative inventory:

$36,000 × 48.7% = $17,532

Determine the cost of the total merchandise handled:

$54,000 × 46.5% = $25,110

Find the open-to-buy at cost:

Total merchandise handled at cost	$25,110
Less cost of the cumulative inventory	17,532
	$ 7,578

The markon on remaining open-to-buy must be:

$$\frac{\text{Retail} - \text{Cost}}{\text{Retail}} = \text{Markon \%}$$

$$\frac{\$18,000 - \$7,578}{\$18,000} = 57.9\%$$

Thus:

	Cost	Retail	Markon
Cumulative inventory	$17,532	$36,000	51.3%
Remaining open-to-buy	7,578	18,000	57.9%
Total merchandise handled	$25,110	$54,000	53.5%

	Cost	Retail	Markon
3. Inventory on hand	?	$11,250	37.3%
Planned purchases	?	7,250	?
Total merchandise handled	?	$18,500	38.3%

Find the cost of the inventory on hand:

$11,250 × 62.7% = $7,054

Determine the cost of the total merchandise handled:

$18,500 × 61.7% = $11,415

Total cost of the merchandise handled	$11,415
Less cost of the inventory on hand	7,054
The cost of the planned purchase	$ 4,361

$$\frac{\text{Retail} - \text{Cost}}{\text{Retail}} = \text{Markon \%}$$

$$\frac{\$7,250 - \$4,361}{\$7,250} = 39.8\%$$

Thus:

	Cost	Retail	Markon
Inventory on hand	$ 7,054	$11,250	37.3%
Planned purchases	4,361	7,250	39.8%
Total merchandise	$11,415	$18,500	38.3%

Determination of the Markon Required on a Purchase When the Cost Value of That Purchase and the Average Markon for the Period have Been Planned (p. 95)

	Cost	Retail	Markon
1. Spent	$ 9,000	?	35.5%
Remaining purchases	6,000	?	?
Open-to-buy	$15,000	?	38.0%

Find the retail for the $9,000 spent at cost:

$9,000 ÷ (100% − 35.5%) = $9,000 ÷ 64.5% = $13,953

Determine the retail price of the open-to-buy:

$15,000 ÷ (100% − 38%) = $15,000 ÷ 62% = $24,194

Define the retail price of the remaining purchases:

Open-to-buy at retail	$24,194
Less retail for $9,000, spent at cost	13,953
Remaining purchases at retail	$10,241

Calculate the markon for the remaining purchases:

$$\frac{Retail - Cost}{Retail} = Markon \%$$

$$\frac{\$10,241 - \$6,000}{\$10,241} = 41.4\%$$

Thus:

	Cost	Retail	Markon
Spent	$ 9,000	$13,953	35.5%
Remaining purchases	6,000	10,241	41.4%
Open-to-buy	$15,000	$24,194	38.0%

		Cost	Retail	Markon
3.	First purchase	$ 4,800	?	38.5%
	Second purchase	6,300	?	45.7%
	Total purchases to date	$11,100	?	?
	Third purchases	5,300	?	?
	Total purchases	$16,400	?	43.0%

Find the retail value of the first purchase:

$4,800 ÷ 61.5% = $7,805

Find the retail value of the second purchase:

$6,300 ÷ 54.3% = $11,602

Calculate the retail value of the total purchases to date and the average markon percentage:

First purchase at retail	$ 7,805
Second purchase at retail	11,602
Total purchases at retail to date	$19,407

The average markon percentage:

$$\frac{\$19{,}407 - \$11{,}100}{\$19{,}407} = 42.8\%$$

Determine the total purchases at retail:

$$\$16{,}400 \div 57\% = \$28{,}772$$

Calculate the retail value of the third purchase:

Total purchases at retail	$28,772
Less total purchases at retail to date	19,407
Retail value of the third purchase	$ 9,365

Find the markon on the third purchase:

$$\frac{\$9{,}365 - \$5{,}300}{\$9{,}365} = 43.4\%$$

Thus:

	Cost	Retail	Markon
First purchase	$ 4,800	$ 7,805	38.5%
Second purchase	6,300	11,602	45.7%
Total purchases to date	$11,100	$19,407	42.8%
Third purchase	5,300	9,365	43.4%
Total purchases	$16,400	$28,772	43.0%

Maintaining the Average Markon When There Is One Cost and Two Retail Prices (p. 98)

1. Determine the average retail price:
   $$\$10.00 \div 52\% = \$19.23$$
   Establish the ratio between the average retail price and the established retail price points:

	$18.00	$22.00
Established retail price points		
Less average retail price	19.23	19.23
Gain or (loss)	($ 1.23)	$ 2.77

Thus, multiplying the gain (loss) by 100 we determine that 123 jackets retailed at $22 will produce a gain of $340.17 (123 × $2.77 = $340.71). And 277 jackets retailed at $18 will produce a loss of $340.71 (277 × −$1.23 = −$340.71). The buyer breaks even, or achieves the average markon of 48%, when the ratio of established retail price is 123 at $22 and 277 at $18. The proportion in which the jackets must be priced in order to achieve the average markon of 48% is:

$$\frac{123 \ (at \ \$22)}{400 \ (the \ sum \ of \ 123 \ + \ 277)} = 31\%, \ and$$

$$\frac{277 \ (at \ \$18)}{400 \ (the \ sum \ of \ 123 \ + \ 277)} = 69\%$$

3. The average retail $= \dfrac{\$5}{62.5\%} = \$8$

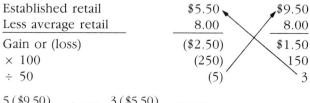

Established retail	$5.50	$9.50
Less average retail	8.00	8.00
Gain or (loss)	($2.50)	$1.50
× 100	(250)	150
÷ 50	(5)	3

$$\frac{5\,(\$9.50)}{8\,(5+3)} = 62.5\%, \ \frac{3\,(\$5.50)}{8\,(5+3)} = 37.5\%$$

144 × 62.5% = 90 ties retailed at $9.50

144 × 37.5% = 54 ties retailed at $5.50

Proof:

90 × $9.50 = $855
54 × $5.50 = $297
144   = $1,152   (Total retail)

144 × $5 = $720 (Total cost)

$$\frac{\$1,152 \ - \ \$720}{\$1,152} = 37.5\%$$

Maintaining the Average Markon When There Is One Cost and Three or More Retail Prices (p. 100)

1. Determine the total retail price of the 500 dresses:

   Total cost = 500 × $46.83 = $23,415

   Total retail = $23,415 ÷ 58% = $40,370.69

   Calculate the number of dresses allocated and their total retail value:

   100 × $99 = $ 9,900
   150 × $69 = 10,350
   250           $20,250   (Total retail)

Find the number of remaining dresses and their total retail value:

$$
\begin{array}{ll}
500 & \$40,370.69 \\
-250 & -20,250.00 \\
\hline
250 & \$20,120.69
\end{array}
$$

The average retail price per remaining unit is:

$\$20,120.69 \div 250 = \$80.48$

Allocate the remaining 250 dresses to the $79 and $89 retail price points:

	$79.00	$89.00
Established price points		
Less average price point	80.48	80.48
Gain or (loss)	(1.48)	8.52
Lowest terms	(37)	213

The ratio is 37 ($89):213 ($79):

$$\frac{37\ (\$89)}{250\ (\text{Total})} = 14.8\% \text{ at } \$89$$

$$\frac{213\ (\$79)}{250\ (\text{Total})} = 85.2\% \text{ at } \$79$$

$250 \times 14.8\% = 37$ dresses at $89

$250 \times 85.2\% = 213$ dresses at $79

Proof:

Unit Retail	Units	Total Retail	Total Cost	Markon
$69	150	$10,350	$ 7,024.50	32.1%
79	213	16,827	9,974.79	40.7%
89	37	3,293	1,732.71	47.4%
99	100	9,900	4,683.00	52.7%
	500	$40,370	$23,415.00	42.0%

$$\frac{\$40,370 - \$23,415}{\$40,370} = 42\%$$

	Unit Retail		Units		Total Retail
3.	$17	×	150	=	$2,550
	14	×	100	=	1,400
	12	×	200	=	2,400
	20	×	50	=	1,000
			500	=	$7,350

Total cost $= \$8 \times 500 = \$4,000$

$$\frac{\$7,350 - \$4,000}{\$7,350} = 45.6\%$$

The average achieved markon is only 43.3%; the answer is no!

Maintaining the Average Markon When There Are Two Costs and One Retail Price (p. 102)

1. The average cost price = $4.50 × 52% = $2.34.
   Compare the average cost price to the established costs:

Established cost	$2.25	$2.64
Less average cost	2.34	2.34
Gain or (loss)	($ .09)	$ .30
Lowest terms	(3)	10

   For every 3 pairs purchased at $2.64, 10 must be purchased at $2.25, because at $2.25 the buyer loses $.09 and 10 × ($.09) = ($.90), and at $2.64 $.30 is gained, and 3 × $.30 = $.90. In other words:

   $$\left.\begin{array}{l} 3 \times \$.30 = \$.90 \\ 10 \times (\$.09) = (\$.90) \end{array}\right\} \text{Break even}$$

   The ratio is therefore 3 (at $2.64):10 (at $2.25).

   $$\frac{3 \ (\$2.64)}{13 \ (3 + 10)} = 23\% \text{ at } \$2.64, \text{ and}$$

   $$\frac{10 \ (\$2.25)}{13 \ (3 + 10)} = 77\% \text{ at } \$2.25$$

   Proof: Assume the $4.50 price line consists of 130 units:

130 × 23% =	30 units	×	$2.64	=	$ 79
130 × 77% =	100 units	×	$2.25	=	$225
Total cost =	130 units				$304

   Total retail = 130 × $4.50 = $585

   $$\frac{\$585 - \$304}{\$585} = 48\%$$

3. The average cost is $50 × 50.5% = $25.25:

Established cost	$23.50	$28.95
Less average cost	25.25	25.25
Gain or (loss)	($ 1.75)	$ 3.70
Lowest terms	(35)	74

74 sweaters purchased at $23.50 will "save" the buyer ($1.75) on each sweater, or ($1.75) × 74 = ($129.50), and 35 sweaters purchased at $28.95 will "cost" the buyer $3.70, or $3.70 × 35 = $129.50. Thus:

$$\left.\begin{array}{l} 74 \times (\$1.75) = (\$129.50) \\ 35 \times \$3.70 = \$129.50 \end{array}\right\} \text{Break even}$$

The proportion in which the buyer is to purchase the sweaters is:

$$\frac{74\ (\$23.50)}{109\ (74 + 35)} = 67.9\% \text{ at } \$23.50, \text{ and}$$

$$\frac{35\ (\$28.95)}{109\ (74 + 35)} = 32.1\% \text{ at } \$28.95$$

Proof: Assume that the buyer's $50 price line is to consist of 90 sweaters. Total cost equals:

90 × 67.9% = 61 sweaters × $23.50 = $1,433.50
90 × 32.1% = 29 sweaters × $28.95 =   839.55

Total cost   = $2,273.05

Total retail equals:

90 × $50 sweaters = $4,500

$$\frac{\$4,500 - \$2,273.05}{\$4,500} = 49.5\%$$

Maintaining the Average Markon When There Are Three or More Costs and One Retail Price (p. 104)

1. Average cost = $3

   Total cost = $3 × 300 = $900

   Units obtained and dollars spent at Vendor A:

   $900 × 20% = $180 spent

   $180 ÷ $4 = 45 candles

   Balance to be distributed between Vendors B and C:

	Units	Dollars
Total to be purchased	300	$900
Less amount committed to Vendor A	45	180
Balance	255	$720

Determine the average cost of the remaining 255 units:

$720 ÷ 255 = $2.82

Calculate the ratio of units to be purchased:

Established cost	$2.50	$3.50
Less average cost	2.82	2.82
Gain or (loss)	($ .32)	$ .68
Lowest terms	(8)	17

The ratio is therefore 8 (at $3.50):17 (at $2.50).
Establish percentage distribution:

$$\frac{8\ (at\ \$3.50)}{25\ (8 + 17)} = 32\% \text{ from Vendor C at } \$3.50$$

$$\frac{17\ (at\ \$2.50)}{25\ (8 + 17)} = 68.0\% \text{ from Vendor B at } \$2.50$$

The actual distribution is:

255 units × 32% = 82 units at $3.50

255 units × 68% = 173 units at $2.50

or

82 units × $3.50 =	$287
173 units × $2.50 =	433
255	$720

Thus we have: 45 candles at a $4 cost, 82 candles at a $3.50 cost, and 172 candles at a $2.50 cost.

Proof:

Unit Cost	Units	Total Cost	Total Retail	Markon
$4.00	45	$180	$ 270	33.3%
3.50	82	287	492	41.7%
2.50	173	433	1,038	58.3%
	300	$900	$1,800	50.0%

3. The average unit cost:

$12.88 × 47.5% = $6.12

Total cost:

$6.12 × 250 = $1,530

The amount of purchase dollars and units to be distributed between the $4.84 and $7.92 costs are:

30% × 250 = 75 units at $4.84 cost

75 × $4.84 = $363.00 total cost

20% × 250 = 50 units at $7.92 cost

50 × $7.92 = $396.00 total cost

Total units and dollars thus far committed:

$$
\begin{array}{lll}
75 \text{ units} & \text{at } \$4.84 = & \$363 \\
\underline{50 \text{ units}} & \text{at } \$7.92 = & \underline{\$396} \\
125 \text{ units} & & \$759
\end{array}
$$

Balance to be spent at $5.90 and $6.50 is:

$$
\begin{array}{ll}
250 & \$1,530 \\
\underline{-125} & \underline{-759} \\
125 & \$771
\end{array}
$$

Average cost of the remaining belts per unit is:

$771 ÷ 125 = $6.17

Determine the ratio of $5.90 belts to $6.50 belts:

	$5.90	$6.50
Established cost		
Less average cost	$6.17	$6.17
Gain or (loss)	($ .27)	$ .33
Lowest terms	(9)	11

The ratio is 11 (at $5.90):9 ($6.50). The percentage distribution is:

$$\frac{9\ (\$6.50)}{20\ (9 + 11)} = 45\% \text{ at } \$6.50, \text{ and}$$

$$\frac{11\ (\$5.90)}{20\ (9 + 11)} = 55\% \text{ at } \$5.90$$

The number of belts to be purchased at each cost is:

125 × 45% = 56 belts at $6.50

125 × 55% = 69 belts at $5.90

Proof:

Unit Cost	Units	Total Cost	Total Retail	Markon
$4.84	75	$ 363	$ 966	62.4%
5.90	69	407	889	54.2%
6.50	56	364	721	49.5%
7.92	50	396	644	38.5%
	250	$1,530	$3,220	52.5%

Topics for Discussion and Review

1. What is an average markon? What factors contribute to the concept?
2. How is the average markon calculated?
3. What is price lining?
4. Explain what is meant by price zones.
5. What are the advantages and disadvantages of price lining?
6. How would you explain the process of obtaining an average markon for two or more retail prices, when those prices are derived from one cost price?
7. Explain how an average markon is to be maintained when the merchant must deal with fluctuating wholesale costs.
8. Explain the concept of a price range.
9. How would you explain the concept of maintaining a predetermined markon when you have one cost and two retail prices?
10. Discuss how you would maintain a predetermined markon if you were forced to purchase similar items from two different vendors.
11. Identify some of the causes for the fluctuation of the cost price.
12. How would you explain the procedure for maintaining a predetermined markon when there are three cost prices and one retail price?
13. Explain the concept of the "breakeven point," in averaging the markon.
14. Assuming that you had to sell one tie at $12.80 for every three ties at $18.40, how would you establish the percentage relationship?
15. Discuss the promotional price zone; how could you establish the price zone and still maintain a required markon?
16. What is a job lot?
17. Why is the average markon not a mathematical average of many established markons?

18. What is stock turnover?

19. Define open-to-buy.

20. Explain how you would determine an average unit cost on purchases so as to achieve a predetermined retail price and markon percent.

21. You are a men's shirt buyer planning to replenish inventory, and find that your current merchandise costs are different from your previous costs; how would you determine the unit retail price on your purchases to support the planned markon percent?

22. You are a women's shoe buyer and have the following data: planned cumulative markon percent, total units required, retail price per unit, units purchased to date, and cost per unit purchased to date. Explain how you would determine the average cost per unit on the remaining purchases.

23. You know the retail value of your cumulative inventory and it's markon percent to-date. You also know the retail value of your planned purchases, and the required markon for the period. Explain how you would arrive at the markon for your purchases that would support the planned markon for the period.

24. Explain how you would distribute an assortment of merchandise with one cost across four different price lines and still maintain a given markon percent.

25. The difference between the established price points and the average price point is defined as a *gain* or a *loss;* what is gained, and what is lost?

Chapter 5
Determination of the Initial Markon

Learning Objectives

- Explain why the achieved markon is markedly different from the originally planned markon.

- Discuss the conceptual differences between the initial markon and the maintained markon.

- Supply two formulas for the maintained markon and explain how they relate to each other.

- Provide the formula for the initial markon in terms of dollars and percentage.

- Calculate the maintained markon.

- Identify the criteria for the establishment of the initial markon.

- Identify the components of the initial markon.

- Calculate the initial markon as a percentage of planned sales, using both dollars and percentages.

Key Terms

Alteration Costs: The net cost of altering merchandise for customers and inventory repair. Includes all supplies, labor, and costs for this service, whether performed within or outside the retail store.

Cash Discounts: A percentage of the billed cost price of the merchandise given as a concession by the vendor for the payment of the invoice within a specified period of time.

Gross Cost of Merchandise Sold: The accumulated inventory at cost plus additions at billed cost, less the closing inventory at cost. The gross cost of merchandise sold is subtracted from net sales to provide for the maintained markon, which is in turn adjusted by cash discounts and alteration costs to provide the gross margin.

Gross Margin: The difference between net sales and the total cost of merchandise sold.

Gross Profit: The difference between net sales and the cost of goods sold; another term, although technically erroneous, for maintained markon or gross margin.

Initial Markon: The difference between the billed cost of the merchandise and the first, or original, retail price at which the goods are offered for sale.

Inventory Turnover: The number of times an average inventory is sold and replaced; normally, but not necessarily, on an annual basis.

Maintained Markon: The difference between net sales and the gross cost of merchandise sold.

Operating Expenses: All the expenses incurred in the processing and sale of merchandise. Includes all administrative and general expenses other than the cost of merchandise itself.

Operating Profit: That profit derived solely from merchandising activities.

Retail Reductions: The total of markdowns, inventory shortages, and sales discounts.

Sales Discounts: A discount on retail sales, normally given to employees of a retail store and other designated persons and institutions.

Total Cost of Merchandise Sold: The gross cost of merchandise sold plus net alteration costs less any cash discounts earned.

5.1

Achieved Markon Is Relative to Time

The function of the markon is to provide the merchant with sufficient income to cover all operating expenses and to supply a reasonable amount of profit as compensation for incurred risk (see Chapter 3). The concept of the markon is essentially the difference between the retail selling price and the cost of the merchandise sold at that price. However, this is not to imply that the markon placed on the merchandise when it first enters the store will be the same markon achieved when those goods are sold. Indeed, just the opposite is true; time changes things, and time has a particularly debilitating effect upon a retail inventory. Thus, the merchant quickly becomes aware of the fact that the first markon placed on an inventory assortment will, over time, deteriorate to a point well below that which was hoped for. That markon which was "hoped for" we define as the *initial* or *purchase markon;* that markon which is actually achieved is called the *maintained markon,* or that addition to the cost price sustained over a period of time. The essential difference between the two markons is the concept of retail reductions, previously noted and further discussed in Chapter 6.

The Relationship Between the Initial and the Maintained Markon

The genesis of the initial markon lies with the maintained markon, in that the maintained markon forms the conceptual basis for the determination of the initial markon. While the maintained markon will be discussed in greater detail in Chapter 7, it is necessary to achieve a basic comprehension of maintained markon to understand how to determine the initial markon.

The maintained markon is a historical figure in the sense that it defines past merchandising activities in terms of the gross profit derived from the sale of merchandise. Because maintained markon is derived from actual sales and represents only that profit realized from the price received, it is calculated without regard for retail reductions (markdowns, sales discounts, and anticipated shortages). Thus, the maintained markon is always a downward revision of the first, or initial, markon because it is, in effect, the initial markon minus the retail reductions. Conceptually, we define the maintained markon as

> The initial markon − (Sales discounts + Markdowns + Estimated shortages)

or

> Maintained markon = Initial markon − Reductions

Conversely, the initial markon may be explained as

> The maintained markon + (Sales discounts + Markdowns + Estimated shortages)

or

> Initial markon = Maintained markon + Reductions

Figure 5.1 illustrates the relationship between the initial markon and the maintained markon.

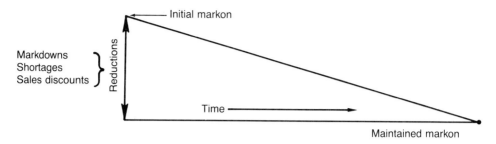

Figure 5.1 The relationship between initial markon, retail reductions, and maintained markon.

The Maintained Markon Defined

Because the initial markon is essentially a product of the maintained markon plus retail reductions, it is appropriate at this point to establish a conceptual understanding of maintained markon; an operational approach will be undertaken in the following chapter.

Specifically the maintained markon is defined as the difference between the actual price at which the merchandise is sold and the gross cost of that merchandise sold. In this sense,

Maintained markon = Net sales − The gross cost of merchandise sold

The gross cost of the merchandise sold differs from the total cost of the merchandise sold as a result of the impact of earned cash discounts and alteration expenses on the cost of sales. Earned cash discounts will decrease the cost of goods sold, while alteration expenses will increase their cost:

Gross cost of merchandise sold
Less earned cash discounts
Net cost of merchandise sold
Alteration expense
Total cost of merchandise sold

As will be further explained in the following chapters, it is precisely these alteration costs and cash discounts that differentiate the maintained markon from the gross margin. When there are no cash discounts and alteration expenses, the maintained markon and the gross margin are one and the same thing.

Assuming the absence of any cash discount or alteration costs, the maintained markon is the final and only profit realized by the merchant on the sale of merchandise. Therefore, if the retail store is to prosper and grow, the maintained markon must cover the operating expenses and provide the merchant with a fair profit. Thus, the maintained markon must be equal to (in addition to sales less the gross cost of sales) the operating expenses plus the operating profit and the alteration costs, if any[1]:

$$\text{Maintained markon} = \text{operating expenses} + \text{operating profit} + \text{alteration costs}^2$$

As a result, the maintained markon is a key ratio in the determination of profitability; it not only defines the profit derived from merchandising activities but also sets the limits on the overall corporate profitability. Also, because it is a true reflection of actual business acumen, the maintained markon is far more important than the initial markon, which is based on planned figures and is therefore only hypothetical.

The strategic importance of the maintained markon is illustrated as follows:

Net sales	$500	100%
Less gross cost of sales	300	60
Maintained markon	200	40
Less operating expenses	160	32
Less alteration costs	15	3
Operating profit	$ 25	5%

Note that, of necessity, the maintained markon of $200, or 40%, must be a result of both net sales less the gross cost of sales and operating expenses plus alteration costs (if any) plus operating profit, if the merchant is to be successful on a corporate basis.

▪ Study Problem

Given: You are planning to open your own retail store. Sales volume for the first year is estimated at $100,000. The following operating expenses have been planned:

Payroll	15,000
Alteration costs	2,000
Advertising	3,000
Utilities	1,400
Supplies	3,000

---

[1] Some claim that cash discounts should be considered as a deduction in the maintained markon formula because they are a part of the merchant's profit. However, they are *not* part of the *operating* profit and are considered as "earned" *additional* income. By deducting the cash discount, the maintained markon will be decreased by that amount, thus weakening the entire profit structure.

[2] Alteration cost are only incurred when "form utility" is required in the sale of merchandise, such as men's alterations. They are costs that relate to merchandising activities and thus are not included with operating expenses (although theoretically, and in the interest of simplicity, they could be).

Travel	700
Communication	800
Depreciation	900
Rent	4,000

Profit is anticipated to be $4,500.

Find: What is the required maintained markon, in dollars and percentage, that must be achieved if you are to be successful during the first year of business? What will your gross cost of sales be in dollars and percentage?

Solution:

Total of all expenses	$28,800
Alteration costs	2,000
Profit	4,500
Maintained markon	$35,300

$$\frac{\$35,300}{\$100,000} = 35.3\% \text{ Maintained markon}$$

$100,000	Sales
35,300	Less maintained markon
$64,700	Gross cost of sales

$$\frac{\$64,700}{\$100,000} = 64.7\% \text{ Gross cost of sales}$$

because:

$100,000	Sales
64,700	Less gross cost of sales
35,300	Maintained markon
2,000	Less alteration costs
28,800	Less operating expenses
$ 4,500	Operating profit

Note that the maintained markon is the pivotal figure in the equation; it is both the product of

Sales	−	Gross cost of sales	=	Maintained markon
$100,000	−	$64,700	=	$35,300

and

Operating expenses	+	Alteration costs	+	Operating profit	=	Maintained markon
$28,800	+	$2,000	+	$4,500	=	$35,300

While the maintained markon theoretically may be derived from either sales less gross cost of sales or operating expenses plus profit, the latter equation is preferred, simply because it is the most practical for the established retail merchant. It is far easier to adjust the cost of sales to a relatively fixed operational structure than it is to modify that structure to conform to the perceived demands of a volatile wholesale market. Therefore, maintained markon is essentially defined in dollars and percentage as

$$\frac{\text{Operating expenses} + \text{Operating profit}}{\text{Net sales}}$$

■ Application Exercise

1. A department manager calculates operating expenses for the spring season to be 42% of sales, with alteration costs of 2% and a planned operating profit of 6%. Assuming planned sales to be $300,000 what is the required maintained markon in dollars and percentage?

2. The owner of a gift shop desires a profit of $8,000 on net sales of $250,000. Operating expenses are planned to be 30% of sales. What is the maintained markon percentage required?

3. Given:

Payroll	14.0%
Rent	2.0%
Advertising	1.8%
Utilities	.5%
Other expenses	2.3%
Profit	3.2%
Markdowns	8.0%
Sales	$12,000

Find: (a) the percentage of maintained markon, (b) maintained markon dollars, (c) gross cost of sales dollars, and (d) gross cost of sales percentage.

5.2
Planning the Initial Markon

Criteria for the Establishment of the Initial Markon

Remembering that the markon is the amount that the merchant adds to the billed cost price of merchandise in order to achieve the initial, or original, retail price, the amount of that markon should meet the following criteria:

1. It must cover all operating expenses, retail reductions, and freight charges, while at the same time providing for a reasonable amount of operating profit.

2. It should result in a selling price that is competitive in the retail marketplace.

3. It must prompt customer acceptance of the merchandise offering.

4. It should contribute to a decrease in markdown dollars.

5. It must result in a gross margin that is compatible with a desired inventory turnover.[3]

Components of the Initial Markon

Because the initial markon anticipates the maintained markon, in the sense that the maintained markon is the actual selling price achieved at some future date, the initial markon must contain the following components:

1. The total nonmerchandise cost of conducting the retail transaction, defined as operating expenses.

2. The anticipated reductions in the retail value of the inventory. Collectively defined as retail reductions, they include:
   a. markdowns
   b. expected inventory shortages
   c. sales discounts to employees and special customers.

3. A satisfactory return on the investment in merchandise, defined as profit.

4. Alteration costs or those expenses incurred when the form of merchandise is changed to develop and close a sale, for example, the installation of carpeting, the hemming of men's trousers, or the repair of owned merchandise damaged in inventory.

The components of the initial markon and their interrelationship are illustrated as follows:

$$
\left.\begin{array}{l}
\text{Operating expenses} \\
\text{Alteration costs} \\
\text{Operating profit}
\end{array}\right\} = \text{Maintained markon}
$$
$$+$$
$$
\left.\begin{array}{l}
\text{Markdowns} \\
\text{Sales discounts} \\
\text{Inventory shortage}
\end{array}\right\} = \text{Retail reductions}
$$
$$
\left.\begin{array}{l} \\ \\ \\ \\ \\ \\ \end{array}\right\} = \text{Initial markon}
$$

---

[3] Normally, the higher the gross margin, the lower the inventory turnover, and vice versa. This concept is discussed further in Chapter 8.

The Relationship Between the Retail Price and the Initial Markon

Because the retail price desired is a product of the markon plus the cost of the merchandise, any reductions in that price must of necessity affect only the markon; obviously, the cost will remain constant regardless of any fluctuation in the selling price. If the selling price fails to cover the components of the maintained markon—operating expenses, alteration cost, and operating profit—operating profit will decline and could well result in an operating loss. For example, the merchant plans a markon of

Operating expenses	$35
Alteration costs	7
Profit	3
Total markon	$45

Assuming that the merchandise costs $55, then the retail price must be

Markon	$ 45
Cost	55
Retail	$100

If the retail price is reduced by $5, it is the markon that suffers, and the merchant not only is deprived of the $3 profit but is also unable to cover $2 in operating expenses. Consider the following illustration comparing the effects of the $100 and $95 retail prices:

	$100	$95
Retail price		
Less merchandise cost	55	55
Maintained markon	$ 45	$40
Less operating expenses plus alteration costs	42	42
Profit or (loss)	$ 3	($ 2)

It is, therefore, absolutely necessary to include as part of the initial markon a dollar amount equal to the anticipated difference between the original retail price and that price at which the goods are finally sold. This difference is the previously defined retail reductions, or the discrepancy between what was "hoped for" and what was actually achieved. Thus, in order for the merchant to achieve the markon percentage dictated by the maintained markon, the initial retail price must be equal to the actual net sales plus the anticipated retail reductions, or

The initial retail price = Net sales + Markdowns + Stock shortages + Sales discounts

because

Net sales = Original retail price − Retail reductions

▪ Study Problem

Given: A merchant experienced an average markdown of $3 on a classification of shirts, an inventory shortage of $2, and sales discounts of $1.

Find: Assuming that a customer purchased a shirt from this classification at $14, what was the original retail price of the shirt?

Solution:

	Net sales	$14
Reductions	Markdowns	3
	Shortages	2
	Sales discounts	1
	Original retail price	$20

because:

The original retail price	$20
Less retail reductions	6
Net sales	$14

    The initial retail price must be sufficient to cover the retail reductions accumulated up to the actual point of sale, so that the dollars returned to the merchant pay for the operating expenses and supply the desired operating profit. Thus, in effect, at the point of sale the maintained markon is technically achieved. The initial retail price is therefore simply the maintained markon dollars plus the dollars planned to be consumed through the retail reductions.

Stated quantitatively,

    $Initial markon = $Maintained markon + $Reductions

because

    $Maintained markon = $Initial markon − $Reductions

▪ Application Exercise

1. A customer purchased a tie for $7. Markdowns were $2, shortages were $.25, and sales discounts were $.75. What was the initial retail price of the tie?

2. A merchant planned an initial markon of $18. Markdowns were projected at $3, shortages at $1, and sales discounts anticipated to be $1.50. What were the maintained markon dollars expected by the merchant?

3. A shoe buyer planned an initial retail price of $70, based on operating expenses of $20, a planned profit of $5, and a $35 cost of sales. What are the anticipated net sales and the retail reductions?

The Calculation of the Initial Markon as a Percentage of the Original Retail Price

As we have previously discussed, the markon is always expressed as a percentage of the retail price from which it was derived, that is, retail dollars minus cost dollars divided by retail dollars. It has also been noted that

$$\$Initial\ markon = \$Maintained\ markon + \$Reductions$$

and that

$$The\ initial\ retail\ price = Net\ sales + Markdowns + Stock\ shortages + Sales\ discounts$$

Therefore, the formula for the determination of the initial markon percentage may be stated

$$Initial\ markon\ \% = \frac{\$Maintained\ markon + \$Retail\ reductions}{\$Net\ sales + \$Retail\ reductions}$$

By expanding the components of the initial markon percentage, we have the following formula:

$$Initial\ Markon\ \% = \frac{\$Maintained\ markon\ (\$Operating\ expenses,\ \$Alteration\ costs,\ \$Operating\ profit)}{\$Net\ sales} + \frac{\$Retail\ reductions\ (\$Markdowns,\ \$Sales\ discounts,\ \$Stock\ shortages)}{+\ \$Retail\ reductions\ (\$Markdowns,\ \$Sales\ discounts,\ \$Stock\ shortages)}$$

The numerator of this initial markon equation is explained by virtue of the fact that the markon, as previously discussed, must cover the operating expenses, including any alteration costs, operating profit, and all the reductions in the retail value of the merchandise up to the point of sale. In order to calculate the percentage of initial markon, these markon dollars must be placed over the original retail value of the merchandise to be sold, which necessarily consists of the actual sales dollars realized plus the total of the retail reductions. In short, when the maintained markon dollars are increased by anticipated reductions, the "hoped for" planned sales must be increased by the same dollar amount; obviously, if the customer accepts the higher retail price, sales volume will increase accordingly.

■ **Study Problem**

Given: A misses' dress buyer is planning an initial markon for the spring season. The following information is available:

Planned sales	$160,000
Operating expenses	56,000
Operating profit	8,000
Stock shortages	4,800
Markdowns	28,000
Sales discounts	2,000

Find: What is the required dollar amount of maintained markon? What is the initial markon percentage required to achieve the maintained markon?

Solution:

$$\text{Initial markon \%} = \frac{\$\text{Maintained markon} + \$\text{Reductions}}{\$\text{Planned sales} + \$\text{Reductions}}$$

The maintained markon = Expenses + Profits

The maintained markon = $56,000 + $8,000 = $64,000

Reductions = Stock shortages + Markdowns + Sales discounts

Reductions = $4,800 + $28,000 + $2,000 = $34,800

Therefore:

$$\text{Initial markon \%} = \frac{\$64,000 + \$34,800}{\$160,000 + \$34,800} = \frac{\$98,800}{\$194,800} = 50.7\%$$

■ **Application Exercise**

1. Given the following information, determine the initial markon percentage:

Maintained markon	$42
Retail reductions	8
Net sales	90

2. What is the initial markon percentage required for a department having the following planned figures?

Net sales	$50,000
Operating profit	7,000
Operating expenses	11,000

Alterations	2,000
Markdowns	3,000
Shortages	1,000
Sales discounts	500

3. A men's clothing store has a planned sales volume of $500,000, with an anticipated operating profit of $35,000. Given the following data, what is the initial markon percentage required to produce the desired dollar profit?

Operating expenses	$190,000
Alterations	10,000
Stock shortages	7,500
Markdowns	50,000
Sales discounts	5,000

4. The markon requirements for a unit of merchandise that may sell at $3.50 are:[4]

Operating profit	$ .18
Operating expenses	1.20
Alteration costs	.02
Sales discounts	.03
Markdowns	.42
Stock shortages	.07

Find the maintained markon dollars required, the initial retail price, and the initial markon percentage required to ensure the $.18 operating profit.

5. Given the following information, what is the maintained markon percentage, and the initial markon percentage required to achieve that maintained markon?

Alteration costs	$ 22,500
Sales discounts	7,500
Markdowns	90,000
Stock shortages	15,000
Operating profit	37,500
Operating expenses	270,000
Net sales	750,000

---

[4] The $3.50 is an anticipated, or net, sales figure predicated upon operating expenses and operating profit. It is the retail price below which the merchant will encounter profit difficulties. The $3.50 is not to imply that the merchandise will not or cannot sell at a higher retail price; the higher price will simply enhance the maintained markon. Remember, net sales equal initial retail minus reductions, or initial retail equals net sales plus reductions.

Calculation of the Initial Markon Utilizing All
Planned Elements as a Percentage of Net Sales

The initial markon percentage is normally derived from its component parts when those values are expressed as a percentage of net sales.[5] Not only does the magnitude of the dollar figures involved in the retail accounting process dictate the use of the relatively simpler percentage basis,[6] but the dissemination of merchandising data through trade associations is always expressed as a percentage of net sales. This provides for the exchange of merchandising and operating information on a ratio basis, but limits the knowledge of specific dollar values to only those parties to whom it is of immediate concern. For example, the merchant probably would not want to reveal the actual dollar value of operating profit, but would be willing to indicate that operating profit, as a percentage of net sales, was 4.3%.

Essentially, the method of calculating the initial markon remains the same, whether using dollars or a percentage. However, as discussed in Chapter 3, it must be remembered that net sales or the retail price, although apparently not given, must necessarily be equal to 100%. Because the retail price or net sales is always equal to 100%, and retail is the generally accepted base from which the markon is derived, all percentages are requisite portions of that 100%.

▪ Study Problem

Given:

Net sales	$3,000
Operating expenses	1,200
Operating profit	150
Alterations	45
Markdowns	390
Sales discounts	15
Shortages	60

Find: Convert the dollar figures to percentages and calculate the initial markon.

---

[5] Net sales are the actual retail dollars achieved by the merchant, as opposed to the initial retail price, or that which is "hoped for." The percentage elements of the initial markon are therefore always based on net sales.

[6] For example, sales discounts of $3,000,000 may be expressed as 1% of a $300,000,000 sales volume. Obviously, 1% is far easier to work with than $3,000,000.

Solution:

Operating expenses	=	$1,200	÷	$3,000	=	40.0%
Operating profit	=	150	÷	$3,000	=	5.0
Alterations	=	45	÷	$3,000	=	1.5
Maintained markon	=	$1,395	÷	$3,000	=	46.5%
Markdowns	=	$390	÷	$3,000	=	13.0%
Sales discounts	=	15	÷	$3,000	=	.5
Shortages	=	60	÷	$3,000	=	2.0
Reductions	=	$465	÷	$3,000	=	15.5%

$$\text{Initial markon \%} = \frac{\text{Maintained markon \% + Reductions \%}}{100\% + \text{Reductions \%}}$$

$$\text{Initial markon \%} = \frac{46.5\% + 15.5\%}{100\% + 15.5\%} = \frac{62\%}{115.5\%} = 53.7\%$$

By substituting the dollar equivalent of the percentage values, we arrive at the identical initial markon percentage.

$$\text{Initial markon \%} = \frac{\$1,395 + \$465}{\$3,000 + \$465} = \frac{\$1,860}{\$3,465} = 53.7\%$$

▪ Application Exercise

1. Determine the initial markon percentage from the following data:

Operating profit	5.0%
Operating expenses	45.0%
Alteration costs	2.0%
Markdowns	15.0%
Shortages	1.5%
Sales discounts	1.0%

2. Planned sales for a classification of men's hosiery is $8,000. The operating profit desired is $680. Given the following information, what should the initial markon percentage be?

Operating expenses	47%
Markdowns	12%
Shortages	2%
Sales discounts	1%

3. Given the following information, determine the initial markon percentage for a small independent merchant:

Sales	$500,000	Markdowns	11.0%
Annual rent	40,000	Profit	10.0%
Utilities	18,000	Shortages	1.5%
Miscellaneous expenses	6,000	Payroll	20.0%
Sales discounts	3.0%	Alterations	2.0%

4. Given the following information, determine the initial markon percentage and the resulting percentage allowable for the cost of merchandise.

Maintained markon	42%
Reductions	8%

5. The owner of a small women's specialty store is planning sales of $650,000 for the fall season. Given the following planned figures, determine the initial markon percentage that needs to be employed.

Markdowns	12.0%	Shortages	1.8%
Sales discounts	.6%	Alterations	.4%
Advertising	3.0%	Payroll	17.0%
Utilities	1.3%	Rental	4.0%
Supplies	1.1%	Travel	.5%
Communications	.7%	Insurance	.8%
Taxes	1.8%	Miscellaneous	1.0%
		Profit	4.5%

▪ Solutions to the Application Exercises

Maintained Markon (p. 127)

1.
Expenses	42%
Alteration costs	2%
Profits	6%
Maintained markon	50%

50% × $300,000 = $150,000

3.
Payroll	14.0%	×	$12,000	=	$1,680
Rent	2.0	×	12,000	=	240
Advertising	1.8	×	12,000	=	216
Utilities	.5	×	12,000	=	60
Other	2.3	×	12,000	=	276
Total expenses	20.6%				$2,472
Profit	3.2	×	12,000	=	384
Maintained markon	23.8%[a]				$2,856[b]

Sales − Gross cost of sales = Maintained markon

or

Gross cost of sales = Sales − Maintained markon:

$12,000 − $2,856 = $9,144[c]

$$\frac{\$9,144}{\$12,000} = 76.2\%^{(d)}$$

Because markdowns, as part of retail reductions, have already been used up, they do not figure in the calculation of maintained markon. The maintained markon and the gross cost of sales total 100%, or $12,000, and maintained markon equals sales minus the cost of sales, and expenses plus profit.

Sales	$12,000	100.0%
Less gross cost of sales	9,144	76.2
Maintained markon	2,856	23.8
Less operating expenses	2,472	20.6
Operating profit	384	3.2%

Components of the Initial Markon (p. 130)

1. Net sales	$ 7.00
Markdowns	2.00
Sales discounts	.75
Shortages	.25
Initial retail price	$10.00

$$3.\ \frac{Profit}{\$5} + \frac{Expenses}{\$20} = \frac{Maintained\ markon}{\$25}$$

$$\frac{Maintained\ markon}{\$25} + \frac{Cost\ of\ sales}{\$35} = \frac{Net\ sales}{\$60}$$

$$\frac{Initial\ retail\ price}{\$70} - \frac{Net\ sales}{\$60} = \frac{Reductions}{\$10}$$

The Calculation of the Initial Markon as a Percentage of the Original Retail Price (p. 132)

$$1.\ Initial\ markon = \frac{\$Maintained\ markon + \$Reductions}{\$Sales + \$Reductions}$$

$$Initial\ markon = \frac{\$42 + \$8}{\$90 + \$8} = 51\%$$

3. Maintained markon $=\begin{cases} \$190,000 & \text{Operating expenses} \\ 35,000 & \text{Operating profit} \\ 10,000 & \text{Alterations} \\ \hline \$235,000 & = \text{Maintained markon} \end{cases}$

Reductions $=\begin{cases} \$\ 7,500 & \text{Stock shortages} \\ 50,000 & \text{Markdowns} \\ 5,000 & \text{Sales discounts} \\ \hline \$62,500 & = \text{Reductions} \end{cases}$

Therefore:

$$\text{Initial markon \%} = \frac{\$235,000 + \$62,500}{\$500,000 + \$62,500} = \frac{\$297,500}{\$562,500} = 52.9\%$$

5. $$\text{Maintained markon \%} = \frac{\text{Expenses} + \text{Alterations} + \text{Profits}}{\text{Net sales}}$$

$$\text{Maintained markon \%} = \frac{\$270,000 + \$22,500 + \$37,500}{\$750,000} =$$

$$\frac{\$330,000}{\$750,000} = 44\%$$

$$\text{Initial markon \%} = \frac{\$\text{Maintained markon} + \$\text{Reductions}}{\$\text{Net sales} + \$\text{Reductions}}$$

Stock shortages	$ 15,000
Markdowns	90,000
Sales discounts	7,500
Reductions	$112,500

$$\text{Initial markon \%} = \frac{\$330,000 + \$112,500}{\$750,000 + \$112,500} =$$

$$\frac{\$442,500}{\$862,500} = 51.3\%$$

Calculation of the Initial Markon Utilizing All Planned Elements as a Percentage of Net Sales (p. 135)

1.		
Operating profit		5%
Operating expenses		45%
Alteration costs		2%
Maintained markon		52%

Markdowns	15.0%
Shortages	1.5%
Sales discounts	1.0%
Reductions	17.5%

$$\text{Initial markon \%} = \frac{52\% + 17.5\%}{100\% + 17.5\%} = \frac{69.5\%}{117.5\%} = 59.1\%$$

3.
Annual rent ($40,000 ÷ $500,000)	8.0%
Utilities ($18,000 ÷ $500,000)	3.6%
Miscellaneous expenses ($6,000 ÷ $500,000)	1.2%
Payroll	20.0%
Alterations	2.0%
Profit	10.0%
Maintained markon	44.8%

Sales discounts	3.0%
Markdowns	11.0%
Shortages	1.5%
Reductions	15.5%

$$\text{Initial markon \%} = \frac{44.8\% + 15.5\%}{100\% + 15.5\%} = \frac{60.3\%}{115.5\%} = 52.2\%$$

Or:

Annual rent	$40,000
Utilities	18,000
Miscellaneous expenses	6,000
Payroll ($500,000 × 20%)	100,000
Alterations ($500,000 × 2%)	10,000
Profit ($500,000 × 10%)	50,000
Maintained markon	$224,000

Markdowns ($500,000 × 11%)	$55,000
Shortages ($500,000 × 1.5%)	7,500
Sales discounts ($500,000 × 3%)	15,000
Reductions	$77,500

$$\text{Initial markon \%} = \frac{\$224,000 + \$77,500}{\$500,000 + \$77,500} =$$

$$\frac{\$301,500}{\$577,500} = 52.2\%$$

5.

Advertising	3.0%
Utilities	1.3
Supplies	1.1
Communications	0.7
Taxes	1.8
Alterations	0.4
Payroll	17.0
Rental	4.0
Travel	0.5
Insurance	0.8
Miscellaneous	1.0
Profit	4.5
Maintained markon	36.1%
Markdowns	12.0%
Sales discounts	0.6
Shortages	1.8
Reductions	14.4%

$$\text{Initial markon \%} = \frac{36.1\% + 14.4\%}{100\% + 14.4\%} = \frac{50.5\%}{114.4\%} = 44.1\%$$

Or:

Advertising ($650,000 × 3%)	$ 19,500
Utilities ($650,000 × 1.3%)	8,450
Supplies ($650,000 × 1.1%)	7,150
Communications ($650,000 × 0.7%)	4,550
Taxes ($650,000 × 1.8%)	11,700
Alterations ($650,000 × 0.4%)	2,600
Payroll ($650,000 × 17.0%)	110,500
Rental ($650,000 × 4.0%)	26,000
Travel ($650,000 × 0.5%)	3,250
Insurance ($650,000 × 0.8%)	5,200
Miscellaneous ($650,000 × 1.0%)	6,500
Profit ($650,000 × 4.5%)	29,250
Maintained markon	$234,650
Markdowns ($650,000 × 12%)	$78,000
Sales discounts ($650,000 × 0.6%)	3,900
Shortages ($650,000 × 1.8%)	11,700
Reductions	$93,600

$$\text{Initial markon \%} = \frac{\$234,650 + \$93,600}{\$650,000 + \$93,600} =$$

$$\frac{\$328,250}{\$743,600} = 44.1\%$$

Topics for Discussion and Review

1. Discuss the initial markon and the maintained markon. What is the essential difference between the two concepts?

2. What factors translate the gross cost of the merchandise sold into the net cost of the merchandise? Illustrate your answer with a specific illustration.

3. Explain the function of the maintained markon.

4. Under what conditions would the maintained markon be equivalent to gross margin?

5. Explain why the maintained markon is the key profitability ratio; illustrate your answer with a specific mathematical example.

6. Why is maintained markon normally derived from operating expenses plus profit, rather than sales minus the cost of sales?

7. What criteria should guide the retail merchant in constructing the initial markon?

8. What specific elements comprise the initial markon?

9. Explain why the initial retail price must be equal to net sales plus markdowns, stock shortages, and sales discounts.

10. At the point of sale, what markon is achieved? Explain your answer.

11. Why is the initial markon equal to the maintained markon plus retail reductions?

12. Explain why planned sales are increased by the amount of retail reductions in the formula for the calculation of the initial markon percentage.

13. Explain the concept of retail reductions.

14. Conceptually, what happens to retail reductions during the accounting period for which they were planned?

15. You are planning to open your own store. Explain how you would construct the initial markon and use it as a pricing mechanism.

16. Discuss the difference between the initial markon, the cumulative markon, and the average markon?

17. Given the maintained markon and reductions in percentages, explain how you would calculate the initial markon.

18. Explain why cash discounts are *not* a deduction in the calculation of the maintained markon.

19. Conceptually, what are alteration costs, and why are they not included in the operating expenses?

20. Given net sales and reductions, how would you construct the initial retail price? Explain your answer.

21. Discuss the relationship between the initial markon and the retail price at which the merchandise is finally sold.

22. Shortages, as part of retail reductions, can only be a historically based estimate. Why is this so?

23. When constructing the initial markon in percentages, why is sales volume of no consequence?

24. Discuss the gross cost of the merchandise sold. How does it affect the maintained markon?

25. Explain the difference between a cash discount and a sales discount.

Chapter 6
Markdown Analysis

Learning Objectives

- Explain the four classes of price changes.

- Discuss the concept of markdowns.

- Identify the advantages and disadvantages of markdowns.

- Identify and discuss the various causes of markdowns.

- Discuss the factors that influence the timing of markdowns.

- Explain the advantages of early markdowns and late markdowns.

- Discuss some considerations on the size of the markdown.

- Calculate the markdown in dollars.

- Calculate the markdown as a percentage of net sales.

- Calculate the markdown as a percentage of the original retail price.

- Calculate the markdown based upon the original retail price, when the markdown on net sales is known.

- Determine the original retail price when the markdown dollars and markdown percentage are known.

- Calculate the required increase in sales volume necessary to offset a reduction in the retail price.

- Explain the relationship between gross markdowns, markdown cancellations, net markdowns, and markup.

Key Terms

Automatic Cancellation Date: The date specified on the retail buyer's purchase order as the latest acceptable shipment date.

Classification: All merchandise of a given type or use, regardless of size, color, style, model, or price—for example, women's shoes.

Distress Merchandise: Merchandise marked down to ensure its rapid disposal. From the merchant's perspective, it includes merchandise that is broken, soiled, or otherwise shopworn.

FIFO: First-in, first-out method of assigning the cost value of a retail inventory. It is assumed that the oldest merchandise is sold first, thus making the ending inventory a composite of the most recent purchase costs.

Forward Stock: Merchandise carried on the selling floor rather than in a reserve stock area.

Gross Markdowns: The original sum of the accumulated markdowns before subtraction of any markdown cancellations to determine net markdowns.

Keystone Markon: Doubling of the merchant's cost price, resulting in an arbitrary 50% markon based upon the retail method.

Maintained Markon: The difference between net sales and the gross cost of merchandise sold.

Markdown: The downward revision of the retail price at which an item(s) is currently marked; normally expressed as a percentage of planned net sales.

Markdown Allowance: The monthly allotment of markdowns as shown on the six-month merchandise plan, in dollars and as a percentage of net sales.

Markdown Cancellation: An upward revision of the current retail price that normally results in the restoration of the original selling price; normally employed when merchandise has been reduced in price for a special sales event, after which the initial retail price is restored.

Marking: Placing the original retail price on new merchandise.

Markup: An upward revision of initial markon, resulting in a higher than original retail price.

Markup Cancellation: A price reduction method whereby the markon is cancelled, thus repricing the merchandise at its original planned markon.

Net Markdowns: Gross markdowns less the markdown cancellations.

Net Sales: Within the context of this chapter, the actual retail price at which the merchandise is finally sold. This is meant to differentiate the planned net sales, or the original retail price, from the final retail selling price.

Odd Lot: An unbalanced assortment of styles, colors, sizes, fabrics, and quality.

Off-Retail Markdown Percentage: The markdown as a percentage of the original retail price, rather than as a percentage of net sales.

Open-to-Buy: The amount of retail dollars available for the purchase of merchandise during a specific period of time, normally a month.

Original Retail Price: The planned net sales or the retail price that the merchant hopes to achieve.

Preretailing: Placing the retail price on the purchase order at the time that the order is placed.

Price Change: The raising or lowering of the current selling price of merchandise.

Purchase Order: A record of agreement made with the vendor that includes merchandise cost, discount terms, and method of shipping.

Rate of Sale: The number of units, or pieces of an item, sold during a given period.

Reserve Stock: Merchandise not on the selling floor but available if needed.

Retail Method of Inventory Valuation: The taking of a physical inventory at retail and then estimating its cost by means of the complement of the cumulative markon.

Salvage Goods: Merchandise damaged beyond reclamation for salable purposes that must be disposed of through other channels.

Season: General record keeping and planning divides the merchandising year into two basic seasons, spring and fall. Spring accounts for the first 26 weeks, approximately February through July; fall accounts for the balance of the year, roughly, August through January. It is significant that inventory levels are at their lowest points during January and July (end of the season), thus affording a minimum of carryover merchandise from one season to another.

Selling Cost: The percentage relationship existing between selling payroll and the net sales generated by those salespeople paid; determined by dividing net sales into the gross salary for any defined period of time.

Stock-to-Sales Ratio: The relationship between the stock on hand at the beginning of a period and the planned sales for that period; determined by dividing inventory for the period at retail by net sales for that period.

Stock Turnover: The number of times within a given time frame, normally a year, that an inventory is sold and replaced.

Visual Merchandising: A merchandising technique based upon nonpersonal informative devices and/or self-service displays.

6.1

Price Change

The retail price is a highly volatile phenomenon; it is rare indeed that an inventory assortment is sold in its entirety at the original, or initial, retail valuation. One of the major functions of efficient merchandise management is the constant adjustment of the retail price to meet or modify customers' expectations of perceived value. Such price changes may either increase or decrease the retail value of the inventory and may be technically classified four ways:

1. Markdown: reduction in the currently marked retail price to some lower price point.

2. Markdown cancellation: an upward revision in the price of merchandise previously marked down; normally a restoration of the immediate past higher selling price.

3. Markup: an increase in the original, or initial, retail price.

4. Markup cancellation: a reduction in the retail price of merchandise on which a markup has been taken; generally a restoration of the initial markon price due to repricing errors or some predetermined tactical considerations. Although in a technical sense the markup cancellation may be viewed as a markdown in that it does reduce the current retail price, its function is to reduce the amount of markups previously taken; the two concepts are not to be confused.

The most common retail price change, and certainly the one that has the greatest impact on the retail value of the inventory, is the markdown. In Chapter 5, we briefly discussed the markdown as the major portion of retail reductions and those reductions as they contribute to the requirements of the initial markon. It is now appropriate to explore the concept of the markdown itself as a major tactic of merchandising strategy.

6.2

Markdowns

The essence of the markdown is, in effect, the merchant's manner of adjusting a retail price to bring it in line with the customer's perception of a lesser value. Thus, the markdown represents a depreciation in the retail value of the merchant's inventory. The concept of the markdown should not be viewed negatively; indeed, it is one of the merchant's most effective tactics for achieving strategic goals. As you recall from the discussion of the initial markon, the merchant should expect, and intelligently plan for, a specific amount of markdowns over a stated period of time. The obvious effect of such an approach to the inevitability of markdowns is to transfer the cost of the markdown to the customer via the initial markon. Thus, when the merchandise goes "on sale," it is the aggregate customer who in effect has paid for the required price reduction far in advance of the sale date. It is only when the merchant fails to anticipate the price reduction that markdown becomes a dirty word, for then the merchant must sustain the loss and the customer truly acquires a bargain. From a merchandising perspective, the sale price must somehow contribute to profitability, and that profitability must ultimately derive from the current retail price, however defined. Thus, again from a merchandising point of view, there can be no such thing as a sale, because a "sale" implies "something for nothing" for the customer, and no merchant can stay in business supplying something for nothing to the customer!

Advantages and Disadvantages of Markdowns

Because markdowns represent a quantitative reality in the world of retail merchandising, their effects, both positive and negative, are predictable and controllable. Consider the advantages of timely, planned markdowns:

1. Increased departmental or storewide traffic.

2. Increased total dollar and unit sales as a product of increased traffic.

3. "Cleaner" stocks through the timely disposal of odds and ends and outdated merchandise.

4. Increased stock turnover.

5. Improved gross margin.[1]

6. Increased cash flow.

7. Additional open-to-buy, thus assuring acquisition of attractive, but not necessarily planned for, market offerings.

8. Increase in goodwill by offering the customer "something for nothing," or at least the perception of a bargain.

On the other hand, markdowns inherently possess potential disadvantages, especially when they come as a surprise:

---

[1] In the sense that there would be no gross margin at all if the markdown had not induced the sale of the merchandise.

1. Gross margin is reduced.[2]

2. If the markdowns are excessive or continuous, the store image may be harmed by giving it a promotional rather than a quality appearance.

3. The sale of regularly priced merchandise may be hampered due to customers' expectations and their seeking out only the marked-down merchandise.

The Causes of Markdowns

Philosophically, the ultimate cause of all markdowns is the abrasion of merchandise as it moves through a time frame. As we have previously noted, time destroys things, whether those things are understood to be perceptions formed by the human psyche or the materialist elements of the real world from which those perceptions are ultimately derived. Our beliefs concerning what is fashionable are no less subject to modification through the impingement of time than is the object of those beliefs. Thus, markdowns are a fact of life for the retail merchant. To question the probability of markdowns is foolish; the only legitimate question to ask is, "How large will they be?"

There are four major factors that dictate the taking of markdowns: merchandising errors, operational errors, uncontrollable circumstances, and the policy dictates of the store management. The first three categories are inevitable and are to be expected; the fourth is a result of the management decision process and eventually manifests itself as the previously discussed retail image.

Merchandising Errors Contributing to Markdowns

Merchandising errors include buying and pricing errors, both of which contribute to the greatest portion of the merchant's markdowns.

Buying errors

The essence of all buying mistakes is the merchant's failure to recognize definite and specific fashion trends and plan the open-to-buy accordingly. Thus, the merchant may be either over- or understocked, not only in demanded styles of merchandise, but also in size ranges, colors, and price lines. This inability, or failure, to define a specific fashion trend may also cause the merchant to invest in a shallow assortment of merchandise spread across a wide variety of items, which eliminates any meaningful assortment of demanded goods. Today, more than ever,

---

[2]The percentage reduction in gross margin is not as great as the percentage of the markdown itself. This will be seen as we progress further into the chapter. Also, the reduction in gross margin dollars may be more than offset by an increased inventory turnover.

the economic aspect of the retail marketplace dictates merchandise assortments that are narrow and deep rather than broad and shallow.

Specific Buying Errors Contributing to Markdowns

1. Buying in excess of customer demand as a result of
   a. Failure to analyze that demand in terms of sales volume, as indicated through classification, style, price, size, and color.
   b. Failure to consider the relationship between the inventory and customer demand as measured by sales volume. This pertains to the stock-to-sales ratio, discussed further in Chapter 12.
   c. Failure to test the consumer market with a sampling of merchandise prior to the placing of a large order.
   d. Failure to monitor fashion trends and buying after the culmination stage has been reached.
   e. Failure to distinguish between a fad and a bona fide fashion trend, and buying into the fad rather than the trend.

2. Failure to anticipate a decline in the wholesale market price of merchandise.

3. Poor timing of merchandising activities:
   a. Ordering goods priced to the peak selling season either too early or too late relative to that season.
   b. Failure to recognize the automatic cancellation date on the purchase order and accepting merchandise too late after placing the order.
   c. Again, the failure to relate a style to its accepted position in the fashion cycle.

4. Failure to develop a close working relationship with key vendors, whose advice will help avoid buying errors.

5. Overdependence on too few resources, with a high portion of the merchant's inventory invested with vendors' mistakes.

6. Failure to examine goods at their point of receipt, thus relaxing quality control standards and inviting poor workmanship, not to mention the possibility of accepting incomplete or incorrect merchandise orders.

Pricing errors

The merchandising axiom defining the conditions prerequisite to a retail transaction—that is, the right merchandise, at the right time, in the right quantities, and in the right place—is solely dependent upon the right price. As we have previously discussed, that retail price is a quantitative dollar value, qualitatively perceived by the retail customer—that is, the merchant sells things for dollars, while the consumer trades value (their dollars) for utility.

Specific Pricing Errors Contributing to Markdowns

1. Failure to recognize the customer's perception of value, thus establishing an initial markon that is either too high or too low.

2. Failure to recognize or accept competitive prices for the same or similar merchandise.

3. Proliferation of price lines, eventually necessitating consolidation. Through the act of consolidation, intermediate price lines must be eliminated, thereby dictating markdowns.[3]

4. Failure to construct the markon using sound merchandising principles:
   a. Indiscriminant use of the keystone markon.
   b. Failure to properly average the markon.
   c. Failure to accurately incorporate all elements of the markon into a unified, realistic pricing structure (e.g., neglect of retail reductions, overstatement of profit).

5. Failure to reprice merchandise correctly:
   a. Failure to make the initial markdown large enough so that the customer can actually perceive a difference between the new selling price and the previous retail price. Everything being relative, a 20% differential between the old and new price constitutes the minimum at which the customer will notice the difference. Markdowns of less than 20% will not be perceived by the customer, and sales objectives will not be achieved, thus necessitating further markdowns. For example, an item gradually reduced from $100 to $80 through a series of $5 markdowns will probably not sell at $80 because the 5.9% differential between $85 and $80 is too small to be meaningful to the customer. However, if that same item is initially reduced from $100 to $80, we have a customer-perceptible price differential of 20% and the sales objective will probably be realized.
   b. Failure to admit a buying error and deferring the markdown to a time when merchandise will have lost most if not all of its potential value. Obviously, at this point the markdown will be far greater than it would have been if the buying error had been rectified through an immediate price reduction.

Operational Errors Contributing to Markdowns

Operational errors are those mistakes affecting the retail price incurred outside of the merchandising division, or in the day-to-day operations of the retail store, such as receiving, checking, and marking, interstore transfers, warehousing, and the general handling of merchandise by both customers and employees. Included

---

[3]To add markup to the representative merchandise of the price lines to be eliminated would be to damage the merchant's credibility in the customer's eyes.

with operational errors are selling-related errors, because increasingly the buying and merchandising activities are being divorced from the selling responsibilities, each function developing as a specialized unit in its own right. Thus, direct contact between the merchant and the sales manager is virtually eliminated; this is especially true in the organizational structure of large department stores and the major retail chains such as Sears and K-mart.

Operational errors

Operational errors that contribute to markdowns generally result from the system that processes the incoming merchandise and delivers it to either a forward stock area or a reserve stock area. Such errors contribute to distressed goods, which include broken, soiled, shopworn, or otherwise damaged merchandise. While these errors are as varied as the personnel responsible for the system, some specific causes stand out.

Specific Operational Causes of Markdowns

1. Failure to efficiently move incoming merchandise through the receiving, checking, and marking processes as a result of
   a. The inability to match the buyer's purchase order with incoming shipments of merchandise, due to faulty information on the order, inadequate information on the merchandise, or the lack of a purchase order. As a result, the movement of that merchandise to the selling floor may be delayed for weeks. Subsequently, markdowns may be required due to poor timing, excessive handling, and the increased probability of damages.
   b. Failure to inspect incoming merchandise, leading to the receipt of damaged goods and subsequent markdowns.
   c. Failure to physically mark the merchandise in accordance with the preretailed price on the purchase order.

2. Inadequate supervision of stockrooms: Failure to inspect or recognize slow-selling merchandise in stock areas disallows any compensating effort on the selling floor, thus increasing the probability of even higher markdowns.

3. Failure to accurately determine the appropriate cost and retail values of inter-store transfers.

Specific selling causes of markdowns

If merchandise is not properly promoted and sold on the selling floor, it will remain in inventory longer than anticipated and deteriorate in value, thus dictating markdowns to stimulate a sales response. On the other hand, high-pressure selling can lead to an increased rate of returns that may have to be marked down for sale at some future date. Nothing actually happens in a retail store until the merchandise is sold, and as a result the importance of effective sales personnel cannot be overemphasized. While the merchant may move merchandise thousands of miles from its point of origin to the retail store, if the salesperson cannot move it two feet across a sales counter, that merchant's efforts are all in vain!

Specific Selling Errors Contributing to Markdowns

1. High-pressure or careless selling.

2. Failure to provide salespeople with adequate merchandise information.

3. Poor stockkeeping on the part of salespeople and the failure to maintain a periodic checkup of slow-moving items.

4. The salesperson's lack of respect for the merchandise, leading to careless handling and subsequent damages.

5. Failure on the part of salespeople to follow the principle of first in, first out (FIFO). This deficiency promotes the sale of newer merchandise at the expense of that received at an earlier date.

6. The failure to employ the principles of visual merchandising or sales-effective merchandise presentation.[4] Visual merchandising is in effect a manner of display designed to supplement or augment the retail salesperson. As such, its mission is to "present merchandise for maximum appeal and easy and quick selection while answering customers' questions with appropriate signing."[5] Thus to ignore the concept of visual merchandising is tantamount to disregarding the role of the salesperson in completing a retail transaction.

Uncontrollable Causes of Markdowns

Although the uncontrollable causes of markdowns may appear fairly obvious, they are mentioned here because of their relationship with the other causes and to emphasize the inevitability of markdowns as a way of life. Even under ideal merchandising conditions, which rarely exist, some contingency for markdowns must always be allowed for.

Seasonal factors

Seasonal factors and inclement weather have a direct bearing on the sale of many merchandise classifications. For example, snow tires will not sell in a dry winter; a warm fall can be disastrous for the outerwear buyer.

---

[4]See *Visual Merchandising* (New York: National Retail Merchants Association, 1976).
[5]See the foreword to *Visual Merchandising.*

Handling

Normal handling will always produce a certain amount of shopworn, broken, and damaged merchandise, which many times results in 100% markdowns and relegation of the goods to salvage status.

Market shifts

Market shifts, or the sudden change in the customer's demand level for certain merchandise classifications, can render current inventories relatively obsolete, whether those changes are new in function or design. Consider the effect of the electronic calculator upon the slide rule or the fickleness of the consumer's acceptance and/or rejection of innovative design in fashion apparel.

Policy Dictates of Store Management

Assuming that all operational and merchandising errors have been kept to a minimum, including the ability to accurately forecast future phenomena, markdowns must still continue to be a significant tactical factor underlying the retail merchandising strategy. Here the store policy comes into play, introduced in the interests of enhanced sales volume and the promotion of a specific and unique store image. Consider the following examples:

1. Maintaining a policy of high initial markons in conjunction with large markdowns, thus exploiting the customer's perception of the relative difference existing between regular prices and "sale" prices.

2. Supplying customers with free samples of merchandise—for example, fancy wines, gourmet cheese.

3. Promoting the store image through the display of innovative and high-fashion merchandise. The intention here is not so much to sell merchandise as it is to tell a story or convey an image. Within this context, markdowns are an inherent risk, but considered worth the cost if, hopefully, the customer receives the "message." One merchandising authority, advocating only a 5% investment in "new fashion" or innovative merchandise, puts it this way:

> This is to tell customers that the store is a real 'with it' store. That while the store may be selling a lot be basic goods and a lot of established goods it has an awareness of the silhouette, or the new fabric, or the new color. For this reason you put it in the window.[6]

---

[6]*The Buyers Manual,* R. Patric Cash, ed. (New York: National Retail Merchants Association, 1979), p. 293.

4. Establishment of a "never undersold" policy. Obviously, if management decides to meet all competition head on, the unforeseeable pricing activities of other stores will force markdowns. However, to the extent that such reductions build goodwill, they are to be considered wise investments.

5. Maintaining balanced stocks, or a reasonable assortment of merchandise, until late into a particular season. Although this sound merchandising strategy contributes to a higher in-season sales volume, it also increases postseason markdowns, due to the larger quantities of carry-over merchandise.

6. Frequent sales of promotional merchandise will always result in some goods not being sold; the odds and ends, or promotional remainders, thus require additional markdowns to clear the inventory completely.

7. Adhering to a "satisfaction guaranteed" policy, whereby price allowances and/ or return privileges are granted to complaining customers regardless of justification. Again, to the extent that goodwill is generated and store image reinforced, the markdown is justified.

When to Take the Markdown

The function of the markdown is to attract attention, arouse interest, and create desire by modifying the customer's perception of value. However, in order to achieve the markdown's objective, that is, the sale of merchandise, the timing of the markdown must coincide with the customer's mood to buy. The less interested the customer is in the merchandise, the more drastic the markdown required to influence a purchasing decision. Thus, timing is a crucial factor in determining the markdown's size and effectiveness.

While it is relatively easy for the merchant to build the markdowns into the initial markon, that markon itself provides no guidelines as to exactly when the markdowns should be taken during a particular selling season. Again, retail merchandising is part art and part science; while we may scientifically construct the initial markon, the timing of the markdowns continues to remain an art. Thus, opinions differ on the timeliness of the markdown. There are several factors that strongly influence the timing of markdowns, all of which ultimately revert to the type of store image to be projected:

1. The promotional strategy of the merchant: major storewide sales events held on an infrequent basis versus the more frequent use of a series of department-oriented minisales.

2. The nature of the merchandise under consideration: seasonal, basic, fashion, or faddish.

3. The length of the selling season and the amount of time remaining at the point-of-markdown consideration.

4. The price sensitivity of the target customer: highly aware of price or generally indifferent to price.

5. The size of the selling space and the availability of storage facilities.

6. The rate of turnover and percentage of gross margin desired.

7. The percentage of the initial markon relative to the required maintained markon.

8. The status of the merchant's open-to-buy.[7]

In essence, the timing of the markdown revolves around two major considerations:

1. The early markdown, taken on individual styles as soon as the rate of sales slows down or after a predetermined length of time in inventory; or,

2. The late markdown, where the reductions are incurred at the end of a season and the merchandise disposed of through clearance sales.

Most merchants favor the concept of the early markdown on individual items taken as the need arises, on the theory that the longer the goods remain in inventory, the less they will eventually be worth. There are others who endorse a late markdown policy. They point out that the accumulation of a large amount of slow-selling merchandise permits the store to stage a clearance event of major importance at the end of the season, thus attracting bargain hunters and building a new clientele from those who do not normally patronize that store.

While the reliance upon seasonal clearance sales may have some basis for acceptance by the exclusive specialty stores due to their limited merchandise assortment and relatively low levels of traffic, the generally accepted practice is an eclectic approach of early markdowns on individual items, monthly merchandise reviews, and a semiannual, storewide clearance sale, usually at the end of the spring and fall seasons.

Advantages of Early Markdowns

Most department stores and popularly priced chain stores would agree on the early markdown, applied when required, on individual items or classifications of merchandise. The following advantages are offered:

1. The dollar amount of the markdown per unit is less, because demand for the goods is still active. A relatively small markdown in an environment of still

---

[7]Markdowns will increase the merchant's open-to-buy by the dollar amount of the markdown. See Chapter 11.

active demand may be sufficient to move the merchandise. Thus, both gross margin and turnover are enhanced.

2. Early markdowns clear the inventory and make room for more-salable goods.

3. Should early markdowns fail to move the merchandise, there is ample time prior to the end of the season to take more-drastic reductions.

4. The fashion integrity of the store is enhanced; the current selling price should reflect the position of a particular style in its fashion cycle. To do otherwise is to court disaster, especially when the competition has already taken a markdown on the same merchandise!

5. The selling cost ratio is reduced, because early price reductions normally sell quickly and extra salespersons do not have to be employed for a massive clearance sale.

6. Goodwill is generated through the customer's perception of "bargain" prices.

Advantages of Late Markdowns

While most merchants insist that the early markdown is the most advantageous, the late markdown, that taken at the end of a season, is highly favored by the smaller specialty stores and the status-oriented, prestige merchants, whose clientele are seasonally oriented to quality and a high level of "good taste." The advocates of the late markdown stress the following advantages:

1. The image of the store is reinforced and preserved. In effect, most prestige, status-oriented patrons are segmented away from the lower-end customers who shop the store only twice a year in search of bargains. Thus, the price-value appeal is subordinated to that of quality and exclusiveness, and the desired image is maintained.

2. The quantities of merchandise accumulated over the length of a season permit the store to advertise a meaningful sales event that is eagerly anticipated by bargain seekers.

3. The relatively lower level of traffic density in the smaller specialty store means that some merchandise may require longer periods of time to sell. No buying or merchandising errors have been made—the right customer just has not yet come in. Thus, in this type of retail environment, the late markdown may contribute to higher net sales through an extended period of initial price maintenance.

4. The credibility of the initial markon is upheld, contributing to the more immediate sale of regularly priced merchandise. When the customer tends to believe that early markdowns are a distinct probability, they mistrust the orig-

inal retail price and are inclined to postpone their purchase decision until midseason, anticipating substantial price reductions.

5. By extending the lifetime of the initial markon, various creative sales and promotional techniques may be employed to enhance the potential customer's perception of value, thus contributing to demand and increasing the possibilities of sales at regular prices.

Some Considerations on the Size of the Markdown to Be Taken

As previously noted, the reason for taking the markdown is to move the merchandise as quickly as possible, so obviously the size of the reduction relative to the current selling price must be sufficient to accomplish that end. Beyond specifically stating that customers generally tend not to recognize price differentials of less than 20%, it is impossible to define the correct percentage of markdown applicable to any given classification of merchandise. The proper amount of the markdown depends entirely upon the correct "timing" of the markdown and its antecedent variables, such as store policy and the original cause of the markdown. Contrary to the calculation of the initial markon, the determination of the markdown is essentially a value judgment, predicated upon all available facts seasoned with ingenuity, past experience, and a gut feeling, all within the following parameters:

1. The markdown must be just large enough to move out a substantial amount of merchandise in a relatively short period of time and still preserve the required maintained markon dollars.

2. The dollar amount of the markdown must not be too great. An excessive amount of markdown may (*a*) perceptually deny value to the merchandise and thus generate a skeptical rather than a positive customer response and (*b*) dangerously erode the profit component of the desired maintained markon.

3. The dollar amount of the markdown must not be too small. As previously discussed, small markdowns are normally ineffective, and having to take a succession of them in order to move out the merchandise may actually increase the required amount of total markdown dollars involved.

Calculation of the Markdown

Markdowns may be expressed in dollars, as a percentage of net sales, or as a percentage of the original retail price of the goods marked down.

The Dollar Expression of Markdowns

The dollar expression of markdown is simply the difference between the retail price of an item or groups of items as currently marked and a new, reduced selling price.

■ Study Problem

Given: Planning for an end-of-the-month clearance, a buyer makes the following price reduction decisions:

1. 450 blouses will be reduced from $38 to $28.50.
2. 600 skirts will be reduced from $50 to $35.

Find: The dollar value of the resulting markdowns.

Solution:

Step 1. Determine the dollar value of the markdown per unit:

$Markdown per unit = Original selling price − Marked-down price

For the blouses, the markdown per unit is

$38 − $28.50 = $9.50

For the skirts, the markdown per unit is

$50 − $35 = $15

Step 2. Calculate the total value of the markdown per classification. For the classification "blouses," the total value of the reduction is

$9.50 × 450 = $4,275

For the classification "skirts," the cost of the markdown is:

$15 × 600 = $9,000

Step 3. Find the total value of the buyer's planned markdowns for the coming sales event:

Markdowns on blouses	$ 4,275
Markdowns on skirts	9,000
Total markdowns	$13,275

▪ Application Excercise

1. A July 4th celebration sale is planned by the owner of a small men's specialty store according to the following schedule: 76 ties will be marked down from $10 to $7.50, 107 shirts will be reduced to $16 from $23, and 35 sport jackets will be marked down to $115 from $165. What is the total markdown cost to be sustained to support the merchant's celebration sale?

Markdown Expressed as a Percentage of Net (Actual) Sales

For the purpose of internal record keeping under the retail method of inventory, the markdown is always expressed as a percentage of net sales.[8] That is, the dollar markdown is always related to the actual price at which the merchandise is finally sold. Thus, if the original retail price of an item is $100, and after a $25 markdown it is finally sold at $75, the markdown percentage would be stated:

$$\frac{\$100 \text{ (Original retail)} - \$75 \text{ (Net sales)}}{\$75 \text{ (Net sales)}} = \frac{\$25}{\$75} = 33.3\%$$

Therefore, as a percentage of net sales,

$$\text{The markdown \%} = \frac{\text{Net markdown dollars}}{\text{Net sales}}$$

As we have previously noted in our study of the initial markon, this concept of the markdown percentage as a function of net sales, or the final retail selling price, is employed to plan the total markdown allowance, to guide the merchant toward the maintained markon objective, and to measure the achieved degree of merchandising efficiency.

While it may be evident at this point that the markdown percentage (for internal record purposes) is indeed a derivative of net sales, it may not be quite so obvious that the planned net sales are not necessarily synonymous with the achieved, or actual, net sales. Planned net sales relate to the initial or cumulative markon and therefore define those net sales that the merchant hopes to obtain; the net sales actually achieved pertain to the maintained markon and are therefore the result of the original planned sales (or retail price) less the markdown dollars. In effect, this provides two bases for the derivation of markdown percentage, the original retail price of the planned sales and those sales dollars actually received,

---

[8] As are all ratios, with the exception of returns and allowances, as previously discussed.

or the net sales. Conceptually, we arrive at two distinct understandings of the markdown percentage:

$$\text{Markdown \%} = \frac{\text{Markdown dollars}}{\text{Net sales}}$$

or:

$$\text{Markdown \%} = \frac{\text{Markdown dollars}}{\text{Original retail price}}$$

The following study problem is essentially an exercise designed to illustrate the determination of the markdown percentage as a product of net sales. However, in the calculation process, the markdown percentage achieved on net sales is always greater than the markdown percentage derived from the original retail price. Of necessity, this must be true, because planned sales, or the original retail price, are always greater than the actual achieved net sales, obviously because of the markdown differential.

The translation of the net sales–based markdown percentage into its original retail equivalent will be discussed in the remainder of the chapter.

▪ Study Problem

Given: A china buyer decided to reduce 50 English teapots by 25% for a spring clearance sale. The current retail selling price (original retail) is $29.

Find: The anticipated net sales per unit and the markdown as a percentage of net sales, assuming that all of the merchandise is sold.

Solution:

Find the markdown dollars per unit:

$29 × 25% = $7.25

Determine the new retail price (net sales per unit):

$29 − $7.25 = $21.75

Calculate the markdown as a percentage of net sales:

$$\frac{\$7.25}{\$21.75} = 33.3\%$$

The markdown defined in terms of net sales differs significantly from the planned markdown of 25%. This comes about because the buyer's planning is predicated upon the $29 original retail price, whereas, in fact, at the point of sale that price no longer exists; it has been reduced by the amount of the markdown to net sales, or

$29 − $7.25 = $21.75

Thus, it does not follow that the markdown predicated upon the current, or original, retail price is commensurate with that markdown percentage achieved from net sales.

■ Application Excercise

1. A quantity of merchandise is to be reduced by 30% of the current selling price. What is the resulting percentage of markdown in terms of net sales?

2. Thirty-five occasional chairs were to be reduced for a fall clearance sale. The current retail price of the individual chairs is $150, and the sale price is planned at $99. Assuming that all of the chairs are sold, what is the planned markdown per unit and the markdown percentage actually achieved on net sales?

3. A gift buyer planned to reduce 50 music boxes 20% in order to make room for incoming merchandise. The current selling price of the music boxes is $80. What is the total markdown in dollars and as a percentage of net sales?

4. One hundred $60 skirts are to be reduced by 20%. However, only 50 of the skirts are sold at the reduced price. What was the markdown percentage achieved on net sales?

5. A major appliance dealer decided to clear out six floor-sample refrigerators by marking them down 30%. Two units currently retail for $350 each, one is priced at $300, another is marked at $200, and two are priced at $180 each. Assuming that all six units were sold, what was the markdown percentage achieved?

Markdowns Expressed as a Percentage of the Original Retail Price

The second method by which the markdown may be calculated is the off-retail percentage, where the markdown calculation is based on the original retail price, rather than net sales. This formula complements the net sales formula and defines the proper philosophy for the buyer's consideration of markdowns.

$$\text{Off-retail markdown \%} = \frac{\text{Original price} - \text{New price}}{\text{Original price}}$$

The off-retail markdown is the determination of the total reduction percentage for an individual item, whereas the net sales–based calculation provides for the average markdown percentage of many items. For example, if a merchant initially sold 50 items at $40, reduced the items to $30, and sold another 25 of the same item, the off-retail markdown percentage (per item marked down) would be:

$$\frac{\$40\ (\text{Original retail}) - \$30.00\ (\text{New retail})}{\$40\ (\text{Original retail})} = 25\%$$

whereas the "average" markdown percentage (for the entire sale) would be:

$$\frac{\$250\ (\text{Total markdown: } \$10 \times 25)}{\$2{,}750\ (\text{Net sales: } \$40 \times 50 + \$30 \times 25)} = 9\%$$

When used in conjunction with each other, the two formulas provide the merchant with the tactical insight to guide the internal operations of the "retail system," as well as to manipulate the customer's perception of value. Essentially, the net sales–based markdown percentage is a statement of merchandising expertise and buying skills, whereas the off-retail percentage defines the size of the markdown in the shopper's psyche; it indicates the relative dollar amount to be "saved" by purchasing at the reduced price and is thus indispensable in the promotional tactics of merchandising strategy. The off-retail markdown can also provide the merchant with a more detailed analysis of specific items and merchandise classifications by defining markdown per item, as well as the total cost of the markdown and the percentage of items marked down to the total sold. For example, the previous illustration of the off-retail markdown permits the following analysis.

The markdown per item is:

$$\frac{\$40 - \$30}{\$40} = \frac{\$10}{\$40} = 25\%$$

The percentage of marked-down items is:

$$\frac{25\ (\text{Items marked down})}{75\ (\text{Total items sold})} = 33.3\%$$

The dollar value of the markdown is:

$$25\ \text{items} \times \$10 = \$250$$

Calculation of the Markdown Based upon the Original Retail Price When the Markdown on Net Sales is Known

The merchant's ultimate markdown objective is to achieve an off-retail price reduction consistent with a predetermined markdown defined in terms of net sales. In short, the markdown based upon the original retail price must finally translate into the markdown percentage compatible with the corporate determinants of profitability; again, all merchandising ratios are percentages of net sales.

▪ Study Problem

Given: A women's shoe buyer carries a classification of sandals currently retailing at $20. The season is about to end, and the buyer desires to clear out the inventory with a price reduction equivalent to 25% of net sales.

Find: The required amount of markdown in dollars and percentage of the original retail price.

Solution:

Step 1. Net sales equals 100%. The markdown to be covered by net sales equals 25%. Therefore original retail must equal 125%, or 125% of net sales equals $20.

Step 2.

Net sales = 125% of $20

Net sales = $20 ÷ 125% = $16

Step 3.

Markdown dollars = $20 − $16 = $4

Markdown percentage = $4 ÷ $20 = 20%

Proof:

20% × $20 (Original retail) = $4

25% × $16 (Net sales) = $4

or:

$$\frac{\$4 \ (Markdown)}{\$20 \ (Original \ retail)} = 20\%$$

$$\frac{\$4.00 \ (Markdown)}{\$16.00 \ (Net \ sales)} = 25\%$$

Alternate Solution:

$$\frac{25\%}{125\%} = 20\%; \ 20\% \times \$20 = \$4$$

▪ Application Exercise

1. A stationery store decides to mark down $550 worth of slow-selling merchandise by 10% of net sales. What should the markdown percentage of the original retail price be?

2. A merchant has some goods in inventory that are to be marked down to 20% of sales. The current retail price is $12 per unit. Assuming that all of the merchandise will be sold, determine the dollar amount of the markdown and the required markdown as a percentage of the original retail price.

3. An assortment of exterior paint retailing at $13.50 per gallon is to be marked down by 30% of sales. Assuming that all the paint is sold, find the new retail price, the dollar amount of the markdown, and the off-retail markdown percentage.

4. A better-dress department planned a markdown of 25% of net sales. The original retail value of the inventory was $5,000. Calculate the new retail value of the inventory, the dollar amount of the markdown, and the off-retail markdown percentage.

5. An inexperienced boys'-clothing buyer was instructed to take a 30% markdown on a particular classification of blazers. The buyer determined that 83 blazers were in the inventory with a total retail value of $2,490 and, following orders, promptly reduced the goods by $747, or 30%, of the original retail price. Will the buyer achieve the desired markdown? If not, what percentage of markdown will be achieved? What procedure should the buyer have used? What is the correct percentage of markdown required to achieve the desired markdown of 30% of sales? Prove your results.

Application of the Off-Retail Markdown to Promotional Tactics

Because the off-retail expression of markdown percentage is most often perceived by the customer to be greater than the dollar differential existing between the old and new retail price, it is common practice for the merchant to advertise:

SALE!

25% OFF

REDUCED TO $2.98

While most readers will be acquainted with this concept, one may not be so familiar with the answer to the question, "25% off what?"

■ Study Problem

Given: An item is reduced by 25% to $2.98.

Find: The original selling price.

Solution:

Original retail	100%
Less reduction	25%
New retail	75%

If 75% equals $2.98 (new retail), then the original retail must be equal to

$\frac{\$2.98}{75\%}$, or $3.97[9]

because $3.97 × 25% = $.99, and $3.97 − $.99 = the sale price of $2.98.

The above calculations mathematically define only a previous selling price; they make no statement concerning the validity of that price or its point of origin. Thus the $3.97 may indeed represent the original retail price, or it could have been the last price in a series of markdowns that originated from a $5.96 retail price. If such had been the case, the markdown percentage should have been stated as "$2.98—50% off the original retail price," rather than 25% off a previous retail price, which the customer obviously found unacceptable. The fact that everything is relative should stand as a reminder that the merchant should select that price relationship that tends to convey the greatest perception of value to the customer, by avoiding the fact that the merchandise is worth no more than its current offered price. (Otherwise, it would have been sold at the higher price and thus would be unavailable at the lower price.)

■ Application Exercise

1. Determine the initial retail price of an item currently on sale at $12, advertised as being "reduced 30%."

2. What was the original retail price of a sofa reduced 40% to $398? What was the percentage of markdown actually achieved by the merchant?

---

[9]$.01 is lost in the rounding process. Also, this is the same concept of going from cost to the retail price discussed in Chapter 3.

3. "Big Sale!—prices slashed a "huge" 33%—sale-priced today only at $17.88!" What was the original retail price?

Determining the Required Increase in Sales Volume Necessary to Offset a Reduction in the Retail Price

As we shall see in Chapter 9, the gross margin dollars—that is, the excess of sales over the total cost of sales—is largely determined by the retail price and the resulting maintained markon plus the rate of inventory turnover. Assuming that for some classifications of merchandise, basic stock for example, a lower retail price will result in a higher turnover or rate of sale,[10] it is important that we consider the relationship existing among markdowns, the rate of sale, and net sales.

∎ Study Problem

Given: A merchant purchased an item for $2 and retailed it at $4; it is currently selling at 150 units per week. Desirous of increasing sales volume, the merchant is contemplating a 20% reduction in the current selling price.

Find: What increase in the current rate of sale is necessary to maintain the same dollar amount of maintained markon? What increase in net sales is required to achieve the current amount of maintained markon?

Solution:

Step 1. Define the new retail price:

$4 × 20% = $.80 (Markdown)

Original retail	$4.00
Less markdown	.80
New retail	$3.20

Step 2. Determine the difference in the markon dollars between the new retail price and the original retail price:

---

[10]Turnover defines the sale and replacement of merchandise over a given period of time, whereas the rate of sale implies only the number of units sold in a particular period of time. However, for the purpose of illustration the two terms are here used synonymously.

Original markon   = $4.00 − $2.00 = $2.00
Less new markon   = $3.20 − $2.00 =   1.20

Markon differential $ .80

Step 3. Calculate the difference in markon as a percentage of the new markon:

$$\frac{\$.80 \ (\text{Markon differential})}{\$1.20 \ (\text{New markon})} = 66.7\%$$

Step 4. What is the required increase in the current rate of sale (150 units per week) to sustain the maintained markon dollars? Because the difference in markon constitutes 66.7% of the new markon, the rate of sale must be increased by a like amount. Therefore:

66.7% × 150 units = 100 units

150 units + 100 units = 250 units (that must be sold in order to yield the original maintained markon)

Step 5. The increase in net sales required to achieve the current level of maintained markon is:

250 units × $3.20 = $800

or, sales volume must be increased by

$$\frac{\$800 - \$600 \ (150 \times \$4)}{\$600} = 33.3\%$$

in order to compensate for the 66.7% decline in the new markon from the prior markon.

Proof:

$600 × 33.3% = $200

$200 + $600 = $800

$800 ÷ $3.20 (New retail) = 250 units per week

Also:

150 units per week × $2 (Markon) = $300 (Maintained markon)

250 units per week × $1.20 (Markon) = $300 (Maintained markon)

▪ Application Exercise

1. T-shirts that retail for $8 and cost $3.75 are selling at the rate of 300 per week. The buyer is considering reducing the price by 20% in order to stimulate sales.

Determine (*a*) the required increase in unit sales that would result in the same maintained markon dollars and (*b*) the increase in net sales necessary to maintain the current maintained markon dollars.

2. The cost of a particular stereo set is $216. At the retail price of $300, the buyer is currently selling 15 sets per week. Considering this rate of sale to be "sluggish," the buyer reduces the price to $269, anticipating that the increased rate of sales will result in the maintenance of the current maintained markon. Find (*a*) the number of units to be sold and (*b*) the required increase in sales volume, in both dollars and percentage.

3. An item retails at $30 with a 40% markon. The rate of sale is 200 items per week. The anticipated markdown is 20%. Find (*a*) the increase in unit sales required to yield the current maintained dollar markon and (*b*) the increase in sales volume in both dollars and percentage necessary to maintain the current dollar amount of maintained markon.

Gross Markdowns, Markdown Cancellations, and Net Markdowns

The original or total dollar amount of markdowns taken during a particular period of time by a store, department, or classification	Gross markdowns
Less the restoration of marked-down merchandise to its original selling price within the same classification and time frame results in	Markdown cancellation
The modification, or reduction, of the original amount of planned markdown	Net markdowns

Therefore:

Net markdowns = Gross markdowns − Markdown cancellations

A markdown cancellation is a revocation of a markdown previously taken; whereas a markdown decreases the retail value of an inventory, the markdown cancellation increases the value of that inventory. Markdowns, in conjunction with markdown cancellations, are normally employed to define the pricing parameters of some type of special sales event over a specified period of time. Consider the following illustration:

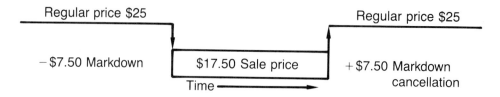

Rules Governing the Use of Markdown Cancellations

1. The dollar value of a markdown cancellation cannot exceed the amount of the preceding markdown. If a $30 item is reduced by $9 to $21, and the price is later increased to $32, $9 of the new retail price is the markdown cancellation and the additional $2 is defined as markup, the upward revision of the initial markon. For example:

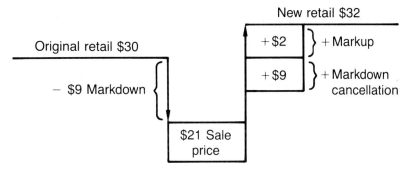

2. Markdown cancellations can only be applied to those items that were originally marked down; cancellation of markdown cannot be applied to a pair of shoes if the markdown was originally taken on a blouse.

3. Markdown cancellations can only apply to merchandise within the time frame of a particular season. If an upward revision of the retail price is desired after the season has ended, then an additional markup is required.

■ Study Problem

Given: A jewelry buyer reduced 75 watches from $90 to $59 for a three-day promotional event. At the end of the third day, 60 watches had been sold at the sale price, and the remaining 15 watches were repriced to retail at $95.

Find: What were the buyer's gross markdowns, total amount of markdown cancellations, net markdowns, and total additional markup dollars?

Solution:

Step 1. Determine gross markdowns:

Original retail	$ 90
Less new retail	59
Markdown	$ 31
Unit markdown	$ 31
Watches	× 75
Gross markdowns	$2,325

Step 2. Find the amount of markdown cancellations. Cancellation of markdown represents the number of watches to be repriced times the amount of the original markdown. Thus,

Markdown	$31
Watches	× 15
Markdown cancellations	$465

Step 3. Calculate the buyer's net markdowns. Net markdowns are equal to the difference existing between the gross markdowns and the markdown cancellations. Therefore:

Gross markdowns	$2,325
Less markdown cancellations	465
Net markdowns	$1,860

Step 4. Define the additional markup dollars. Markup is the upward revision of the original retail price or the initial markon. As a result:

New price revision	$95
Less original retail	90
Markup per watch	$ 5
Markup	$5
Watches repriced	× 15
Markup	$75

▪ Application Exercise

1. 100 pairs of socks were reduced from $5 to $3.50 for a "back to school" sale. At the end of the sale, 65 pairs were sold and the balance was returned to inventory at the regular $5 price. Find the gross markdowns, the markdown cancellations, and the net markdowns.

2. An independent merchant is planning a one-day sale according to the following schedule:

Classification X:	35 units to be reduced from $18 to $14
Classification Y:	75 units to be reduced from $39.98 to $24
Classification Z:	86 units to be reduced from $24.50 to $15

At the end of the day, the following results were realized:

Classification X:	Sold 25 units
Classification Y:	Sold 50 units
Classification Z:	Sold 75 units

Find the net markdowns per classification and the total net markdowns required to support the merchant's one-day sale.

3. To partially offset the effects of the net markdowns (in problem 2), the buyer decided to reprice the sale merchandise after the sale as follows:

Classification X: $20
Classification Y: $44.98
Classification Z: $30

Find the additional markup per classification and for the total remaining inventory assortment.

▪ Solutions to the Application Exercises

The Dollar Expression of Markdowns (p. 158)

1. Determine the dollar value of the markdown per unit:

Ties: $10 − $7.50 = $2.50 Markdown
Shirts: $23 − $16 = $7 Markdown
Jackets: $165 − $115 = $50 Markdown

Find the total value of the markdown per classification and the total cost required to support the "celebration" sale.

Ties:	76 × $2.50	= $ 190
Shirts:	107 × $7	= $ 749
Jackets:	35 × $50	= $1,750
Total cost of markdown		= $2,689

Markdowns Expressed as a Percentage of Net (Actual) Sales (p. 159)

1.
Retail	100%	$\dfrac{30\%}{70\%} = 42.9\%$
Less markdown	30	
New retail	70%	

3. Current retail value = $80 × 50   = $4,000
   Less $markdown = $4,000 × 20% =   800
   New retail price $3,200

$$\frac{\text{Markdown}}{\text{New retail}} = \text{Markdown \%}, \frac{\$800}{\$3,200} = 25\%$$

	Original Retail	Markdown %	$Markdown	New Retail
5.	$ 350	30	105	$ 245
	350	30	105	245
	300	30	90	210
	200	30	60	140
	180	30	54	126
	180	30	54	126
Total	$1,560	30%	$468	$1,092

$$\frac{468 \text{ (Total markdown)}}{\$1,092 \text{ (New retail)}} = 42.9\%$$

Calculation of the Markdown Based upon the Original Retail Price When the Markdown on Net Sales Is Known (p. 164)

1. Sales $= 100\% + 10\% = 110\%$

   $110\% = \$550.00$

   Sales $= \dfrac{\$550}{110\%} = \$500$

   The markdown $= \$550 - \$500 = \$50$

   The markdown off-retail % $= \dfrac{\$50}{\$550} = 9.1\%$

3. Sales $= 100\% + 30\% = 130\%$

   $130\% = \$13.50$

   Sales $= \dfrac{\$13.50}{\$130\%} = \$10.38$ (New retail)

   Markdown $= \$13.50 - \$10.38 = \$3.12$

   Off-retail markdown % $= \dfrac{\$3.12}{\$13.50} = 23.1\%$

5. The buyer will not achieve the desired 30% markdown; the achieved markdown will be:

   $$\frac{\$747 \text{ (Markdown)}}{\$1,743 \text{ (Net sales)}} = 42.9\%$$

   The buyer should have used the off-retail percentage method; accordingly, the correct procedure and resulting percentage of markdown is:

Sales $= 100\% + 30\% = 130\%$

$130\% = \$2,490$

Sales $= \dfrac{\$2,490}{130\%} = \$1,915.38$

Markdown $= \$2,490 - \$1,915.38 = \$574.62$

Markdown off-retail % $= \dfrac{\$574.62}{\$2,490} = 23.1\%$

Proof:

$30\% \times \$2,490$ (Original retail) $= \$747$

$30\% \times \$1,915.38$ (New retail) $= \$574.61$

Or:

$$\dfrac{\$747 \text{ (Markdown)}}{\$2,490 \text{ (Original retail)}} = 30\% = \dfrac{\$574.62 \text{ (Markdown)}}{\$1,915.38 \text{ (New retail)}}$$

Application of the Off-Retail Markdown to Promotional Tactics (p. 165)

1. $\dfrac{\$12}{70\%} = \$17.14$

   because $\$17.14 \times 30\% = \$5.14$, and $\$17.14 - \$5.14 = \$12.00$

3. $\dfrac{\$17.88}{67\%} = \$26.69$

   because $33\% \times \$26.69 = \$8.81$, and $\$26.69 - \$8.81 = \$17.88.$

Determining the Required Increase in Sales Volume Necessary to Offset a Reduction in the Retail Price (p. 167)

1. $\$8 \times 20\%$ $= \$1.60$ (Markdown)
   $\$8 - \$1.60$ $= \$6.40$ (New retail price)

   $\$8 - \$3.75$ $= \$4.25$ (Original markon)
   $\$6.40 - \$3.75 = \underline{\$2.65}$ (Less new markon)
   $\qquad\qquad\quad \$1.60$ (Markon differential)

   $\dfrac{\$1.60 \text{ (Markon differential)}}{\$2.65 \text{ (New markon)}} = 60.4\%$

(a) 60.4% × 300 (Units) = 181 (Units)

    300 (Units) + 181 (Units) = 481 (Units)

(b) 481 (Units) × \$6.40 = \$3,078

or sales volume must be increased by

$$\frac{\$3,078 - \$2,400 \ (\$8 \times 300)}{\$2,400} = 28.3\%$$

Proof:

\$2,400 × 28.3% = \$679.20

\$2,400 + \$679.20 = \$3,079.20

\$3,079.20 ÷ \$6.40 = 481 units per week

Also:

300 units per week × \$4.25 (Markon) = \$1,275

481 units per week × \$2.65 (Markon) = \$1,275

3. The cost of the item is:

\$30 × (100% − 40%) = \$18

\$30 − \$18 = \$12 (Original markon)

\$30 × 20% = \$6 (Amount of reduction)

\$30 − \$6 = \$24 (New retail)

\$24 − \$18 = \$6 (New markon)

\$12	(Original markon)
6	(Less new markon)
\$ 6	(Markon differential)

$$\frac{\$6 \ (\text{Markon differential})}{\$6 \ (\text{New markon})} = 100\%$$

(a) 100% × 200 (Items) = 200 (Items)

    200 (Items) + 200 (Items) = 400 (Items to be sold)

(b) 400 (Items) × \$24 (New retail) = \$9,600

or a sales increase of:

$$\frac{\$9,600 - \$6,000 \ (\$30 \times 200)}{\$6,000} = 60\%$$

Proof:

$6,000 × 60% = $3,600

$6,000 + $3,600 = $9,600

$9,600 ÷ $24 = 400 Items

Or:

$12 (Original markon) × 200 units = $2,400

$6 (New markon) × 400 units = $2,400

Gross Markdowns, Markdown Cancellations, and Net Markdowns (p. 170)

1. $5 − $3.50 = $1.50

   $1.50 × 100 pairs of socks = $150 (Gross markdowns)

   100 − 65 = 35 pairs of socks upon which the markdown was cancelled. Thus, the markdown cancellations are:

$1.50	Markdown per unit
× 35	Units
$52.50	Markdown cancellations

   Therefore, the net markdown is:

$150.00	Gross markdowns
52.50	Less markdown cancellations
$97.50	Net markdowns

3. Classification *X*:

   Markup = $20 − $18 = $2 × 10 units = $20

   Classification *Y*:

   Markup = $44.98 − $39.98 = $5 × 25 units = $125

   Classification *Z*:

   Markup = $30 − $24.50 = $5.50 × 11 units = $60.50

   Total additional markup = $20 + $125 + $60.50 = $205.50

Topics for Discussion and Review

1. Define and explain the four classifications of retail price revisions.
2. How is the cost of the markdowns transferred from the merchant to the consumer?

3. Discuss the advantages of planned markdowns. What are the disadvantages?

4. What is the essential cause of markdowns? Why are they inevitable?

5. Define and discuss the four factors dictating the taking of markdowns.

6. What are the pricing errors contributing to unplanned-for markdowns?

7. Discuss ways of reducing the operational causes of markdowns.

8. How can markdowns be minimized on the selling floor?

9. Discuss markdowns as a management tool to modify or reinforce the retail image.

10. What factors influence the timing of markdowns? What are some of the advantages of early markdowns and late markdowns?

11. What are some of the considerations that determine the size of the markdown?

12. What is a markdown cancellation? What are net markdowns?

13. Distinguish between a markon and a markup.

14. When does a markdown become a markup?

15. Explain the concept of net markdowns; illustrate your answer.

16. Internal record keeping dictates that markdowns are always to be recorded as a percentage of net sales rather than of the original retail price. Why is this so?

17. What is meant by the expression "off-retail markdown"? How does this type of markdown differ from the sales-based markdown? What functions does the off-retail markdown normally serve?

18. Explain how you would convert a markdown percentage based upon original retail to a markdown percentage derived from planned net sales.

19. Assuming that markdowns will increase the rate of sale, discuss the relationship between markdowns and sales volume.

20. How could the dictates of store policy influence the amount of markdowns that are taken?

21. What are the three ways of expressing a markdown?

22. How would you calculate the amount of increased sales volume you would need to offset a planned markdown?

23. What would happen if you took an $8 markdown on a $20 item, and two weeks later effected a $10 markdown cancellation?

24. Explain how you would determine the original retail price if you knew the markdown percent and the current selling price.

25. Explain the effect of markdowns on the rate of turnover and gross margin.

Chapter 7
Markdown and Maintained Markon

Learning Objectives

- Discuss the concept of the maintained markon, and provide two formulas for its definition.

- Explain how the cost of the markdown is arrived at.

- Explain the relationship between the initial markon, the markdown, and the maintained markon.

- Calculate the maintained markon when the initial markon and the markdown are known.

- Calculate the markdown when the initial markon and the maintained markon are known.

- Determine the maintained markon in dollars, given the initial markon, sales, and retail reductions in dollars.

- Calculate the maintained markon percentage, given the initial markon, sales, and retail reductions as a percentage of sales.

- Determine the markdowns allowable for the balance of a period, given the planned maintained markon and activity to date.

Key Terms

Alteration Costs: The net cost of altering merchandise for customers and merchandise in stock but not yet sold.

Cash Discounts: A discount granted to the merchant by the vendor for the merchant's payment of an invoice within an agreed upon, specific period of time. Cash discounts are not to be taken for granted; they must be "earned" by the merchant.

Cost of the Markdown: The value of the cost portion of the markdown. Determined by multiplying the retail markdown times the complement of the initial or cumulative markon. Also, the cost of the markdown is equal to the difference between the initial markon and the maintained markon.

Gross Cost of Merchandise Sold: The accumulated inventory at cost plus additions at billed cost minus the closing inventory at cost. Subtracted from net sales, the gross cost of merchandise sold provides for the maintained markon. The maintained markon, subsequently adjusted by cash discounts and workroom costs, defines the gross margin of profit on the merchandise sold.

Gross Margin: The difference between net sales and the total cost of merchandise sold.

Gross Sales: The total amount of merchandise sold over a given period of time.

Initial Markon: The difference between the cost and the retail price placed upon the merchandise; the first markon, or that which is "hoped for." Note that the cumulative markon is the average of many initial markons; thus, the two concepts are mathematically treated in the same manner.

Maintained Markon: The difference between net sales and the gross cost of merchandise sold.

Markdown: A reduction in the retail price of the merchandise, normally expressed as a percentage of planned sales.

Net Sales: Those sales actually achieved by the retail merchant; determined by deducting returns and allowances from gross sales.

Operating Expenses: All nonmerchandising expenses incurred in the selling of goods; those costs acquired below the determination of gross margin.

Operating Profit: The difference between gross margin and total operating expenses.

Planned Sales: Anticipated sales over a given period of time. In effect, planned sales is that income "hoped for" by the merchant.

Retail Method of Accounting: An accounting system in which all percentages are relative to the retail price rather than the cost price.

Retail Reductions: The total of markdowns, sales discounts, and either estimated or actual inventory shortages.

Total Cost of Merchandise Sold: Defines the gross cost of merchandise sold plus net workroom charges less the cash discounts earned.

7.1

The Concept of Maintained Markon

In Chapter 5, we saw that the initial markon contained the elements of operating expenses, profit, and retail reductions. The interaction of these components resulted in a percentage or dollar amount that, when added to the billed cost of the merchandise, determined the original value of the merchant's inventory. However, this initial markon is simply a hypothetical statement concerning an assumption yet to be proved; it is an assertion of the merchant's hope, subject to future verification by the customer's activities in the retail marketplace. Thus, it remains for net sales to prove or disprove the hypothesis of the initial markon.

While it is theoretically possible and indeed highly probable that the initial markon will be achieved on some of the merchandise all of the time, and on all of the merchandise some of the time, it is in fact impossible to attain that markon on all of the merchandise all of the time. The initial markon falls when the customer fails to support it; in effect, the initial markon, when not supported, will "float" downward to meet the acceptable level of customer demand. At this point, the maintained markon has been achieved, as evidenced by net sales. Thus, the maintained markon represents the reality of a retail price originally "hoped for"; that difference between what was hoped for and reality is defined as retail reductions, the essence of which is markdowns.

A more precise definition of the maintained markon is that difference between net sales and the gross cost of merchandise sold, wherein net sales represents the actual price received, and the gross cost of merchandise sold defines the billed cost of the merchandise plus any added incidentals, such as transportation, special packaging, and so forth. Quantitatively stated,

Maintained markon = Net sales − Gross cost of merchandise sold

Therefore, the maintained markon defines the profit actually achieved on the sale of merchandise.

The gross cost of merchandise sold is not the same as the total cost of merchandise sold. The gross cost of merchandise refers to the billed cost, whereas the total cost defines the absolute or final cost of the merchandise sold—that is, the gross cost modified by the impact of alteration expenses and cash discounts. Thus,

Net sales − Maintained markon = Gross cost of merchandise sold

and,

Gross cost of merchandise sold + Alteration costs − Cash discounts
earned = Total cost of merchandise sold

Or,

Net sales
Less maintained markon

Gross cost of merchandise sold
Plus alteration costs
Less cash discounts earned

Total cost of merchandise sold

As we shall see in Chapter 8, it is exactly these cash discounts and alteration expenses that differentiate the maintained markon from the gross margin; when there are no alteration costs and cash discounts, the maintained markon is the same as the gross margin.

From a planning perspective, the objective of the maintained markon is to provide sufficient funds to cover the operating expenses and operating profit. However, while this objective is obviously not always achieved, it is still theoretically correct to also define the maintained markon as the product of operating expenses plus operating profit. To neglect this concept is to deprive the maintained markon of the essence of its basic function and fundamental value.

7.2

The Maintained Markon as a Product of the Markdown[1] and the Initial Markon

The retail method of accounting dictates that all percentage figures must be based on net sales.[2] For accounting purposes, the markdown is no exception,[3] and this leads to the unique relationship among the initial markon, the markdown, and the resulting maintained markon. In order to better comprehend and appreciate this relationship, consider the following comparative illustrations:

Situation 1

A department had a total amount of merchandise available for sale at a cost of $6,000 with a retail value of $10,000. Net sales were $8,000, and no markdowns were taken. The following conditions would then exist:

---

[1]Because markdowns are by far the greatest and the most manipulable portion of the retail reductions, the two terms are used synonymously in this chapter.
[2]Except the initial markon, which is based upon planned sales or the original retail, and returns and allowances, which are derived from gross sales.
[3]While markdown may be predicated upon original retail for promotional or planning purposes, that markdown actually achieved is always expressed as a percentage of net sales.

	Cost	Retail	Markon $	Markon %
Total merchandise[4] handled and initial markon	$6,000	$10,000	$4,000	40%
Net sales[5]		8,000		
Markdowns		0		
Total retail reductions and net sales		8,000		
Closing inventory	1,200[6]	2,000		
Gross cost of merchandise sold	4,800			
Maintained markon[7]			3,200	40%

Maintained markon = Net sales − Gross cost of merchandise sold

Thus,

$3,200 = $8,000 − $4,800

and,

$$\text{Maintained markon\%} = \frac{\$3,200 \ (\text{Maintained markon})}{\$8,000 \ (\text{Net sales})} = 40\%$$

Notice that in this case the initial markon of 40% is the same as the maintained markon; this is because no markdowns were taken, thus leaving the percentage relationship between cost and retail intact.

Situation 2

Consider the same situation as previously discussed, only this time assume that the department had markdowns of $1,000. We would then have this situation:

---

[4]The correct terminology here is "cumulative markon." However, it will be recalled that cumulative markon is the average of many initial markons; thus, for illustrative purposes only, the term "initial markon" is used.

[5]Net sales are reductions in the total amount of merchandise handled and reduce only the amount of inventory on hand. Net sales are not to be confused with retail reductions, i.e., markdowns, shortages, and sales discounts, which reduce the "value" of the inventory, regardless of whether it is sold.

[6]Closing inventory is reduced to cost by:
$2,000 × (100% − 40%) = $2,000 × 60% = $1,200.

[7]Maintained markon here is the same as gross margin because of the absence of workroom costs and earned cash discounts.

	Cost	Retail	Markon $	Markon %
Total merchandise handled and initial markon	$6,000	$10,000	$4,000	40%
Net sales		{ 8,000		
Markdowns		{ 1,000		
Total retail reductions and net sales		9,000		
Closing inventory	600	1,000		
Gross cost of merchandise sold	5,400			
Maintained markon			2,600	32.5%

Now, consider the relationship between the initial markon, the maintained markon, and the markdown. In the first situation, the maintained markon is $3,200. In the second situation, after taking a $1,000 markdown, the maintained markon is $2,600. Note that the $1,000 markdown did not reduce the maintained markon by the same amount; despite the $1,000 markdown, the maintained markon was reduced by only $600 ($3,200 − $2,600).

Translated into percentages, the 40% maintained markon achieved in the first situation was reduced in the second situation to 32.5% by the taking of a 12.5% markdown.[8] In other words, a 12.5% markdown only reduced the maintained markon by 7.5% (40% − 32.5%)! This phenomenon requires additional explanation.

The markdown essentially reflects the customer's lack of support for the current selling price, thus forcing the merchant to depreciate the retail value of the inventory. When this occurs, the retail accounting procedure requires a corresponding devaluation in the cost of that inventory.[9] For example, in comparing the two previous situations we find in the latter that the closing inventory at retail is reduced by sales and the amount of the markdown to $1,000. This figure is in turn reduced to cost, or $600 (60% of $1,000), thus increasing the cost of goods sold from $4,800 to $5,400. As a result, the maintained markon will be decreased in proportion to the cost of goods sold as dictated by the original markon (40%) and not the total amount of the markdown itself.

This brings us to a further consideration of the concept of the markdown. Because the original retail price is a proportional distribution of billed cost and initial markon, any part of that original price, such as the markdown, must be constituted in the same proportional ratios. For example, in the second situation we find

---

[8] $\text{Markdown \%} = \dfrac{\$1,000\,(\$\text{Markdown})}{\$8,000\,(\text{Net sales})} = 12.5\%$

[9] This concept will be further developed in Chapter 11.

Initial markon = 40%
Original cost = 60%
Original retail = 100%

Therefore, the markdown must consist of a cost and markon component, distributed in the same proportional ratios as found in the original retail price.

Markon component of markdown = 40%
Cost component of markdown = 60%
Total markdown = 100%

Because the markdown as operationally used is always defined as a percentage of net sales, the dollar cost of the markdown to the merchant is determined in the same manner as any other cost figure would be. That is,

Markdown cost = Dollar markdown (100% − Initial markon)

By applying the above formula to the second situation, we find that the cost of the markdown is

$1,000 (100% − 40%) = $1,000 × 60% = $600.

Because of the lack of markdowns in the first situation, the percentage of maintained markon achieved on sales of $8,000 is 40%, or the same as the initial markon; in other words, the markon "hoped for" was actually accomplished, and $3,200 ($8,000 × 40%) was obtained in markon dollars.

The second situation illustrates the effect of the markdown on the initial markon and defines the relationship between the initial markon and the maintained markon. Here we find that the maintained markon is $2,600, or $600 less than the maintained markon in the first situation. This has come about because the cost of the markdown, $600, has increased the cost of the closing inventory by a like amount, thus decreasing the maintained markon in the first situation from $3,200 to the $2,600 maintained markon found in the second situation. Thus, we see that the essential difference between the initial markon and maintained markon is the cost of the markdown. We may therefore conclude that

$Initial markon − $Cost of the markdown = $Maintained markon
$3,200 − $600 = $2,600

And

$$\text{Maintained markon\%} = \frac{\$ \text{ Maintained markon}}{\$ \text{ Net sales}} = \frac{\$2,600}{\$8,000} = 32.5\%$$

The same reasoning and procedure are to be followed when working with percentages. Utilizing the data in the second situation, we find that

$$\text{Markdown \%} = \frac{\$1,000 \text{ (Markdown)}}{\$8,000 \text{ (Net sales)}} = 12.5\%$$

The initial markon % = 40%

Therefore,

Cost of the markdown = 12.5% (100% − 40%) = 7.5%

Then,

Initial markon% − Cost of markdown% = Maintained markon%
40%   −   7.5%   =   32.5%

Determination of the Maintained Markon When the Initial Markon and Markdown Are Known

We have previously stated that the maintained markon is equal to the initial markon less the cost of the markdown. There is, however, another formula, derived from the equation for initial markon. It will be recalled from Chapter 5 that

$$\text{Initial markon} = \frac{\text{Maintained markon} + \text{Reductions}}{100\% + \text{Reductions}}$$

Therefore, by transposition, it may be stated that

Maintained markon = Initial markon (100% + Reductions) − Reductions

Either formula is acceptable, and both are illustrated in the following study problem.

▪ Study Problem

Given: The initial markon was 44% and markdowns amounted to 12%.

Find: The maintained markon percentage achieved.

Solution:

Cost of markdown = 12% (100% − 44%) = 6.7%

Initial markon % − Cost of markdown % = Maintained markon %
44%   −   6.7%   =   37.3%

Alternate Solution:

Initial markon % (100% + Reductions) − Reductions = Maintained markon %
44%   (100% + 12%)   −   12%   =   37.3%

▪ Application Exercise

1. Find the percentage of maintained markon in a department that had an initial markon of 38% and markdowns of 12%.

2. The initial markon was planned at 45% and retail reductions at 14%. What is the resulting percentage of maintained markon?

3. The housewares department had net sales of $80,000, with a cumulative markon[10] of $37,600 and markdowns of 7%. Calculate the maintained markon in terms of dollars and percentage. Show both methods of calculation.

4. Given net sales of $65,000, total merchandise handled of $90,000, markdowns of $7,150, and a cumulative markon of 46%, find the gross margin[11] in dollars and percentage. Prove your answer.

5. Given operating expenses of 35%, markdowns of 8%, and initial markon of 48%, find the percentage of operating profit and the gross cost of merchandise sold.

Determination of the Markdown When the Initial Markon and the Maintained Markon Are Known

In order to maintain profitability, merchandise must be priced within the parameters established by the initial markon and the maintained markon. The maintained markon sets the bottom limits of a price range by defining the expenses and profits to be covered. The initial markon states the upper limits of the retail price by adding to the maintained markon an amount sufficient to cover the estimated markdowns. Thus, the markdown is obviously the difference between the initial markon and the maintained markon. However, this difference only represents the cost portion of the markdown, or that fixed amount already paid to the vendor. It is this cost of merchandise in the markdown that needs to be covered by the initial markon and not the total markdown itself. Consider the following situations.

Situation 1

Calculation of the maintained markon:

Net sales	$80	100%
Less cost of sales	48	60
Maintained markon	$32	40%

---

[10] The cumulative markon is simply the average sum of many individual initial markons.

[11] Gross margin is equal to maintained markon when there are no workroom costs or earned cash discounts.

Situation 2

Interject a $10 markdown and determine the initial markon:

Planned sales (Markdown + Net sales)	$90	100.0%
Less cost of sales	48	53.3
Initial markon	$42	46.7%

Or,

$$\text{Initial markon \%} = \frac{\$32 + \$10}{\$80 + \$10} = \frac{\$42}{\$90} = 46.7\%$$

And

$$\text{Initial markon \%} = \frac{40\% + 12.5\%^{12}}{100\% + 12.5\%} = \frac{52.5\%}{112.5\%} = 46.7\%$$

Notice that in both situations the cost of sales remains constant in dollars but varies in its percentage relationship to sales. It is precisely this percentage differential between the cost of sales in the maintained markon and the cost of sales in the initial markon that defines the cost of the markdown. Consider:

Cost of sales in maintained markon	60.0%
Less cost of sales in initial markon	53.3
Cost of markdown	6.7%

The resulting difference between the initial markon and the maintained markon is the cost of the markdown, or:

Initial markon	46.7%
Less maintained markon	40.0
Cost of markdown	6.7%

Proof:

$$\text{Cost of markdown} = 12.5\% \ (100\% - 46.7\%) = 6.7\%$$

∎ Study Problem

Given: A buyer is required to price merchandise within the confines of an initial markon of 48% and a maintained markon of 42%.

---

[12]Markdown % = $10 (Markdown) ÷ $80 (Net sales) = 12.5%.

Find: What is the retail value of the markdown or the maximum amount of markdown that may be allowed?

Solution:

Initial markon − Cost of markdown = Maintained markon

Then,

Initial markon − Maintained markon = Cost of markdown

Initial markon	48%
Less maintained markon	42
Cost of markdown	6%

Convert the cost portion of the markdown (6%) to its full retail value (the markdown as a percentage of original retail or planned sales). The procedure to be followed is the same as that outlined in Chapter 3 for converting the cost price to the retail price. Thus,

$$\text{Markdown at retail} = \frac{\text{Cost of markdown}}{(100\% - \text{Initial markon})}$$

$$\text{Markdown at retail} = \frac{6\%}{100\% - 48\%} = \frac{6\%}{52\%} = 11.5\%$$

In effect, the buyer may take markdowns up to 11.5% of the retail value of the inventory and still achieve the 42% maintained markon, because the cost of the markdown equals 6% (11.5% × 52%) and

Initial markon − Maintained markon = Cost of markdown

▪ Application Exercise

1. Determine the maximum markdown that can be taken in a department where the average initial markon is 46% and the required maintained markon is 41%.

2. Given a maintained markon of 35% and an initial markon of 42%, indicate the maximum markdown allowable for the coming season. Prove your answer.

3. An independent merchant has determined the following:

Cost of sales	55%
Initial markon	52%

Determine the retail value of the markdown.

4. What is the maximum amount of markdown as a percentage of retail that may be taken, given the following situation?

Initial markon	48%
Operating profit	5%
Operating expenses	35%

5. A small women's off-price specialty shop achieved a gross margin of 33%. No alteration services were offered; no cash discounts were earned due to a poor cash flow. If the cumulative markon to date is 40%, what is the maximum amount of markdown available at retail to stimulate sales and increase the inadequate cash flow?

Calculating the Maintained Markon in Dollars, Given the Initial Markon, Sales, and Retail Reductions in Dollars

The essence of the maintained markon is the difference between net sales and the gross cost of merchandise sold, wherein the gross cost of merchandise sold is equal to the cost of net sales plus the cost of retail reductions. That is, retail reductions (i.e., markdowns, estimated shortages, and sales discounts), in effect, represent an increase in the cost of goods sold, because they represent merchandise the buyer paid for but that generates no sales volume. Therefore, we may state that the

Maintained markon = Net sales − Gross cost of merchandise sold

And

Gross cost of merchandise sold = Cost of net sales + Cost of reductions

Therefore,

Maintained markon = Net sales − (Cost of net sales + Cost of retail reductions)

▪ Study Problem

Given: A men's shoe department had net sales of $100,000, net markdowns of $11,000, sales discounts of $1,000, and estimated inventory shortages of $1,200.

Find: What was the dollar amount of maintained markon if the initial markon was 50%?

Solution:

Find gross cost of merchandise sold:

Cost of sales = $100,000 (100% − 50%) = $100,000 × 50% = $50,000

Markdowns + Sales discounts + Shortages = Reductions
  $11,000 + $1,000   + $1,200 = $13,200

Cost of reductions = $13,200 (100% − 50.0%) =
  $13,200 × 50% = $6,600

Cost of   Cost of   Gross cost of
reductions + sales = merchandise sold
  $6,600 + $50,000 = $56,600

Determine the maintained markon dollars:

Net   Gross cost of   Maintained
sales − merchandise sold = markon
$100,000 − $56,600   = $43,400

Proof:

$$\text{Maintained markon \%} = \frac{\$43,400}{\$100,000} = 43.4\%$$

Initial   Maintained   Cost of
Markon % − markon % = reductions
  50%   −   43.4%   =   6.6%

Retail value of reductions = 6.6% ÷ (100% − 50%) = 13.2%

13.2% × $100,000 = $13,200 (the sum of the markdowns [$11,000] + discounts [$1,000] + shortages [$1,200] at retail)

Alternate Solution:

A simpler method of determining the maintained markon in either dollars or percentage, without the same explicable characteristics of the former method, is derived from the formula for the initial markon.

$$\text{Initial markon} = \frac{\text{Maintained markon + Reductions}}{100\% + \text{Reductions}}$$

By transposition, we find that the formula for the maintained markon appears as

Maintained markon = Initial markon % (100% + Reductions) − Reductions[13]

By substituting the dollar figures found in the study problem, we more efficiently arrive at the $43,400 maintained markon:

Maintained markon = 50% ($100,000 + $13,200) − $13,200

= $56,600 − $13,200 = $43,400

---

[13]This formula is applicable to both percentage figures and dollars, as we shall see in the following section.

▪ Application Exercise

1. A department with an initial markon of 44% achieved a net sales volume of $50,000. If markdowns were $4,000, sales discounts were $500, and the estimated inventory shortages were $1,000, what was the maintained markon in dollars?

2. A china department anticipates sales of $80,000, with an initial markon of 35%. Due to the nature of the merchandise, inventory shortages are nil and the low initial markon precludes any sales discounts. What will the maintained markon be if markdowns are planned at $4,000?

3. Considering the following information, determine the dollar value of the maintained markon.

Net sales	$230,000
Markdowns	$27,000
Estimated shortages	$9,200
Sales discounts	$2,300
Initial markon	51%

4. Given the following departmental figures, calculate the achieved maintained markon.

Gross sales	$90,000
Returns and allowances	$5,000
Gross markdowns	$8,500
Markdown cancellations	$1,500
Sales discounts	$900
Estimated inventory shortages	$1,700
Initial markon	47%

5. A small shop owner has planned the coming season according to the following figures.

Gross sales	$200,000
Returns and allowances	1%
Net markdowns	12.5%
Estimated shortages	1.3%
Sales discounts	1.2%
Operating expenses	$69,300
Operating profit	$9,900
Initial markon	42%

Calculate the maintained markon derived from the sale of merchandise. Analyze your results in terms of required operating expenses and desired operating profit. What are your recommendations?

Determination of the Maintained Markon Percentage, Given the Initial Markon, Sales, and Retail Reductions as a Percentage of Sales

The determination of maintained markon percentage follows the same procedure used to calculate the maintained markon dollars.

▪ Study Problem

Given: A toy department had an initial markon of 40%, markdowns of 10%, sales discounts of 2%, and inventory shortages of 1%.

Find: The department's maintained markon.

Solution:

Determine the cost of merchandise sold: Since the cost percentage and the markon percentage must equal 100% (the retail price), the cost percentage must be the complement of markon percentage. If

Cost % + Markon % = 100%

then

Cost % = 100% − Markon %

Therefore:

Cost of sales = 100% − 40% = 60%

Determine the total cost of the reductions:

Retail reductions = 10% + 2% + 1% = 13%

Cost of reductions = 13% (100% − 40%) = 7.8%

Find the gross cost of merchandise sold:

Cost of sales	60.0%
Cost of reductions	7.8
Gross cost of merchandise sold	67.8%

Calculate the maintained markon:

Net sales	100.0%
Less gross cost of merchandise sold	67.8
Maintained markon	32.2%

Alternate Solution:
Use the maintained markon formula discussed in the previous section on the derivation of maintained markon dollars:

Maintained markon = Initial markon % (100% + Reductions) − Reductions

Maintained markon % = 40% (100% + 13%) − 13%

Maintained markon % = 45.2% − 13% = 32.2%

Proof:

Initial markon − Maintained markon = Cost of reductions
        40%   −   32.2%   =   7.8%

7.8% ÷ (100% − 40%) = 13% (Retail reductions)

■ Application Exercise

1. A notions department with an initial markon of 49.5% anticipates retail reductions to be 8%. What will the resulting maintained markon be?

2. Determine the percentage of maintained markon achieved by a store that had an initial markon of 43%, markdowns of 8%, stock shortages of 1.5%, and sales discounts of 0.5%.

3. With a cost of sales of 56% and retail reductions of 9%, what was the maintained markon in the housewares department?

4. Given initial markon of 46%, markdowns of 8.3%, operating expenses of 33%, sales discounts of 1.5%, and inventory shortages of 3%, find the resulting operating profit.

5. The owner of a small boutique is planning for the fall season; markdowns are anticipated to be 11%, sales discounts 2%, and inventory shortages 1.5%. An initial markon of 48.5% is established so as to "ensure" an operating profit of 7%. In this particular case, what is the maximum percentage allowance for operating expenses?

Determination of the Markdowns Allowable for the Balance of a Period, Given the Planned Maintained Markon and Activity to Date

The remaining markdowns allowable for the balance of any given period are equal to the difference between the total markdowns planned for that period and the actual markdowns realized to date. By now, you should be well aware of the relationship between the retail reductions, especially markdowns, and the maintained markon and the ultimate impact of this relationship upon operating profit. It is therefore of the utmost importance that the retail merchant should be able at any time to determine the current amount of markdown available for the period and its relationship to the balance of planned sales. It is only through such analysis that the objective of the maintained markon can be achieved, thus preserving or enhancing the operating profit.

▪ Study Problem

Given: The planned sales in a toy department for the Christmas season are $300,000, with an initial markon of 42% and a maintained markon of 35%. By December 10th, sales have reached $200,000, with accumulated markdowns of $14,000.

Find: The remaining markdowns in dollars and percentage allowable for the balance of the season that will ensure the realization of the 35% maintained markon.

Solution: Determine the total retail value of the markdown for the season:

Initial markon − Maintained markon = Cost of markdown
    42%   −   35%   =   7%

Retail value of markdown for the Christmas season =
7% ÷ (100% − 42%) = 12.1%, or 12.1% × $300,000 = $36,300

Find the markdowns, in dollars and percentage allowable, for the balance of the season:

Markdowns allowed for Christmas season	$36,300
Less markdowns as of December 10th	14,000
Markdowns allowable for balance of season	$22,300

$$\frac{\$22,300 \quad \text{Markdowns for balance of season}}{\$100,000 \quad \text{Balance of sales } (\$300,000 - \$200,000)} = 22.3\%$$

Proof:

	$Markdown	÷	Sales	=	Markdown %
To date	$14,000	÷	$200,000	=	7.0%
Balance	22,300	÷	100,000	=	22.3%
Total	$36,300	÷	$300,000	=	12.1% (Retail)

■ Application Exercise

1. A costume jewelry department had an initial markon of 51% and a planned maintained markon of 45%. To date, sales total $80,000 and markdowns $4,000. Planned sales for the remainder of the season are $25,000. What are the dollar markdowns allowable for the balance of the season?

2. A sporting goods department planned the following figures for the spring season: maintained markon 33%, initial markon 44%, sales for season $200,000. To date, sales are $125,000 and markdowns are 10%. Determine the percentage of markdown allowable for the balance of the period in order to preserve the maintained markon.

3. In order to achieve a maintained markon of 48%, a women's handbag department established the initial markon at 53.5%. Sales for the season are planned at $12,000; to date, sales total $7,500 and markdowns are $700. What are the markdowns allowable in dollars and percentage if the maintained markon is to be achieved?

4. A junior dress department planned a 50.6% initial markon in order to achieve a maintained markon of 43.6%. To date, sales total $11,500, with markdowns thus far of $2,000. Planned sales for the balance of the period are $7,300. Find the remaining markdowns allowable to sustain the maintained markon.

5. Given operating expenses of 38%, operating profit of 5%, initial markon of 47.7%, sales for the season of $15,000, sales to date of $10,000, and markdowns to date of $800, find the maximum markdowns allowable for the balance of the season in both dollars and percentage.

■ Solutions to the Application Exercises

Determination of the Maintained Markon When the Initial Markon and Markdown Are Known (p. 185)

1. Cost of markdown = 12% (100% − 38%) = 7.4%

   Maintained markon = 38% − 7.4% = 30.6%

3. Markdowns = 7% × $80,000 = $5,600

   Initial markon % = $37,600 ÷ $80,000 = 47%

   $Cost of markdowns = $5,600 (100% − 47%) = $2,968

   Dollars of maintained markon = $37,600 − $2,968 = $34,632

   Percentage of maintained markon = $\dfrac{\$34,623}{\$80,000}$ = 43.3%

Or,

Cost of markdown = 7% (100% − 47%) = 3.7%

Maintained markon = 47% − 3.7% = 43.3%

5. Cost of markdown = 8% (100% − 48%) = 4.2%

Initial markon %	−	Markdown cost %	=	Maintained markon %
48%	−	4.2%	=	43.8%

Maintained markon	43.8%
Less operating expenses	35.0
Operating profit	8.8%

If the maintained markon is 43.8%, then 100% − 43.8% = Gross cost of merchandise sold = 56.2%.

Determination of the Markdown When the Initial Markon and the Maintained Markon Are Known (p. 187)

1. 46% − 41% = 5% (Cost of markdown)

$$\text{Markdown at retail} = \frac{5\%}{(100\% - 46\%)} = \frac{5\%}{54\%} = 9.3\%$$

3. Net sales − Cost of sales = Maintained markon
   100% − 55% = 45%

   Initial markon − Maintained markon = Cost of markdown
   52% − 45% = 7.0%

$$\text{Markon at retail} = \frac{7\%}{(100\% - 52\%)} = \frac{7\%}{48\%} = 14.6\%$$

Proof:

14.6% × 48% = 7%

52% − 45% = 7%

5. When there are no cash discounts and alteration costs, gross margin is equal to the maintained markon. The cumulative markon is the sum of the opening inventory at retail plus the aggregate purchase markon, including additional markups. Thus, the cumulative markon, in this instance, is equivalent to the initial markon.

   Initial markon − Maintained markon = Cost of markdown
   40% − 33% = 7%

$$\text{Retail value of markdown} = \frac{7\%}{(100\% - 40\%)} = \frac{7\%}{60\%} = 11.7\%$$

Calculating the Maintained Markon in Dollars, Given the Initial Markon, Sales, and Retail Reductions in Dollars (p. 190)

1. Cost of merchandise sold = $50,000 (100% − 44%) = $28,000

Markdowns	$4,000
Sales discounts	500
Inventory shortages	1,000
Reductions at retail	$5,500

Cost of reductions = $5,500 (100% − 44%) = $3,080

$$\begin{array}{ccccc}
\text{Cost of} & + & \text{Cost of} & = & \text{Gross cost of} \\
\text{reductions} & & \text{sales} & & \text{merchandise sold} \\
\$3,080 & + & \$28,000 & = & \$31,080
\end{array}$$

$$\begin{array}{ccccc}
\text{Net sales} & - & \text{Gross cost of} & = & \text{Maintained} \\
 & & \text{merchandise sold} & & \text{markon} \\
\$50,000 & - & \$31,080 & = & \$18,920
\end{array}$$

Alternate Solution:

Maintained markon = 44% ($50,000 + $5,500) − $5,500

Maintained markon = $24,420 − $5,500 = $18,920

Proof:

$$\text{Maintained markon \%} = \frac{\$18,920}{\$50,000} = 37.8\%$$

$$\begin{array}{ccccc}
\text{Initial} & - & \text{Maintained} & = & \text{Markon} \\
\text{Markon \%} & & \text{Markon \%} & & \text{Cost \%} \\
44\% & - & 37.8\% & = & 6.2\%
\end{array}$$

6.2% ÷ (100% − 44%) = 11% (Markdown at retail)

$50,000 × 11% = $5,500 (Reductions at retail)

3. Cost of merchandise sold = $230,000 (100% − 51%) = $112,700

Markdowns	$27,000
Shortages	9,200
Sales discounts	2,300
Total reductions	$38,500

Cost of reductions = $38,500 (100% − 51%) = $18,865

$112,700 + $18,865 = $131,565 (Gross cost of merchandise sold)

$230,000 − $131,565 = $98,435 (Maintained markon)

Alternate Solution:

Maintained markon = 51% ($230,000 + $38,500) − $38,500

Maintained markon = $136,935 − $38,500 = $98,435

Proof:

Maintained markon % = $\dfrac{\$98,435}{\$230,000}$ = 42.8%

51% − 42.8% = 8.2% (Cost of reductions)

Reductions at retail = 8.2% ÷ (100% − 51%) = 16.7%

$\dfrac{\text{Total reductions}}{\text{Net sales}} = \dfrac{\$38,500}{\$230,000}$ = 16.7% (Reductions at retail)

5. $200,000 × 1% = Returns and allowances = $2,000

Net sales = $200,000 − $2,000 = $198,000

Cost of sales = $198,000 (100% − 42%) = $114,840

Retail reductions = 12.5% + 1.3% + 1.2% = 15%

$198,000 × 15% = $29,700

Cost of reductions = $29,700 (100% − 42%) = $17,226

Gross cost of merchandise sold = $114,840 + $17,226 = $132,066

Maintained markon = $198,000 − $132,066 = $65,934

Alternate Solution:

Maintained markon = 42% ($198,000 + $29,700) − $29,700

Maintained markon = $95,634 − $29,700 = $65,934

Proof:

Maintained markon % = $\dfrac{\$65,934}{\$198,000}$ = 33.3%

42% − 33.3% = 8.7% (Cost of reduction)

Reduction at retail = 8.7% ÷ (100% − 42%) = 15%

$198,000 × .15% = Retail reductions = $29,700

Analysis: The maintained markon achieved on sales is insufficient to cover the demands of operating expenses and profit:

Net sales	$198,000	100.0%
Less gross cost of sales	132,066	66.7%
Maintained markon	65,934	33.3%
Less operating expenses	69,300	35.0%
Operating profit (loss)	($ 3,366)	(1.7%)

Recommendations: Essentially, the maintained markon must be increased through the initial markon.[14] Consider the following:

$$\text{Expenses} + \text{Profit} = \text{Maintained markon}$$
$$\$69,300 + \$9,900 = \$79,200$$

$$\frac{\text{Initial}}{\text{markon \%}} = \frac{(\text{Maintained markon}) \ \$79,200 + (\text{Reductions}) \ \$29,700}{(\text{Net sales}) \ \$198,000 + (\text{Reductions}) \ \$29,700} =$$

$$\frac{\$108,900}{\$227,700} = 47.8\% \text{ (required to cover the expenses, profit, and reductions)}$$

Apply the new initial markon of 47.8% to the previously given situation:

Cost of sales = $198,000 (100% − 47.8%) = $103,356

Cost of reductions = $29,700 (100% − 47.8%) = $15,503

Gross cost of merchandise sold = $103,356 + $15,503 = $118,859

Maintained markon = $198,00 − $118,859 = $79,141

Thus:

Maintained markon = Expenses + Profit

$79,000[15] = $69,300 + $9,900

As a percentage of sales, maintained markon must be equal to 40% ($79,200 ÷ $198,000) in order to cover expenses and profit, as the following figures illustrate:

---

[14]Obviously, operating profit can be enhanced by decreasing the retail reductions, increasing net sales, reducing returns and allowances, and tightening up on operating expenses. However, our immediate concern is only with maintained markon, its derivation, and its impact on operating profit.
[15]Corrected for rounding deficiencies: $79,141 = $79,200.

Net sales	$198,000	100%
Less gross cost of sales	118,859	60
Maintained markon	79,141	40
Less operating expenses	69,300	35
Operating profit	$9,841[16]	5%

Determination of the Maintained Markon Percentage, Given the Initial Markon, Sales, and Retail Reductions as a Percentage of Sales (p. 192)

1. Cost of sales = 100% − 49.5% = 50.5%

   Cost of reductions = 8% (100% − 49.5%) = 4%

   Gross cost of sales = 50.5% + 4% = 54.5%

   Maintained markon = 100% − 54.5% = 45.5%

   Alternate Solution:

   Maintained markon = 49.5% (100% + 8%) − 8%

   Maintained markon = 53.5% − 8% = 45.5%

   Proof:

   $$\frac{\text{Initial}}{\text{markon}} - \frac{\text{Maintained}}{\text{markon}} = \frac{\text{Cost of}}{\text{reductions}}$$

   49.5% − 45.5% = 4%

   Retail reductions = 4% ÷ (100% − 49.5%) = 8%

3. Initial markon = 100% − 56% = 44%

   Cost of reductions = 9% (100% − 44%) = 5%

Cost of sales	56%
Cost of reductions	5%
Gross cost of merchandise sold	61%

Net sales	100%
Less gross cost of merchandise sold	61%
Maintained markon	39%

[16]Again, the rounding process differentiates the actual operating profit ($9,841) from the planned figure ($9,900).

Alternate Solution:

Maintained markon = 44% (100% + 9%) – 9%

Maintained markon = 48% – 9% = 39%

Proof:

44% – 39% = 5% (Cost of reductions)

5% ÷ (100% – 44%) = 9% (Retail reductions)

5. Cost of sales = 100% – 48.5% = 51.5%

   Reductions = 11% + 2% + 1.5% = 14.5%

   Cost of reductions = 14.5% (100% – 48.5%) = 7.5%

   Gross cost of merchandise sold = 51.5% + 7.5% = 59%

   Maintained markon = 100% – 59% = 41%

   Alternate Solution to Maintained Markon:

   Maintained markon = 48.5% (100% + 14.5%) – 14.5%

   Maintained markon = 55.5% – 14.5% = 41%

   Proof of Maintained Markon:

   48.5% – 41% = 7.5% (Cost of reductions)

   Retail reductions = 7.5% ÷ (100% – 48.5%) = 14.5%

   Maximum percentage allowance for operating expenses:

$$\begin{matrix} \text{Maintained} \\ \text{markon} \\ 41\% \end{matrix} - \begin{matrix} \text{Operating} \\ \text{profit} \\ 7\% \end{matrix} = \begin{matrix} \text{Operating} \\ \text{expenses} \\ 34\% \end{matrix}$$

   Proof:

Net sales	100%
Less gross cost of merchandise sold	59%
Maintained markon	41%
Less operating expenses	34%
Operating profit	7%

Determination of the Markdowns Allowable for the Balance of a Period, Given the Planned Maintained Markon and Activity to Date (p. 194)

1. $$\begin{matrix} \text{Initial} \\ \text{markon} \\ 51\% \end{matrix} - \begin{matrix} \text{Maintained} \\ \text{markon} \\ 45\% \end{matrix} = \begin{matrix} \text{Cost of} \\ \text{markdown} \\ 6\% \end{matrix}$$

Markdown at retail = 6% ÷ (100% − 51%) = 12.2%

Markdowns for season = Sales for the season ($80,000 + $25,000 = $105,000) × 12.2% = $12,810

Markdowns for season	$12,810
Less markdowns to date	4,000
Markdown balance	$ 8,810

Proof:

$8,810 + $4,000 = $12,810 ÷ ($80,000 + $25,000) = 12.2%

3. Initial markon − Maintained markon = Cost of markdown
   53.5% − 48.0% = 5.5%

Markdown at retail = 5.5% ÷ (100% − 53.5%) = 11.8%

Seasonal markdown = $12,000 × 11.8% = $1,416

Seasonal − Markdown = Markdown
markdown   to date   balance
$1,416 − $700 = $716

Seasonal sales − Sales to date = Balance of sales
  $12,000 − $7,500 = $4,500

Markdown % allowable = $\dfrac{\$716}{\$4,500}$ = 15.9%

Proof:

	$Markdown ÷	*Sales*	= *Markdown %*
To date	$ 700 ÷	$7,500	= 9.3%
Balance	716 ÷	4,500	= 15.9%
Total	$1,416 ÷	$12,000	= 11.8% (Retail)

5. Operating + Operating = Maintained
   profit   expenses   markon
   5% + 38% = 43%

Cost of markdown = 47.7% − 43% = 4.7%

Retail value of markdown = 4.7% ÷ (100% − 47.7%) = 9%

Markdown for season = $15,000 × 9% = $1,350

Markdown balance of season = $1,350 − $800 = $550

Sales balance of season = $15,000 − $10,000 = $5,000

Markdown % balance of season = $\dfrac{\$550}{\$5,000}$ = 11%

Proof:

	$Markdown	÷	Sales	= Markdown %
To date	$ 800	÷	$10,000	= 8%
Balance	550	÷	5,000	= 11%
Total	$1,350	÷	$15,000	= 9% (Retail)

Topics for Discussion and Review

1. What is the difference between the initial markon and the maintained markon?

2. Explain the difference between the gross cost of merchandise sold and the total cost of merchandise sold.

3. What is the difference between the maintained markon and gross margin?

4. What is meant by the cost of the markdown?

5. Given the initial markon and maintained markon percentages, how would you determine the amount of markdown allowable at retail?

6. What are retail reductions?

7. What is the effect of cash discounts and alteration costs on the gross cost of the merchandise sold?

8. Why does the maintained markon represent the reality of a retail price originally "hoped for"?

9. Essentially, what is the function of the maintained markon?

10. Why do we say that the initial markon is based upon planned sales and the maintained markon is based upon net sales?

11. Why is the actual markdown always expressed as a percent of *net* sales?

12. Explain what reduces the quantity of an inventory and what reduces the quality of an inventory.

13. If merchandise were sold immediately after it was placed on the selling floor, what would be the relationship between the initial markon and the maintained markon?

14. What do we mean by the cost of the markdown?

15. Explain the mathematical difference between the initial markon and the maintained markon. How would you convert this "diffference" to its full value?

16. How would you determine the maintained markon if you knew the initial markon and the markdown percent?

17. Assuming that you knew the values of the initial and maintained markons, explain how you would determine the retail value of the available markdown?

18. Explain how you would determine the maintained markon in dollars and percent, given sales, retail reductions, and the percentage of initial markon.

19. Given planned sales and markdowns for a period, sales to date, initial markon and maintained markon, and the amount of markdowns to date, explain how to determine the amount of markdown money available for the balance of the period.

20. Discuss the concept of the maintained markon.

21. Differentiate between the gross cost of the merchandise sold and the total cost of the merchandise sold.

22. Explain why a 25% off sale does not cost the merchant 25%.

23. Given the cost of sales in the initial markon and maintained markon, how would you determine the markdown at cost and at retail?

24. In a situation where there is an initial markon of 48% and a markdown of 20%, explain why the difference between the initial markon and the maintained markon will be only 10.4%.

25. Explain how you would determine the maintained markon percentage, given the initial markon, sales, and reductions, all in percentages.

Chapter 8
The Determinants of Gross Margin

Learning Objectives

- Explain and define the concept of gross margin.

- Derive gross margin from the maintained markon, cash discounts, and alteration costs.

- Derive gross margin and maintained markon percentages from the known reductions, initial markon, cash discounts, and alteration costs.

- Calculate maintained markon, given the gross margin, cash discounts, and alteration costs.

- Calculate the allowable markdown dollars, given net sales, initial markon, cash discounts, alteration costs, and gross margin.

- Itemize, define, and explain the elements of the gross margin statement.

- Compute the gross margin statement.

- Explain the significance of the gross margin return per dollar of cost inventory ratio.

- Explain the calculation of the average inventory.

Key Terms

Alteration Costs: The net cost of altering merchandise for customer and stock repair.

Average Inventory: The average amount of inventory on hand at either cost or retail over a specific period of time—normally, but not necessarily, one year;

computed by adding the sum of the ending inventories for the time period under consideration to the beginning inventory for the period and dividing by the total number of inventories involved.

Beginning Inventory: The opening inventory or the merchandise available for sale at the beginning of a specific period of time.

Book Inventory: The retail value of an inventory at a specific point in time as shown by the perpetual inventory system.

Cash Discounts: A percentage reduction in the billed cost price offered by the vendor for payment of the invoice within a specific period of time.

Gross Cost of Merchandise Sold: The accumulated inventory to date plus additions at billed cost, less the closing inventory at cost. Deducted from net sales, the gross cost of merchandise sold provides for the maintained markon. The maintained markon, when adjusted by the cash discounts earned and workroom costs, determines the gross margin of profit derived from the sale of merchandise.

Gross Margin: The difference between net sales and the total or net merchandise cost.

Gross Margin Return per Dollar of Cost Inventory: The amount of gross margin dollars earned by the merchant per cost dollar invested in inventory. This ratio measures the degree of efficiency of the funds invested in the cost inventory. It is computed by dividing the gross margin dollars by the average cost inventory.

Maintained Markon: The difference between net sales and the gross cost of merchandise sold.

Markup: The upward revision of the original retail price (not synonymous with markon).

Markup Cancellation: A method of price reduction that restores the original retail price or revokes the markup; not chargeable against the buyer's markdown sales allowance, therefore subject to strict control.

Net Cost of Merchandise Sold: The gross cost of the merchandise sold less the earned cash discounts.

Net Markups: The excess of markup over markup cancellations.

Net Purchases: As used in the computation of gross margin and the operating statement, the value of gross purchases plus transportation less returns to, and allowances from, the vendor.

Net Transfers In: The balance of merchandise moved into a department from other departments after deducting the goods transferred out.

Operating Expenses: All expenses incurred in the sale of merchandise, excluding the cost of the goods sold.

Operating Profit: Profit derived from the merchandising function of the store.

Perpetual Inventory: A retail accounting method of controlling inventory whereby a beginning inventory is revalued on a daily basis according to net additions and net reductions.

Retail Reductions: The sum of markdowns, sales discounts, and inventory shortages, the greatest of which are markdowns.

Total Cost of Merchandise Sold: Gross cost of merchandise sold plus net workroom costs less the amount of cash discounts earned.

Total Merchandise Handled: The sum of the beginning inventory, net purchases, and transportation charges.

8.1

The Concept of Gross Margin

After all the transactional activity of buying and selling merchandise is completed, the amount of dollars remaining in the hands of the merchant is defined as the gross margin. The term *gross margin* is not to be confused with *gross profit;* profit defines the excess of dollars beyond that which is required to cover operating expenses, whereas margin implies the dollar amount sufficient to pay for the expenses plus provide for an operating profit. If the gross margin is not at least equal to the expenses incurred in operating the store, a loss takes place. In other words, the determinant of profit is the excess of gross margin beyond the requirements of operating expenses, or

Gross margin − Operating expenses = Operating profit

It has been previously established that the maintained markon is equal to the net sales minus the gross cost of merchandise sold, wherein the gross cost of merchandise sold is the product of the billed cost of the merchandise, including transportation, plus retail reductions (markdowns, shortages, and sales discounts). Therefore,

Maintained markon = Net sales − Gross cost of merchandise sold

Gross margin, on the other hand, is to be distinguished from the maintained markon by the impact of alteration costs and earned cash discounts upon the gross cost of merchandise sold. That is to say, by increasing the gross cost of merchandise sold by the net amount of alteration cost and subsequently decreasing it by the cash discounts earned, the gross cost of merchandise sold is translated into the total cost of merchandise sold. Thus,

Total cost of merchandise sold = Gross cost of merchandise sold +
Net alterations − Cash discounts

Therefore,

> Gross margin = Sales − (Gross cost of merchandise sold + Net alterations − Cash discounts)

By removal of the parentheses, the signs in the equation are changed to indicate the impact of the alterations and cash discounts on the gross margin. Note that it is only reasonable to state that alteration costs will decrease the gross margin while cash discounts earned will increase its value. In essence, alteration costs represent additional expenses, whereas earned cash discounts are a type of additional income. Therefore,

> Gross margin = Sales − Gross cost of merchandise sold − Net alterations + Cash discounts

However,

> Maintained markon = Net sales − Gross cost of merchandise sold

As a result, we may define gross margin as follows:

> Gross margin = Maintained markon − Net alterations + Cash discounts

8.2
Gross Margin as a Product of the Maintained Markon

The determination of gross margin is best illustrated by the calculation of the maintained markon and the transformation of that maintained markon into the gross margin through the impact of the known alteration costs and earned cash discounts.

Gross Margin Derived from the Maintained Markon, Known Cash Discounts, and Alteration Costs

Recall from Chapter 7 that earned cash discounts and alteration costs are what differentiate gross margin from maintained markon. The next study problem illustrates this concept.

▪ Study Problem

Given:

Net sales	$300
Gross cost of merchandise sold	165
Cash discounts	15
Alteration costs	3

Find: The maintained markon and gross margin in dollars and percentages.

Solution:

Net sales	$300
Less gross cost of merchandise sold	165
Maintained markon	135
Cash discounts	15
Less alteration costs	3
Gross margin	$ 147[1]

$$\text{Maintained markon } \% = \frac{\$135}{\$300} = 45\%$$

$$\text{Gross margin } \% = \frac{\$147}{\$300} = 49\%$$

Proof:

Taking the dollar figures as a percentage of sales we find:

Net sales	100%
Less gross cost of merchandise sold	55
Maintained markon	45%
Cash discounts	5
Less alteration costs	1
Gross margin	49%

▪ Application Exercise

1. Given net sales of $45,000, gross cost of merchandise sold of $27,000, cash discounts of $2,700, and alteration costs of $675, find the maintained markon and gross margin in dollars and percentages.

2. Given the following data, determine the maintained markon and gross margin in dollars and percentages for the luggage department.

Net sales	$83,000
Gross cost of merchandise sold	48,140
Earned cash discounts	1,660

---

[1]As previously mentioned, gross margin normally exceeds maintained markon because of the excess of earned cash discounts over the alteration costs.

3. A book department had net sales of $123,000, inventory shortages were 2%, cash discounts totaled 3.2%, and the gross cost of merchandise sold was 65%. What were the maintained markon and gross margin in dollars and percentages?

4. Determine the gross cost of sales and gross margin in dollars and percentages in a department with the following figures:

Maintained markon	$120,000
Net sales	250,000
Markdowns	13,800
Cash discounts	17,500
Alteration costs	8,250

5. Given the following information, find the maintained markon percentage.

Alteration costs	1.5%
Cash discounts	5.0%
Gross margin	46.5%

Gross Margin and Maintained Markon Percentages Derived from the Known Reductions, Initial Markon, Cash Discounts, and Alteration Costs

As in the previous study problem, the calculation of gross margin is best illustrated by first determining the maintained markon, then adding the cash discounts and subtracting alteration costs.

▪ Study Problem

Given: A boys' clothing department had an initial markon of 48%, markdowns of 12%, cash discounts of 3%, and alteration costs of 1%.

Find: Determine the percentages of maintained markon and gross margin earned by the department.

Solution:

Determine the maintained markon percentage:

Initial markon − Maintained markon = Cost of markdown[2]

---

[2]Because the markdown is a part of the retail price, it has a cost and markon component in the same proportion as the retail price from which it was derived.

Therefore,

Initial markon − Cost of markdown = Maintained markon

Cost of markdown = $12\%(100\% - 48\%) = 6.2\%$[3]

Then,

Determine gross margin percentage:

$$\underset{\substack{\text{markon} \\ 41.8\%}}{\text{Maintained}} + \underset{\substack{\text{discounts} \\ 3\%}}{\text{Cash}} - \underset{\substack{\text{costs} \\ 1\%}}{\text{Alteration}} = \underset{\substack{\text{margin} \\ = 43.8\%}}{\text{Gross}}$$

Alternate Solution:

Maintained markon = Initial markon $(100\% + \text{Reductions}) - \text{Reductions}$[4]

$$= 48\% \; (100\% + 12\%) - 12\%$$

$$= 53.8\% - 12\%$$

$$= 41.8\%$$

$$\underset{\substack{\text{markon} \\ 41.8\%}}{\text{Maintained}} + \underset{\substack{\text{discounts} \\ 3\%}}{\text{Cash}} - \underset{\substack{\text{costs} \\ 1\%}}{\text{Alteration}} = \underset{\substack{\text{margin} \\ = 43.8\%}}{\text{Gross}}$$

■ Application Exercise

1. Determine the maintained markon and gross margin in a television department with the following figures:

Initial markon	25.0%
Retail reductions	6.7%
Cash discounts	3.5%
Alteration costs	.8%

---

[3]The cost of the markdown is derived as set forth in Chapter 7: 6.2% represents the cost portion of the markdown. Therefore, $12\% - 6.2\% = 5.8\%$, or the markon portion; $6.2\% + 5.8\% = 12\%$, or 100% of the markdown, which is its retail value.
[4]This formula is derived from the formula for the calculation of initial markon discussed in Chapter 5:

$$\frac{\text{Initial}}{\text{markon}} = \frac{\text{Maintained markon \% + Reductions \%}}{100\% + \text{Reductions \%}}$$

Maintained markon % + Reductions% = Initial markon % $(100\% + \text{Reductions \%})$
Maintained markon % = Initial markon % $(100\% + \text{Reductions \%}) - \text{Reductions \%}$

2. A sporting goods store has planned an initial markon of 43.3% predicated upon markdowns of 12.3%, sales discounts of 1.5%, and estimated inventory shortages of 4.2%. Assuming that cash discounts earned will be 4%, what percentages of maintained markon and gross margin may be anticipated?

3. What are the maintained markon and gross margin percentages for a costume jewelry department, given the following data?

Cumulative markon	53.0%
Stock shortages	12.2%
Markdowns	5.3%
Cash discounts	8.3%

4. A bath shop planned the following figures:

Initial markon	51.0%
Retail reductions	6.5%
Cash discounts	2.5%
Operating expenses	40.2%

What is the anticipated operating profit?

5. Given the following data for a children's clothing store, what is the maximum amount of operating expense that can be incurred?

Cumulative markon	50.0%
Markdowns ·	12.3%
Estimated inventory shortages	2.2%
Sales discounts	1.3%
Operating profit	6.3%
Cash discounts	8.3%
Alteration costs	.5%

8.3
Maintained Markon as a Product of the Gross Margin

Just as the gross margin may be derived from the maintained markon, so the maintained markon may be calculated as a product of the gross margin, given the cash discounts and alteration costs.

Calculation of the Maintained Markon Given the Gross Margin, Cash Discounts, and Alteration Costs

The maintained markon may be simply found by transposing the elements of the gross margin formula, taking particular note of the change in signs.

■ Study Problem

Given:

Gross margin	$48,000
Earned cash discounts	6,000
Alteration costs	2,500

Find: The maintained markon.

Solution:

Gross margin = Maintained markon + Cash discounts − Alteration costs

Therefore:

Maintained markon = Gross margin − Cash discounts + Alteration costs[5]

Then,

Maintained markon = $48,000 − $6,000 + $2,500 = $44,500

■ Application Exercise

1. Define the maintained markon in a women's hosiery department with a gross margin of 47%, cash discounts of 4%, and no workroom costs.

2. What was the maintained markon in a small leather goods department with a gross margin of $48,200 and cash discounts of $5,000?

3. A men's clothing department achieved a gross margin of $40,500. If alteration costs were $2,500 and cash discounts $5,500, what was the maintained markon?

4. A junior sportswear department's net sales for the fall season were $600,000. The gross margin was 47%, net alteration charges were 0.3%, and cash discounts amounted to 10%. What was the maintained markon in dollars and percentage?

5. Given the following data for men's casual wear, determine the maintained markon, gross cost of merchandise sold, and resulting operating profit.

---

[5]Note the relationship between the gross margin and maintained markon in this instance and in the study problem on page 208.

Operating expenses	36.3%
Gross margin	43.5%
Alteration costs	2.4%
Cash discounts	7.3%
Net sales	$250,000

Calculation of the Allowable Markdown Dollars, Given Net Sales, Initial Markon, Cash Discounts, Alteration Costs, and Gross Margin

It is often necessary to determine the amount of markdown allowable, either in the planning stage or in the course of an accounting period. This is particularly true when the initial markon and gross margin are firmly established objectives.

■ Study Problem

Given:

Net sales	$300,000
Initial markon	48.0%
Gross margin	43.0%
Cash discounts	7.0%
Alteration costs	1.5%

Find: The maximum amount of markdown, in both dollars and percentage, that may be taken.

Solution:

In order to first determine the percentage of markdown allowable, we must first calculate the maintained markon:

Maintained markon = Gross margin − Cash discounts + Alteration costs

Maintained markon % = 43% − 7% + 1.5% = 37.5%

Calculate the cost of the markdown:

Cost of markdown = Initial markon − Maintained markon

Cost of markdown = 48% − 37.5% = 10.5%

Determine the retail value of the markdown:[6]

---

[6]In this instance, we move from the cost of the markdown to its total retail value (not to be confused with the markon component). Follow the same procedure as described in Chapter 3.

$10.5\% \div (100\% - 48\%) = 10.5\% \div 52\% = 20.2\%$

Then, \$ markdown $= \$300,000 \times 20.2\% = \$60,600$

The formula for the more immediate calculation of the retail value of the markdown may be derived from:

$$\frac{\text{Initial}}{\text{markon\%}} = \frac{\text{Maintained markon} + \text{Reductions}[7]}{100\% + \text{Reductions}}$$

By substitution we find that:

$$\text{Reductions}[8] = \frac{\text{Initial markon} - \text{Maintained markon}}{100\% - \text{Initial markon}}$$

Thus:

$$\frac{48\% - 37.5\%}{100\% - 48\%} = \frac{10.5\%}{52\%} = 20.2\%$$

▪ Application Exercise

1. What is the maximum amount of markdown, in percentage and dollars, that a buyer may take if the following planned figures are to be achieved?

Net sales	$380,000
Initial markon	44.0%
Cash discounts	3.0%
Alteration costs	1.0%
Gross margin	38.5%

2. A women's specialty store planned the following figures for the spring season:

Gross sales	$650,000
Returns and allowances	8.4%
Initial markon	50.5%
Earned discounts	7.2%
Net alteration costs	.9%
Gross margin	45.3%

What is the total allowable amount of markdown dollars?

---

[7]See initial markon, Chapter 3.
[8]Markdowns are reductions and are treated as such.

3. How much additional dollar markdown can a buyer take given the following data?

Total sales for the season	$300,000
Markdowns to date	12,000
Planned initial markon	45.3%
Planned gross margin	42.4%
Earned cash discounts	4.3%
Alteration costs	1.7%

4. Midway through the fall season, a merchant determines that markdowns to date amount to $6,000; planned sales achieved so far are $65,000. In conjunction with the following data, determine the remaining markdowns permissible for the balance of the season in dollars and percentage.

Planned sales for season	$150,000
Planned initial markon	48.7%
Planned gross margin	45.2%
Planned cash discounts	5.8%
Planned alteration costs	1.3%

5. To date a buyer has achieved 80% of planned sales and consumed 74% of planned markdowns. Given the following data, what is the maximum percentage of markdown remaining for the balance of the season?

Total planned sales	$550,000
Planned initial markon	51.0%
Planned gross margin	46.8%
Planned cash discounts	4.3%
Planned alteration costs	.8%

8.4
Computation of Gross Margin

So far we have concerned ourselves with the applications of the principle of gross margin and its relationship to maintained markon, retail reductions, cash discounts, and alteration costs. It is now time to consider the computation of gross margin as it would appear on the periodic merchandise statement according to the retail method of inventory.[9]

Gross margin is the excess of net sales over the total costs of sales, where the total cost of sales includes the cost of the merchandise sold plus alteration costs, cash discounts, and retail reductions, including a retail shortage provision. In effect,

---

[9]The retail method of inventory will be discussed in detail in Chapter 11.

what happens is that the merchant begins a specific period or season with an opening inventory that has been carried over from the previous period at both cost and retail; that inventory is increased at both cost and retail by specific additions and decreased at cost and retail by net sales and retail reductions. The difference at the end of the period between net sales and the total cost of merchandise sold during that period is equal to the gross margin or the "profit" achieved from the sale of merchandise. The balance of the total merchandise handled for that period, that is, the unsold portion, becomes the opening or beginning inventory at cost and retail for the ensuing period. Thus, the process of deriving gross margin is continuous on a periodic basis, either monthly, seasonally, or annually, with the closing inventory of any given period determining the opening inventory of the following period. With this concept in mind, let us proceed with the detailed calculation of the gross margin as illustrated in Table 8.1.

▪ **Study Problem**

Given:

Period: 6/1–6/30

	Cost	Retail
Beginning inventory	$32,000	$67,000
Net purchases	6,000	11,500
Net transfers in	3,500	7,322
Net markups	-0-	2,500
Transportation	1,500	-0-
Net sales	-0-	15,000
Net markdowns	-0-	1,050
Sales discounts	-0-	450
Estimated shortages	-0-	300
Cash discounts earned	1,000	-0-
Alteration costs	500	-0-

Find: The gross margin for the period of 6/1 through 6/30.

Solution:

Step 1. Total Merchandise Handled and Cumulative Markon.

The total merchandise handled (Table 8.1, Line 7) is the beginning inventory (Line 1) plus the total additions to that inventory (Line 6). The beginning inventory consists of the closing inventory from the prior period, and the additions are

Table 8.1

Computation of gross margin for period of 6/1–6/30

	Items	1 Cost	2 Retail	3 $Markon	4 % of Sales	5 Cumulative Markon %
1.	Beginning inventory	$32,000	$67,000	$35,000		
2.	Net purchases	6,000	11,500	5,500		
3.	Net transfers in	3,500	7,322	3,822		
4.	Net markups		2,500	2,500		
5.	Transportation	1,500		(1,500)		
6.	Total additions	$11,000	$21,322	$10,322		
7.	Total merchandise handled and cumulative markon	43,000	88,322	45,322		51.3
8.	Net sales		15,000			
9.	Net markdowns		1,050		7.0	
10.	Sales discounts		450		3.0	
11.	Estimated shortages		300		2.0	
12.	Total retail reductions		$16,800			
13.	Book inventory at retail		71,522			
14.	Book inventory at cost	34,831				
15.	Gross cost of merchandise sold and maintained markon	$8,169		6,831	45.5	
16.	Earned cash discounts	(1,000)		1,000	6.7	
17.	Net cost of merchandise sold	$7,169		$7,831	52.2 %	
18.	Alteration costs	500		(500)	(3.3)	
19.	Total cost of merchandise sold and gross margin	$7,669		$7,331	48.9 %	

conceptually any factors that increase the cost and retail value of that beginning inventory. Therefore,

Total merchandise handled = Beginning inventory + Additions

Notice that only tangible merchandise, that is, the "net purchases" and "net transfers in," have a cost and retail value; transportation is simply an additional cost devoid of any actual retail value, which serves only to reduce the value of the markon. The net markups are an arbitrary management decision to increase the markon on merchandise already purchased, thus increasing retail value with no additional cost.

The difference between the total merchandise handled at cost and retail (Line 7, Columns 1 and 2) is equal to the cumulative markon dollars (Line 7, Column 3), which in turn translates into the cumulative markon of 51.3% (Line 7, Column 5), or the average percentage of markon achieved for the period 6/1 through 6/30.

$$\frac{\$88,322 - \$43,000}{\$88,322} = \frac{\$45,322}{\$88,322} = 51.3\%$$

Step 2. Determination of the Book Inventory at Retail.

The book inventory is in effect the closing inventory at retail for the period, as defined by the perpetual inventory.[10] The book inventory at retail is the total merchandise handled at retail (Line 7, Column 2) less the total retail reductions for the period (Line 12, Column 2). The total retail reductions consist of net sales (Line 8), net markdowns (Line 9), sales discounts (Line 10), and estimated shortages (Line 11). Thus,

Book inventory at retail = Total merchandise handled at retail − Total retail reductions

The book inventory at retail, $71,522, is shown on Line 13, Column 2.

Step 3. Conversion of the Book Inventory at Retail to the Book Inventory at Cost.

In order to calculate the cost of the merchandise that was sold and the resulting gross margin, it becomes necessary to determine the cost value of the remaining inventory; thus, the book inventory at retail must be converted to the book inventory at cost. This is accomplished by multiplying the book inventory at retail by the cost complement of the cumulative markon[11] (Line 7, Column 5). Thus,

Book inventory at cost = Book inventory at retail (100% − Cumulative markon %)

Therefore, the book inventory at cost (Line 14, Column 1) is $34,831, or $71,522 × 48.7%. The value of the closing (book) inventory at cost is not the

---

[10]This concept will be further developed in Chapter 11. Suffice it here to say that the book inventory is the retail value of the stock shown to be on hand at any particular time as a product of the perpetual inventory. The perpetual inventory is a retail method of accounting whereby a beginning inventory is adjusted upward for "additions" and downward for net sales and retail reductions. The effect is to produce a running (daily) total of the retail value of the inventory; on the date at which the period ends, this retail value is defined as the book inventory.

[11]The cumulative markon may be considered the same as the initial markon, in the sense that the cumulative markon is the average of many initial markons to date.

actual or true cost of the remaining merchandise; it is a computed estimate of approximate value, based upon the average relationship between the cost and retail price of the total merchandise handled for the period. While this procedure has obvious limitations (to be discussed in detail in Chapter 11), it is generally considered to be accurate enough for business and taxation purposes.

Step 4. Determination of the Gross Cost of Merchandise Sold and Maintained Markon.

The gross cost of merchandise sold (Line 15, Column 1) is the total merchandise handled at cost (Line 7, Column 1) minus the book inventory at cost (Line 14, Column 1). Thus, the

Gross cost of merchandise sold = Total merchandise handled at cost − Book inventory at cost

or

$$\$43,000 - \$34,831 = \$8,169$$

The maintained markon dollars (Line 15, Column 3) are calculated by subtracting the gross cost of merchandise sold (Line 15, Column 1) from net sales (Line 8, Column 2); the maintained markon percentage (Line 15, Column 4) is simply arrived at by dividing the maintained markon dollars by net sales. Thus, we find that

$$\text{Maintained markon \%} = \frac{\$15,000 - \$8,169}{\$15,000} = \frac{\$6,831}{\$15,000} = 45.5\%$$

In support of our previous discussion of the relationship among the cumulative (or initial) markon, retail reductions, and the maintained markon, your attention is directed to that relationship as exhibited in this computation of gross margin. Simply as a point of interest and reinforcement, notice that the percentage of retail reductions, that is, 7%, 3%, and 2% (Lines 9 to 11, Column 4), total 12%. The cost value of these retail reductions, as determined by the initial markon, is 5.8%.

$$12\% \ (100\% - 51.3\%) = 12\% \times 48.7\% = 5.8\%$$

And because the difference between the initial or cumulative markon and the maintained markon also represents the cost of the reductions, we may arrive at the maintained markon in the following alternate manner:

Initial markon	−	Maintained markon	=	Cost of markdown
51.3%	−	45.5%	=	5.8%

Therefore,

Initial markon	−	Cost of markdown	=	Maintained markon
51.3%	−	5.8%	=	45.5%

Step 5. Calculation of Net Cost of Merchandise Sold.

The net cost of merchandise sold represents the difference between the gross cost of merchandise sold and the cash discounts earned. Notice that the earned cash discounts (Line 16, Column 1) reduce the gross cost of the merchandise sold by $1,000 and thus increase the maintained markon by 6.7%. The cash discounts earned are to be considered as an additional type of "income" that in effect tends to reduce the gross cost of merchandise sold by the dollar amount of the discount (Line 15, Column 1 minus Line 16, Column 1); consequently, the maintained markon will be increased by a like amount (Line 15, Column 3 plus Line 16, Column 3). We may therefore state that the

Net cost of	=	Gross cost of	−	Cash
merchandise sold		merchandise sold		discounts
$7,169	=	$8,169	−	$1,000

At this point in our calculations, the achieved markon (Line 17, Column 3) as a percentage of sales (Line 17, Column 4) is determined as follows:

$$\frac{\$15,000 - \$7,169}{\$15,000} = \frac{\$7,831}{\$15,000} = 52.2\%$$

Step 6. Determination of Gross Margin.

The final step in the calculation of gross margin is to add the alteration costs (Line 18, Column 1) to the net cost of the merchandise sold (Line 17, Column 1). We then arrive at the total cost of merchandise sold (Line 19, Column 1), which when subtracted from net sales (Line 8, Column 2) equals the gross margin dollars (Line 19, Column 3). The alteration costs have the opposite effect of the cash discounts on the gross margin. The cash discounts decrease the cost of merchandise sold and increase the markon; the alteration costs increase the cost of merchandise sold and decrease the markon.

The gross margin percentage (Line 19, Column 4) is computed as follows:

$$\frac{\$15,000 - \$7,669}{\$15,000} = \frac{\$7,331}{\$15,000} = 48.9\%$$

▪ Application Exercise

1. Given:

	Cost	Retail
Beginning inventory	$48,000	$80,000
Net purchases	18,000	32,700
Net transfers in	4,300	7,800
Net markups		2,100
Transportation	900	
Net sales		43,000

	Cost	Retail
Net markdowns		5,160
Sales discounts		520
Estimated shortages		1,300
Earned cash discounts	2,150	
Alteration costs	700	

Determine:

a. total merchandise handled and cumulative markon.

b. total retail reductions.

c. book inventory at cost and retail.

d. gross cost of merchandise sold and maintained markon.

e. net cost of merchandise sold.

f. total cost of merchandise sold and gross margin in dollars and percentage.

Use the gross margin statement at right as a guide for your calculations.

2. As the assistant buyer for a small, independently owned bridal shop, you are asked to determine the percentage of gross margin achieved during the month of April. The following information is made available to you. What is your answer?

	Cost	Retail
Beginning inventory	$122,321	$240,000
Net sales		78,000
Net purchases	12,400	24,800
Transportation	1,500	
Net markups		2,300
Net markdowns		10,530
Alteration costs	4,680	
Estimated shortages		400
Earned cash discounts	6,630	
Sales discounts		235

8.5

Gross Margin Return per Dollar of Cost Inventory

Gross margin is the excess of net sales over the cost of those sales, or the amount of profit derived from the sale of an inventory. As such, gross margin dollars define the merchant's return on an inventory investment and are therefore a percentage or ratio of that investment. Such a ratio is known as the gross margin return per dollar of cost inventory and establishes a measure for the efficiency of the funds invested in inventory. Quantitatively stated, gross margin return per dollar of cost inventory is simply a percentage figure derived as follows:

$$\frac{\text{Gross margin dollars}}{\text{Average inventory investment at cost}}$$

Gross Margin Statement

Period _____

	Items	Cost	Retail	$Markon	% of Sales	Cumulative Markon %
1.	Beginning inventory					
2.	Net purchases					
3.	Net transfers in					
4.	Net markups					
5.	Transportation					
6.	Total additions					
7.	Total merchandise handled and cumulative markon					
8.	Net sales					
9.	Net markdowns					
10.	Sales discounts					
11.	Estimated shortages					
12.	Total retail reductions					
13.	Book inventory at retail					
14.	Book inventory at cost					
15.	Gross cost of merchandise sold and maintained markon					
16.	Earned cash discounts					
17.	Net cost of merchandise sold					
18.	Alteration costs					
19.	Total cost of merchandise sold and gross margin					

The significance of the ratio is that it represents a percentage return on funds invested in inventory and thus defines merchandising acumen in terms of profit relative to investment, rather than profit dollars per se. The objective of the merchant, especially in times of tight money and high interest rates, is to constantly strive to achieve the maximum amount of gross margin dollars with the minimum amount of inventory investment. Thus, the higher the gross margin return per invested cost dollar, the greater the potential for increased merchandising profit. Compare the percentage return derived from equivalent gross margin dollars with variable investments in the cost inventory:

$$\frac{\$150\,(\text{Gross margin})}{\$100\,(\text{Average inventory})} = 150\%$$

$$\frac{\$150\,(\text{Gross margin})}{\$125\,(\text{Average inventory})} = 120\%$$

In the first example, $150 in gross margin was derived from an inventory investment of $100, thus producing a return of 150%, or $1.50, in gross margin for every dollar invested in inventory. While the gross margin dollars remained the same in the second example, the increased inventory costs have reduced the gross margin return to $1.20 per dollar of cost inventory investment; obviously, the second investment is less efficient than the first.

Calculation of the Average Inventory

Before we can actually determine the gross margin return, it is necessary to define and calculate the average cost inventory. The average inventory, whether at cost or retail, and for any given period of time, is the sum of the beginning inventory plus the number of ending inventories in the designated time frame, divided by the total number of inventories involved. Any period of time, from one month to a year, must have a beginning and ending inventory; thus, the sum of the inventories must include one more inventory than the actual number of periods involved. For example, consider the fall season, which consists of the following six months:[12]

	BOM[13]	EOM[14]
August	$9,000	$10,000
September	(10,000)	12,000
October	(12,000)	15,000
November	(15,000)	14,000
December	(14,000)	12,000
January	(12,000)	10,000
(February)	(10,000)	
	$9,000 +	+ $73,000 = $82,000

$82,000 ÷ 7 (Number of inventories) = $11,715 (The average inventory for the six-month fall season)

---

[12]The fall season runs August through January; the spring season is February through July.
[13]Beginning of the month.
[14]End of the month.

Notice that the total inventory of $82,000 actually consists of the BOM for August, $9,000, plus the sum of the ending inventories, $73,000, for the six-month period. This is because the BOM inventory for any one month is the same as the EOM for the month directly preceding it. In other words, the EOM inventory for August, $10,000, is in reality the BOM inventory for September. Thus, while it may initially appear that the BOM inventories other than August are not used, they are actually represented by the EOM inventories for the number of months in the season, in this case six. As a result, we have one BOM inventory and six EOM inventories in a six-month season, or a total of seven inventories, always one more inventory than the number of months in the time period. Conceptually, this may be shown as follows:

	BOM		*EOM*	
August	$9,000		$10,000[15]	
September			12,000	
October			15,000	
November			14,000	
December			12,000	
January			10,000	
Total	$9,000	+	$73,000	= $82,000
	(1)	+	(6)	= (7)

This principle holds true regardless of the number of months in any given period of time. Consider the following, for example:

$$\text{Average inventory (per month)} = \frac{1 \text{ BOM} + 1 \text{ EOM}}{2}$$

$$\text{Average inventory (per quarter)} = \frac{1 \text{ BOM} + 3 \text{ EOMs}}{4}$$

$$\text{Average inventory (annual)} = \frac{1 \text{ BOM} + 12 \text{ EOMs}}{13}$$

Conversion of the Average Inventory at Retail to the Average Inventory at Cost

Because the value of the inventories is normally expressed in terms of retail dollars, it becomes necessary to translate the average inventory into its cost complement by means of the cumulative or initial markon. Applying an arbitrary 40%

---

[15]Note that the August EOM inventory of $10,000 must of necessity be the BOM inventory for September; what August ends with, September must obviously begin with.

cumulative markon to the previously calculated fall season average inventory, we find that:

$$\frac{\text{Cost of the}}{\text{average inventory}} = \$11,715\,(100\% - 40\%) = \$7,029$$

■ Study Problem

Given: A men's tie department has a BOM inventory of \$24,000 and an EOM inventory of \$18,000 for the month of May. The cumulative markon was 54%, and the achieved gross margin was 53%.

Find: What was the gross margin return per dollar of cost inventory if net sales were \$51,000?

Solution:

$$\text{Average inventory} = \frac{\$24,000 + \$18,000}{2} = \$21,000$$

$$\frac{\text{Cost of the}}{\text{average inventory}} = \$21,000\,(100\% - 54\%) = \$9,660$$

$\$\text{Gross margin} = \$51,000 \times 53\% = \$27,030$

$$\frac{\text{Gross margin}}{\text{return}} = \frac{\$27,030\,(\text{Gross margin})}{\$9,660\,(\text{Cost average inventory})} = \$2.80$$

Note that the \$2.80 represents the gross margin dollars obtained on each dollar invested in inventory.

■ Application Exercise

1. The beginning inventory for September in a girls' clothing department was \$36,400, and the closing inventory was \$28,000. The cumulative markon was 50%, with an achieved gross margin of 47.7%. Net sales for the period were \$116,300. Define the gross margin dollars returned as a percentage of the average cost inventory.

2. Given the following information, determine the gross margin dollar return per dollar of cost inventory for the period February through April.

	BOM	EOM
February	$10,000	$11,000
March	11,000	12,000
April	12,000	13,000
May	13,000	14,000

Gross margin	$12,000
Cumulative markon	45%

3. Determine the gross margin return as a percentage of cost inventory for the fall season for a cosmetics department with the following planned figures:

Planned sales	$100,000
Cumulative markon	39.7%
Gross margin	39.1%

	BOM
August	$23,000
September	30,000
October	35,000
November	50,000
December	45,000
January	30,000
February	35,000

Rearrange the opening inventory data to show the proper BOM/EOM relationship for the fall season.

4. An independently owned men's specialty store had an annual sales volume of $1,000,000. The cumulative markon was 51.5%, with a gross margin of 43.5%. Given the following beginning and ending inventories, determine the gross margin return per dollar of cost inventory.

	BOM	EOM
February	$450,000	$480,000
March	480,000	490,000
April	490,000	500,000
May	500,000	575,000
June	575,000	600,000
July	600,000	650,000
August	650,000	680,000
September	680,000	700,000
October	700,000	750,000
November	750,000	850,000
December	850,000	600,000
January	600,000	450,000

5. After five months of operation, the owner of a new children's clothing store decided to evaluate the gross margin return per dollar of cost inventory to date.[16] Given the following data, what figure was arrived at?

Net sales to date	$167,000
Gross margin achieved to date	45.5%
Cumulative markon	50.0%

	BOM	EOM
May	$32,000	$33,000
June	33,000	37,250
July	37,250	38,000
August	38,000	39,000
September	39,000	40,000

▪ Solutions to the Application Exercises

Determination of the Maintained Markon and Gross Margin When the Net Sales, Gross Cost of Merchandise Sold, Cash Discounts, and Alteration Costs Are Known (p. 209)

1.

Net sales	$45,000
Less gross cost of merchandise sold	27,000
Maintained markon	$18,000
Cash discounts	2,700
Less alteration costs	675
Gross margin	$20,025

$$\frac{\text{Maintained}}{\text{markon \%}} = \frac{\$18,000}{\$45,000} = 40\%$$

$$\frac{\text{Gross}}{\text{margin \%}} = \frac{\$20,025}{\$45,000} = 44.5\%$$

Proof: All figures as a percentage of sales:

Net sales	100.0%
Less gross cost of merchandise sold	60.0
Maintained markon	40.0%
Cash discounts	6.0
Less alteration costs	1.5
Gross margin	44.5%

---

[16]While this ratio can be defined for any period of time, it is normally considered an annual figure, using one BOM inventory and twelve EOM inventories.

3. Gross cost of merchandise sold = $123,000 × 65% = $79,950

Net sales	$123,000
Less gross cost of merchandise sold	79,950
Maintained markon	43,050
Cash discounts ($123,000 × 3.2%)	3,936
Gross margin	$46,986

$$\text{Maintained markon \%} = \frac{\$43,050}{\$123,000} = 35\%$$

$$\text{Gross margin \%} = \frac{\$46,986}{\$123,000} = 38.2\%$$

The inventory shortages in this instance have no bearing on the maintained markon as they already have been accounted for as a portion of the total retail reductions. Therefore, they are no longer a part of the closing inventory and resulting maintained markon. This holds true for markdowns as well as sales discounts. See "Situation 2," Chapter 7, page 181.

Proof: All figures as a percentage of sales:

Net sales	100.0%
Less gross cost of sales	65.0
Maintained markon	35.0%
Cash discounts	3.2
Gross margin	38.2%

5. $\dfrac{\text{Gross}}{\text{margin}} = \dfrac{\text{Maintained}}{\text{markon}} + \dfrac{\text{Cash}}{\text{discounts}} - \dfrac{\text{Alteration}}{\text{costs}}$

Therefore,

$\dfrac{\text{Gross}}{\text{margin}} - \dfrac{\text{Cash}}{\text{discounts}} + \dfrac{\text{Alteration}}{\text{costs}} = \dfrac{\text{Maintained}}{\text{markon}}$

46.5% − 5% + 1.5% = 43%

Proof:

$\text{Net sales} - \dfrac{\text{Maintained}}{\text{markon}} = \text{Gross cost of sales}$

100% − 43% = 57%

Net sales	100.0%
Less gross cost of sales	57.0
Maintained markon	43.0%
Cash discounts	5.0
Less alteration costs	1.5
Gross margin	46.5%

Gross Margin and Maintained Markon Percentage Derived from the Known Reductions, Initial Markon, Cash Discounts, and Alteration Costs (p. 211)

1. Cost of reductions = 6.7% (100% − 25%) = 5%

$$\frac{\text{Initial}}{\text{markon}} - \frac{\text{Cost of}}{\text{reductions}} = \frac{\text{Maintained}}{\text{markon}}$$
$$25\% \quad - \quad 5\% \quad = \quad 20\%$$

$$\frac{\text{Maintained}}{\text{markon}} + \frac{\text{Cash}}{\text{discounts}} - \frac{\text{Alteration}}{\text{costs}} = \frac{\text{Gross}}{\text{margin}}$$
$$20\% \quad + \quad 3.5\% \quad - \quad .8\% \quad = 22.7\%$$

Alternate Solution:

Maintained markon = Initial markon (100% + Reductions) − Reductions
$$= 25\% \ (100\% + 6.7\%) - 6.7\%$$
$$= 26.7\% - 6.7\%$$
$$= 20\%$$

$$\frac{\text{Maintained}}{\text{markon}} + \frac{\text{Cash}}{\text{discounts}} - \frac{\text{Alteration}}{\text{costs}} = \frac{\text{Gross}}{\text{margin}}$$
$$20.0\% \quad + \quad 3.5\% \quad - \quad .8\% \quad = 22.7\%$$

3. Markdowns   5.3%
   <u>Stock shortages</u>   <u>12.2</u>
   Retail reductions   17.5%

   Cost of reductions = 17.5% (100% − 53%) = 8.2%

   Maintained markon = 53% − 8.2% = 44.8%

   Gross margin = 44.8% + 8.3% = 53.1%

   Alternate Solution:

   Maintained markon = 53% (100% + 17.5%) − 17.5% = 44.8%

   Gross margin = 44.8% + 8.3% = 53.1%

5. Reductions = 12.3% + 2.2% + 1.3% = 15.8%

   Cost of reductions = 15.8% (100% − 50%) = 7.9%

   Maintained markon % = 50% − 7.9% = 42.1%

   or,

   Maintained markon % = 50% (100% + 15.8%) − 15.8% = 42.1%

   Gross margin = 42.1% + 8.3% − .5% = 49.9%

   Gross margin − Operating profit = Operating expenses
   $$49.9\% \quad - \quad 6.3\% \quad = \quad 43.6\%$$

Calculation of the Maintained Markon Given the Gross Margin, Cash Discounts, and Alteration Costs (p. 213)

1. $\frac{\text{Gross}}{\text{margin}} - \frac{\text{Cash}}{\text{discounts}} + \frac{\text{Alteration}}{\text{costs}} = \frac{\text{Maintained}}{\text{markon}}$

    $47\%\ -\ \ 4\%\ \ +\ \ 0\%\ \ =\ \ 43\%$

3. | | |
    |---|---|
    | Gross margin | $40,500 |
    | Less cash discounts | 5,500 |
    | Alteration costs | 2,500 |
    | Maintained markon | $37,500 |

5. Maintained markon = 43.5% − 7.3% + 2.4% = 38.6%
    $250,000 × 38.6% = $96,500

Net sales	−	Maintained markon	=	Gross cost of sales
100%	−	38.6%	=	61.4%
$250,000	−	$96,500	=	$153,500

Gross margin	−	Operating expenses	=	Operating profit
43.5%	−	36.3%	=	7.2%
$108,750	−	$90,750	=	$18,000

    Proof:[17]

Net sales	$250,000	100.0%
Less gross cost of sales	153,500	61.4
Maintained markon	$ 96,500	38.6%
Cash discounts	18,250	7.3
Less alteration costs	6,000	2.4
Gross margin	$108,750	43.5%
Less operating expenses	90,750	36.3
Operating profit	$ 18,000	7.2%

Calculation of the Allowable Markdown Dollars, Given Net Sales, Initial Markon, Cash Discounts, Alteration Costs, and Gross Margin (p. 215)

1. Maintained markon = 38.5% − 3% + 1% = 36.5%

    $$\text{Markdown (at retail)} = \frac{44\% - 36.5\%}{100\% - 44\%} = \frac{7.5\%}{56\%} = 13.4\%$$

    $Markdown = $380,000 × 13.4% = $50,920

---

[17]This is not so much to prove the answers as it is to illustrate the interrelationship of the various elements of the problem.

3. Maintained markon = 42.4% − 4.3% + 1.7% = 39.8%

$$\text{Markdown} = \frac{45.3\% - 39.8\%}{100\% - 45.3\%} = \frac{5.5\%}{54.7\%} = 10\%$$

Total markdown = $300,000 × 10% = $30,000

Balance of markon = $30,000 − $12,000 = $18,000

5. Maintained markon = 46.8% − 4.3% + .8% = 43.3%

$$\text{Seasonal markdown \%} = \frac{51\% - 43.3\%}{100\% - 51\%} = \frac{7.7\%}{49.0\%} = 15.7\%$$

$Seasonal markdown = $550,000 × 15.7% = $86,350

$Markdown consumed to date = $86,350 × 74% = $63,899

$Markdown remaining = $86,350 − $63,899 = $22,451

Achieved sales = $550,000 × 80% = $440,000

Sales remaining = $550,000 − $440,000 = $110,000

$$\frac{\$\text{Remaining markdown}}{\$\text{Remaining sales}} = \frac{\$22,451}{\$110,000} = 20.4\%$$

Thus, for the balance of the season, the buyer is permitted to take $22,451 in markdowns, which represents 20.4% of the remaining planned sales.
Proof:

	$Markdown	÷	*$Sales*	=	*Markdown %*
To date	$63,899	÷	$440,000	=	14.5%
Balance	22,451	÷	110,000	=	20.4%
Total	$86,350	÷	$550,000	=	15.7%

Computation of Gross Margin (p. 221)

1.   Gross Margin Statement

Period _____

	Items	Cost	Retail	$Markon	% of Sales	Cumulative Markon %
1.	Beginning inventory	$48,000	$80,000	$32,000		
2.	Net purchases	18,000	32,700	14,700		
3.	Net transfers in	4,300	7,800	3,500		
4.	Net markups		2,100	2,100		
5.	Transportation	900		(900)		
6.	Total additions	$23,200	$42,600	$19,400		

	Items	Cost	Retail	$Markon	% of Sales	Cumulative Markon %
7.	Total merchandise handled and cumulative markon	71,200	122,600	51,400		41.9
8.	Net sales		43,000			
9.	Net markdowns		5,160		12.0	
10.	Sales discounts		520		1.2	
11.	Estimated shortages		1,300		3.0	
12.	Total retail reductions		$49,980			
13.	Book inventory at retail		72,620			
14.	Book inventory at cost	42,192				
15.	Gross cost of merchandise sold and maintained markon	$29,008		13,992	32.5	
16.	Earned cash discounts	(2,150)		2,150	5.0	
17.	Net cost of merchandise sold	$26,858		$16,142	37.5%	
18.	Alteration costs	700		(700)	(1.6)	
19.	Total cost of merchandise sold and gross margin	$27,558		$15,442	35.9%	

Gross Margin Return per Dollar of Cost Inventory (p. 226)

1. Average inventory $= \dfrac{\$36,400 + \$28,000}{2} = \$32,200$

Average inventory at cost $= \$32,200 \,(100\% - 50\%) = \$16,100$

Gross margin $= \$116,300 \times 47.7\% = \$55,475$

The gross margin return per dollar of cost inventory $= \dfrac{\$55,475}{\$16,100} = \$3.45$

3. Although technically you may add the seven BOM inventories and divide by 7 to obtain the six-month average, theoretically the point of deriving the average inventory from one beginning inventory and six ending inventories is missed. The concept is to "blanket" the season with a beginning inventory and the subsequent ending inventories, not just to add up a series of beginning inventories. Thus, the opening inventory is derived as follows:

	BOM	*EOM*
August	$23,000	$30,000
September		35,000
October		50,000
November		45,000
December		30,000
January		35,000

Notice that the EOM figures are the BOM inventories for the coming month. For example, September's EOM of $35,000 is also the $35,000 October BOM; thus, January's EOM is derived from February's BOM.

$$\text{Average inventory} = \frac{\$23,000 + \$30,000 + \$35,000 + \$50,000 + \$45,000 + \$30,000 + \$35,000}{7} =$$

$$\frac{\$248,000}{7} = \$35,429$$

Average inventory at cost = $35,429 (100\% - 39.7\%) = $21,364

Gross margin = $100,000 \times 39.1\% = $39,100

$$\text{Gross margin return per dollar of cost inventory} = \frac{\$39,100}{\$21,364} = \$1.83$$

5. Gross margin = $167,000 \times 45.5\% = $75,985

$$\text{Average inventory} = \frac{\$32,000 + \$33,000 + \$37,250 + \$38,000 + \$39,000 + \$40,000}{6} = \$36,542$$

Average cost inventory = $36,542 (100\% - 50\%) = $18,271

$$\text{Gross margin return per dollar of cost inventory to date} = \frac{\$75,985}{\$18,271} = \$4.16$$

Topics for Discussion and Review

1. Explain the difference between the concepts of margin and profit.

2. What considerations distinguish gross margin from maintained markon?

3. How would you explain the determination of markdown, given net sales, initial markon, cash discounts, alterations, and gross margin?

4. Explain the concept of gross margin.

5. How is the total merchandise handled determined, and how does it relate to the cumulative markon?

6. What is the difference between the perpetual inventory and the book inventory? Quantitatively, how would you define the book inventory at retail?

7. Why must the book inventory at retail be converted to cost, and how is this accomplished?

8. Why is the book inventory at cost not the merchant's true, or actual, cost?

9. Define the gross cost of merchandise sold and its contribution to maintained markon.

10. Explain why cash discounts reduce the gross cost of merchandise sold and increase gross margin.

11. How do the alteration costs increase the cost of merchandise sold and decrease the gross margin?

12. Discuss the significance of the gross margin return per dollar of cost inventory ratio.

13. Explain the concept of the average inventory. How is it converted to cost?

14. Explain how to determine gross margin dollars and percentage, assuming that you know new sales, gross cost of merchandise, cash discounts, and alterations, all in dollars.

15. Why is gross margin normally higher than the maintained markon?

16. How would you determine the gross margin and maintained markon, if the retail reductions, initial markon, cash discounts, and alteration costs are known?

17. Explain the calculation of the maintained markon, given gross margin, cash discounts, and alteration costs.

18. You are part way through period III; how would you determine the amount of markdowns remaining in dollars and percentage given net sales, initial markon, cash discounts, alteration costs, and gross margin?

19. What do we mean when we talk of the profit derived from the sale of merchandise?

20. How do net markups affect total additions to the beginning inventory?

21. Explain how to determine the gross margin return per dollar of cost inventory.

22. What is the net cost of merchandise sold?

23. In the gross margin statement, explain the relationship between the initial markon, the maintained markon, and retail reductions.

24. In the gross margin statement, explain the effect of transportation costs on the total merchandise handled and the cumulative markon percent.

25. What happens to the book inventory at the end of an accounting period?

Chapter 9
Turnover: The Relationship Between Inventory and Net Sales

Learning Objectives

■ Define the concept of productivity in terms of the retail merchant.

■ Explain the concept of inventory turnover.

■ Explain the concept of inventory turnover in terms of capital turnover and GMROI.

■ Explain why there is no such thing as the ideal turnover ratio.

■ Discuss methods of improving turnover.

■ Discuss the advantages and limitations of a rapid turnover rate.

■ Define hand-to-mouth buying.

■ Calculate turnover for one or more months.

■ Plan net sales using the turnover formula.

■ Calculate the reduction in inventory necessary to increase turnover by a specific amount.

■ Determine the amount of sales increase required to raise the stock turn by a specific amount.

■ Determine the average inventory turnover for a whole unit, given the sales and stockturns for the constituent parts of this unit.

■ Calculate the average turnover for the unit, given the percentage of net sales and the turnover for the fractional parts of the unit.

- Find the turnover for one part of a unit, given the average unit turnover, percentage of net sales, and the turnover for each component part.

- Determine capital turnover for any given period of time.

- Calculate the initial markon, given capital turnover and inventory turnover.

- Find capital turnover, given the initial markon and inventory turnover.

- Calculate the inventory turnover, given the capital turnover and initial markon.

- Explain the concept of GMROI.

- Calculate the GMROI.

Key Terms

Average Inventory: The BOM inventory plus the sum of the EOM inventories for a given period of time, divided by the total number of inventories.

BOM: The merchant's abbreviation for the *beginning of the month*.

Cancellation Date: The date specified by the buyer on the merchandise purchase order as the latest acceptable date of shipment.

Capital Turnover: The ratio between net sales and the average inventory valued at cost. It provides a means of evaluating the dollars invested in inventory (at cost) with the net sales produced by that inventory.

EOM: The merchant's abbreviation for the *end of the month*.

Gross Margin: The difference between net sales and the total cost of merchandise sold, expressed in dollars or as a percentage of net sales.

Gross Margin Return on Investment (GMROI): The rate of return (gross margin) derived from the investment in inventory. GMROI measures the efficiency of the merchandise investment at cost.

Hand-to-Mouth Buying: Buying in small quantities for immediate use.

Inventory Turnover: The number of times within a specific period of time that an average inventory is sold and replaced. Inventory turnover is normally calculated on an annual basis; however, it may be determined for any given period of time.

Operating Profit: The profit derived from merchandising operations.

Return on Investment: The amount of dollars realized above the original dollar investment.

Returns to Vendor: Shipments of merchandise returned by the merchant to the vendor.

Seasonal Discount: A special discount to all merchants who place orders for seasonal merchandise well in advance of the normal selling season.

Selling Cost Ratio: The relationship between selling payroll and net sales, determined by dividing gross selling payroll by net sales.

SKU: An abbreviation for *stock-keeping unit,* which defines the lowest level of merchandise identification for the management of inventory—normally size and color within a style.

Total Assets: The sum of the owned physical objects (tangible) and/or rights (intangible) having a monetary value expressed in terms of cost or depreciated cost.

Working Capital: The difference between current assets and current liabilities.

9.1
Productivity: The Key to Profitability

In Chapter 1, retail merchandising was essentially defined as a management system of tactical planning and control, directed toward the financial enhancement and profitable sale of a retail inventory to the ultimate consumer. Thus, the essence of retail merchandising is the profitable relationship between net sales and the inventory from which those sales were derived.

The merchant's inventory investment represents the single greatest portion of a store's working capital, the largest part of its total assets. The sale of merchandise from this inventory defines the store's major source of operating profit. Thus, the ultimate success of merchandising management depends upon the productivity of the dollar investment in the retail inventory. That is, for every dollar committed to an inventory, the merchant should expect, indeed demand, a profitable return both in terms of net sales and gross margin dollars.

9.2
Inventory Turnover

Inventory turnover is defined as the number of times that an average inventory is sold and replaced within a specified period of time; it measures the speed with which merchandise passes through the hands of the retail merchant into those of the ultimate consumer. In essence, inventory turnover defines the measure of the correctness of the merchant's ratio, or balance, between net sales and the inventory that produced those sales.

The rate of stock turnover is not the determinant of merchandising activity but the by-product of the merchant's efficient management and control of the retail inventory. Hence, the rate of inventory turnover is a vital yardstick in measuring the performance of a store, department, or classification in terms of management acumen. Consider, for example, the following situation:

A specialty store owner (A) carries an average inventory at retail of $300,000, which generates an annual sales volume of $750,000 and an operating profit of $45,000. However, a more astute competitor (B), using essentially the same merchandise inventory, is able to produce $900,000 in sales volume and net an operating profit of $54,000.

A comparative analysis of the individual operating data highlights the differences between the two retail stores:

	$Operating Profit	÷	*$Net Sales*	=	*Operating Profit %*
Store B	$54,000	÷	$900,000	=	6%
Less Store A	45,000	÷	750,000	=	6%
Difference	$ 9,000		$150,000		0%

Notice that both stores A and B derive the same percentage of operating profit from a similar investment in inventory; however, B has $150,000 more in net sales than A, and thus $9,000 more in operating profit. This is because A achieved an inventory turnover of 2.5, whereas B was able to turn over the same inventory investment 3 times. How this was accomplished is the subject of this chapter and will be explained as we progress. A higher ratio of sales to inventory, or stock turnover, tends to enhance merchandising profitability, the ultimate goal of the retail merchant.

Inventory turnover, or stock turn, may be expressed in terms of retail dollars, cost dollars, or units. However, because the retail method of inventory prevails among the major retail establishments, the concept as herein used is always assumed to be at retail unless specifically stated otherwise.

The Concept of Inventory Turnover: Productivity

Turnover, in effect, is a simple fraction in which the numerator represents the net sales for a specific period of time and the denominator defines the average inventory used to produce those sales within the same time frame. Thus,

$$\frac{\text{Net sales}}{\text{Average inventory}} = \text{Turnover}$$

Turnover therefore represents the ratio of the inventory to sales and designates the number of times that an inventory must be sold, replaced, and resold to produce a net sales volume in a given period of time. If the annual net sales for a particular operation were $200,000 and the required average retail inventory were $50,000, the turnover would be 4 times, or

$$\frac{\$200,000 \,(\text{Net sales})}{\$50,000 \,(\text{Average inventory})} = 4$$

The above fraction is not an abstract figure; it represents productivity ratios that measure the returns on various types of investment. Depending upon the classification of merchandise, the turnover (productivity) ratio will vary. For example, fine jewelry turns about 1.5 times, whereas women's gloves turn about 4.2 times. Consider the following examples using the above conceptual formula:

1. *Inventory turnover.* "Four times" essentially means that the average dollar of inventory investment at retail generated $4 in net sales.

2. *Capital turnover.*[1] This represents the relationship between the cost of the inventory and net sales. Assuming that the cumulative markon[2] is 40% in the above situation, we may reduce the $50,000 average retail inventory to cost ($50,000 × 60% = $30,000) and thus obtain the following result that indicates the turnover on the invested capital, or the ratio of dollars invested in inventory at cost to net sales.

$$\frac{\$200,000 \,(\text{Net sales})}{\$30,000 \,(\text{Average cost inventory})} = 6.7$$

The equation now states that the average dollar invested in the cost inventory (the actual capital investment) produced $6.70 in net sales or that the capital turn was 6.7 times.[3]

3. *GMROI.* This represents the gross margin dollars returned per dollar of cost inventory, or gross margin dollars divided by the average cost inventory. Because the GMROI is essentially a ratio of profit dollars to cost dollars, that same ratio may be derived from capital turnover if the gross margin percentage is known. For example, assume that along with a capital turnover of 6.7 times, or a $6.70 return per invested cost dollar, the profit derived from the sale of the merchandise, or gross margin, is known to be 36%. Then, because $6.70 defines the sales dollars returned, and gross margin represents the percentage of merchandising profit derived from those sales dollars, the GMROI may be expressed as capital turnover times gross margin. Or,

GMROI = Capital turnover × Gross margin %

The above capital turnover of $6.70 may be translated into a GMROI figure simply by multiplying $6.70 times the percentage of achieved gross margin:

---

[1]This will be discussed in greater detail further into the chapter.
[2]The cumulative markon is the average of multiple initial markons. Therefore, cumulative markon as used in this chapter is synonymous with initial markon.
[3]This ratio may also be derived by dividing the stock turn at retail by the cost complement of the cumulative markon: 4 times ÷ 60% = 6.7 times.

GMROI $= \$6.70 \times 36\% = \$2.41$

In effect, the net sales dollars returned per dollar of inventory investment (capital turnover) have been reduced to the gross margin dollars returned per dollar of inventory investment (GMROI).

The concept of turnover, then, is that it is a ratio of profit dollars to investment dollars, and it therefore represents productivity, or the number of times within a given period of time that the initial investment can be reworked into profit dollars. Profit margins are therefore the product of the initial investment times the frequency of reinvestment. By improving turnover, the merchant's return on invested capital is enhanced. Consider the following examples:

1. If the gross margin is 50% and the turnover rate is 1, the gross margin return is 50% (50% $\times$ 1). However, if the turnover is increased by a one-quarter turn, then the gross margin return is increased by 12.5% to 62.5% (50% $\times$ 1.25).

2. By reducing the gross margin to 40% and increasing the stock turn to 2.5 times, we are able to increase the gross margin return to 100% (40% $\times$ 2.5). But, should the turnover ratio happen to fall to 2.2 times, the gross margin return will be reduced by 12% to 88% (40% $\times$ 2.2).

This concept of inventory turnover, in effect, defines merchandising profit not only in terms of the retail price and merchandise costs, but also as a result of the frequency with which the inventory is sold and replaced. In the final analysis, merchandising profits are essentially determined by the gross margin per item sold times the number of items sold within a specific period of time.

Although turnover is a leading measure of the efficiency with which the merchant manages the retail inventory, it is in no way to be construed as an objective of merchandising strategies. The achievement of the "right" turnover rate is simply a corollary benefit that accrues to the merchant as a result of the correct alignment of consumer demand with the availability of a corresponding inventory assortment.

Determinants of Increased Turnover

Defining Proper Turnover

The ideal turnover ratio per se is nonexistent. It is only when turnover is related to a particular type of retail operation, and specific merchandise classifications within the inventory assortments of that operation, that the turnover ratio becomes meaningful. For example, women's hosiery in a specialty store may turn 2.7 times annually, whereas in a major department store that same classification may turn 3.7 times or better. Within the same department store, the turnover ratio for junior sportswear may exceed 5.4, while if the pattern department turns its average stock 0.8 times, that is considered to be a superior achievement.[4] Such variations exist in the turnover ratio because the projected image of the particular store, department, or classification is a manifestation of unique merchandising tactics. Consider, for example, the following:

Variations in the merchandise mix, including price differentials, size ranges, and color availability.

Emphasis on the advertising philosophy, that is, institutional versus the promotional approach.

Interior promotional efforts such as display techniques and personalized selling.

In the final analysis, the individual merchant must determine the unique ratios of inventory turnover most compatible with a particular retail image and do so by item, classification, department, and store. As previously mentioned, the "proper" turnover ratio in any given situation is achieved as a by-product of astute merchandise management; it is a reflection of the merchant's ability to realistically translate a minimum investment in inventory into a maximum volume of net sales. Therefore, the "right" turnover ratio is the correct balance between an inventory assortment and a sales volume, the "correct balance" definable only in terms of the objectives and goals of the retail firm.

Methods of Improving the Turnover Ratio

As previously defined, the basic turnover ratio is the product of

$$\frac{\text{Net sales}}{\text{Average inventory}}$$

From an inspection of the relationship between net sales and the average inventory, it becomes clear that there are essentially only three ways by which turnover may be increased:

1. Increase net sales relative to the average inventory.
   a. Study merchandise performance by classification in terms of price, size, and color; take relevant markdowns[5] where necessary.

---

[4]For a more comprehensive view of stock turn ratios in terms of classifications and store sizes, see the current edition of *Department and Specialty Store Merchandising and Operating Results* published yearly by the Financial Executives Division, National Retail Federation, Inc., 100 West 31st Street, New York, NY 10001.

[5]Markdowns will increase sales at the expense of planned gross margin. On the other hand, the sale of formerly unwanted merchandise through the stimulus of a price reduction will at least generate some gross margin where none previously existed. Also, there is the distinct possibility that the increased turnover will allow the GMROI to remain virtually intact.

     b. Consider promotional tactics, advertising, display, etc.

     c. Evaluate the image of the retail store in terms of customer "wants."

     d. Study operating expense ratios; ratios that are too low, for example the selling cost ratio,[6] can hinder the sales effort.

     e. Scrutinize retail reductions, particularly in the areas of markdowns and inventory shortages.

     f. Ensure that sales personnel are well trained, supplied with adequate merchandise information, and possess the positive attitude necessary to "close the sale."

2. Decrease the average inventory relative to the net sales.

     a. Avoid duplication of styles, brands, and classifications of merchandise; for example, men's colognes in both the cosmetics and men's furnishings departments.

     b. Eliminate useless price lines; the test of a good price line is the rapidity with which it moves merchandise and satisfies customer wants.

     c. Merchandise "narrow and deep."[7]

     d. Carefully weigh the pros and cons of seasonal discounts.[8]

     e. Adhere to purchase order cancellation dates; merchandise received well into a selling season denies those goods the required exposure for adequate sales, and thus they must be carried over to the subsequent season or end up on the markdown racks.

     f. Purchase goods in less quantity but more frequently.

     g. Process incoming merchandise more efficiently and thus reduce the transit time to the selling floor.

3. Obtain a larger sales volume with a proportionally lower average inventory; although this is conceivable and represents the best of both worlds, it is obviously difficult to achieve except in situations of highly inept merchandise management.

Advantages of Rapid Inventory Turnover

It is generally accepted that, within the limitations to be discussed shortly, the higher the turnover ratio the more profitable the operation is likely to be. This is true so long as there is a constructive balance between net sales and the average inventory. To be more specific, as long as the relationship between sales and

---

[6]The dollars expended in selling payroll divided by net sales. For example, given a sales volume of $3,000 and a selling payroll of $210, the selling cost ratio would be $210 ÷ $3,000, or 7%.

[7]Few product categories (classifications) and a large assortment in each category, as opposed to "wide and shallow."

[8]Special discounts to the merchant from the vendor for ordering merchandise well in advance of the normal season. Buying too far in advance of the season will increase the average inventory and thus decrease the turnover.

inventory contributes to merchandising profitability, the resulting turnover ratio is perceived to be desirable and possesses the following advantages:

1. *The return on inventory investment is increased.* Only when merchandise is sold does "return on inventory investment" occur; thus, the higher the rate of sale, the better the return (assuming, of course, an adequate gross margin).

2. *Operating expenses are decreased.* Smaller inventories require fewer storage facilities, both on the selling floor and in the reserve stock areas. This released space may be used in the expansion of the business without the necessity of leasing or constructing additional facilities. Also, there are savings in taxes, insurance costs, and interest expenses, all resulting from the reduced requirements of smaller inventories.

3. *Markdowns and shortages are decreased.* Because markdowns and inventory shortages are at least partially a function of time, it follows that the longer the merchandise remains in inventory, the greater the opportunity for obsolescence to occur. Thus the higher the rate of turnover, the less chance the merchandise has of becoming shopworn, aged, and pilfered.

4. *The sales volume is enhanced.* The objective of improved stock turn is to balance the inventory assortment to the vagaries of consumer demand. As a by-product of this matching process, the customer is exposed to new and more complete merchandise assortments, thus stimulating customer interest and attracting those who must always seek that which is perceived to be new.

5. *Cash flow is increased.* A rapid turnover frees up a greater amount of investment capital that can be employed in the acquisition of new merchandise, or be used to take advantage of special buying opportunities that may arise during the course of the selling season.

Hand-to-Mouth Buying

In conjunction with the determinants of increased turnover, the concept of hand-to-mouth buying should be mentioned at this point. Here we speak of a rapid turnover policy carried to its extreme, wherein the merchant carefully watches the level of inventory on hand and orders replenishment quantities in frequent but small amounts. In effect, the merchant attempts to eliminate, or at least minimize, the risks inherent in relatively larger inventories by purchasing only what is needed, in terms of classification and quantity, when it is needed. The essence of hand-to-mouth buying involves two conditions:

1. The placing of frequent, small orders rather than fewer but larger orders.

2. The ordering of merchandise for immediate delivery rather than a future delivery date.

Hand-to-mouth buying contributes to the advantages of rapid inventory turnover by eliminating the risk of commitments to long-term investments that may contribute to markdowns, shortages, returns to vendors, and order cancellations.

Hand-to-mouth buying has serious limitations in that it adds to the merchant's operating expense through increased clerical costs and the physical work of shipping and receiving many small units. Indirectly, merchandise costs are also increased because the vendor must produce in anticipation of the merchant's requirements rather than in fulfillment of specific purchase orders.

Limitations of a Rapid Inventory Turnover

While the benefits to be derived from a higher inventory turnover are beyond dispute, most merchants would agree that a rapid turnover policy can be carried too far and do harm to the retail store. Such a point is reached when profitability is impaired. For example, when sales volume suffers as a result of inadequate inventories, a high stock turn ceases to be advantageous and, in fact, requires immediate reappraisal. As a case in point, consider the following. A department may be achieving a net sales volume of $200,000 with an average inventory of $50,000, representing a turnover ratio of 4. In order to increase the rate of turnover, the average inventory is reduced to $40,000 and, as a result, net sales fall to $180,000. Now, while the turnover may be increased to 4.5, the savings in inventory can in no way compensate the merchant for a $20,000 loss in sales volume. The danger of lost sales due to an out-of-stock condition is probably the greatest disadvantage of a rapid inventory turnover. However, there are others:

1. *The cost of merchandise is increased.* By purchasing in small quantities, the merchant is deprived of quantity discounts. Also, higher transportation costs resulting from many small shipments add to the cost of the merchandise. Thus, gross margin is reduced by the increased cost of the inventory.

2. *Correspondence, clerical, and handling cost are increased.* The cost of processing thirteen weekly reorders in a three-month period will be thirteen times as great as placing one reorder per quarter. Thirteen purchase orders have to be written, thirteen invoices have to be paid, thirteen shipments have to be received, checked, and marked. Also, the merchant's time will be taken up with more inventory and sales analysis and reordering, leaving less time for the other management aspects of the business.

Determination of Turnover for One Month

The essence of turnover is that sales are divided by an average inventory for any given period of time. The average inventory always consists of the sum of the BOM inventories plus the EOM inventory, divided by the total number of inventories.

▪ Study Problem

Given: A candy department had an opening inventory of $8,000 on June 1 and closed the period on June 30 with an inventory of $7,200. Sales for June amounted to $2,300.

Find: The turnover ratio for the candy department during the month of June.

Solution:

$$\text{Turnover} = \frac{\text{Net sales}}{\text{Average inventory}}$$

$$\text{The average inventory}^9 = \frac{\text{BOM} + \text{EOM}}{2}$$

$$= \frac{\$8,000 + \$7,200}{2} = \$7,600$$

$$\text{Turnover for June} = \frac{\$2,300}{\$7,600} = .30^{10}$$

▪ Application Exercise

1. A budget shoe buyer had a BOM inventory of $18,000. Net sales amounted to $3,435, leaving a closing inventory of $15,000. What was the stock turnover for the month?

2. A small leather goods buyer closed the month of December with an inventory of $22,000. With a BOM of $30,000, the buyer had managed to achieve net sales of $13,000. Determine the buyer's ratio of inventory to net sales for December.

3. Gross sales in a children's clothing store for the month of September were $70,000. Returns were 7%, the BOM stock was $179,000, and the ending inventory amounted to $140,500. What was the rate of turnover achieved for the month of September?

---

[9]Refer to Chapter 8 ("Gross Margin Return per Dollar of Cost Inventory") for the calculation of the average inventory.
[10]"Thirty" represents 3/10, or 30% of one turn. Assuming that the inventory turned 0.30 for twelve months (although possible, highly improbable), the annual turnover rate would be 0.30 × 12, or 3.6 times.

4. The owner of a junior sportswear boutique had a BOM inventory of $36,400. Net sales for the period were $15,700, and the EOM inventory was $38,500. What was the rate of stock turnover for the period?

5. A gourmet food shop experienced sales for the month of April of $45,350. The BOM inventory was $84,750, and the EOM inventory was $79,800. What was the rate of turnover achieved?

Determination of Turnover at Cost for One Month

The method for determining turnover at cost is the same as that for turnover at retail, except that the figures must all be at cost. Therefore,

$$\text{Turnover at cost} = \frac{\text{Cost of merchandise sold}}{\text{Average cost inventory}}$$

▪ Study Problem

Given: A floor-covering department had a BOM inventory at cost of $63,000 and an EOM inventory at cost of $57,300.

Find: If the cost of sales was $15,000, what was the turnover at cost?

Solution:

$$\text{Average cost inventory} = \frac{\$63,000 + \$57,300}{2} = \$60,150$$

$$\text{Turnover at cost} = \frac{\$15,000}{\$60,150} = .25 \text{ times}$$

▪ Application Exercise

1. A sporting-goods department had a BOM stock of $142,500 at cost. Cost of sales for the period was $32,000, and the ending inventory at cost was $136,100. What was the turnover at cost for the period?

2. The cost of sales for a drug department was $18,000 for October. The inventory at cost on October 1 was $31,500; the cost inventory on October 31 was $40,500. Determine the turnover at cost for October.

3. Given net sales of $13,000, maintained markon[11] of 40%, BOM inventory at cost of $17,000, and EOM inventory at cost of $10,000, find turnover at cost.

---

[11]The maintained markon is the difference between net sales and the gross cost of merchandise sold and is therefore applied to net sales to determine the cost of sales.

4. Given cost of sales of $18,000, cumulative markon[12] of 43%, BOM inventory at retail of $78,000, and EOM inventory at retail of $72,100, find turnover at cost.

5. Given the following information for the month of July,

Net sales	$83,500
BOM inventory July 1 (retail)	$272,500
EOM inventory July 31 (retail)	$283,300
Cumulative markon July 31	42.5%
Maintained markon July 31	39.2%

Determine the stock turnover for July at (A) retail and (B) cost.[13]

Computation of Inventory Turnover for a Period of Several Months

▪ Study Problem

While monthly, or periodic, turnover ratios have their place in tactical planning, the development of seasonal turnover figures is of greater importance in the implementation of merchandising strategy. This is especially true in the construction of the six-month merchandise plan, discussed in Chapter 12.

Given:

	Inventory		
	BOM	*EOM*	*Net Sales*
August	$25,000	$28,000	$12,000
September	28,000	35,000	13,000
October	35,000	34,000	18,000
November	34,000	33,000	15,000
December	33,000	30,000	14,000
January	30,000	24,000	11,000

---

[12]The cumulative markon is the difference between the total cost and the total original retail value of the merchandise handled to date. Expressed as a percentage of original retail, it is the factor that translates the retail inventories into cost inventories.

[13]The correct computation of this exercise will demonstrate that the inventory turnover at cost is greater than the stock turnover at retail. This is because the cumulative markon, or the spread between the cost and retail inventories, exceeds the maintained markon, which is the difference between the cost of sales and the final retail price, or net sales. You will recall from Chapter 7 that this difference between the cumulative (or initial) markon and the maintained markon is the cost of the retail reductions.

Find: A department's turnover for the fall season.[14]

Solution:

$$\text{Turnover} = \frac{\text{Net sales}}{\text{Average inventory}}$$

Average inventory = The sum of the ending inventories for the season plus the beginning inventory for the season divided by 7.[15]

August	BOM	$25,000
August	EOM	28,000
September	EOM	35,000
October	EOM	34,000
November	EOM	33,000
December	EOM	30,000
January	EOM	24,000
Total inventories		= $209,000

$$\text{Average inventory} = \frac{\$209,000}{7} = \$29,857$$

Total sales = $83,000

$$\text{Turnover for the fall season} = \frac{\$83,000}{\$29,857} = 2.8 \text{ (times)}$$

■ **Application Exercise**

1. A department had the following inventory and net sales figures for the first three months of the year. Determine the turnover for this first quarter.

BOM Inventories		Net Sales
January	$5,667	$2,500
February	6,467	3,500
March	7,533	4,500
April	7,400	

2. For the last quarter of the year, a Christmas shop showed the following figures. What was the achieved rate of inventory turnover?

---

[14]The fall season runs from August through January.
[15]For a more detailed explanation of average inventory, see Chapter 8.

	Inventory		
	BOM	EOM	Net Sales
October	$60,500	$68,300	$49,500
November	68,300	45,200	65,000
December	45,200	-0-	59,500

3. Determine the turnover at cost, given the following information:

Cost of Inventory		Net Sales	
August 1	$4,924	August	$2,902
September 1	4,220	September	2,600
October 1	4,910	October	3,100
October 31	4,870		

Maintained markon is 45%.

4. What is the departmental turnover at retail for the period January 1 through May 31, given the following data?

	Inventory		
	BOM	EOM	Cost of Sales
January	$33,380	$34,260	$8,542
February	34,260	35,160	9,124
March	35,160	36,890	9,682
April	36,890	37,370	10,209
May	37,390	39,500	10,998

Maintained markon is 41.5%.

5. A hobby shop exhibited the following figures for the fall season. Determine the rate of turnover at both (A) retail and (B) cost.

	Inventory		
	BOM	EOM	Net Sales
August	$354,800	$354,200	$80,920
September	354,200	356,200	81,730
October	356,200	357,700	82,810
November	357,700	358,600	84,320
December	358,600	359,100	84,620
January	359,100	358,500	85,600

Cumulative markon is 42.8%, and maintained markon is 39.6%.

Determination of Net Sales and the Average Inventory

From the formula,

$$\text{Turnover} = \frac{\text{Net sales}}{\text{Average stock}}$$

the following equations can be derived:

$$\text{Average stock} = \frac{\text{Net sales}}{\text{Turnover}}$$

$$\text{Net sales} = \text{Turnover} \times \text{Average stock}$$

■ Study Problem

Given: A furniture store has an average inventory of $100,000 with a turnover of 2.

Find: The store's net sales.

Solution:

Net sales = Turnover × Average stock

Net sales = 2 × $100,000 = $200,000

Assume in the above problem that net sales and turnover are known and we wish to solve for the average stock. Then,

$$\text{Average stock} = \frac{\text{Net sales}}{\text{Turnover}}$$

$$\text{Average stock} = \frac{\$200,000}{2} = \$100,000$$

■ Application Exercise

1. The owner of an intimate-apparel shop had an inventory turnover of 3 and an average inventory of $166,000. What were the net sales?

2. A junior sportswear department is planning an average stock at retail for the fall season of $130,000, with turnover anticipated to be 5.5. What net sales should be expected?

3. A coat buyer planned net sales for the spring season at $325,000 with a turnover of 2.2. What will the average stock at cost be if the cumulative markon is established at 49.5%?

4. Given the following data, define the planned sales for the last quarter of the year.

	Inventory	
	BOM	EOM
October	$25,500	$30,800
November	30,800	22,300
December	22,300	18,400

Turnover = 1.3

5. The owner of a health food store has planned an annual turnover of 7.7 and an average inventory at cost of $26,475. If the cumulative markon is to be 41%, what amount of net sales can be expected?

Improving the Turnover Ratio by Reducing the Average Inventory While Maintaining a Constant Level of Net Sales

It is often desirable or necessary to increase the stock turn without a corresponding increase in sales volume. Because turnover reflects the relationship between inventory and sales, the merchant is faced with this question: By how much should the average inventory be decreased so as to increase the turnover ratio by a specific amount?

▪ Study Problem

Given: A costume jewelry department experienced a net sales volume last year of $300,000 with a stock turn of 2.5. This year, the sales volume is again planned at $300,000; however, the stock turn is to be increased from 2.5 to 3 times.

Find: How much must the average inventory be reduced, in terms of dollars and percentage, to achieve the increased turnover?

Solution:

Average stock last year = $\frac{\$300,000}{2.5}$ = $120,000

Planned average stock = $\frac{\$300,000}{3}$ = $100,000

Reduction in average stock = $120,000 − $100,000 = $20,000

Percentage reduction in average stock =
$\frac{\$120,000 - \$100,000}{\$120,000} = \frac{\$20,000}{\$120,000}$ = 16.7%

▪ Application Exercise

1. A buyer of sheets and pillowcases achieved net sales of $208,500 and a turnover of 2.6 at the end of the past season. For the coming season, sales are expected to remain the same. However, in order to increase productivity the buyer seeks to raise the rate of turnover to 3. By how much, in terms of dollars and percentage, must the average inventory be decreased?

2. A buyer achieved a turnover of 1.2 for the first quarter as a result of the following inventory/sales relationship:

	Inventory		
	BOM	EOM	Net Sales
January	$13,500	$15,000	$5,650
February	15,000	14,200	6,100
March	14,200	13,500	5,110

For the second quarter, the turnover is planned at 1.5 with no change in the volume of net sales. By how much, in dollars and percentage, must the average inventory be reduced to achieve the 1.5 stock turn?

3. The annual turnover of a luggage department was 2.5. Net sales for the year were $123,000. Determine by how much the inventory should be reduced in dollars and percentage in order to achieve a stock turn of 3 with the same level of sales.

4. A floor-covering buyer was informed by the merchandise manager that the turnover for the fall season of 1.1 on net sales of $300,000 was totally unacceptable. Advised to seek a 1.4 turnover for the spring season and unable to foresee any improvement in net sales, the buyer decided to reduce the amount of inventory on hand. By how much should the average inventory for the spring season be reduced, in dollars and percentage, in order to achieve the 1.4 stock turn?

5. Last May, the achieved turnover was 0.4. The BOM inventory for the month was $30,000, and for June the BOM stock was $20,000. This May, the turnover is planned at 0.6. Assuming that the net sales are the same this May as last May, define the required decrease in the average inventory in both dollars and percentage.

Improving the Turnover Ratio by Increasing Net Sales While Maintaining a Constant Level of Inventory

It is not uncommon for the merchant to be in a situation where a reduction in average inventory is impractical, but an increase in turnover is nevertheless required. It therefore becomes necessary to determine a specific amount of sales increase, in both dollars and percentage, to effect the desired increase in stock turnover.

■ Study Problem

Given: A little girls' clothing department had an average inventory of $43,000 and an inventory turnover of 4.3 last year. This year, a stock turn of 4.8 is planned by means of increased sales and the maintenance of the same average inventory as last year.

Find: The required amount of sales increase, in terms of dollars and percentage, to achieve the higher stock turn.

Solution:

Net sales = Turnover × Average inventory

Therefore,

Last year's sales = 4.3 × $43,000 = $184,900

And,

Planned sales = 4.8 × $43,000 = $206,400

Dollar sales increase required = $206,400 − $184,900 = $21,500

Percentage increase required = $\dfrac{\$206,400 - \$184,900}{\$184,900} = \dfrac{\$21,500}{\$184,900} = 11.6\%$

■ Application Exercise

1. A major-appliance department had an annual stock turn of 4.2 derived from an average inventory of $190,500. Assuming that the average inventory remains constant, how much should sales be increased in order to raise the stock turn from 4.2 to 4.7?

2. The owner of a men's clothing store desires to improve the profitability of the operation by increasing the stock turn from 5 to 5.5. Through better service, advertising, and merchandise selection, it is believed that sales can be increased without affecting the average inventory of $100,000. By how much should sales be increased, in dollars and percentage, to achieve the desired turnover of 5.5?

3. The buyer of television sets desired to increase the departmental turnover from 4.2 to 5.3 without further increasing the cost of inventory, which is cur-

rently $300,000. The cumulative markon is to remain at 26.5%. By how much must net sales be increased, in dollars and percentage, if the new turnover goal is to be achieved?

4. A boys' furnishings buyer wishes to increase turnover from 3.5 to 3.9 while maintaining the average inventory of $163,000. By how many dollars, and by what percentage, must sales be increased in order to achieve the higher stock turn?

5. The buyer of women's gloves currently turns the average inventory of $23,000 4 times annually. Because this rate of stock turn is considerably below the industry average, a 10% increase is sought. Assuming a constant level of inventory, define the percentage increase in sales necessary to produce a 10% increase in turnover.

Determination of the Average Inventory Turnover for a Whole Unit, Given the Net Sales and the Stock Turns for the Constituent Parts of the Unit

Here we define the whole unit as a store, selling department, or merchandise classification. The store is a unit composed of selling departments, the selling department is a unit made up of merchandise classifications, and the merchandise classification is a unit derived from many subclassifications. This sequential process of redefining units in terms of component parts eventually terminates in the stock-keeping unit, or SKU. An SKU defines the lowest level of merchandise identification for the purposes of inventory control; within a particular style of a classification (itself a unit), the SKU normally refers to a unique size within a unique color.

Profitability, to a large extent, is dependent upon unit turnover however defined; unit turnover is an average turnover, derived from the individual turnovers of that unit's constituent parts.

Armed with this understanding, the merchant is better able to zero in upon the specific strengths and weaknesses of any aspect of the merchandising function of the retail store.

∎ Study Problem

Given: An independent merchant owned a small menswear store consisting of four departments exhibiting the following data:

	Net Sales	Turnover
Suits	$200,000	2.0
Furnishings	100,000	2.5
Sportswear	150,000	3.0
Shoes	50,000	1.5

Find: The inventory turnover for the entire store.

Solution:

$$\text{Inventory turnover} = \frac{\text{Total sales}}{\text{Total average inventory}}$$

Therefore,

$$\text{Average inventory} = \frac{\text{Sales}}{\text{Turnover}}$$

Department	Net Sales	Turnover	Average Inventory
Suits	$200,000	2.0	$100,000
Furnishings	100,000	2.5	40,000
Sportswear	150,000	3.0	50,000
Shoes	50,000	1.5	33,333
Total store	$500,000	?	$223,333

$$\text{Total store turnover} = \frac{\$500,000}{\$223,333} = 2.2 \text{ (average turnover)}$$

▪ Application Exercise

1. Determine the turnover for a store, given the following data:

	Net Sales	Turnover
Dept. A	$150,300	1.5
Dept. B	50,500	3.0
Dept. C	250,800	2.4
Dept. D	175,700	1.8
Dept. E	280,300	4.3

2. A classification of men's shirts consisted of six sizes and exhibited the following activity:

Size	Net Sales	Turnover
14	$2,800	1.8
14½	4,300	2.6
15	5,500	4.1
15½	5,800	4.5
16	4,300	3.8
16½	4,000	3.2

What was the turnover for the entire classification?

3. A men's furnishings department consists of four classifications of merchandise, performing as follows:

Classification	Net Sales	Turnover
Shirts	$8,000	3.2
Ties	6,000	4.0
Hosiery	3,000	3.7
Jewelry	7,500	3.5

What is the departmental turnover?

4. A family-owned shoe store carries men's, women's, and children's footwear. Calculate the storewide turnover, using the following data:

Classification	Net Sales	Turnover
Men's shoes	$10,500	1.9
Women's shoes	18,300	2.6
Children's shoes	9,400	1.7

5. A jewelry department carried watches at four price points; given the following data, determine the turnover of the watch classification.

Price Points	Net Sales	Turnover
$23.98	$8,300	4.2
45.50	10,500	2.9
65.90	9,300	2.5
85.00	12,200	1.5

Calculation of the Average Turnover for the Unit, Given the Percentage of Net Sales and the Turnover for the Fractional Parts of the Unit

Unit sales, the ultimate determinant of turnover whether derived from the store, department, classification, or whatever, are always considered to be a "whole." That is, the unit, when defined in terms of net sales, is composed of various fractional components, the sum of which must always be equal to 100%; as previously discussed, net sales must always equal 100%.

▪ Study Problem

Given: A classification of men's shirts consisted of four colors; red, blue, white, and yellow. Net sales and turnover were apportioned in the following manner:

	Percentage of Total Sales	Turnover
Red	15	2.5
Blue	30	3.9
White	35	4.3
Yellow	20	2.7

Find: The average turnover for the men's shirt classification.

Solution:

Because we know that net sales are always 100% and that each color comprises a proportion of that percentage, any dollar value may be assigned to net sales because the ratio of colors sold is always constant to total sales. In this instance, assume sales to be $1,000 and proceed to solve the problem in exactly the same manner as the previous study problem.

	Percentage of Total Sales	$Sales	Turnover	Average Inventory
Red	15	150	2.5	$60
Blue	30	300	3.9	77
Yellow	20	200	2.7	74
White	35	350	4.3	81
Total	100	$1,000	?	$292

Classification turnover $= \dfrac{\$1,000}{\$292} = 3.4$

▪ Application Exercise

1. A major appliance store consisted of five departments, with net sales and turnover distributed as follows:

	Sales %	Turnover
Ranges	20	3.8
Washers	30	4.2
Dryers	25	4.5
Small electrics	10	3.5
Televisions	15	5.0

What is the average turnover for the major appliance store?

2. A music department consisted of three classifications of merchandise exhibiting the following characteristics:

	Percentage of Total Sales	Turnover
Instruments	60	2.8
Records and tapes	25	3.5
Sheet music	15	1.7

What is the average turnover in the music department?

Finding Turnover for One Part of a Unit, Given Average Unit Turnover, and Percentages of Net Sales and Turnover for Each Component Part

The essence of the concept is the determination of the turnover of a fractional part of a unit, when the average stock for the balance of the parts and the entire unit are known. Essentially, we proceed as in the previous study problem, but with a few minor variations.

▪ Study Problem

Given: A department that has three classifications, A, B, and C, is to be enlarged to include a fourth classification, D. It is planned that Classification A will do 35% of the department's volume with a turnover of 6.5, Classification B will do 20% of the volume with a stock turn of 4.5, and C will do 30% of the volume on a stock turn of 3.

Find: If Classification D is to consume the balance of the planned volume, or 15%, what must its turnover be to ensure a departmental turnover of 4?

Solution:

Assume the net sales to be $1,000, and determine the average stock for the store and Classifications A, B, and C.

	Percentage of Total Sales	$Sales	Turnover	Average Stock
Class. A	35	$350	6.5	$54
Class. B	20	200	4.5	44

Class. C	30	300	3.0	100
Class. D	15	150	?	?
Total	100	$1,000	4	$250

The total average stock for Classifications A, B, and C equals $198. The average stock for the department is $250. Therefore, the average stock for D must be equal to the difference between $250 and $198, or $52. And because

$$\text{Turnover} = \frac{\text{Sales}}{\text{Average stock}}$$

the turnover for Classification D will have to be

$$\frac{\$150}{\$52} = 2.9$$

∎ Application Exercise

1. A women's shoe store consists of three departments: shoes, hosiery, and slippers. The owner is contemplating adding handbags as a fourth department. Given the following information, determine the required turnover for the new handbag department if the store is to maintain an average turnover of 3.

	Sales %	*Turnover*
Shoes	40	2.5
Hosiery	30	4.0
Slippers	20	3.2
Handbags	10	?
Total store	100	3.0

2. The owner of a men's apparel shop has decided to increase the store's average turnover from 2.6 to 3. The inventory currently consists of merchandise divided into five departments exhibiting the following activities.

	Sales %	*Turnover*
Furnishings	10	3.7
Casual wear	25	3.3
Dress shirts	20	3.5
Outerwear	15	3.0
Suits	30	1.7

It has been determined that the 3 turnover goal can best be achieved by reducing the average inventory in the suit department while maintaining that department's current level of sales. By what percentage should the average suit inventory be decreased in order to achieve the total store turnover objective? What will the new turnover be for the suit department?

9.3

Capital Turnover

In contrast to inventory turnover, which defines the number of times that the average stock at retail has been sold and replaced, capital turnover measures the rate of return, in terms of retail dollars, achieved on the cost investment in inventory. Simply stated, inventory turnover expresses the relationship between net sales and the average stock at retail; capital turnover is the ratio of the average stock at cost to net sales, thus measuring the efficiency of cost dollars in the generation of retail dollars. Quantitatively stated,

$$\text{Capital turnover} = \frac{\text{Net sales}}{\text{Average inventory at cost}}$$

Capital turnover differs from inventory turnover in three essential ways.

1. While inventory turnover measures the number of times that the average stock at retail is converted to net sales, capital turnover defines the frequency with which the cost inventory is translated into retail dollars.

2. Inventory turnover requires that both the numerator and the denominator of the equation are always the same, either at retail or at cost. Capital turnover, however, dictates a retail numerator (net sales) and a cost denominator (inventory).

3. The ratio of capital turnover will always exceed the ratio of inventory turnover.

As an index of merchandising efficiency, the ratio of capital turnover should be of interest to the retail merchant because the values of the cost and retail inventories will directly correlate by means of the initial markon. This relationship will be further developed in the determination of the initial markon from capital and inventory turnover, to be discussed shortly.

Determination of Capital Turnover for a Given Period of Time

The essence of capital turnover lies in the number of times within a given period of time that a cost investment in inventory can be translated into net sales. Thus, it is not to be confused with the merchant's total capital commitment. We are only concerned with the dollar cost of net sales.

▪ Study Problem

Given: A gift shop had an opening inventory of $20,000 at cost and a closing inventory of $28,000 at cost.

Find: If net sales for the period amounted to $36,000, what was the capital turnover for the shop?

Solution:

As previously discussed, the average inventory, whether at cost or retail, is a product of the beginning inventory plus the sum of ending inventories divided by the number of inventories in the period. In this instance,

$$\text{Average cost inventory} = \frac{\$20,000 + \$28,000}{2} = \$24,000$$

$$\text{Capital turnover} = \frac{\$36,000 \text{ (Net sales)}}{\$24,000 \text{ (Average cost inventory)}} = 1.5$$

▪ Application Exercise

1. A candy department had an opening inventory at cost of $8,000. The closing cost inventory was $6,000. Net sales for the period totaled $21,000. What was the capital turnover?

2. Given the following information, determine the capital turnover for a women's coat department.

	Cost Inventory		Net Sales
	BOM	EOM	
February	$8,000	$7,000	$6,800
March	7,000	9,000	7,300
April	9,000	10,000	8,200

3. A candle shop had an opening inventory of $6,500 at cost. Additional cost purchases amounted to $22,800. Net sales for the period amounted to $23,800, leaving an ending inventory at cost of $4,900. What was the capital turnover experienced by the candle shop for this period of time?

4. On July 1, the inventory in a notions department was $23,000 at cost and $44,200 at retail. During the course of the month, additional purchases of $7,200 were made, markdowns amounted to $3,200, and net sales totaled $16,000. As of July 31, the book inventory revealed a stock on hand of $19,800 at cost and $39,600 at retail. What was the capital turnover for the notions department for the month of July?

5. A shoe department experienced the following merchandise activity for the first quarter of the year. Determine the capital turnover for the period.

BOM at Retail

January	$10,300
February	11,800
March	9,900
April	12,300

Gross sales	$8,400
Returns	10%
Cumulative markon	51%

Determination of the Initial Markon, Given Capital Turnover and Inventory Turnover

It has been previously stated that the values of the cost and retail inventories will directly correlate by means of the initial markon. These relationships are now explored in detail in this and the following two sections. The essential difference between stock turnover and capital turnover lies in the nature of the denominator of each equation:

$$\text{Stock turnover} = \frac{\text{Net sales}}{\text{Average stock at retail}}$$

$$\text{Capital turnover} = \frac{\text{Net sales}}{\text{Average stock at cost}}$$

The basic markon formula (see Chapter 2) is:

$$\text{Markon \%} = \frac{\$\text{Retail} - \$\text{Cost}}{\$\text{Retail}}$$

Therefore,

$$\text{Initial markon \%} = \frac{\$\text{Average stock at retail} - \$\text{Average stock at cost}}{\$\text{Average stock at retail}}$$

■ Study Problem

Given: A junior sportswear department had an inventory turnover of 5 and a capital turnover of 10.2.

Find: The percentage of initial markon.

Solution:

Assume net sales to be $1,000.[16]

$$\text{Average retail stock} = \frac{\text{Net sales}}{\text{Inventory turnover}} = \frac{\$1,000}{5} = \$200$$

$$\text{Average cost stock} = \frac{\text{Net sales}}{\text{Capital turnover}} = \frac{\$1,000}{10.2} = \$98$$

$$\text{Average retail stock} - \text{Average cost stock} = \text{Initial markon}$$

Therefore;

$$\text{\$Initial markon} = \$200 - \$98 = \$102$$

$$\text{Initial markon \%} = \frac{\$102}{\$200} = 51\%$$

Proof (and Alternate Solution):

$$\frac{\text{Capital turnover} - \text{Inventory turnover}}{\text{Capital turnover}} = \text{Initial markon \%}$$

Thus,

$$\text{Initial markon \%} = \frac{10.2 - 5}{10.2} = \frac{5.2}{10.2} = 51\%$$

■ Application Exercise

1. A men's shoe classification had an inventory turnover of 2.5 and a capital turnover of 5. Determine the initial markon percentage.

2. A linens and domestics department had a capital turnover of 5.5 and a stock turn of 3. What was the department's cumulative markon?

3. A jewelry shop had an inventory turnover of 5 and a capital turnover of 8. What was the initial markon percentage?

4. A men's tie classification had a capital turnover of 4 and an inventory turnover of 2.5. Calculate the initial markon percentage.

---

[16]Because the initial markon is a product of the relationship between inventory turnover and capital turnover, no specific sales volume is required. Thus, $1,000 is an arbitrary figure, selected for convenience. See proof and alternate solution.

5. A fur department had an inventory turnover of 1.5 and a capital turnover of 2.7. Define the cumulative markon.

Determination of Capital Turnover, Given the Initial Markon and Inventory Turnover

Capital turnover is the product of the initial markon and inventory turnover. Thus, it may be used not only to individually evaluate the correctness of the markon and turnover, but also the relationship between the two concepts.

■ Study Problem

Given: A men's clothing store had an inventory turnover of 5. The initial markon was 40%.

Find: The capital turnover.

Solution: Assume net sales to be $1,000.

$$\text{Average retail stock} = \frac{\text{Net sales}}{\text{Stock turnover}} = \frac{\$1,000}{5} = \$200$$

$$\text{Average cost stock} = \$200 \times (100\% - 40\%) = \$120$$

$$\text{Capital turnover} = \frac{\text{Net sales}}{\text{Average cost stock}} = \frac{\$1,000}{\$120} = 8.3$$

By reducing the average stock at retail to cost we have increased the turnover ratio by the amount equivalent to the cost complement of the initial markon, that is, $100\% - 40\% = 60\%$. In other words, by decreasing the retail inventory by 60%, we have increased the rate of turnover by a like amount.

The same results may be obtained by increasing the turnover ratio itself by dividing it by the cost complement of the initial markon.

Proof (and Alternate Solution):

$$5 \div (100\% - 40\%) = 8.3$$

■ Application Exercise

1. The inventory turnover in a maternity department is 4.2. The average initial markon is 53%. Determine the capital turnover.

2. A housewares department had a cumulative markon of 43% and a stock turn of 2. What was the capital turnover?

3. Determine the capital turnover of a lamp department with an initial markon of 46% and an inventory turnover of 2.5.

4. A classification of upholstered furniture turned its inventory 2.3 times annually. If the cumulative markon was 46.5%, what was the capital turnover?

5. The cumulative markon for a toy store was 40% with an inventory turnover of 3.3. What was the capital turnover?

Determination of the Inventory Turnover, Given the Capital Turnover and the Initial Markon

A predetermined rate of capital turnover and percentage of initial markon dictates a precise ratio of inventory turnover. Therefore, the merchant must be able to calculate the ratio of inventory turnover necessary to support the markon and rate of capital turnover.

▪ Study Problem

Given: A classification of men's ties had a capital turnover of 8 with an initial markon of 51%.

Find: The inventory turnover necessary to support the capital turnover and markon percentage.

Solution:

Assume net sales to be $1,000.

$$\text{Average cost stock} = \frac{\text{Net sales}}{\text{Capital turnover}} = \frac{\$1,000}{8} = \$125$$

$$\text{Average retail stock} = \$125 \div (100\% - 51\%) = \$255$$

$$\text{Inventory turnover} = \frac{\text{Net sales}}{\text{Average retail stock}} = \frac{\$1,000}{\$255} = 3.9$$

Proof (and Alternate Solution):

$$8 \times (100\% - 51\%) = 3.9$$

▪ Application Exercise

1. A small leather goods department had a cumulative markon of 52% and a capital stock turn of 7.7. What was the inventory turnover?

2. A classification of children's clothing had a 50% markon and a capital turnover of 8.4. Calculate the stock turn.

3. The capital turnover in a women's boutique was 9.8 with a cumulative markon of 51%. Determine the inventory turnover at retail.

4. A particular style of misses' suits carried an initial markon of 49.5% and experienced a capital turnover of 9.5. What was the stock turn?

5. A selection of men's red ties had a capital turnover of 8.7 and a cumulative markon of 54%. What was the stock turn for these red ties?

9.4

Gross Margin Return on Inventory (GMROI)

Gross margin return on inventory is a relatively new concept of inventory analysis that attempts to provide the merchant with a comprehensive index of product or classification performance, in terms of gross margin percentages and the rate of capital turnover. The objective of the GMROI index is to project and/or review inventory results from a return-on-investment point of view, wherein gross margin defines "return" and "investment" is simply the number of dollars the merchant has tied up in inventory. In essence, the GMROI index tries to measure the productivity of an inventory investment, using the model illustrated in Figure 13.1.

Figure 9.1 demonstrates that the GMROI index may be determined in either one of two ways:

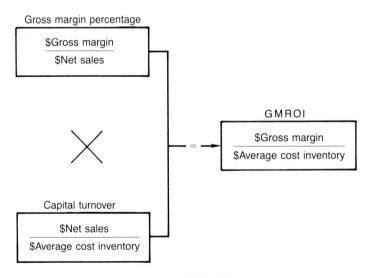

Figure 9.1 Gross margin return on inventory (GMROI)

1. Gross margin percentage times capital turnover.

2. Gross margin dollars divided by the average cost inventory.

For example, given the following data, the gross margin return on inventory may be calculated in the following two ways:

Gross margin   40%
Net sales $600
Stock turnover   3
Cumulative markon   45%

1. Gross margin = $600 × 40% = $240
   Average retail inventory = $600 ÷ 3 = $200
   Average cost inventory = $200 (100% − 45%) = $110
   Capital turnover = $600 ÷ $110 = $5.45[17]
   GMROI = $5.45 × 40% = $2.18[18]

2. GMROI = $240 ÷ $110 = $2.18[19]

   A third method for the determination of the GMROI is predicated on page 266. Capital turnover may be found by dividing inventory turnover (net sales ÷ average retail inventory) by the cost complement of the initial or cumulative markon percentage. Thus, in the above example, capital turnover is equal to the stock turnover (3) divided by 55% (100% − 45%), or $5.45. And because the GMROI is equal to capital turnover times the gross margin percentage, we find again that:

$$\text{GMROI} = \$5.45 \times 40\% = \$2.18$$

This concept provides us with the third, and most concise, formula for the calculation of the GMROI:

$$\text{GMROI} = \frac{\text{Inventory turnover}}{\text{Complement of initial markon \%}} \times \text{Gross margin \%}$$

   The above relationships sharply define the factors that contribute to a high GMROI—gross margin and the rate of inventory turnover. While circumstances may not permit the merchant to achieve a higher markon or reduction in oper-

---

[17]The actual turnover ratio is 545%, or 545 "times." However, it is here expressed as $5.45, indicating that for every $1.00 invested in inventory $5.45 is achieved in terms of net sales.
[18]Because gross margin is 40% of sales, it is of necessity also 40% of capital turnover. Therefore, the GMROI, or the gross margin dollars returned per dollar of cost inventory, is 40% of $5.45, or $2.18.
[19]Here we see that the gross margin is 218% of the cost inventory, or the gross margin return per dollar of cost inventory is $2.18.

ating expenses, this does not preclude a greater return on investment based upon an enhanced turnover ratio.

Using this formula in conjunction with previous observations, note the three-fold relationship between

1. Gross margin as a percentage of net sales,

2. Gross margin return on inventory (GMROI), and

3. Capital turnover.[20]

Given any two factors, the third may be readily established, either as projected goals or the product of past merchandise activities.

▪ Study Problem

Given: The following data:

Planned sales	$80,000
Gross margin	$33,600
Cumulative markon	$38,400
Stock turn	4

Find: The GMROI for a classification of men's suits.

Solution:

Gross margin % = $33,600 ÷ $80,000 = 42%
Cumulative markon % = $38,400 ÷ $80,000 = 48%

Average retail stock = $80,000 ÷ 4 = $20,000
Average cost stock = $20,000 × 52% = $10,400
Capital turnover = $80,000 ÷ $10,400 = $7.69

GMROI = $7.69 × 42% = $3.23

Proof (and Alternate Solution):

$$\text{GMROI} = \frac{\text{Gross margin dollars}}{\text{Average cost inventory}}$$

$$\text{GMROI} = \frac{\$33,600}{\$10,400} = \$3.23$$

---

[20]Capital turnover implies a knowledge of the initial or cumulative markon percentage and the rate of inventory turnover.

■ Application Exercise

1. A handbag and small-leather-goods department had a gross margin of $495 on net sales of $1,000. The average cost inventory was $127. What was the GMROI?

2. Net sales for a girls' clothing classification were planned at $12,000, using an average inventory at retail of $4,000. The cumulative markon was to be 51% and the gross margin was anticipated to be 47.5%. Assuming that all the planned figures materialized, what would be the expected GMROI?

3. A department planned a total cost of sales of 55% with a capital turnover of $8.60. Determine the anticipated GMROI.

4. The average inventory at cost is planned at $3,000 for a classification of china. Stock turn is expected to be 1.7 with a cumulative markon of 47%. Cost of sales is forecasted at 54%, with no cash discounts or workroom costs. What is the expected ratio of GMROI?

5. Given the following data, determine the GMROI for a men's furnishings department.

Net sales	$50,000
Cost of merchandise sold	$27,000
Average inventory at retail	$14,290
Cumulative markon	51%

6. An independent merchant planned activities for the spring season as follows:

Gross sales	$250,000
Returns and allowances	10%
Maintained markon	43%
Cash discounts	5%
Alteration costs	3%
Inventory turnover	3.5 times[21]
Cumulative markon	51%

Define the anticipated GMROI.

7. A merchant has set an annual GMROI goal of $3 for every $1 invested in inventory. Sales are planned at $800,000, with an inventory turnover of 4 times and a cumulative markon of 47%. What is the gross margin required to achieve the GMROI goal?

8. Given the following figures, what is the projected rate of inventory turnover for a junior sportswear department during the coming fall season?

---

[21]While inventory turnover is the ratio of the average inventory to net sales, it is normally expressed in terms of "times."

GMROI	$2.50
Gross margin	48%
Cumulative markon	55%

9. A costume jewelry department exhibited the following merchandising results last year:

Cumulative markon	52%
Net sales	$180,000
Stock turnover	3
Gross margin	49%

This year, the planned figures are as follows:

Cumulative markon	52%
Net sales	$200,000
Stock turnover	4
Gross margin	49%

Find the percentage of increase in the GMROI this year over last year.

■ Solutions to the Application Exercises

Determination of Turnover for One Month (p. 247)

1. Average inventory $= \dfrac{\$18,000 + \$15,000}{2} = \$16,500$

   Turnover $= \dfrac{\$3,435}{\$16,500} = .21$ (times)

3. Returns $= \$70,000 \times 7\% = \$4,900$

   Net sales $= \$70,000 - \$4,900 = \$65,100$

   Average inventory $= \dfrac{\$179,000 + \$140,500}{2} = \$159,750$

   Turnover $= \dfrac{\$65,100}{\$159,750} = .41$ (times)

5. Average inventory $= \dfrac{\$84,750 + \$79,800}{2} = \$82,275$

   Turnover $= \dfrac{\$45,350}{\$82,275} = .55$ (times)

Determination of Turnover at Cost for One Month (p. 248)

1. Average cost inventory $= \dfrac{\$142,500 + \$136,100}{2} = \$139,300$

   Turnover at cost $= \dfrac{\$32,000}{\$139,300} = .23$ (times)

3. Cost of sales $= \$13,000 \times 60\% = \$7,800$

   Average cost inventory $= \dfrac{\$17,000 + \$10,000}{2} = \$13,500$

   Turnover at cost $= \dfrac{\$7,800}{\$13,500} = .58$ (times)

5. Average retail inventory $= \dfrac{\$272,500 + \$283,300}{2} = \$277,900$

   (A) Turnover at retail $= \dfrac{\$83,500}{\$277,900} = .30$ (times)

   Cost of sales $= \$83,500 \times 60.8\% = \$50,768$

   BOM at cost $= \$272,500 \times 57.5\% = \$156,688$

   EOM at cost $= \$283,300 \times 57.5\% = \$162,898$

   Average cost inventory $= \dfrac{\$156,688 + \$162,898}{2} = \$159,733$

   (B) Turnover at cost $= \dfrac{\$50,768}{\$159,733} = .32$ (times)

Computation of Inventory Turnover for a Period of Several Months (p. 250)

1. Determine the average inventory, which consists of January's BOM plus the sum of the EOMs for January, February, and March. (The EOM is equal to the BOM for the following month.)

January	BOM	$5,667
January	EOM	6,467
February	EOM	7,533
March	EOM	7,400

   Total inventories $= \dfrac{\$27,067}{4} = \$6,767$ (average inventory)

Net sales total = $10,500

$$\text{Turnover} = \frac{\$10,500}{\$6,767} = 1.6 \text{ times}$$

3. Total sales at retail = $8,602

Total cost of sales = $8,602 × 55% = $4,731

$$\text{Average cost inventory} = \frac{\$4,924 + \$4,220 + \$4,910 + \$4,870}{4} = \$4,731$$

$$\text{Turnover at cost} = \frac{\$4,731}{\$4,731} = 1 \text{ (time)}$$

5. Average inventory at retail =

$$\frac{\$354,800 + \$354,200 + \$356,200 + 357,700 + \$358,600 + \$359,100 + \$358,500}{7} = \frac{\$2,499,100}{7} = \$357,014$$

Total net sales = $500,000

(A) $$\text{Turnover at retail} = \frac{\$500,000}{\$357,014} = 1.4 \text{ (times)}$$

Average cost inventory = $357,014 × 57.2% = $204,212

Cost of sales = $500,000 × 60.4% = $302,000

(B) $$\text{Turnover at cost} = \frac{\$302,000}{\$204,212} = 1.5 \text{ (times)}$$

Determination of Net Sales and the Average Inventory (p. 252)

1. Net sales = $166,000 × 3 = $498,000

3. $$\text{Average stock} = \frac{\$325,000}{2.2} = \$147,727$$

Average stock at cost = $147,727 × 50.5 = $74,602

5. Average retail inventory = $26,475 ÷ 59% = $44,873

Net sales = $44,873 × 7.7 = $345,522

Improving the Turnover Ratio by Reducing the Average Inventory While Maintaining a Constant Level of Net Sales (p. 254)

1. Average stock currently required $= \dfrac{\$208,500}{2.6} = \$80,192$

   Planned average stock $= \dfrac{\$208,500}{3} = \$69,500$

   Reduction in average stock $= \$80,192 - \$69,500 = \$10,692$

   Percentage reduction $= \dfrac{\$80,192 - \$69,500}{\$80,192} = \dfrac{\$10,692}{\$80,192} = 13.3\%$

3. Average inventory at 2.5 turns $= \dfrac{\$123,000}{2.5} = \$49,200$

   Average inventory at 3 turns $= \dfrac{\$123,000}{3} = \$41,000$

   Dollar reduction in inventory $= \$49,200 - \$41,000 = \$8,200$

   Percentage reduction $= \dfrac{\$49,200 - \$41,000}{\$49,200} = \dfrac{\$8,200}{\$49,200} = 16.7\%$

5. Last May average inventory $= \dfrac{\$30,000 + \$20,000}{2} = \$25,000$

   Last May net sales $= .4 \times \$25,000 = \$10,000$

   Average inventory this May $= \dfrac{\$10,000}{.6} = \$16,667$

   Dollar decrease in inventory $= \$25,000 - \$16,667 = \$8,333$

   Percentage decrease in inventory $= \dfrac{\$25,000 - \$16,667}{\$25,000} = \dfrac{\$8,333}{\$25,000} = 33.3\%$

Improving the Turnover Ratio by Increasing Net Sales While Maintaining a Constant Level of Inventory (p. 255)

1. Past sales $= 4.2 \times \$190,500 = \$800,100$

   Planned sales $= 4.7 \times \$190,500 = \$895,350$

   Dollar increase required $= \$895,350 - \$800,100 = \$95,250$

   Percentage increase required $= \dfrac{\$895,350 - \$800,100}{\$800,100} = \dfrac{\$95,250}{\$800,100} = 11.9\%$

3. Cost inventory must be converted to retail:

Retail inventory = $300,000 ÷ 73.5 = $408,163

Then,

Past sales = $408,163 × 4.2 = $1,714,285

Planned sales = $408,163 × 5.3 = $2,163,264

Dollar increase = $2,163,264 − $1,714,285 = $448,979

$$\text{Percentage increase} = \frac{\$2,163,264 - \$1,714,285}{\$1,714,285} = \frac{\$448,979}{\$1,714,285} = 26.2\%$$

5. Current sales = $23,000 × 4 = $92,000

Planned turnover ratio = 4 + (4 × 10%) = 4.4

Planned sales = $23,000 × 4.4 = $101,200

Required percentage increase in sales =
$$\frac{\$101,200 - \$92,000}{\$92,000} = \frac{\$9,200}{\$92,000} = 10\%$$

In other words, as long as the average inventory remains constant, the percentage increase (or decrease) in turnover will produce an equal percent of increase (or decrease) in net sales.

Determination of the Average Inventory Turnover for a Whole Unit, Given the Net Sales and the Stock Turns for the Constituent Parts of the Unit (p. 257)

		Net Sales	Turnover	Average Inventory
1.	Dept. A	$150,300	1.5	$100,200
	Dept. B	50,500	3.0	16,833
	Dept. C	250,800	2.4	104,500
	Dept. D	175,700	1.8	97,611
	Dept. E	280,300	4.3	65,186
	Total	$907,600	?	$384,330

$$\text{Turnover} = \frac{\$907,600}{\$384,330} = 2.4$$

	Classification	Net Sales	Turnover	Average Stock
3.	Shirts	$8,000	3.2	$2,500
	Ties	6,000	4.0	1,500
	Hosiery	3,000	3.7	811
	Jewelry	7,500	3.5	2,143
	Total	$24,500	?	$6,954

$$\text{Departmental turnover} = \frac{\$24,500}{\$6,954} = 3.5$$

	Price Points	Net Sales	Turnover	Average Stock
5.	$23.98	$8,300	4.2	$1,976
	45.50	10,500	2.9	3,621
	65.90	9,300	2.5	3,720
	85.00	12,200	1.5	8,133
	Total	$40,300	?	$17,450

$$\text{Watch classification turnover} = \frac{\$40,300}{\$17,450} = 2.3$$

Calculation of the Average Turnover for the Unit, Given the Percentage of Net Sales and the Turnover for the Fractional Parts of the Unit (p. 259)

1. Assume net sales to be $5,000. Then:

	Percentage of Total Sales	$Sales	Turnover	Average Stock
Ranges	20	$1,000	3.8	$263
Washers	30	1,500	4.2	357
Dryers	25	1,250	4.5	278
Small electrics	10	500	3.5	143
Televisions	15	750	5.0	150
Total	100%	$5,000	?	$1,191

$$\text{Average store turnover} = \frac{\$5,000}{\$1,191} = 4.2$$

Finding Turnover for One Part of a Unit, Given Average Unit Turnover, and Percentage of Net Sales and Turnover for Each Component Part (p. 261)

1. Assume net sales to be $1,000. Then:

	Percentage of Total Sales	$Sales	Turnover	Average Inventory
Shoes	40	$ 400	2.5	$160
Hosiery	30	300	4.0	75
Slippers	20	200	3.2	63
Handbags	10	100	?	?
Total store	100%	$1,000	3.0	$333

Average handbag stock = $333 − ($160 + $75 + $63) = $35

$$\text{Required handbag turnover} = \frac{\$100}{\$35} = 2.9$$

Determination of Capital Turnover for a Given Period of Time (p. 263)

1. $\text{Average cost inventory} = \dfrac{\$8,000 + \$6,000}{2} = \$7,000$

$$\text{Capital turnover} = \frac{\$21,000}{\$7,000} = 3$$

3. $\text{Average cost inventory} = \dfrac{\$6,500 + \$4,900}{2} = \$5,700$

$$\text{Capital turnover} = \frac{\$23,800}{\$5,700} = 4.2$$

5. $\text{Average cost inventory} = \dfrac{\$10,300 + \$11,800 + \$9,900 + \$12,300}{4}$

$$= \$11,075 \times 49\% = \$5,427$$

Net sales = $8,400 × 10% = $840
= $8,400 − $840 = $7,560

$$\text{Capital turnover} = \frac{\$7,560}{\$5,427} = 1.4$$

Determination of the Initial Markon, Given Capital Turnover and Inventory Turnover (p. 265)

1. Assume net sales to be $1,000.

$$\text{Average retail stock} = \frac{\$1,000}{2.5} = \$400$$

$$\text{Average cost stock} = \frac{\$1,000}{5} = \$200$$

$$\text{Initial markon \%} = \frac{\$400 - \$200}{\$400} = 50\%$$

Proof:

$$\frac{5 - 2.5}{5} = 50\%$$

3. Assume net sales of $1,000.

   Average retail stock $= \dfrac{\$1,000}{5} = \$200$

   Average cost stock $= \dfrac{\$1,000}{8} = \$125$

   Initial markon % $= \dfrac{\$200 - \$125}{\$200} = \dfrac{\$75}{\$200} = 37.5\%$

   Proof:

   $\dfrac{8 - 5}{8} = \dfrac{3}{8} = 37.5\%$

5. Assume net sales to be $1,000.

   Average retail stock $= \dfrac{\$1,000}{1.5} = \$666.67$

   Average cost stock $= \dfrac{\$1,000}{2.7} = \$370.37$

   Cumulative markon % $= \dfrac{\$666.67 - \$370.37}{\$666.67} = 44.4$

   Proof:

   $\dfrac{2.7 - 1.5}{2.7} = 44.4$

Determination of Capital Turnover, Given the Initial Markon and Inventory Turnover (p. 266)

1. Assume net sales to be $1,000.

   Average retail stock $- \dfrac{\$1,000}{4.2} = \$238$

   Average cost stock $= \$238 \times (100\% - 53\%) = \$112$

   Capital turnover $= \dfrac{\$1,000}{\$112} = 8.9$

   Proof:

   $4.2 \div (100\% - 53\%) = 8.9$

3. Assume net sales to be $1,000.

$$\text{Average retail stock} = \frac{\$1,000}{2.5} = \$400$$

Average cost stock = $400 × (100% − 46%) = $216

$$\text{Capital turnover} = \frac{\$1,000}{\$216} = 4.6$$

Proof:

2.5 ÷ (100% − 46%) = 4.6

5. Let net sales equal $1,000.

$$\text{Average retail stock} = \frac{\$1,000}{3.3} = \$303$$

Average cost stock = $303 × (100% − 40%) = $182

$$\text{Capital turnover} = \frac{\$1,000}{\$182} = 5.5$$

Proof:

3.3 ÷ (100% − 40%) = 5.5

Determination of the Inventory Turnover Given the Capital Turnover and the Initial Markon (p. 267)

1. Let net sales be equal to $1,000.

$$\text{Average cost stock} = \frac{\$1,000}{7.7} = \$130$$

Average retail stock = $130 ÷ (100% − 52%) = $271

$$\text{Inventory turnover} = \frac{\$1,000}{\$271} = 3.7$$

Proof:

7.7 × (100% − 52%) = 3.7

3. Net sales equal $1,000.

$$\text{Average cost stock} = \frac{\$1,000}{9.8} = \$102$$

Average retail stock = $102 ÷ (100% − 51%) = $208

$$\text{Inventory turnover} = \frac{\$1,000}{\$208} = 4.8$$

Proof:

$$98 \times (100\% - 51\%) = 4.8$$

5. Net sales are $1,000.

$$\text{Average cost stock} = \frac{\$1,000}{8.7} = \$115$$

$$\text{Average retail stock} = \$115 \div (100\% - 54\%) = \$250$$

$$\text{Stock turn} = \frac{\$1,000}{\$250} = 4$$

Proof:

$$8.7 \times (100\% - 54\%) = 4$$

Gross Margin Return on Inventory (GMROI) (p. 271)

1. $\dfrac{\$495}{\$1,000} \times \dfrac{\$1,000}{\$127} = 49.5\% \times \$7.87 = \$3.90$

3. Gross margin $= 100\% - 55\% = 45\%$

   GMROI $= 45\% \times \$8.60 = \$3.87$

5. Gross margin $\% = \dfrac{\$50,000 - \$27,000}{\$50,000} = 46\%$

   Average cost inventory $= \$14,290 \times 49\% = \$7,002$

   Capital turnover $= \$50,000 \div \$7,002 = \$7.14$

   GMROI $= \$7.14 \times 46\% = \$3.28$

   Or:

   $\text{GMROI} = \dfrac{\$23,000\,(\text{Gross margin})}{\$\,7,002\,(\text{Average cost stock})} = \$3.28$

7. $\text{Capital turnover} = \dfrac{\text{Inventory turnover}}{100\% - \text{Cumulative markon }\%}$

   GMROI $=$ Capital turnover $\times$ Gross margin $\%$

   Then,

   Gross margin $\% =$ GMROI $\div$ Capital turnover

   Capital turnover $= 4 \div 53\% = \$7.55$

Gross margin % $= \dfrac{\$3.00}{\$7.55} = 39.7\%$

Proof:

GMROI = $Gross margin ÷ Average cost inventory

Gross margin = $800,000 × 39.7% = $317,600

Average retail inventory = $800,000 ÷ 4 = $200,000

Average cost inventory = $200,000 × 53% = $106,000

GMROI = $317,600 ÷ $106,000 = $3.00

Or,

GMROI = Gross margin % × Capital turnover

GMROI = 39.7% × $7.55 = $3.00

9. Find the GMROI for last year:

Gross margin = $180,000 × 49% = $88,200

Average retail inventory = $180,000 ÷ 3 = $60,000

Average cost inventory = $60,000 × 48% = $28,800

GMROI = $88,200 ÷ $28,800 = $3.06

Planned GMROI this year:

Gross margin = $200,000 × 49% = $98,000

Average retail inventory = $200,000 ÷ 4 = $50,000

Average cost inventory = $50,000 × 48% = $24,000

GMROI = $98,000 ÷ $24,000 = $4,08

Percentage of increase $= \dfrac{\$4.08 - \$3.06}{\$3.06} = \dfrac{\$1.02}{\$3.06} = 33.3\%$

∎ ━━━

Topics for Discussion and Review

1. Discuss the concept of inventory turnover.

2. What is capital turnover?

3. Explain the concept of gross margin return on investment (GMROI).

4. What are the major elements of the profit margin?

5. How would you explain the "ideal" turnover ratio?

6. Discuss in detail the three methods of increasing stock turnover.

7. What are the advantages of a rapid inventory turnover?

8. What is hand-to-mouth buying? Discuss advantages and disadvantages.

9. Discuss the greatest disadvantage of a rapid stock turnover. What are some of the other problems that may result from a turnover that is too high?

10. How does capital turnover differ from stock turnover?

11. Why is the merchant able to obtain the initial markon from the relationship existing between stock turn and capital turn?

12. How would you explain the relationship between stock turnover and capital turnover? Why is it that if the two ratios are known, the initial markon may be computed?

13. What three methods may be used to compute the GMROI index? What are the three concepts that underlie those methods?

14. Explain the concept of merchandising productivity.

15. Explain turnover at cost and at retail. What is the essential difference, and what is the cause of this difference?

16. How would you calculate turnover for a fall season?

17. How would you forecast sales, if you know a department's average inventory and stock turn for the coming season?

18. How do you determine a department's average stock at cost for the coming season, if you know the cumulative markon, sales and stock turnover?

19. Assume that you want to increase your turnover from 1.8 to 2.3 and still maintain a sales volume equal to last year's. Explain how you would do this.

20. Explain how you would increase your turnover for next year and still maintain the current level of average inventory.

21. Explain how you would determine the average turnover for an entire store or department if you know the net sales and turnover for each department or classification.

22. Assuming that you know the percentage distribution of sizes and turnover within a classification, explain how you would determine the turnover for the entire classification.

23. Assuming that all the necessary information were available, explain how you would determine the turnover ratio for a new classification to be added to your department.

24. Given the initial markon and inventory turnover, how would you determine capital turnover?

25. If you know the initial markon and capital turnover, how would you determine the inventory turnover?

Chapter 10
Measuring Profit According to the Cost Method of Inventory

Learning Objectives

- Discuss the effects of inventory valuation on gross margin and operating profits.

- Explain the concept of inventory valuation in a rising wholesale market.

- Explain the concept of inventory valuation in a falling wholesale market.

- List the objectives of the dollar control of the retail inventory.

- Define the concept of the physical inventory.

- Define the concept of the perpetual inventory.

- Discuss the reasons for the determination of the book inventory.

- Explain the concept of the cost method of inventory valuation.

- Explain those types of situations where the cost method of inventory is best applied.

- Explain why, under the original-cost method without book inventory, the physical inventory is rarely, if ever, taken.

- Explain how the original-cost value of the inventory is determined.

- Identify the three major deficiencies inherent in the original-cost method without the book inventory.

- Describe five disadvantages of the original-cost method without book inventory.

- Explain how the book inventory at cost is calculated.

- Explain the effects of inventory shortage on operating profit.

- Discuss three methods of determining the market value of the physical inventory.

- Explain the effect of freight charges on the ending inventory.

Key Terms

Billed Cost: The cost price appearing on the vendor's invoice before the deduction of cash discounts but after any deductions for trade and/or quantity discounts (the term is herein used synonymously with "original cost").

Book Inventory: The amount of inventory at cost or retail shown to be on hand at any given time as a product of a perpetual inventory system.

Cost Method of Inventory: The determination of the original-cost value of the merchandise on hand by means of decoding the cost of each item on its individual price tag and totaling the results.

Cost of Net Sales: The difference between the beginning inventory at cost plus purchases at cost and the ending inventory at cost. In effect, the cost of net sales defines the individual or cumulative cost of merchandise sold to produce a specific amount of net sales.

Dollar Control: The management and control of retail inventories, including sales volume, in terms of dollars, rather than in terms of pieces, items, or units.

Gross Margin: The difference between net sales and the total merchandise cost.

Inventory: The composite cost or retail value of all the individual units of merchandise on hand at any given time.

Invoice: An itemized statement from a vendor that details merchandise charges and purchase items.

Invoice Cost: The merchandise cost incurred by a buyer and stated on an invoice; under a cost system of accounting, the invoice cost is net to the buyer after deducting trade, quantity, and cash discounts. Under the retail method of accounting, the invoice or billed cost is not affected by the cash discounts and is thus net to the buyer after deducting only the trade and quantity discounts.

Market Value: The wholesale value of an item of merchandise at any given time or place.

Marking Procedure: Preparing the retail price tags with pertinent selling information such as price, classification, style, color, size, cost (where appropriate) and attaching them to the merchandise.

One-Price Concept: A policy by which, at the same time, all customers pay the identical price for any given item of merchandise.

Open-to-Buy: When stated at the beginning of an accounting period, the concept is synonymous with planned purchases. The concept is normally defined as the dollar amount of merchandise that the merchant may order during the balance of a given accounting period.

Original Cost: The cost price originally paid to a vendor for an item of merchandise.

Periodic Inventory: The physical inventory conducted on a random basis, that is, from time to time; normally, fall and spring.

Perpetual Inventory: An ongoing accounting system of inventory control and analysis, normally maintained on a daily basis. Daily sales and retail reductions are subtracted from a beginning inventory, while purchases and other additions are added to it; the resulting figure at any given point in time is the book or ending inventory. While normally associated with the retail method of inventory, it is theoretically possible to maintain a perpetual inventory at cost.

Physical Inventory: The actual count of each item of merchandise on hand, normally at the end of an accounting period, compiled and totaled in terms of dollars and units, at either cost or retail.

Planned Purchases: The value of merchandise (normally, but not necessarily, stated at retail) that may be purchased during a given accounting period (usually one month).

Retail Method of Inventory: A method of estimating the cost of an ending inventory by translating the sum of the merchandise on hand at retail at the end of the period into its cost equivalent by use of the complement of the cumulative markon percentage.

Total Cost of Merchandise Sold: All expenses involved in the selling of merchandise. Determined by adding the billed cost of the merchandise to the transportation and workroom costs and deducting the cash discounts earned.

Total Merchandise Handled: The total of the opening inventory and additions to date.

Transaction: The business conducted between the retail merchant and the customer, defined as the sale, return, or exchange of merchandise, including the adjustment of the current selling price.

10.1

Inventory Control and the Valuation of the Ending Inventory

For any retail firm, regardless of its degree of complexity, the proper valuation of the merchandise on hand at the end of a fiscal period is essential, not only for the determination of immediate profitability, but also for the control and management of the ongoing inventory. As we have seen, the ending inventory for a given period is the beginning inventory for the ensuing period; thus, the incorrect valuation of the merchant's ending inventory tends to not only distort the current operating figures but also carries forward to adversely affect the profitability of the succeeding periods.

As a matter of practicality, the process that controls the merchant's inventory also dictates the value of the ending inventory, and it is this valuation of the closing inventory that is a vital consideration in the determination of merchandising profit. The valuation of the ending inventory involves far more than a consideration of the purchase price or retail price of the merchandise contained therein.

The Effects of Inventory Valuation on Gross Margin and Operating Profit

From our discussion of gross margin in Chapter 8, you will recall that the (gross) cost of merchandise sold is essentially the total merchandise handled minus the ending (or book) inventory, and the gross margin dollars result from subtracting the total cost of merchandise sold from net sales. The following abbreviated gross margin statement will serve to illustrate the point and refresh our memories:

	Cost	*Retail*
Net sales		$100,000
Total merchandise handled	$125,000	
Less ending inventory	70,000	
Less cost of merchandise sold		55,000
Gross margin		$45,000

In effect, gross margin is equal to net sales minus the cost of merchandise sold. However—and this is the major point to be made—the value placed upon the ending inventory will directly determine the cost of merchandise sold and thus indirectly influence the profits, or the gross margin, derived from the sale of that merchandise.

Let us assume that in the above example the ending inventory is correctly appraised at $70,000. Now consider the effects of overstating and understating the value of that closing inventory:

| | Overstated | | Understated | |
	Cost	Retail	Cost	Retail
Net sales		$100,000		$100,000
Total merchandise handled	$125,000		$125,000	
Less ending inventory	80,000		60,000	
Less cost of merchandise				
sold		45,000		65,000
Gross margin		$ 55,000		$ 35,000

It becomes readily apparent that to overstate the value of the closing inventory is to understate the cost of goods sold and thus to overstate gross margin and the resulting operating profit.[1] Conversely, to understate the value of the ending inventory increases the cost of goods sold and correspondingly decreases the gross margin and operating profit.

Either extreme in the valuation of the ending inventory is to be scrupulously avoided by the retail merchant, as the consequences can only negatively impact the true results of the merchandising operations. For example, overstatement of profits results in unnecessarily higher income tax liabilities, increased insurance costs, and capital expenditures and profit distributions predicated upon "paper profits," which in reality are illusory and thus contribute to a false sense of financial security. On the other hand, the undervaluation of the closing inventory tends to create the perception of a dearth of profit, which may well contribute to the unrealistic conservation of capital and operating expenditures, thus limiting the future growth of the retail firm.

Thus, the valuation of the ending inventory presents a real problem for the merchant, especially when required to report the correct profit figures for federal and state income tax purposes. Moreover, the merchandise planning process is directly affected because, to reiterate, the ending inventory for the current period is always the beginning inventory for the succeeding period. It is therefore incumbent upon the merchant to select a method of inventory valuation that realistically reflects the actual value of the inventory without the distortions of "paper" profits or losses.

Conservative Valuation of Inventory

Given the aforementioned consequences of a distorted inventory valuation, the merchant is advised to value the closing inventory so that the figures are realistically as low as possible, yet in accordance with sound legal and accounting practices. Under these circumstances, "realistic" is defined as "conservative," where the valuation of the closing inventory takes into consideration paper losses

---

[1]Operating expenses are not affected, and therefore operating profit will be distorted in relationship to the gross margin.

but not paper profits. The rule of thumb for the conservative valuation of the inventory is the "original cost or current market value, whichever is lower." Thus, each item in the ending inventory is to be appraised at what the merchant originally paid for it, or its current wholesale or replacement value, whichever figure is the more conservative amount. Consider the following two examples.

Inventory valuation in a rising wholesale market

A merchant is taking inventory on a classification of $10 ties. The original assortment consisted of 100 units at a cost of $4.50 each; the current inventory on hand is found to be 40 pieces; however, the market or replacement value of the ties has now risen to $5. Thus, given the choice between listing the remaining ties at the $4.50 cost or the $5 market value, the merchant elects the $4.50 cost for the following reasons:

1. $4.50 realistically represents the merchant's original-cost investment and is therefore the most conservative basis for the inventory valuation.

2. Using the $5 replacement value would increase the unit cost by $0.50, thus inflating the ending inventory by $20 (40 ties × $0.50), from $180 (40 ties × $4.50) to $200 (40 ties × $5). Accordingly, gross margin and operating profit would be increased by a like amount, resulting in a higher tax liability on an unrealistic "paper" profit. By valuing the inventory on a conservative basis, the merchant is anticipating losses, not gains, in the merchandising and operating profit.

Consider the financial ramifications of the merchant's decision to value the inventory at its original-cost price ($4.50) rather than the current market value ($5):

	Original Cost ($4.50)		Market Value ($5)	
	Cost	Retail	Cost	Retail
Net sales[2]		$600		$600
Total merchandise handled[3]	$450		$450	
Less ending inventory[4]	180		200	
Cost of goods sold		270		250
Gross margin		330		350
Less operating expenses		300		300
Operating profit		$ 30		$ 50

---

[2]100 ties − 40 ties = 60 ties sold. 60 × $10 = $600.
[3]$4.50 cost per tie × 100 ties.
[4]40 ties × $4.50 = $180; 40 ties × $5 = $200.

Notice that by electing to value the inventory at its original cost, the merchant has legitimately reduced the tax liabilities on both the ending inventory and the operating profit. Insurance costs on the inventory will also be proportionately decreased, thus, in theory (although not shown for the sake of simplicity), reducing operating costs and thereby further enhancing the real operating profit.

Inventory valuation in a falling wholesale market

In this instance, inventory is again being taken in the same department as previously described and under similar conditions, with the exception that the wholesale price of the merchandise has now fallen from $4.50 to $4. Once more, faced with a choice between the original cost ($4.50) and the current price ($4) with which to value the inventory, the merchant selects the lower $4 market valuation for the following reasons:

1. The rule, "original cost or current market value, whichever is lower," still prevails; $4, as the lower replacement cost, represents the most conservative price at which to value the closing inventory.

2. Again, valuing the inventory at the higher $4.50 cost would inflate the ending inventory and the succeeding gross margin and operating profits. By the conservative valuation of the inventory at current market prices, the merchant anticipates losses rather than profits and thus legitimately avoids the higher tax liabilities incurred through higher "paper" profits.

The following example demonstrates the financial results inherent in the merchant's immediate choice of either the market value or the original-cost basis for the valuation of the inventory:

	Original Cost ($4.50)		Market Value ($4)	
	Cost	*Retail*	*Cost*	*Retail*
Net sales		$600		$600
Total merchandise handled	$450		$450	
Less ending inventory	180		160	
Cost of merchandise sold		270		290
Gross margin		330		310
Less operating expenses		300		300
Operating profit		$ 30		$ 10

Thus, in either a rising or declining wholesale market, the most prudent basis for the valuation of the billed-cost inventory is always the lower of the original cost or the current market value. It is only by means of this conservative valuation of the closing inventory that the merchant can avoid an exaggeration of gross margin on the operating statement and the resulting accountability for higher federal, state, and local taxes. Moreover, operating expenses are reduced and merchandise planning and control are enhanced by using realistic merchandise values as the basis for sound decision making.

10.2

The Elements of Inventory Valuation

There are essentially two bases for the valuation of the retail inventory, either cost or the current selling price, and only three fundamental methods for arriving at that valuation: the physical inventory, the perpetual inventory, or some combination of the two.

Before we can delve into the methods of appraising the cost or retail values of a merchant's inventory, the concepts of the perpetual and physical inventory and their relationship to the dollar control of inventory investment must be discussed.

Dollar Control of the Retail Inventory

Dollar control of the retail inventory is the management of merchandise in stock in terms of dollars or values instead of units or pieces. For the retail merchant, such control implies the following specific objectives:

1. Inventory balanced to net sales.

2. Minimization of stock shortages.

3. Strict control of markdown dollars.

4. Known value of inventory investment by store, department, and classification.

5. Return per dollar of inventory investment by store, department, and classification.

Achieving dollar control objectives depends entirely on the merchant's ability to determine, at any time, the value of the inventory. The merchant's inability to correctly ascertain the value of the inventory on hand precludes an accurate calculation of the cost of goods sold, thus preventing a workable identification of gross margin and operating profit. Inventory dollar control is therefore concerned with the determination, at any specific time, of the value of the merchant's inventory. Two merchandising techniques for making this determination are available: physical and perpetual inventory.

The Physical Inventory

The physical inventory is simply the counting and recording of the unit amount and dollar value of the aggregate stock on hand at any given time. This elementary concept of the physical inventory belies the complexity of its nature and its importance as an essential feature of retail merchandise management. While the physical counting and listing of all the goods in stock at a particular time is an exceedingly costly and time-consuming process, viewed by most merchants as a "necessary evil," the physical inventory still remains as the only exact method of determining the precise quantity and value of the goods on hand. This is not to disallow other methods of inventory valuation, but only to affirm the physical inventory method as the most accurate reflection of the total value of the merchant's stock on hand. The accumulated inventory totals may be defined either in terms of the merchant's original cost or the marked retail prices.[5] The choice of either cost or retail valuation is dictated not so much by the concept of theoretical accuracy as it is by the mechanical process of arriving at a financially sound valuation of the inventory remaining on hand.

The Perpetual Inventory

The perpetual inventory derives its name from the fact that it is an ongoing, or running, inventory derived not from the physical counting of merchandise but from an accounting process whereby a beginning inventory is periodically increased by the total of additions and decreased by the sum of the reductions. When the process terminates, normally at the close of an accounting period, the ending figure is defined as the closing book inventory. Recall the following relationships from the study of gross margin in Chapter 8:

Net purchases	Net sales
Net transfers-in	Net markdowns
Net markups	Sales discounts
Transportation	Estimated shortages
Total additions	Total reductions

Therefore,

Book inventory = Beginning inventory + Additions − Deductions

---

[5]The physical inventory, aside from its cost and retail prices, may also be counted in terms of units. For financial purposes, i.e., dollar control, the value of the inventory is the prime consideration; for merchandise assortment decisions such as inventory replenishment and promotional activities, unit assortments are of major significance.

Book inventory is only an estimate, its accuracy depending entirely upon the recording and accounting process. The degree of correctness notwithstanding, the book inventory is still only an appraisal, or an approximation, of the value of the ending inventory; it remains for the physical inventory to determine by actual count the reality, or true value, of the closing inventory.

Reasons for the determination of the book inventory

Calculation and control of inventory shortages   The physical inventory provides the merchant with the knowledge of *what is* on hand, while the book inventory is a statement of *what should be* on hand. Thus, the difference between the physical inventory (what is) and the book inventory (what should be) is defined either as a shortage or an overage. A shortage occurs when the dollar value of the physical inventory is less than the book inventory; an overage is an excess dollar value of physical inventory over the dollar value of book inventory. Shortages result from clerical errors and physical merchandise losses; overages are almost always due to accounting errors.

Thus, comparing book inventory to physical inventory results provides the merchant with the only means of exposing inventory shortage; the control of inventory shortage depends upon the merchant's knowledge of that loss.

The control and enhancement of gross margin   The book inventory allows for the estimation of merchandising profit, normally done on a monthly basis. This is accomplished by substituting the book inventory amount for the physical inventory that would normally be used.[6] Assuming that the book inventory is free from clerical errors, the estimated cost of goods sold and resulting gross margin will be accurate to the extent of the unknown stock shortages, which should be relatively small.[7]

As opposed to merchandising profits derived from the annual or semiannual physical inventory, the book inventory provides estimated profits on a perpetual basis, thus allowing the merchant to modify tactics and even strategy according to the immediate demands of the retail marketplace.

Control of planned purchases   The book inventory, if determined on a periodic or monthly basis, guides the merchant in the determination of planned purchases, or what is more aptly defined as the open-to-buy.[8] The perpetual inventory provides

---

[6]See Chapter 8, "Computation of Gross Margin."
[7]Roughly 1% to 2.5%, depending upon the type of retail operation, classification, etc.
[8]Planned purchases: the dollar value (normally at retail) of merchandise that may be purchased during a given accounting period. When stated at the beginning of the period, usually a month, planned purchases are equivalent to open-to-buy. Open-to-buy, in the strict sense, defines the amount of merchandise that may be ordered during the balance of a period, whereas planned purchases designate the dollar value of merchandise to be purchased for an entire accounting period.

the merchant with a continuous record of the amount of stock on hand by department and classification at any given time, without the burden of the physical inventory. Thus, the predetermined ratio of inventory to net sales[9] is maintainable throughout the accounting period in accordance with customer demand and the expectations of the dollar return on the inventory investment.

Minimization of loss due to fire or other natural disasters   The book inventory will maximize the settlements obtained from insurance companies as a result of fire or other types of losses. Without the book inventory figure, the merchant lacks any basis for the substantiation of the value of lost or damaged merchandise and thus is legitimately at the mercy of the insurance carriers, which naturally strive to settle at the lowest possible figure.

10.3

The Cost Method of Inventory Valuation

As previously mentioned, there are essentially only two methods, or accounting systems, available to the retail merchant for determining the value of the inventory on hand. These are the cost and retail methods of accounting; the cost method values the merchandise at its original cost plus inbound freight less a consideration for depreciation, whereas the retail method values the inventory at its current selling, or retail, price. While the two systems theoretically achieve the same objective—the cost of the ending inventory—in methodology, they are diametrically opposed. Thus, the application of either system is dictated not so much by the end result but by the procedures required to achieve that result.

The remainder of this chapter will be devoted to an understanding and application of the concepts inherent in the cost method of inventory valuation; Chapter 11 will explore the retail method as an alternative system of inventory valuation.

Introduction

Historically, prior to the "one price for all" concept currently practiced by North American and European merchants, the cost price dominated the retail mentality;

---

[9]Here we speak to the stock-to-sales ratio, which defines the relationship between the stock on hand at the beginning of a period (or the end of a period) and the planned sales (or the net sales) for the period, normally one month. Quantitatively stated, the

$$\text{Stock-to-sales ratio} = \frac{\text{Beginning inventory}}{\text{Net sales}}$$

or

$$\text{Stock-to-sales ratio} = \frac{\text{Ending inventory}}{\text{Net sales}}$$

cost was fixed and known while the retail price (determined by haggling or bargaining) was a relatively unknown quantity. As a result, the small amount of merchandising data that was available was maintained at cost, and the ending inventory was simply an educated guess predicated upon an estimation of the achieved percentage of gross margin and the resulting total cost of merchandise sold.

Essentially, the concept is implemented in the following manner:

	Cost	Retail	$Markon	Markon%
Opening inventory	$40,000			
Additions (including freight)	8,000			
Total merchandise handled	$48,000			
Net sales		$16,000		
Less estimated closing inventory	38,400			
Less estimated cost of merchandise sold		9,600		
Estimated gross margin			$6,400	40%

Notice that the only known values are the cost of the total merchandise handled and net sales; the ending inventory is a relatively unknown value, an estimate, and thus precludes any accurate determination of the cost of goods sold and the ensuing gross margin.

This cost mentality prevails even today, especially among the small, independent retail merchants, due to its simple methodology and ease of comprehension. While it may not be statistically proven, there is little doubt that such a simplistic approach to the inherent complexities of retail merchandise management is the major contributor to the high incidence of retail failures, especially during the first five years of operation.

This is not to imply that the cost method of inventory valuation is essentially wrong, but only that such a system of merchandise control lends itself to false security predicated upon incorrect information. Indeed, the cost method is theoretically the most accurate means of inventory valuation, but only to the degree that the closing inventory is determined by a physical count of the goods on hand. And herein lies the intrinsic difficulty with the cost method of inventory: The realistic valuation of the merchandise remaining in stock is so complicated that it virtually prevents the implementation of any type of periodic inventory system, thus denying the merchant the ability to effectively control and manage the lifeblood of the retail operation—the inventory.

Limitations in Applying the Cost Method

The difficulties encountered in the cost method arise not so much from any theoretical considerations as they do from the indiscriminate application of that theory to all retail operations and merchandise classifications. Such utility is not to be the case; the cost method of inventory valuation yields satisfactory results only when limited in application to specific classifications of merchandise or particular types of retail operations, which are discussed next.

Small stores or shops

The cost method works best when the size of the retail store is relatively small, characterized by limited unit stocks, restricted price lines, and an inventory that is not necessarily defined in terms of departments or classifications. The cost method is particularly suited to a very specialized merchandise operation where the physical inventory at any given time is small in relation to sales and can be readily counted and summarized. Such operations may range in type from a simple retail business such as a newsstand or fruit and produce market to large and busy restaurants or workrooms in major metropolitan department stores.

In short, within those merchandising situations where the amount of the ending inventory is relatively small, so are the attendant management and control problems, and it is in just such an environment that the cost method is not only feasible but may also be the most desirable means of inventory regulation.

Where form utility is created

For certain types of retail stores and departments, the cost method of inventory valuation is mandatory. Here reference is made to any retail establishment or store department engaged in the manufacturing process, wherein merchandise is changed in form or has certain labor inputs that preclude the establishment of a retail price when the goods are received. Bakeries, prescription drug stores, and restaurants can only evaluate their inventories on the basis of the cost of raw materials, rather than the retail price of a product yet to be produced. A pound of flour is one thing; a loaf of bread or a piece of cake is yet another.

In the larger retail stores, form utility is created by the so-called nonretail operations, generally defined as workrooms or cost departments.[10] These operations are designed to provide convenience by means of a store-controlled, manufactured product or service. The concept of convenience aside, the "manufacturing" process, of necessity, implies the utilization of the cost method of inventory valuation and thus explains the origin of the term "cost department." Workroom costs consist of the expenses of labor and materials required to ensure the salability of merchandise; in ready-to-wear, they cover alternations; in furniture, they consist of polishing, finishing, and repairs; in appliances, they mean initial and follow-up servicing; in carpets and draperies, such cost refers to the cutting, sewing, and installation of merchandise; and so on.

---

[10]See Chapter 2.

High unit cost, low turnover inventories

The cost method of inventory valuation is particularly suitable in those situations where the composition and movement of the stock exhibits the following characteristics:

The unit value is high.

The transactions are relatively few.

The number of items carried in stock are limited.

The type of merchandise is not subject to abrupt or rapid changes in style— that is, the influence of fashion may be anticipated, rather than suddenly emerging as an unexpected and disruptive phenomenon.

Therefore, inventories consisting of big-ticket items such as furs, fine jewelry, automobiles, furniture, major appliances, and the like are all readily adaptable to the cost method of valuation.

The essence of the cost method, as the name obviously implies, is the determination of the cost value of the inventory on hand (the ending, or closing, inventory) at the precise time that the physical inventory is taken. This simplicity of concept, which attracts so many unsophisticated small merchants, misrepresents the complexity of implementing and maintaining the cost method in all but the most ideal of situations just described; for the average retail merchant engaged in a high volume of transactions across a multiplicity of merchandise classifications, the cost method is not only complex and burdensome, but it fails in its attempt to fairly and accurately define the value of the merchant's inventory. However, within the overall scheme of retail merchandising, the cost method does have its place and is worthy of consideration, if for no other reason than to lay a foundation for, and serve as a contrast to, the retail method of inventory. With these thoughts in mind, let us examine this concept of inventory valuation.

Essentially, we must look at the cost method from three distinct perspectives: original cost without book inventory; original cost with book inventory; and the lower of original cost, or market.

Original Cost Without Book Inventory

Under the original-cost method without book inventory, the cost value of the inventory may be determined only at the time that a physical inventory is conducted. In other words, the cost value of the inventory on hand remains an unknown quantity at all times except for those specific periods when the individual items of merchandise are counted and their cost value totaled. In theory, sound merchandising practice dictates that such an inventory should be taken at least twice a year, at the end of the spring and fall seasons. Experience indicates, however, that merchants operating under this cost method without book inventory rarely, if ever, engage in the taking of a physical inventory. This is fundamentally the result of the following conditions:

1. Without the book inventory as a basis for comparison, the dollar value of the merchandise on hand is a relatively meaningless figure.

2. The sheer immensity of counting and determining the cost value of literally thousands of units of merchandise totally confounds the average retail merchant.

Valuation of the Inventory at Original Cost

In order to determine the original-cost value of the inventory, the cost price of each individual item must be available at the time that the physical count takes place. This may be accomplished by indicating the cost price in code[11] on the price ticket of each item placed in stock; when the inventory is physically counted, the cost codes are translated into the original cost, posted on the inventory sheet, and totaled to arrive at the aggregate cost value of the inventory.

While again this may initially be perceived as a simple procedure, consider, for example, the arduous task of taking a physical inventory at cost in a women's specialty shop doing a modest $600,000 in net sales annually. Assuming that the cumulative markon is 50% and the turnover is 3, the average cost inventory would be $100,000. Assuming further that the average cost per item in stock is $10, we arrive at 10,000 units[12] to be counted, decoded, and totaled before the cost value of the merchandise on hand can be determined. Each individual item must be specifically accounted for because the same item received into stock at different times may well have a different cost price.[13]

Cost Coding

The cost code, which is placed on the price ticket during the marking procedure, essentially derives from three concepts: words or phrases, symbols, or the mutation of the original cost through the introduction of additional digits.

---

[11]The difference between the original-cost price and the current retail price is the item's gross margin; obviously, this information is not to be available either to the customer or the competition.

[12]Computed as follows:

$$\frac{\$600,000 \times 50\%}{3} = \$100,000$$

$100,000 \div \$10 = 10,000$ units

[13]It is to be remembered that the retail price, as previously discussed, is normally an average of many different cost prices.

Words or phrases

The easiest and most effective method of developing a cost code is to use words or phrases consisting of ten *different* letters corresponding to the digits 0 through 9. Consider the following illustration:

M	O	N	E	Y		T	A	L	K	S
0	1	2	3	4		5	6	7	8	9

Using the above example, the merchant's original-cost price of $12.43 would appear on the price ticket as ONYE. Any word or combination of words is acceptable, as long as the letters are not used more than once; a few additional examples are:

BANKRUPTCY	CALM SPRING	REPUBLICAN
SHOPLIFTER	COLD WATERS	BLUE MONDAY

Symbols

Although symbols may be employed to disguise the cost price, a word or phrase has been found to be easier to decipher and thus less prone to errors in transposition. Also, symbols require more time to write than letters or numbers. Nevertheless, the following is a commonly used example of a symbolic code to conceal the original-cost price.

1	2	3
4	5	6
7	8	9

0 = X

The original-cost price of $23.58 would therefore be written as

When a zero is involved in a cost price, such as $14.50, the code would appear as

Mutation of the original-cost price

The idea here is to translate the cost price into an apparently meaningless number, to both conceal or enhance the cost with additional accounting information. In the former case, a random number from 1 through 9 may be chosen and placed in front of the cost price, and at the same time added to each digit of that price, dropping the tens. For example, by applying the prefix 4 to a cost of $15.98, and also adding it to each of the four digits, that cost will be transformed into:

$$
\begin{array}{r}
\$4\ 1\ 5.9\ 8 \\
+\ \ 4\ 4.4\ 4 \\
\hline
=\ 4\ 5\ 9\ 3\ 2
\end{array}
$$

Decoding the cipher is essentially a process of subtraction, again dropping the tens:

$$
\begin{array}{r}
4\ 5\ 9\ 3\ 2 \\
-4\ 4\ 4\ 4\ 4 \\
\hline
=\ \$1\ 5.9\ 8
\end{array}
$$

In the latter instance, the merchant might decide to prefix the $15.98 with the year (91) and follow it with the month of receipt (09). Thus the original cost would be encoded on the price ticket as:

9 1 1 5 9 8 0 9

■ Application Exercise

1. Using the cost code "CUT FLOWERS," determine the original-cost value of the following items of merchandise currently on hand.[14]

    UTSF   OS
     LTR   UTL

2. Calculate the value of an ending inventory utilizing the symbolic code

$$
\begin{array}{|c|c|c|}
\hline
1 & 2 & 3 \\
\hline
4 & 5 & 6 \\
\hline
7 & 8 & 9 \\
\hline
\end{array}
\quad 0 = X,
$$

to define the cost price of the merchandise remaining in stock.

---

[14]These problems are offered not so much as a test of comprehension as they are an exercise to demonstrate the tediousness of the decoding process, even on an extremely limited basis.

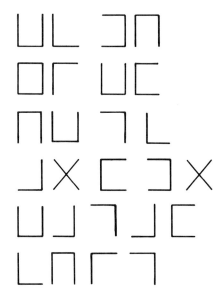

3. The following are original-cost prices encoded by the numeral 5. Decode the ciphers and establish the value of the ending inventory.

5 6 8 3 9	5 6 5 9 8	5 6 4 4 2
5 7 8 2 3	5 8 4 9 3	5 2 4 1 2
5 2 9 0	5 0 3 8	5 6 0 4

4. A furniture dealer is in the process of taking a physical inventory. The original-cost price has been encoded on the price tags, using the year and month of receipt. List the items according to the length of time in inventory, and find the total cost value of the ending inventory.

1 2 1 2 3 7 1 8 5	1 0 8 6 9 2 8 5	1 0 1 0 8 4 3 8 5
0 1 6 3 2 1 8 0	0 5 4 6 3 9 8 2	0 4 8 2 7 3 8 1
0 7 9 6 8 4 8 4	1 1 6 4 7 8 8 5	0 8 7 7 6 3 8 5

Determination of Profitability Using the Original-Cost Method Without Book Inventory

There are three major deficiencies inherent in the original-cost method of inventory valuation, as illustrated in the following study problem. The first shortcoming is that gross margin and operating profit cannot be determined until after the inventory on hand is physically valued. Thus, the merchant using the original-cost method and relying solely upon a physical inventory system can determine profitability only as often as the physical inventory is conducted.

The second defect within the original-cost method lies with its inability to account for retail reductions and transportation costs,[15] therefore failing to define the inventory in terms of its lowest value, either market or cost. In other words, the cost price of the inventory remains stable, or intact, and does not take into consideration the vagaries of the retail price resulting from markdowns, shortages, and sales discounts.

Lastly, a major negative consideration in the original-cost method without book inventory is that it fails to provide the merchant with a measure to define inventory shortages; the physical inventory only tells the merchant what is currently on hand, not what the ending inventory should be. Therefore, inventory shortages, while in reality always a major factor in the evaluation of merchandising effectiveness, always represent an unknown quantity.

▪ Study Problem

Before exploring the following problem, recall the following concepts:

Gross margin = Net sales − Cost of goods sold
Gross margin = Operating profit + Operating expenses
Operating profit = Gross margin − Operating expenses

Given: The following data[16] at cost (except net sales):

Net sales	$80,000	Ending inventory (6/30)	$36,000
Operating expenses	$27,000		
Beginning inventory (1/1)	$50,000	Purchases received	$35,000

Find: A merchant's operating profit for the period 1/1 through 6/30.

---

[15]While transportation charges are theoretically an integral part of the merchandise costs, the impracticality of prorating freight charges per shipment to individual items precludes their inclusion in the coded cost on the price ticket.
[16]Net sales is from the net receipts for the period. Beginning inventory is the ending inventory for the previous period, calculated by a count of the merchandise in stock at cost. Purchases are the total cost of the merchandise received during the period 1/1–6/30, derived from the sum of the invoice costs. The ending inventory is determined by a count of the merchandise on hand at cost as of 6/30.

Solution:

	Cost	*Retail*
Net sales		$80,000
Beginning inventory (1/1)	$50,000	
Purchases received	35,000	
Total merchandise handled	$85,000	
Less ending inventory (6/30)	36,000	
Cost of merchandise sold	$49,000 ⟶	(49,000)
Gross margin		$31,000
Less operating expenses		27,000
Operating profit		$ 4,000

▪ Application Exercise

1. Calculate the gross margin for an independent furniture store exhibiting the following merchandise characteristics:

Opening inventory at cost	$380,000
Merchandise returns and allowances	30,000
Closing inventory at cost	262,000
Gross sales	300,000
Purchases at cost	30,000

2. The ending inventory in a luggage department, derived from the coded cost on the price tags, was $83,000. Net sales for the period were $125,000. The beginning inventory at cost was $130,000, and the cost of additional purchases amounted to $18,000. Assuming that the operating expenses were $55,000, what was the operating profit as a percentage of sales?

Disadvantages of the Original-Cost Method Without Book Inventory

In the light of the foregoing discussion, it may be concluded that for retail establishments with large and/or diversified inventories, the original-cost method without a book inventory has the following limitations and disadvantages:

1. The decoding of the individual cost prices is tedious, time consuming, and highly prone to error.

2. Since the method makes no provisions for the recording and application of markdowns to the cost price, the depreciation of the inventory to the lower cost or market value tends to rest upon subjective value judgments rather than

realistic data. As a result, the value of the ending inventory and ensuing gross margin are subject to a wide range of distortion.[17]

3. The system fails to provide a book inventory against which the physical inventory can be compared to determine the extent of inventory shortage.

4. Financial statements cannot be prepared with any degree of accuracy until the physical inventory is taken.

5. Comparison of merchandising and operating ratios with similar retail establishments cannot be accomplished until the merchandise on hand is physically counted and valued.

As a result of the previous limitations, the original-cost method of inventory valuation without the book inventory generally fails to provide the merchant with the financial tools necessary to control and manage the inventory on a day-to-day basis.

Original Cost with Book Inventory

The introduction of a perpetual inventory system and its resultant book inventory into the original-cost method of inventory management lessens the problems of infrequent financial statements and shortage control by maintaining a running total of the cost value of the inventory on hand at any particular time. However, the essence of the original-cost method remains intact, along with two of its most serious defects: the tedious task of decoding the individual original-cost prices and the failure to define the inventory in terms of its lowest value, cost or market.

Using the original-cost method with a book inventory, the merchant must record each individual sale or transaction at its original-cost price and maintain a perpetual inventory system at cost.[18]

Determination of the Cost of Sales

The costing of each transaction is normally accomplished by either of two methods:

1. A multipart price ticket containing the coded original-cost and retail price is attached to each individual item of merchandise. At the point of sale, a section of the ticket is detached and retained by the merchant for later decoding and posting of the cost price. The total of these cost prices for any given period of time represents the cost of net sales, or the total cost of the merchandise that produced the achieved net sales figure.

---

[17]Specific methods for the determination of market value will be discussed in the following section.
[18]Book inventory is the *product* of a perpetual inventory system, not the system itself.

2. The coded cost price may be recorded on a two-part sales check, the original of which is given to the customer and the duplicate retained by the merchant as a source of costing data.

Calculation of the Book Inventory at Cost

The book inventory at cost is derived from the perpetual cost inventory by adding purchases to the cost value of the beginning inventory and deducting the cost of merchandise sold. The resulting figure is the original-cost value of the merchandise on hand, or the book inventory at cost, which contributes to merchandising efficiency in a two-fold manner:

Financial statements can be prepared on a periodic basis (normally monthly).

Inventory shortages can be determined from a comparison of the physical inventory with the book inventory, thus providing for a more accurate determination of operating profit.

Illustrated below is a perpetual inventory system at cost for the spring season and the application of its consequential book inventory to a six-month operating statement. As you study the calculations, note the absence of any provisions for the determination and inclusion of markdowns, sales discounts, and estimated stock shortages in the system. Thus, the book inventory and the resulting operating statement will be inaccurate to the extent that these factors are present in the merchant's operation.[19]

The perpetual inventory system at cost[20]

Date	BOM Inventory	+	Purchases	–	Sales (Cost of)	=	EOM[21] Book Inventory
2/1–2/28	$400,000		$50,000		$123,000		$327,000
3/1–3/31	327,000		43,000		112,000		258,000
4/1–4/30	258,000		62,000		90,000		230,000
5/1–5/30	230,000		83,000		98,000		215,000
6/1–6/30	215,000		96,000		110,000		201,000
7/1–7/31	201,000		33,000		81,000		153,000
Total (as of 7/31)			$367,000		$614,000		

---

[19]While it is true that the taking of a physical inventory will determine the extent of actual shortage, i.e., the difference between "what is" and "what should be," no inventory taken at original cost can account for the depreciation factor incurred through markdowns, sales discounts, and the general "aging process" of the merchandise.

[20]All figures are at cost, including sales. Note that the EOM inventory is the BOM inventory for the coming month.

[21]The book inventory is the ending inventory in the sense that the book inventory defines the cost value of the merchandise on hand at the end of the month. The book inventory, by definition, is always an ending inventory; however, this is not to imply that an ending inventory is always a book inventory.

By using the data compiled from the above perpetual inventory system and including net sales of $1,023,300 and operating expenses of $359,000 for the spring season, we are able to construct the following operating statement:

	Cost	Retail	Markon %
Sales		$1,023,300	
Beginning inventory	$400,000		
Purchases	367,000		
Total merchandise handled	$767,000		
Less ending (book) inventory (7/31)	153,000		
Cost of merchandise sold	$614,000 ⟶	(614,000)	
Gross margin		$ 409,300	40
Less operating expenses	$359,000 ⟶	(359,000)	
Operating profit		$ 50,300	4.9

Notice the key role that the book inventory plays in the determination of operating profit: It directly defines the cost of merchandise sold and the gross margin, and in conjunction with operating expenses, indirectly controls the amount of operating profit. All else being equal, the operating profit will vary in direct accordance with the accuracy by which the book inventory reflects the true value of the merchandise remaining in the inventory. The book inventory at cost is simply an estimated accounting figure on a financial statement, whereas "the true value of the merchandise remaining in the inventory" implies the physical inventory, wherein

A specific number of items of merchandise are known to be on hand.

The actual utility of those items is collectively defined in terms of its original-cost or existing market value, whichever is currently the lower.

Obviously, the two concepts do not represent the same dollar value under the cost method; as previously mentioned and here reiterated for the sake of emphasis, the book inventory is to be distinguished from "the true value of the merchandise" (i.e., the physical inventory) by

Shortage, the excess of book inventory over the actual physical inventory valued at original cost.

The difference between the current market value of that physical inventory and its original-cost price.

Using "the perpetual inventory system at cost" and its application to the operating statement as study problems, determine the solutions for the following application exercises.

▪ Application Exercise

1. Determine the book inventory at cost for a fur department, using the following cost data:

Cost of sales	$87,000
Opening inventory	103,000
Additional purchases	25,000

2. A fine-jewelry department recorded the following information at cost for the first quarter of the fiscal year. Determine the book inventory at cost at the end of the quarter.

   Beginning inventory = $300,000

	Cost of Sales	Purchases
January	$150,000	$43,000
February	123,000	50,000
March	96,000	85,000

3. Given the following merchandise information, prepare the June operating statement for a small independent furniture and appliance store. All data are at cost except net sales.

Net sales	$800,000
Cost of sales	440,000
Beginning inventory	640,000
Net purchases	150,000
Operating expenses	328,000

4. Determine the profit or loss incurred by a piano/organ department for the fall season, using the following cost data:

Net sales	$1,575,000
Beginning inventory 8/1	500,000

	Purchases	Cost of Sales
August	$97,000	$250,000
September	200,000	320,000
October	350,000	285,000
November	150,000	320,000
December	250,000	225,000
January	130,000	175,000

   Operating expenses = $386,000

The Effects of Inventory Shortage on Operating Profit

The effects of a relatively small percentage of inventory shortage can be extremely detrimental to a small retail merchant's profit structure, particularly when the original-cost method is being used. This is because of the insidious nature of the factors contributing to shortages (pilferage, damages, and poor record keeping) and by the very structure of the cost method itself. As has been pointed out, the valuation of the inventory on an original-cost basis tends to inhibit the taking of the physical inventory and at the same time makes no provision in the perpetual inventory for the anticipation of shortages. More often than not, the awareness of stock shortages comes as a total surprise to the merchant operating under these conditions, frequently with disastrous results.

Consider the effects of inventory shortages as they impinge upon the previously discussed operating statement (p. 307). Assume that a physical inventory has been taken on 7/31 to validate the $153,000 book inventory. By means of decoding and totaling the cost price of each individual item, the original-cost value of the merchandise on hand was found to be $127,500. Thus, the shortage figure is $25,500, the amount by which the stated value of the book inventory exceeds the actual value of the physical inventory. In view of the above shortage figure, the revised operating statement is illustrated as follows:

	Cost	Retail	Markon %
Sales		$1,023,300	
Beginning inventory	$400,000		
Purchases	367,000		
Total merchandise handled	$767,000		
Less ending (book) inventory (7/31)	153,000		
Cost of merchandise sold (unadjusted)	$614,000		
Inventory shortage	25,500		2.5
Cost of merchandise sold (adjusted)	$639,500 ⟶	(639,500)	
Gross margin		$ 383,800	37.5
Less operating expenses	$359,000 ⟶	359,000	
Operating profit		$ 24,800	2.4

Notice that the cost of merchandise sold has been increased by the amount of the shortage and the resulting gross margin and operating profit decreased by a like amount. In other words, under the original-cost method, the inventory shortages must obviously be defined in terms of cost, and as a result, they directly and totally impact the gross margin and ensuing operating profit. As we have seen from our study of gross margin and will see again when we consider the retail method of inventory, this is not the case when stock shortages are recorded in terms of their retail value.

As this revised operating statement shows, what may appear to be a relatively small shortage when compared to net sales can have a devastating effect upon operating profit. The $25,500 in shortages represents only 2.5% of sales, but consider its effect upon gross margin and the operating profit:

1. Gross margin falls from $409,300 to $383,800; this represents the amount of the shortage, $25,500, or a 6.2% decline.

2. Operating profit also drops by $25,500, from $50,300 to $24,800, or a whopping 50.7%!

For the retail merchant, inventory shortages are to be accepted as an essential characteristic of the business; to question the existence of a shortage is simply to ignore the realities of merchandising activities. Thus, the question to be addressed is not so much the presence of shortages but the amount of those shortages already present.

The concept of inventory shortage identifies a major flaw in the original-cost method of inventory, even with the use of the book inventory. That is, the determination of shortages depends upon the taking of a physical inventory, which because of its arduous requirements is seldom if ever carried out in the properly prescribed manner. As a result, the presence of shortages remains largely undetected until the "moment of truth" arrives, at which time remedial action is often "too little, too late."

▪ Application Exercise

1. Determine the actual "cost of merchandise sold" from the following cost information:

BOM inventory	$2,000
Book inventory	$1,600
Purchases	$800
Physical inventory	$1,300

2. An antique dealer experienced net sales of $20,000 for the second quarter. All other data were recorded at cost and offered as follows:

Opening inventory	$7,500
Purchases	$14,000
Cost of sales	$9,000
Operating expenses	$5,800
Ending physical inventory	$11,300

Determine book inventory, stock shortage, actual cost of merchandise sold, gross margin, and operating profit.

Determination of the Market Value of the Physical Inventory

As we have just seen, the higher the value of the ending (book) inventory, the lower the cost of merchandise sold, and thus the greater the gross margin and operating profit. Because the value of the inventory establishes the basis for the rate of real property taxation and insurance premiums, and the amount of net profit determines the liability for income taxes, it obviously follows that, within the limits of legality, the ending inventory should be appraised relative to the lower of its current market (wholesale) value or its original-cost price.

The original-cost method, upon which this chapter has so far been predicated, is entirely satisfactory for basic-type merchandise, where the cost price is stable and depreciation is negligible; the value of such merchandise at the time of inventory reporting is approximately equal to the price that was originally paid for it. However, for fashion merchandise, or basic stock that may have depreciated in value prior to the inventory statement, the original-cost method defers depreciation losses to the period in which the merchandise is sold, rather than to the time frame in which the losses became apparent. For example, if the inventory is currently valued at a $14,000 original-cost figure when it can be replaced today at a market value of $11,000, the operating profit will not be reduced by the $3,000 depreciation that has taken place. Thus, tax liability on both the inventory and profits will be unrealistically high, because it will be predicated upon the "paper" value of an inflated inventory rather than its replacement, or current market, value.

If the physical inventory is taken at the original-cost price, there are generally three methods of distinguishing that cost from the current market value, so as to allow the merchant to apply the advantages of the lower of the two assessments; these are the aging, the quotation, and the markdown methods.

The aging method

The aging method arbitrarily depreciates the original-cost value of the inventory on the basis of predetermined losses accrued over specific periods of time. For example, it may be determined that a particular classification of merchandise may be carried in inventory for up to three months at its original-cost price, after which time a 30% markdown is taken, reducing the value of the inventory to 70% of its original cost, or its currently perceived market value. Given another three-month period during which the merchandise still does not sell, yet another 30% markdown may be taken, thus still further reducing the market value of the inventory to 40% of its original cost. Assuming that the inventory, or any portion of it, still remains unsold, this devaluation process may continue until such time that any remaining merchandise is fully depreciated and its current market value is zero. This is illustrated below:

Age (Months)	Original Cost	Markdown %	Depreciation[22] %	Current Market Value
0–3	$100,000	-0-	-0-	$100,000
3–6	100,000	30	30	70,000
6–9	100,000	30	60	40,000
9–12	100,000	30	90	10,000
Over 12	100,000	10	100	-0-

Given the legality of the situation, the time frame and rate of depreciation are entirely at the individual merchant's discretion. Obviously, fashion merchandise will "age" faster than staple merchandise, and the aging process in general will tend to vary from store to store and within individual stores by department, classification, and style.

▪ Study Problem

The depreciation schedule for a particular classification of merchandise dictated the following course of action:

Given: A 25% markdown was to be taken after merchandise was in inventory three months and an additional 30% was to be taken after five months. Merchandise still on hand between eight and twelve months was to be reduced by another 40%, after which time any remaining stock was to be fully depreciated and donated to charity.

Find: The market value of the following ending inventory, including the percentage of total depreciation from its original-cost value. Assume that the inventory is conducted on an annual basis.

---

[22]The rate of depreciation and the current market values are predicated upon an annual inventory; this is a fair assumption under the cost method. The depreciation rate itself is illustrated as a result of a series of markdowns, or a cumulative markdown, i.e., 30% + 30% + 30% + 10% = 100%, only to demonstrate a "textbook" relationship between markdowns and depreciation to date. Therefore, merchandise found in inventory that is six to nine months old may be assumed to have depreciated 60% only because it has not been previously recognized and reduced, say between three and six months. Had the merchandise been marked down after three months, its market value would have been $70,000 and any subsequent reductions would have to be predicated upon that figure, rather than the $100,000 original cost. That being the case, the markdown percentage would obviously have to change.

Age (Months)	Original Cost
0–3	$43,000
3–5	21,000
5–8	8,000
8–12	3,000
12– +	1,250

Solution:

Set up a schedule of depreciation and determine the market value as follows:

Age (Months)	Original Cost	Markdown %	Depreciation %	Market Value
0–3	$43,000	-0-	-0-	$43,000
3–5	21,000	25	25	15,750
5–8	8,000	30	55	3,600
8–12	3,000	40	95	150
12– +	1,250	5	100	-0-
	$76,250			$62,500

$$\text{Percentage of depreciation} = \frac{\$76,250 - \$62,500}{\$76,250} = 18\%$$

▪ Application Exercise

1. A merchant has determined that after six months in inventory a specific classification of fashion merchandise will have a market value of 73% of its original-cost price. Assuming that the original-cost price of the inventory is $73,500, what is the required markdown, in terms of percentage and dollars, and the resulting market value?

2. Determine the market value of an ending inventory for the spring season, given the following data:

Original-cost value = $83,600

Depreciation Schedule		
Age (Months)	% on Hand	Depreciation %
0–2	60	-0-
2–4	20	40
4–6	15	80
6– +	5	100

3. Calculate the total percentage of depreciation allowable for a sportswear boutique as determined from a closing original-cost inventory of $163,000, using the following depreciation rates:

Age (Months)	Merchandise on Hand	Depreciation %
0–2	$110,000	-0-
2–5	25,000	20
5–8	15,500	40
8–10	10,300	60
10–12	2,200	80

4. A men's clothing store has just completed an annual inventory at original cost. The merchandise is divided into five classifications: shoes, furnishings, sportswear, suits, and outerwear. The cost code being utilized is "MONEY TALKS."[23] The inventory reveals the following merchandise to be on hand:

86	pairs of shoes coded	EMTM
150	suits coded	ONTEM
200	topcoats coded	OTMNT
300	shirts coded	ONNE
250	ties coded	LKM
254	jackets coded	AOEM
200	pairs of slacks coded	ETYT

Because the image of the store projects a total fashion story, the owner believes that all merchandise, regardless of classification, should be depreciated at the same rate. Therefore, a storewide depreciation schedule has been established as follows:

Age (Months)	Depreciation %
2–3	20
3–6	30
6–9	40
9–12	50

The results of the annual inventory reveal: 70% is from two to three months old; 15% is from three to six months old; 10% is from six to nine months old; 5% is from nine to twelve months old.

a. Determine the total original-cost value of the ending inventory by classification.

[23]See page 300.

b. Determine the total market value of the ending inventory and the ratio of depreciation from original cost.

The quotation method

Another widely used method of translating the original-cost value of the physical inventory into its complementary market value is to use the current price quotations available from vendor or market resources. Such information may be obtained from price lists, vendors' catalogs, market quotations in trade publications, or by direct inquiry of primary sources.

This method poses two major problems:

1. It fails to take into consideration damaged, shopworn, or otherwise imperfect merchandise, which could constitute a sizable portion of the merchant's inventory.

2. The magnitude of the task of obtaining and applying market quotations for literally thousands of heterogeneous items in the inventory limits the use of the quotation method primarily to basic items, handled in relatively large unit quantities.

Although not worthy of any mathematical consideration, the essence of the quotation method is to determine the original-cost value of the closing inventory and then to reprice at cost each individual item according to the dictates of the current wholesale market. Obviously, the simplicity of the concept misrepresents the complexity of its application; the task is laborious and time consuming, and the results are generally not satisfactory in all but the most simplistic of merchandising operations.

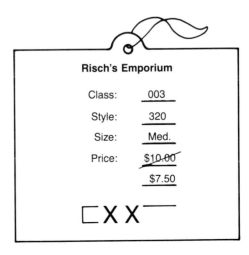

The markdown method

The markdown method of determining the depreciation of the original-cost value of an inventory rests upon the assumption that the market, or wholesale, value of that inventory is a direct function of the current selling price. Simply stated, a 25% reduction in the retail price of an item automatically implies a 25% reduction in its cost, or replacement, value. The logic of the situation is predicated upon the fact that markon determines profitability, and because markon is composed of the difference between the cost and retail price, achieving profitability depends entirely upon the compatibility of cost and retail in terms of a specific percentage of markon. Thus, what the merchant is willing to pay for merchandise (the market value) is totally dependent upon the demands of the retail market, or that retail price actually supported by the store's clientele. For example, operating under the assumption that a 40% markon is required to sustain a particular retail operation, a merchant purchases an item for $6 and plans to retail it for $10.[24] Should the customer fail to accept the $10 price, the merchant may be forced to take a markdown of, say, 25%, thus reducing the original retail price of $10 to $7.50 and the resulting markon from 40% to 15%.[25] Now, while the item may sell well at $7.50, it is currently not worth its original-cost price of $6, nor can the merchant sustain that cost in the event of any future repurchases. As a result, the original-cost value of the item, whether or not currently in inventory, must be reduced by a percentage equivalent to the amount of the markdown. In this instance, the $6 original cost must be depreciated by 25% (or $1.50) to $4.50 so as to reflect its current market value in the inventory and at the same time establish the cost basis for any repurchase decision.[26]

Using this data, consider the following practical application of the markdown method of inventory valuation, as it relates to an individual item of merchandise.[27] Notice that the price tag shows the original retail price of $10 reduced to $7.50, plus the coded original-cost price of $6 at the bottom.[28] Given this data, we may now proceed to determine the dollar amount and percentage by which to depreciate the original-cost value of the item and determine its current market value.

---

[24] $\dfrac{\$10 - \$6}{\$10} = 40\%$

[25] $\dfrac{\$7.50 - \$6}{\$10} = 15\%$

[26] $\dfrac{\$7.50 - \$4.50}{\$7.50} = 40\%$

[27] Under the cost method of inventory valuation, each item must receive individual consideration, clearly an obstacle to its implementation.

[28]

1	2	3
4	5	6
7	8	9

$0 = X$

$$\text{Markdown \% (at retail)} = \frac{\$10 - \$7.50}{\$10} = 25\%$$

Equivalent replacement cost (at the new retail price), or the current market value = $6 (100\% - 25\%) = \$4.50$

$\$\text{Depreciation} = \$6 - \$4.50 = \$1.50$

$$\text{Depreciation \%} = \frac{\$6 - \$4.50}{\$6} = 25\%[29]$$

Alternate solution:

$$\text{Original markon \%} = \frac{\$10 - \$6}{\$10} = 40\%$$

Equivalent cost for new retail and current market value = $7.50 (100\% - 40\%) = \$4.50$

$\$\text{Depreciation} = \$6 - \$4.50 = \$1.50$

$$\text{Depreciation \%} = \frac{\$6 - \$4.50}{\$6} = 25\%$$

The major disadvantage of the markdown method lies not so much with the complexity of the concept as it does with the implementation of the system under the cost method of inventory valuation. Not only are numerous calculations required per unit, but these computations must be multiplied times the number of units in the inventory. Consider, for example, the task of maintaining accurate records for literally thousands of items when each item must be individually and uniquely accounted for:

All price tags must at least carry the original and current retail values along with the coded original-cost price.

Markon percentages must be computed for each item in the inventory that has been marked down.

The current market value for each item reduced must be determined from the existing retail price.

---

[29]Notice that the markdown percentage at cost must be equivalent to that taken at retail, if the markon percentage is to remain intact.

■ Application Exercise

1. The original-cost value of a dress was $32.45, and the first retail price was established at $59. After remaining in inventory for three months, the dress was reduced to $44.25. Determine the dollar amount and percentage of depreciation of the original-cost value and the current market value of the dress.

2. Using the cost code "CALM SPRING," the original cost of a sofa was defined as ANPPC. The price ticket indicates that the original price of the sofa was $331.25, but it is currently on sale for $231.88. For the purpose of inventory valuation, determine the sofa's market value.

3. The original-cost value of an ending inventory was determined to be $86,350. Assume that the original retail value has been reduced to $146,520 as a result of $19,980 in markdowns. Calculate the market value of the ending inventory.

4. A lamp originally cost the merchant

and was retailed to sell at $62.59. After remaining in stock for six months, the price was reduced to $49.99. It still remained unsold, and after three months an additional markdown of 30% was taken. At this point in time, what is the market value of the lamp?

The effect of freight charges on the ending inventory

As discussed in Chapter 2, freight charges are considered to be an integral part of the cost of merchandise and are not to be treated as just another incidental cost of operating the retail store. Freight charges are incorporated into the purchase price of the merchandise, and it therefore follows that a portion of the freight charges paid on purchases should be allocated to the value of the ending inventory, rather than remaining in the cost of merchandise sold.

The original-cost value of the physical inventory is derived from the information on the price ticket, and while it is theoretically possible to prorate freight charges to individual items of merchandise and to indicate those charges on the price tag, the task itself is unwieldy and expensive, with the resulting data extremely prone to human error.[30]

---

[30]Imagine attempting to prorate a freight charge of $3.86 over a gross of men's ties, and then accurately indicating that prorated charge on 144 price tickets.

The correct procedure for the management of freight costs under the cost method is for the merchant to calculate the ratio of those expenses to the total cost purchases for the period and then to apply that ratio by the cost of closing inventory.[31] The effects of such an accounting procedure will be to increase the value of the ending inventory, *thus* decreasing the cost of merchandise sold, *thereby* increasing gross margin and resulting operating profit, as shown below:

| | *Ending Inventory without Freight* | | *Ending Inventory with Freight* | |
	Cost	Retail	Cost	Retail
Beginning inventory	$ 80,000		$ 80,000	
Purchases	45,500		45,500	
Freight charges (2% of purchases)	910		910	
Total merchandise handled	$126,410		$126,410	
Net sales		$100,000		$100,000
Ending inventory	$ 71,300		$ 71,300	
Freight charges	–0–		1,426	
Total ending inventory	$ 71,300		$ 72,726	
Less cost of merchandise sold	$ 55,110		$ 53,684	
Gross margin		$ 44,890		$ 46,316
Less operating expenses		$ 34,660		$ 34,660
Operating profit		$ 10,230		$ 11,656

[31] $\frac{\text{Freight charges}}{\text{Total purchases}}$ = Ratio of freight charges to purchases

The resulting ratio is then multiplied times the value of the ending inventory to determine applicable freight costs; this figure is now added to the ending inventory to determine its original cost value, and the process of depreciation proceeds from this point. Thus, we may state that the market value of the ending inventory equals the billed cost plus freight charges minus depreciation.

Under the retail method of inventory, it is not necessary to calculate and add freight costs to the ending inventory to determine its cost value. This will receive more discussion in Chapter 11.

▪ Application Exercise

1. Based upon the cost codes on the price tags, the value of an ending inventory was initially determined to be $56,600. Purchases for the period amounted to $36,800, with freight charges of $552. What was the actual original-cost value of that ending inventory?

2. Given the following data, determine the original-cost value of the ending inventory:

Beginning inventory	$23,800
Purchases	18,600
Freight costs	279
Billed cost of ending inventory	20,800

3. The closing inventory for a furniture department, as determined from the price tags, was $68,450. An analysis of the coded costs indicated the following data:

   Six sofas totaling $2,400 had depreciated 30%.
   Ten chairs worth $800 had depreciated 40%.
   Twenty-four occasional tables, each costing $78.50, had depreciated by 50%.

   The cost purchases during the period totaled $133,500, and the freight charges on those purchases amounted to $2,670. What was the market value of the ending inventory?

4. Determine the market value of an ending inventory given the following information:

   Closing inventory at billed cost is $75,600.
   The wholesale value of 150 items has dropped from $8.50 to $7.20.
   The replacement cost of 100 items has fallen from $13.85 to $11.40.
   The market value of 23 items has risen from $13.98 to $14.98.
   Purchases for the period were $36,400.
   Transportation on purchases amounted to $637.

▪ Solutions to the Application Exercises

Cost Coding (p. 301)

1. C U T   F L O W E R S
   0 1 2   3 4 5 6 7 8 9

   U T S F = $12.93   O S = $ .59
   L T R   = $4.28   U T L = $1.24

3.
56839	57823	5290
− 55555	− 55555	− 5555
$13.84	$23.78	$7.45

56598	58493	5038
− 55555	− 55555	− 5555
$10.43	$39.48	$5.83

56442	52412	5604
− 55555	− 55555	− 5555
$19.97	$79.67	$1.59

$13.84
23.78
7.45
10.43
39.48
5.83
19.97
79.67
1.59
$202.04 = Cost value of the ending inventory

Determination of Profitability Using the Original-Cost Method Without Book Inventory (p. 304)

	Cost	Retail
1. Gross sales		$300,000
Less returns and allowances		30,000
Net sales		$270,000
Opening inventory	$380,000	
Purchases	30,000	
Total merchandise sold	$410,000	
Less closing inventory	262,000	
Cost of merchandise sold	$148,000 ⟶	(148,000)
Gross margin		$122,000

The Perpetual Inventory System at Cost (p. 308)

1. Under the original-cost method:

Book inventory = BOM inventory + Purchases − Cost of sales

Therefore,

Book inventory = $103,000 + $25,000 − $87,000 = $41,000

3. Determine the book inventory:

$640,000 + $150,000 − $440,000 = $350,000

Formulate the operating statement down to operating profit.

	Cost	Retail
Net sales		$800,000
Beginning inventory	$640,000	
Purchases	150,000	
Total merchandise handled	$790,000	
Less book inventory	350,000	
Cost of merchandise sold	$440,000 ⟶	(440,000)
Gross margin		$360,000
Less operating expenses	$328,000 ⟶	(328,000)
Operating profit		$ 32,000

The Effects of Inventory Shortage on Operating Profit (p. 310)

1. BOM inventory	$2,000
Purchases	800
Total merchandise handled	$2,800
Less book inventory	1,600
Cost of merchandise sold (unadjusted)	$1,200
Shortage ($1,600 − $1,300)	300
Cost of merchandise sold (adjusted)	$1,500[32]

The Aging Method (p. 313)

1. Required markdown percentage = 100% − 73% = 27%

Dollar markdown = $73,500 × 27% = $19,845

Market value = $73,500 − $19,845 = $53,655

Or:

$73,500 × 73% = $53,655

---

[32]Note that the $300 shortage represents an undefined depletion of inventory (e.g., pilferage, account error) and thus adds to the cost of merchandise sold.

$$\frac{\$73,500 - \$53,655}{\$73,500} = 27\%$$

3.

Age (Months)	Merchandise on Hand	Depreciation %	Market Value
0–2	$110,000	-0-	$110,000
2–5	25,000	20	20,000
5–8	15,500	40	9,300
8–10	10,300	60	4,120
10–12	2,200	80	440
Total	$163,000		$143,860

$$\text{Depreciation \%} = \frac{\$163,000 - \$143,860}{\$163,000} = 11.7\%$$

The Markdown Method (p. 318)

1. $$\text{Original markon \%} = \frac{\$59 - \$32.45}{\$59} = 45\%$$

Cost of new retail price and current market value = $44.25 (100% − 45%) = $24.34

$Depreciation = $32.45 − $24.34 = $8.11

$$\text{Depreciation \%} = \frac{\$32.45 - \$24.34}{\$32.45} = 25\%$$

Again, note that the depreciation percentage is equivalent to the markdown percentage, that is, the

$$\text{Markdown \%} = \frac{\$59 - \$44.25}{\$59} = 25\%$$

3. Original retail = $146,520 + $19,980 = $166,500

$$\text{Original markon \%} = \frac{\$166,500 - \$86,350}{\$166,500} = 48.1\%$$

Market value = $146,520 (100% − 48.1%) = $76,044

Proof:

$$\text{Markdown \%} = \frac{\$19,980}{\$166,500} = 12\%$$

$$\text{Depreciation \%} = \frac{\$86,350 - \$76,044}{\$86,350} = 12\%$$

The Effect of Freight Charges on the Ending Inventory (p. 320)

1. The ratio of freight charges to purchases for the period $= \dfrac{\$552}{\$36,800} = 1.5\%$

   $\$56,600 \times 1.5\% = \$849$ (Freight charges applicable to the ending inventory)

   Original-cost value of the ending inventory $= \$56,600 + \$849 = \$57,449$

3. Market value = Billed cost + Freight charges − Depreciation

   Billed cost = $68,450

   Ratio of freight charges to purchases $= \dfrac{\$2,670}{\$133,500} = 2\%$

   Freight charges to be added to closing inventory $= \$68,450 \times 2\% = \$1,369$

   Depreciation:

$2,400 × 30.0% =	$720
800 × 40.0% =	320
1,884 × 50.0% =	942
Total depreciation =	$1,982

   Valuation of the ending inventory:

Closing inventory at billed cost	$68,450
Freight charges	1,369
Less depreciation	1,982
Market value	$67,837

Topics for Discussion and Review

1. Explain how the value of the ending inventory affects gross margin and, ultimately, operating profit.

2. What is meant by the conservative valuation of inventory?

3. Given the opportunity of valuing the ending inventory at a $1,000 original cost or at the current market value of $1,300, what valuation should the merchant select? Why?

4. What are bases for the valuation of an inventory, and what methods may be used to arrive at that valuation?

5. What is the only precise method of determining the value of the merchant's inventory?

6. Explain the concepts of perpetual inventory and book inventory; what is the difference?

7. What is the difference between the physical inventory and the book inventory? Which is theoretically the more accurate?

8. Explain the concept of an inventory shortage. What is an overage?

9. Discuss the reasons why sound merchandising practice dictates the merchant's use of a perpetual inventory system.

10. What is the major difficulty with the cost method of inventory? Explain your answer.

11. What types of retail operations could make best use of the cost method of inventory valuation? In what situation is the cost method mandatory?

12. How would you value an inventory at original cost? Discuss the concept and give specific examples.

13. Explain the three major deficiencies inherent in the cost method of inventory valuation without the book inventory.

14. Discuss the limitations of the cost method of inventory without the book inventory.

15. How is the perpetual inventory at cost maintained, and how is the book inventory determined? What advantages does the merchant derive from this book inventory?

16. Explain the role of the book inventory in the determination of operating profit.

17. Explain, with a specific illustration, the effect of a relatively small inventory shortage on the merchant's operating profit.

18. Discuss the reasons why the merchant should be able to distinguish between the original cost of an inventory and its current market value.

19. What is the aging method, and how is it used to determine the market value of the cost inventory?

20. What are the major problems inherent in the quotation method of determining market value for a cost inventory?

21. How would you explain the markdown method of inventory valuation, and its implementation, as a means of arriving at the market value of a cost inventory?

22. What is the proper method for the allocation of freight charges under the cost method of inventory allocation?

23. Explain the procedure for the determination of the book inventory at cost.

24. Discuss the quotation method for obtaining the market value of an inventory. What are its two basic limitations?

25. What is meant by the "conservative valuation of inventory"?

Chapter 11
Measuring Profit According to the Retail Method of Inventory

Learning Objectives

- Explain the concept of the retail method of inventory valuation.

- Discuss the objectives of the retail method.

- Describe the sequential mechanics of the retail method.

- List the underlying premises of the retail method.

- Identify the classifications of merchandise information necessary to the implementation of the retail method.

- Discuss the advantages and limitations of the retail method of inventory valuation.

- Determine the value of the ending inventory at both retail and cost.

- Calculate the cost of the merchandise sold, gross margin, and operating profit.

- Explain the effects of transportation costs and inventory shortages on the component values of the retail method.

- Explain and discuss the specific elements of the price change concept.

- Describe the effects of markup on the cumulative markon.

- Discuss the effects of markdowns on the value of the book inventory at both retail and cost.

Key Terms

Average Markon: The dollar or percentage differential existing between the cost and retail value of a group of items or an inventory of merchandise.

Book Inventory: The amount of inventory that is shown to be on hand as a result of the perpetual inventory; the perpetual inventory is a retail system of accounting that at any given point in time defines the value of the book inventory; the perpetual inventory is an accounting system, and the book inventory is the result of that system.

Classification: All merchandise of a given type or use, without regard for color, size, style, or price; a specific segment of customer demand—for example, women's bathing suits or men's dress shirts.

Cost Inventory: The actual cost or market value, whichever is the lower, of the inventory on hand at any given time.

Cost of Goods Sold: The total cost of the merchandise handled minus the lower of the book or physical inventory at cost. For the purpose of this chapter, it includes the cost of the merchandise plus transportation costs; normally defined as all expenses incurred in the sale of merchandise, determined by adding billed cost, freight charges, and alteration expenses and subtracting the earned cash discounts.

Cost Method of Inventory Valuation: The determination of the cost value of the merchandise on hand by indicating the actual cost of each item on its attached price ticket and computing the inventory within a specific accounting period.

Cost Price: The price of merchandise charged by a vendor to the merchant. Normally defined as the "billed cost," it is the price appearing on the vendor's invoice before the deduction of cash discounts and after the deduction of trade and quantity discounts.

Cumulative Markon: The average markon achieved in a specific period in time.

Departmentalization: The organization of related merchandise and subsequent identification of that organization as a specific department.

Gross Margin: The difference between net sales and the total cost of the merchandise that produced those sales; the excess of sales over the cost of sales.

Markdown: A reduction of the original retail price. Markdowns include sales discounts and allowances to customers, but never inventory shortages or markup cancellations.

Markdown Cancellation: An upward revision of a current retail price previously marked down; a price change that generally "cancels" a markdown and results in the restoration of the original selling price.

Market Value: The wholesale value of an item of merchandise at any given time.

Market Value of the Ending Inventory: The current depreciated worth of the ending inventory, or the merchandise on hand.

Markup: An addition or series of additions to the original retail price; not to be confused with the concept of markon.

Markup Cancellation: A reduction of all or part of a previously taken markup, serving to reduce a retail price downward toward its original retail price.

Operating Profit: The profit derived from merchandising operations.

Original Retail: The initial, or first, price at which merchandise is offered for sale.

Perpetual Inventory: A system of retail accounting whereby the movement and retail values of the merchandise on hand are maintained daily. In effect, it is a process of adding and deducting specific values to and from the opening inventory at cost and retail.

Physical Inventory: The physical count of each item of merchandise currently on hand.

Retail Method of Inventory Valuation: The taking of the physical inventory at current retail prices and reducing the total retail value to its cost value by means of the cost complement of the cumulative markon percentage.

Retail Price: The price that the merchant puts on goods for resale to the consumer. The retail price reflects the merchant's current perception of the retail value of the goods on hand; thus, the retail price is always subject to modification.

Retail Price Change: The raising or lowering of the current retail price.

Retail Reductions: Generally considered to be the sum of net markdowns, sales discounts, and inventory shortages; in the computation of the retail method, retail reductions also include net sales.

Shortage: The difference between the dollar value of the physical inventory and the book inventory; under the retail method, the dollar value is always defined at retail. When the retail value of the physical inventory exceeds the retail value of the book inventory, an overage occurs; while extremely rare, overages do take place.

Total Merchandise Handled: The sum of the beginning inventory, net purchases, transportation charges, and net markups.

Transportation Costs: All freight charges paid by the merchant and not chargeable to the vendor.

11.1

The Inadequacy of the Cost Method of Inventory

As previously discussed in Chapter 1, the essence of retail merchandising is the "tactical planning and control" of the merchant's inventory, to provide a vehicle for its profitable distribution to the consumer. Planning and control are in effect a series of decisions, the effectiveness of which are totally dependent upon the timely receipt of economically derived, accurate data. In all but the most limited circumstances, the cost method of inventory valuation fails to meet this criterion, in the sense that the costing of each individual item of merchandise in inventory is time consuming, expensive, and often inaccurate, thus precluding any realistic determination of the actual, or market, value of the ending (book) inventory. Given this degree of error, it naturally follows that the ensuing cost of merchandise sold, gross margin, and operating profit will incorporate, perpetuate, and communicate faulty information to the retail merchant, thus distorting the decision process and ultimately undermining the effectiveness of whatever control measures may be desired.

The Retail Method Defined

The retail method of inventory valuation, normally referred to as simply "the retail method," has gradually evolved to its present status and is generally accepted, especially by the mass merchants and department stores, as the most efficient means of overcoming the two major deficiencies of the cost method: the inefficient costing of individual items and the arbitrariness of the determination of market value.

The retail method is defined as a system of merchandise accounting wherein the merchant can, at any given time, determine the market value of the goods on hand by means of the relationship between the average cost and retail prices of all the merchandise available for sale during any given period of time.

The retail method is essentially a perpetual inventory system that permits the merchant to approximate the market value for groups of merchandise that are homogeneous in type and markon.[1] Thus, at any given time, gross margin and operating profit can be determined without the necessity of a physical inventory or the bother of computing the market value of individual items. When the physical inventory is taken,[2] it is done so only to verify the accuracy of the book inventory,[3] and the procedure now is to simply count and list the merchandise at

---

[1]The retail method is essentially a process of averaging individual markons into one cumulative markon; therefore, the integrity of the cumulative markon is solely dependent upon the consistency of the merchandise grouping and the markon of its constituent items.

[2]Normally twice a year, at the end of the fall and spring seasons.

[3]The difference between the physical inventory and the book inventory is called "shortage."

its current selling price and then to convert the total retail value of this physical inventory to its complementary cost.

The concept of the retail method derives from the essential nature of retail merchandise management, in that the goods purchased for resale are immediately repriced to meet the demands of the consumer marketplace. Thus, it is the retail price that dominates the merchant's thinking rather than cost,[4] and it is to this retail price that all merchandising activities are related, from operating ratios to planning and analysis documents. Therefore, at least theoretically, it would appear quite illogical, and to a great extent impractical, to value the merchant's inventory in terms other than its retail price.

The Objectives of the Retail Method

The strategic objective of the retail method is to approximate as closely as possible the lower of cost or the market value for homogeneous clusters of merchandise, without having to calculate the current market value of individual items. The achievement of this objective will in turn supply the merchant with the following tactical advantages:

> The ability to profitably manage and control the ongoing merchandise inventory.

> A convenient, efficient, and perpetual means of appraising and evaluating the effectiveness of merchandising decisions.

> A system of merchandise management capable of exposing current problem areas to immediate remedial action, thus greatly reducing the possibility of unforeseen difficulties.

Analysis of the Retail Method

The design, construction, and application of the various components of the retail method are predicated upon the premise that the average markon of the merchandise currently on hand will closely approximate the cumulative (or average) markon achieved to date on similar merchandise handled during the current selling season. With this concept in mind, the sequential mechanics of the retail method are as follows:

1. The implementation of the retail method begins with the realistic determination and application of a retail price to each individual item of merchandise in stock.

---

[4]While individual merchants may subordinate retail to cost, this does not change the reality of the situation.

2. This is followed by a departmental inventory taken at both retail and cost at the commencement of the accounting period; the cost values are to be determined by reference to actual vendor invoices.

3. Next, all succeeding merchandise purchases[5] are recorded by department at both retail and cost and added to the corresponding cost and retail values of the beginning inventory. At the same time, the retail value of the inventory is to be adjusted so as to reflect the effect of markups and markup cancellations[6] and the cost value increased by the addition of transportation charges on the purchases received.

4. The total merchandise handled at retail for the period now consists of the opening inventory at retail plus the purchases at retail and the net markups. From this total is subtracted the net sales, net markdowns, sales discounts, and a provision for retail shortages (if applicable). The resulting balance is the retail value of the merchandise on hand at the end of the period, or the book inventory at retail.

5. The next step is the determination of the cumulative markon percentage, which is derived from the difference between the retail and cost values of the total merchandise handled to date and expressed as a percentage of the retail value. To reiterate:

Total merchandise handled at retail = The retail value of the opening inventory + Purchases at retail + Net markups

Total merchandise handled at cost = The cost value of the opening inventory + Purchases at cost + Transportation charges

$$\text{Cumulative markon \%} = \frac{\text{Total retail} - \text{Total cost}}{\text{Total retail}}$$

6. We are now in a position to convert the book inventory at retail to the book inventory at cost.[7] This is simply accomplished by multiplying the book in-

---

[5] These are the additions to the beginning inventory at both retail and cost.
[6] A markup is the upward revision of the selling price after the initial markon. It is considered to be a correction of the original retail price and thus figures into the total retail value of the inventory and corresponding cumulative markon. Markup cancellations are normally but not necessarily corrections of error in markon and are thus deducted from markups in deriving the retail value of the ending inventory. Two points are to be noted:
1. Markup cancellations are not markdowns; they are corrections of pricing errors and should be so reflected in the operating statement.
2. Net markups, markups less markup cancellations, affect only the retail value of the inventory, never the cost.
[7] Under the retail method, "cost" does not imply the mathematical sum of the vendor's invoice cost. It is an average cost derived from an average retail adjusted for price changes.

ventory at retail times the cost complement of the cumulative markon percentage as follows:

Book inventory at cost = Book inventory at retail (100% − Cumulative markon %)

This resulting cost inventory always represents the lower value of either cost or market, because the items that have been marked down will be indirectly valued at less than their original cost.[8]

7. At the end of a fiscal period, normally after the spring and fall seasons, the merchant takes a physical inventory of the merchandise on hand by summarizing the marked retail prices.

8. A comparison of the results of the physical inventory at retail with the book inventory at retail reveals the amount of retail inventory overage or shortage. Some degree of shortage is to be expected and is often defined as "shrinkage." Where there is an overage, the fault invariably lies with some discrepancy in the accounting system.

9. The book inventory at retail is now adjusted to agree with the physical inventory at retail; the resulting "new" retail figure, when converted to cost as discussed above, is used to determine the gross margin for the accounting period.

10. The adjusted ending inventory at retail and cost will now serve as the beginning inventory for the coming accounting period, and so the process continues.

In summary, the successful implementation of the retail method depends upon the following:

1. All vendor purchases and related transactions (e.g., freight charges and returns and allowances) must be recorded at both their cost and retail values.

2. All other transactions (e.g., net sales, markdowns) must be recorded at retail.

3. Purchases and net markups are to be treated as an addition to inventory; sales and retail reductions serve to reduce the value of the inventory.

4. The retail method is a system of average values; therefore, the inventory must be developed through the periodic addition and subtraction of aggregate values rather than individual items or unique transactions.

---

[8]When the current retail value of the merchandise is less than the initial retail price, the application of the cost complement of the cumulative markon reduces the cost value of the merchandise in proportion to its current selling price. Thus, depreciation is automatically provided for and the cost value of the inventory is conservatively stated.

5. The validity of the retail method is solely dependent upon the accuracy of the accounting system (perpetual inventory) that ultimately defines the value of the book inventory.

Underlying Premises of the Retail Method

The concept of the retail method of inventory valuation is predicated upon the following five premises:

1. The marked retail prices on the merchandise in stock represent the fair value of those goods in the current retail marketplace.

2. The cumulative markon percentage represents an accurate and equitable relationship between the total merchandise handled at cost and at retail.

3. The goods that make up the inventory are homogeneous in nature and the high-markon and low-markon merchandise will sell in approximately the same proportions in which they were purchased.[9]

4. Merchandise that is offered for sale is initially priced according to the original retail as indicated on the merchant's copy of the purchase order.

5. Markdowns must be promptly executed and duly recorded so as to maintain the integrity of the current retail value of the inventory.

Record Keeping Requirements Under the Retail Method

The retail method is essentially an accounting system based upon the demands of the consumer market, the validity of which is totally derived from the accuracy with which pertinent factors are recognized and incorporated into that system. No method of inventory control will yield satisfactory results if accounting details are compiled carelessly, inaccurately, or with the omission of relevant data.

The sound application of the retail method to the determination of merchandising profitability—that is, gross margin—depends upon the accurate and timely receipt of the following classifications of merchandise information:[10]

---

[9]Should this not be the case, the book inventory at retail would either overstate or understate the actual value of the physical inventory in the retail market. The natural tendency is to overstate the ending inventory because the most desirable merchandise is sold first, while the least desirable and thus less profitable merchandise remains in stock, subject to future markdowns.

[10]Because the thrust of this chapter is an examination of the fundamental determinants of the retail method of inventory control rather than the specific elements of gross margin (in spite of the fact that gross margin is the ultimate objective of the retail method), the following classifications of "merchandise information" are eliminated because of their nonessential nature to an understanding of the concept of the retail method: (a) interdepartmental and interstore transfers; (b) alteration and workroom costs; and (c) earned cash discounts.

1. Purchases at billed cost and marked retail

2. Transportation charges

3. Merchandise returned to vendors and allowances received from vendors

4. Gross sales

5. Merchandise returned by customers and allowances granted to customers

6. Net sales

7. Interdepartmental and interstore transfers

8. Markups and markup cancellations

9. Markdowns and markdown cancellations

10. Sales discounts to employees and privileged customers

11. Alteration and workroom costs applicable to the sale of merchandise at retail

12. Earned cash discounts

The Advantages and Limitations of the Retail Method over the Cost Method

The retail method is a logical extension of the perpetual-inventory concept, applied at the retail level of the price spectrum to which it is most amenable, rather than at original cost, where the valuation of individual items almost entirely precludes the practical application of any perpetual dollar control system. Thus, to contrast the two methods on the basis of "cost" and "retail" is not entirely accurate; the comparison is actually being drawn between a perpetual system of inventory control (the retail method) and a nonperpetual system of inventory valuation (the cost method).

Advantages of the Retail Method

1. It provides a perpetual book inventory; thus, interim financial statements can be prepared without the need of a physical stock count, facilitating financial control and a more precise management of the merchant's inventory.

2. The process of conducting the physical inventory is greatly facilitated, resulting in economy of effort and, by the minimization of clerical error, a higher degree of accuracy.

3. Shortages can be determined and incorporated into operating data, thus fine tuning, so to speak, the validity of financial statements. The essence of the retail method is the book inventory, and only with such a document can shortages (or overages) be determined.

4. The retail method, again because it is predicated upon a book inventory, provides a sound basis for insurance claims as a result of fire or other natural disasters. In cases of such loss, the book inventory provides valid evidence of those goods that "should" have been in the inventory. Because merchandise often comprises the greatest portion of the merchant's assets, insurance coverage is essential, as are the supporting records to substantiate potential losses.

5. Transportation charges are automatically included in the value of the ending inventory; transportation charges are a part of the total cost of merchandise handled; thus, by nature they reduce the cumulative markon[11] and increase the cost value of the ending inventory.

6. The retail method automatically defines the lower of market value or cost for the closing inventory. This is because the cumulative markon percentage represents the merchant's perception of the retail price and thus reciprocally interprets the cost that the merchant is willing to sustain in order to support that price.[12]

Limitations of the Retail Method

No method of inventory system exists without some types of limitations or disadvantages, and the retail method is no exception. However, for the merchant handling general merchandise,[13] the advantages of the retail method far outweigh the following limitations:

1. It is not useful for those merchandising situations where the modification of form utility is required to consummate the retail transaction. Thus, florist shops, bakeries, restaurants, or any retail operation where labor enters into the cost of merchandise sold cannot use the retail method; some form of the cost method must be employed.

2. The maintenance of the perpetual inventory system under the retail method is burdensome, time consuming, and thus expensive. Yet, at the same time, the validity of the book inventory is solely dependent upon the accuracy of the accounting system posting data to that perpetual inventory; the book inventory and resulting cost of merchandise sold may be meaningless figures unless the required data are precisely recorded.

---

[11]The average of multiple initial markons.
[12]For example, if the book inventory at retail is $1,000, predicated upon a cumulative markon of 45%, then the replacement value (the cost that the merchant is willing to incur, i.e., market value) of that merchandise must be $550 (55% × $1,000) if the maintained markon is to remain intact at 45%.
[13]"General merchandise" defines the merchandise assortments offered by department stores, mass merchants, variety, and chain stores. Such offerings include, but are not limited to, apparel, cosmetics, sporting goods, home furnishings, jewelry, luggage, tobacco products, toys, dry goods, and garden equipment.

3. The system is subject to manipulation, especially under the conditions of employee-management, as opposed to owner-management; thus, it requires careful supervision and control.

4. The retail method requires departmentalization, unless only a narrow line of merchandise is to be carried, because of the necessity of goods being similar or homogeneous in nature.

5. The cost complement of the cumulative markon is only an average figure predicated upon the difference between the total cost of the merchandise handled and its retail value. Therefore, it only approximates the cost value of the ending inventory, but never actually defines the merchant's true cost. This is particularly the case if fast-selling merchandise has different markons than slow-selling merchandise and/or if there are significant discrepancies between the markons achieved on various items within the same department.

When classifications, departments, or even small stores fail to achieve homogeneity in markon, the inevitable result is an overstated valuation of the book inventory.[14] To understand why this is so, consider the following illustration:

		Cost	Retail	Markon %
(1)	Beginning inventory	$500	$1,000	50.0
(2)	Purchases to date	400	600	33.3
(3)	Total merchandise handled	$900	$1,600	43.8
(4)	Less net sales		600	
(5)	Book inventory at retail		$1,000	
(6)	Book inventory at cost	$562		

Assume, for the sake of illustration, that the $600 in net sales (Line 4) consisted of all the lowest markon merchandise, that is, purchases to date (Line 2). Then the book inventory at retail (Line 5) must mathematically be $1,000, and its cost equivalent (Line 6), as defined by the retail method, must be $1,000 (100% − 43.8%) or $562. However, the actual cost of the merchandise sold (Line 2) is $400. Therefore, there is an overstatement in the cost value of the book inventory (Line 6) of $162 ($562 − $400). Thus, the retail method cannot be accurately applied to an entire grouping of merchandise unless all the composite items have relatively the same markon percentages.

This may indeed be the greatest deficiency of the retail method; while the cumulative markon percentage may be representative of the cost and retail relationship in the total merchandise handled, it does not necessarily follow that the same percentage relationship applies to the cost and retail value of that ending inventory. This is not to negate the value of the retail method but only to imply that

---

[14]Thus, the cost of the merchandise sold is decreased and gross margin and operating profit are correspondingly increased.

its usefulness is directly dependent upon the merchant's ability to homogeneously classify the unique items of merchandise that constitute the ongoing inventory.

11.2

Profit Calculations According to the Retail Method

The calculations involved in the determination of operating profit under the retail method are essentially a compilation of previously discussed concepts, herein brought together under the "umbrella" of the retail method. The calculation of gross margin in Chapter 8 was in effect an exercise predicated upon the retail method of inventory, in that the ending inventory was derived solely from retail figures and converted to an estimated cost by means of the application of the cost complement of the cumulative markon. Thus, you may find nothing new in this section except the direction of emphasis, which is

1. The key to the derivation of gross margin and, consequently, operating profit derives from the calculation of the cost of merchandise sold, which in turn is a direct function of the cost value of the ending inventory.

2. The fact that the retail method, as the name implies, uses only retail figures to derive the cost value of the ending inventory.

Determination of the Ending Inventory at Both Cost and Retail

The following study problem illustrates how the cost value of the closing inventory is derived from retail figures.

■ Study Problem

Given:

	Cost	Retail
Beginning inventory	$30,500	$57,300
Net purchases	$26,800	$52,900
Net sales		$63,200

Find: A merchant's closing inventory at both cost and retail.

Solution: Set up the problem as follows and solve for cost and retail:

	Cost	Retail	Markon %
Beginning inventory	$30,500	$ 57,300	46.8
Net purchases	26,800	52,900	49.3
Total merchandise handled	$57,300	$110,200	48.0
Less net sales		63,200	
Closing (book) inventory	$24,440	$ 47,000	48.0

Note that the total merchandise handled at both retail and cost is the sum of the beginning inventories plus net purchases and that the cumulative markon of 48% represents the ratio of total markon dollars to the retail value of the total merchandise handled. Thus,

$$\frac{\$110,200 - \$57,300}{\$110,200} = 48\%$$

The closing inventory at retail, or the retail value of the merchandise remaining at the end of the period, is equivalent to the total merchandise handled for the period at retail, less the retail value of the merchandise sold during the period, or

$$\$110,200 - \$63,200 = \$47,000$$

The closing inventory at cost (book inventory at cost) is simply the cost complement of the closing inventory at retail (book inventory at retail) as determined by the cumulative markon percentage. The calculation is as follows:

Closing inventory at cost = $47,000 (100% − 48%) = $24,440

The markon achieved on the closing inventory is the same as that derived from the total merchandise handled for the period. This, in effect, is a statement of the assumption that the markon achieved on the merchandise sold (net sales) is consistent with the original (cumulative) markon placed upon the total merchandise handled.[15] While this may not be the actual case, it is the basic premise upon which the retail method is based. Thus,

---

[15]Recall that the markon achieved on the total merchandise handled is defined as the cumulative markon, or the markon achieved to date. Because the cumulative markon is used to evaluate the total amount of merchandise handled over a specific period of time, logic dictates that that same markon percentage be employed to determine the value of the ending inventory, i.e., the cost value of the book inventory. The one alternative choice would be the lesser maintained markon (see Chapter 7), which would only serve to increase the cost value of the book inventory (thus reflecting a smaller markon) and invalidate the principle that the valuation of an inventory should be at cost or market value, whichever is lower.

$$\text{Markon on closing inventory} = \frac{\$47,000 - \$24,440}{\$47,000} = 48\%$$

▪ Application Exercise

1. Given the following information, determine the book inventory at cost for a shoe department:

	Cost	Retail
Opening inventory	$26,000	$43,600
Purchases to date	15,200	29,300
Net sales		53,900

2. Determine the EOM inventory at cost for a classification of blouses, given the following data:

	Cost	Retail
BOM stock	$18,300	$36,500
Purchases	10,200	21,000
Sales		41,800

3. A men's shirt department opened the season with an $8,300 inventory at cost and a planned markon of 48%. Additional purchases were retailed at $5,800 based on a 43.5% markon. Net sales for the season were $15,700. What was the buyer's book inventory at cost?

4. A jewelry department experienced gross sales of $53,800 for the month of June, with returns and allowances amounting to 2%. The inventory as of 6/1 was $73,800 at retail, predicated upon a cumulative markon of 52%. Purchases as of 6/30 cost $15,300 and had an average markon of 50%. What was the book inventory at cost as of 6/30?

5. A men's tie shop, because of homogeneous inventory classifications, was able to consistently maintain a 42% markon on all merchandise sold. Given the following information, what was the owner's book inventory at cost at the end of the spring season?

	Retail
Gross sales	$83,200
Returns	1,300
Inventory 2/1	43,800
Purchases 2/1–7/31	72,100

Determination of the Cost of Merchandise Sold, Gross Margin, and Operating Profit

The cost and retail value of the book inventory are the crucial determinants of gross margin and operating profit. The following study problem illustrates this concept.

▪ Study Problem

Given:

	Cost	Retail
Net sales		$200,000
BOM inventory	$84,600	154,300
Net purchases	58,400	115,700
Operating expenses	89,400	

Find: The merchant's (a) cost of goods sold, (b) gross margin, and (c) operating profit.

Solution:

The solution to this problem begins with the same procedure as set forth in the previous example:

	Cost	Retail	$Markon	Markon %
BOM inventory	$ 84,600	$154,300	$ 69,700	45.2
Net purchases	58,400	115,700	57,300	49.5
Total merchandise handled	$143,000	$270,000	$127,000	47.0
Less net sales		200,000		
Book inventory	$ 37,100	$ 70,000		
Cost of merchandise sold	$105,900[a]			
Gross margin			$94,100[b]	
Less operating expenses	$ 89,400	⟶	(89,400)	
Operating profit			$ 4,700[c]	

The total merchandise handled is the product of the sum of the BOM inventory plus net purchases; the cumulative markon of 47% represents the average markon achieved to date. The complement of this markon, 53%, translates the book inventory from retail into cost. Then,

(a) The cost of the merchandise sold is the difference between the total merchandise handled at cost and the book inventory at cost, or

Cost of merchandise sold = $143,000 − $37,100 = $105,900

(b) The gross margin is the net sales minus the cost of the merchandise sold, or

Gross margin = $200,000 − $105,900 = $94,100

(c) Operating profit is equal to the gross margin less the operating expenses. Thus,

Operating profit = $94,100 − $89,400 = $4,700

The cost of merchandise sold and the ensuing profit dollars are entirely dependent upon the cost value of the book inventory, which in turn is predicated entirely on retail figures and their degree of accuracy.

■ Application Exercise

1. A toy buyer achieved a cumulative markon of 40% for the fall season. If the ending inventory at retail is $123,800, what is its average cost value?

2. The following data are available for a classification of major appliances:

	Cost	Retail
Opening inventory	$32,800	$42,600
Net purchases	15,600	20,800
Net sales		43,700
Operating expenses	10,000	

Determine (a) cost of merchandise sold, (b) gross margin, and (c) operating profit.

3. A small specialty store exhibited the following operating data for the month of July:

	Cost	Retail
Gross sales		$45,000
Purchases as of 7/31	$23,800	45,500
Returns and allowances		500
Inventory 7/1	15,500	30,200
Operating expenses	18,800	

For the month of July, what was the (a) cost of merchandise sold, (b) gross margin, and (c) operating profit?

4. A dress buyer purchased $15,800 worth of merchandise during the month of October upon which was realized a 47.6% markon. The inventory as of 10/1 had a retail value of $37,800 and an average markon of 45.3%. Net sales for the

month were $43,200, and departmental operating expenses amounted to $17,815. What was the percentage of operating profit achieved by the buyer for October?

5. A handbag buyer achieved net sales of $432,000 for the spring season. The opening inventory at retail was $327,000 with a 51.5% markon. Purchases at retail throughout the season amounted to $278,600 with an average markon of 49.6%. Assuming that operating expenses were 42.6% of net sales and that no extraneous factors impinged upon operating profit, what was the percentage of net profit achieved by the handbag buyer?

The Effect of Transportation Costs and Inventory Shortages on the Component Values of the Retail Method

As we have previously established from our study of gross margin, transportation costs paid by the merchant are an element of merchandise expense; as such, they increase the cost of the total merchandise handled and decrease the markon dollars by a like amount. Thus, from the mechanical aspect of retail accounting, transportation charges affect only the cost of merchandise purchased and have no direct bearing upon the retail value of that merchandise.[16]

Inventory shortages exist when the retail value of the book inventory exceeds the retail value of the physical inventory.[17] Because the retail method acknowledges the retail value of the physical inventory (as opposed to the book inventory) as the ultimate determinant of profitability, it is that figure which, when converted to its market value, defines the cost of goods sold.

These two concepts are illustrated in the following study problem.

▪ Study Problem

Given:

	Cost	Retail
Beginning inventory	$60,000	$100,000
Net purchases	30,800	58,300
Transportation	500	

---

[16]This does not preclude the fact that the cost of transportation should be included in the initial markon.

[17]Shortages are best classified by their source of origin: those that relate to paperwork errors resulting from employee negligence and/or the deliberate manipulations of the inputs of the perpetual inventory system; and those attributable to internal (employee) and external (nonemployee) theft. Although a rarity, stock overages will occur, but only as a result of clerical error or some miscalculation in a deliberate attempt to alter the value of the book inventory; obviously, the value of the physical inventory cannot legitimately exceed the value of the book inventory.

	Cost	Retail
Operating expenses	39,359	
Net sales		108,200
Ending physical inventory		48,300

Find:

(a) Book inventory at retail
(b) Inventory shortage at retail
(c) Market value of the physical inventory
(d) Cost of merchandise sold
(e) Gross margin
(f) Operating profit

Solution: Set up the problem and solve as follows:

	Cost	Retail	$Markon	Markon %
Beginning inventory	$60,000	$100,000	$40,000	40.0
Net purchases	30,800	58,300	27,500	47.2
Transportation	500		(500)	
Total merchandise handled	$91,300	$158,300	$67,000	42.3
Less net sales		108,200		
Book inventory at retail		$50,100$^{(a)}$		
Less ending physical inventory	$27,869$^{(c)}	48,300		
Inventory shortages		$1,800$^{(b)}		
Cost of goods sold	$63,431$^{(d)}			
Gross margin			$44,769$^{(e)}	
Less operating expenses	$39,359 \longrightarrow		(39,395)	
Operating profit			$5,410$^{(f)}	5.0

■ Application Exercise

1. Given:

	Cost	Retail
Opening inventory	$32,800	$59,600
Net purchases	18,600	35,400
Transportation	840	
Net sales		46,700
Closing physical inventory		46,200

Determine: (a) book inventory at retail, (b) stock shortages, (c) physical inventory at cost, and (d) cost of merchandise sold.

2. Given:

	Cost	Retail
Opening inventory	$ 68,300	$ 97,500
Net purchases	187,600	284,242
Freight charges	2,900	
Operating costs	86,367	
Net sales		300,800
Ending physical inventory		76,500

Determine: (a) book inventory at retail, (b) inventory shortage, (c) physical inventory at cost, (d) cost of goods sold, (e) gross margin, and (f) operating profit for a toy department at the end of the fall season.

3. A luggage buyer closed out the spring season with a physical inventory valued at $16,800. Net sales for the period amounted to $53,600. The inventory as of 2/1 was $47,700 at retail and $26,235 at cost, with additional net purchases at cost and retail of $12,400 and $23,600, respectively; transportation costs amounted to 1.8% of net purchases. What was the buyer's (a) inventory shortage figure and (b) cost of goods sold as of 7/31?

4. A small bookstore had an opening inventory of $13,800 at cost with an average markon of 38%. Purchases for the period amounted to $11,300 at retail and carried an initial markon of 36.5%; freight charges on purchases amounted to $225. A physical inventory indicated that the value of the stock on hand at the close of the period was $9,100. If gross sales for the period were $25,000 and returns and allowances totaled 3.7%, what was the achieved percentage of gross margin?

5. Determine a buyer's gross margin, given the following data:

	Cost	Retail	Markon %
BOM inventory	$83,600	$143,700	41.8
Purchases	23,800	$ 41,800	43.0
Freight charges		$ 500	
Net sales		$ 87,300	
Physical inventory		$106,300	

The Effects of Price Changes on the Component Values of the Retail Method

Retail prices must obviously fluctuate in response to the vagaries of consumer demand, and such price changes must be reflected in the calculations involved in the retail method of inventory. Of crucial importance to the realistic valuation of the merchant's inventory in terms of market value or original cost is the manner in which retail price changes are classified and recorded into the perpetual inventory system. This in turn requires a conceptual grasp of retail price changes, including an understanding of the appropriate terminology.

The Concept of Retail Price Changes

The essential nature of all retail price changes (as they pertain to the retail method) is that they must of necessity relate to the initial, or original, retail price. That is, the original retail value of the merchandise is the focal point towards which, or away from which, all price changes gravitate. Price changes are therefore to be defined in terms relative to their point of origin or their initial retail price.

Figure 11.1 schematically depicts the concept of a sequential progression of price changes defined in terms applicable to the retail method. Note that the initial retail price of $20 forms the base value for the merchandise and that all subsequent price changes occur with respect to this particular point of reference. This concept will be developed as we progress further into this chapter.

The Mathematical Sequence of Retail Price Changes

Figure 11.2 further expands the concept of retail price changes shown in Figure 11.1 by means of the mathematical definition of terms and the sequential application of those values to the initial retail price. A more detailed explanation of these numerical changes and the proper definition of terminology follow.

Definition and Explanation of Price Change Terminology

The various types of price changes as depicted by the numbered arrows in Figure 11.1, and expanded in Figure 11.2, are defined and explained.

Markon

As previously discussed, the markon is essentially the difference between the original cost of an item and its initial selling price. However, if and when that initial retail price should be increased, the difference between the original cost and the new selling price is still defined as the markon. Thus, the markon, as depicted in Figure 11.1, may be defined as

Arrow 1: The difference between original cost and the initial retail price—$8.

Arrow 3: The difference between original cost and an increase in the initial retail price—$11.

Arrow 5: The difference between original cost and a further increase in the initial retail price—$13.

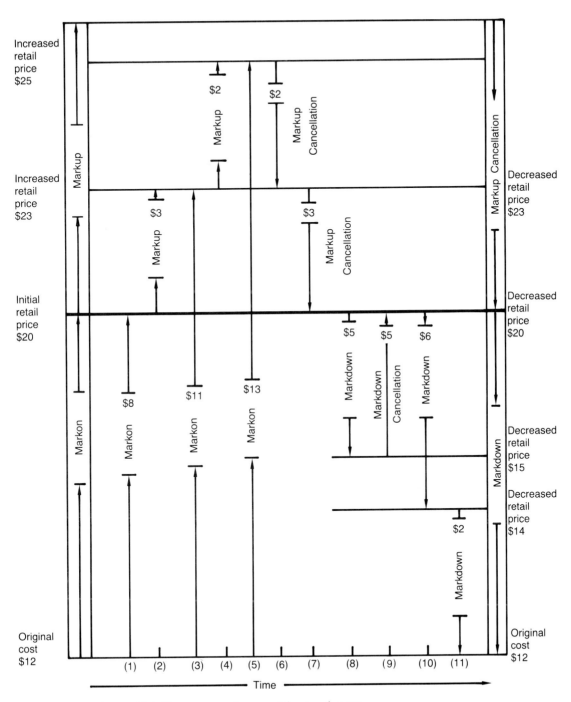

Figure 11.1 The concept of sequential price changes

Arrow Number		
	Original cost	$12
1	+ Markon	8
	Initial retail price	$20
2	+ Markup	3
	Increased retail price	$23
4	+ Markup	2
	Increased retail price	$25
6	− Markup cancellation	2
	Decreased retail price	$23
7	− Markup cancellation	3
	Initial retail price	$20
8	− Markdown	5
	Decreased retail price	$15
9	+ Markdown cancellation	5
	Initial retail price	$20
10	− Markdown	6
	Decreased retail price	$14
11	− Markdown	2
	Decreased retail price (original cost)	$12

Figure 11.2 The mathematical sequence of price changes

Theoretically speaking, we may define the markon as the difference between original cost and the current retail selling price, regardless of where that retail price falls in relationship to the initial retail price.[18] However, within the context of a rising retail price, markon may consist not only of the difference between the original cost and the initial retail price, but that difference plus one or more markups. The concept of markup therefore requires further explanation.

Markup

A markup is an upward revision of the initial retail price and serves to increase (by becoming a part of) the markon; additional markups serve to increase the revised selling price and at the same time proportionally increase the markon. Thus,

---

[18]The markon, however defined in merchandising terminology, is in effect the net gain the merchant realizes over and above the original cost of the merchandise, whether or not that gain is achieved at, above, or below the initial retail price.

Arrow 2 depicts a markup of $3, which increases the markon from $8 to $11 (Arrow 3).

Arrow 4 indicates an additional markup of $2, thus further increasing the markon to $13 (Arrow 5).

Two points are to be noted:

1. A markup can only occur at or above the initial retail price, and thus has no value.

2. While the retail price may be increased by a markup, that markup in no way supplants the concept of the markon as the proper descriptor for the spread between original cost and the current selling price.

Markup cancellation

A markup cancellation is the downward revision of the current selling price from a point above the initial retail price toward that original retail price. In other words, the markup cancellation serves to revoke all or some of the previously taken markup. If the markup cancellation should take the new retail price to a point below the initial selling price, the difference between the current retail price and the original selling price is recorded as a markdown. In short, if the markup cancellation is greater than the value of the markup, the excess amount is to be taken as an ordinary markdown. Markup cancellations are illustrated as follows:

Arrow 6 illustrates a $2 markup cancellation, which nullifies the previous $2 markup (Arrow 4) and decreases the retail price to $23 (Arrow 3).

Arrow 7 indicates a second markup cancellation of $3, which voids another previous markup of $3 (Arrow 2) and subsequently reduces the current selling price of $23 to its initial retail value of $20 (Arrow 1).

Markup cancellations may be the result of any one of several factors. In all cases, however, such downward revisions of the retail price may be taken only when they will not reflect a depreciation in the cost value of the merchandise. Examples are as follows:

1. Failure of the customer to accept a higher retail price than that established by the initial markon.

2. To manipulate the consumer's perception of value by creating artificially high retail prices (initial markon plus markup) and relating those prices to a subsequent "sale price" (initial markon minus the markup).

3. To correct a mechanical error in the original selling price.

4. To compensate for a vendor's reduction of the cost price of merchandise already in inventory.[19]

Markdown

A markdown is a reduction in the initial retail price of merchandise currently offered for sale and thus not only affects the retail value of an inventory but also its cost value.

> Arrow 8 indicates a markdown of $5, thus reducing the original retail price to $15 and the cost or market value to $9.[20]

> Additional markdowns, Arrows 10 and 11, further reduce the original price to $14 and $12 and the corresponding cost values to $8.40 and $7.20.

Markdown cancellation

A markdown cancellation is the upward revision of an existing retail price to offset a previous markdown; it restores all or part of the original selling price after it had been marked down.[21] If, after a markdown cancellation is taken, the resulting retail price is higher than the initial selling price, the difference is to be recorded as a "markup."

> Arrow 9 depicts a markdown cancellation of $5, which serves to offset the previous markdown of $5 (Arrow 8) and restores the initial retail price of $20.

> Subsequent markdowns, Arrows 10 and 11, must commence with the original retail price, as indicated by arrow 10.

The Development and Recording of Cumulative Price Change Data

Figure 11.3 illustrates the accumulation and development of price change data to be incorporated into the retail method. The essential concepts are as follows:

1. Net markup results from an accumulation of markup less the sum of the markup cancellations and thus affects only the retail value of the total merchandise handled.

---

[19]For example, a vendor may grant a cumulative quantity discount on the cost price of merchandise previously purchased and currently in stock.

[20]The markon percentage $= \dfrac{\$20 - \$12}{\$20} = 40\%$

Market value or cost $= \$15\,(100\% - 40\%) = \$9$

[21]The most common example is the restoration of the original selling price of merchandise that had been marked down for a specific sales event.

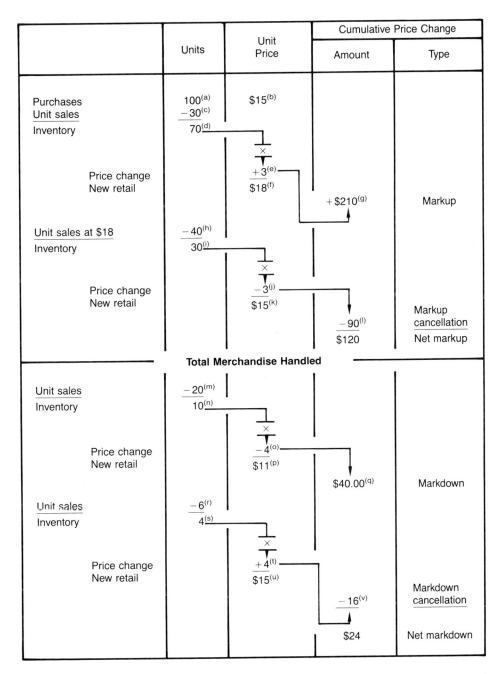

	Units	Unit Price	Cumulative Price Change	
			Amount	Type
Purchases	100[a]	$15[b]		
Unit sales	−30[c]			
Inventory	70[d]			
		×		
Price change		+3[e]		
New retail		$18[f]		
			+$210[g]	Markup
Unit sales at $18	−40[h]			
Inventory	30[i]			
		×		
Price change		−3[j]		
New retail		$15[k]		
			−90[l]	Markup cancellation
			$120	Net markup
Total Merchandise Handled				
Unit sales	−20[m]			
Inventory	10[n]			
		×		
Price change		−4[o]		
New retail		$11[p]		
			$40.00[q]	Markdown
Unit sales	−6[r]			
Inventory	4[s]			
		×		
Price change		+4[t]		
New retail		$15[u]		
			−16[v]	Markdown cancellation
			$24	Net markdown

Figure 11.3 Comulative price changes

2. Net markdowns are the total markdowns minus the amount of markdown cancellations and therefore impinge upon both the retail and cost values of the total merchandise handled.

In short, markup activity affects only the retail value of the merchant's inventory, whereas markdowns affect not only the retail value but also the original cost value. This concept is shown in Figure 11.3 by placing "net markup" above the "total merchandise handled" and "net markdown" below that line. Thus, "net markup" and "net markdown" are not to be integrated into one "net" figure; they stand as separate entities and discretely affect the process of inventory valuation.

The steps in the accumulation of price change data, as set forth in Figure 11.3, are as follows.

Net markup

A merchant purchases (a) 100 units of merchandise to retail at (b) $15 per unit. Subsequent sales amount to (c) 30 units, leaving (d) 70 units in the inventory. These 70 units are now marked up by (e) $3 each to a new retail of (f) $18, thus providing for a cumulative markup of (g) $210 (70 × $3). Of these 70 units, (h) 40 are sold at $18 and the remaining inventory is (i) 30 units; the $3 markup on these 30 units is (j) "cancelled," reducing the price to (k) $15 and establishing a markon cancellation of (l) $90 (3o × $3). The net markup therefore amounts to the $210 "markup" minus the $90 "markup cancellation," or $120.

All this activity occurs at or above the original retail price; thus, from the mechanical aspects of retail accounting, net markup is a factor to be considered only in the determination of the retail value of the "total merchandise handled"; as a determinant, it must obviously lie above, or precede, that which is "determined."

Net markdown

When the sequence of price changes leads to a point below the original retail price, the merchant is confronted with a markdown. A markdown is a downward revision of the initial retail price, which bears directly upon the cost valuation of the inventory. Thus, net markdowns enter into the calculations of the retail method below the determination of the "total merchandise handled."

The succession of price changes resumes with the sale of (m) 20 units from the (i) 30 currently on hand. This leaves an inventory of (n) 10 units, which are all marked down to (o) $4, from (k) $15 to (p) $11; the total markdown is (q) $40 (10 × $4). Assuming that 6 of the remaining (r) 10 units are sold, the inventory is now reduced to (s) 4 units. At this point, the merchant decides to "cancel" the $4 markdown (o) previously taken with a (t) $4 upward revision of (p) the current selling price; this restores the retail price to (u) $15, and the resulting total markon cancellation is (v) $16 (4 × $4). The $24 net markdown is (q) the $40 markdown less (v) the $16 markdown cancellation.

With these concepts in mind, let us proceed to apply them to the retail method.

Integration of Price Change Data into the Retail Method

The effect of markup and markup cancellation on the value of the total merchandise handled and cumulative markon

Net markup, the product of total markup less total markup cancellations, is an addition to the original markon with no corresponding increase in cost. Thus, the cumulative markon is increased by the amount of the net markup.

▪ Study Problem

Given: A classification of women's shoes exhibited the following data:

	Cost	Retail
Net purchases	$23,600	$45,000
Opening inventory	35,000	65,000
Markup		3,500
Markup cancellation		1,800

Find: The value of the total merchandise handled at retail and cost and the cumulative markon percentage.

Solution: Set up the problem and solve as follows:

	Cost	Retail	$Markon	Markon %
Opening inventory	$35,000	$65,000	$30,000	46.2
Net purchases	23,600	45,000	21,400	47.6
Net markup		1,700	1,700	
Total merchandise handled	$58,600	$111,700	$53,100	47.5

Notice that the $1,700 in net markup derives from a $3,500 markup less a markup cancellation of $1,800. Net markup is therefore an upward revision of the retail price and enters into the calculation of the "total merchandise handled" at retail with no corresponding effect on cost. As a result, the original markon dollars ($30,000 + $21,400 = $51,400) are increased by the amount of the net markup ($1,700) to $53,100 and the markon percentage adjusted accordingly.

▪ Application Exercise

1. Given:

	Cost	Retail
Opening inventory	$8,000	$14,300
Purchases	7,600	13,900
Markup		1,100
Markup cancellation		500

Determine (a) total merchandise handled at retail, (b) total merchandise handled at cost, (c) cumulative markon dollars, and (d) cumulative markon percentage.

2. Given:

	Cost	Retail
BOM inventory	$23,700	$45,300
Net purchases	18,200	36,400
Transportation	800	
Markup		3,800
Markup cancellation		1,200
Net sales		63,200

Determine (a) book inventory at cost and (b) book inventory at retail.

3. Given:

	Cost	Retail
Net sales		$43,600
Markup cancellation		2,100
Markup		4,600
Freight in	$1,400	
Gross purchases	16,800	28,700
Purchase returns and allowances	2,800	3,900
BOM inventory	36,700	48,900

Find (a) gross margin dollars and (b) gross margin percentage.

4. Given:

	Cost	Retail
Beginning inventory	$36,400	$70,300
Gross purchases	18,300	35,800
Purchase returns and allowances	2,400	4,100
Freight charges	1,500	

	Cost	Retail
Gross sales		73,000
Markup		6,200
Markup cancellation		1,800
Customer returns and allowances		5,100
Closing physical inventory		36,200

Identify: (a) total merchandise handled at retail, (b) total merchandise handled at cost, (c) cumulative markon percentage, (d) book inventory at retail, (e) physical inventory at cost, (f) stock shortages, (g) cost of merchandise sold, (h) gross margin dollars, and (i) gross margin percentage.

5. A boys' clothing buyer had an opening inventory of $34,800 at retail with a markon of 47%. Additional merchandise was purchased at a cost of $16,500 with a markon of 48%; freight charges on these purchases amounted to $650. Upon receipt, the buyer discovered that part of the shipment was defective and therefore returned some items that had a cost value of $1,200 and a planned retail price of $2,400. Errors in the pricing of the merchandise required a markup cancellation of $1,500. Gross sales for the period amounted to $46,700, with customer returns and allowances totaling $3,300. A physical inventory taken at the end of the period revealed that the retail value of the merchandise on hand was $17,900. Operating expenses for the period were $16,663. What was the buyer's operating profit?

The effect of markdowns and markdown cancellations on the retail value of the book inventory

As we have just seen, markup is an upward revision of the original selling price, or an increase in the initial or cumulative markon, and as such affects only the retail value of the total merchandise handled. Because cost is not affected, net markups increase the retail value of the total merchandise handled and the resulting cumulative markon dollars and percentages. Conversely, net markdowns[22] enter into the calculation of the retail method as a negative factor, below the "total merchandise handled," and thus contribute, along with net sales and sales discounts, to the total amount of retail reductions.[23]

---

[22] Gross markdowns minus markdown cancellations.
[23] Retail reductions, as the concept pertains to the retail method, consist of net sales, net markdowns, and sales discounts (a special form of markdown); anticipated shortages may or may not be included at the discretion of the merchant.

▪ Study Problem

Given: The following merchandise data are offered by a small, independent merchant:

	Cost	Retail
BOM inventory	$38,600	$70,500
Net purchases	23,400	44,700
Transportation	850	
Net sales		92,700
Markdowns		7,500
Markdown cancellations		3,600
Sales discounts		1,800

Find: (a) The value of the book inventory at retail and (b) the value of the book inventory at cost.

Solution:

	Cost	Retail	$Markon	Markon %
BOM inventory	$38,600	$ 70,500	$31,900	45.2
Net purchases	23,400	44,700	21,300	47.7
Transportation	850		(850)	
Total merchandise handled	$62,850	$115,200	$52,350	45.4
Net sales		92,700		
Net markdowns		3,900		
Sales discounts		1,800		
Total retail reductions		$ 98,400		
Book inventory	$ 9,173[(b)]	$ 16,800[(a)]		

The book inventory at retail (a) is the product of the total merchandise handled at retail for the period minus the total amount of retail reductions accrued during the period; retail reductions in this instance refer to the sum of the net sales, net markdowns,[24] and sales discounts. Thus,

---

[24]Net markdowns cannot be deducted prior to the determination of the total merchandise handled because they obviously do not appear on the purchase records and thus have no effect upon the cumulative markon. Markdowns, including sales discounts, reflect the depreciation in the retail value of the merchant's inventory within a specific time frame and thus bear directly upon the subsequent gross margin and operating profit for the period of concern.

Total retail reductions = $92,700 + $3,900 + $1,800 = $98,400

Because the book inventory at retail is equal to the total merchandise handled at retail less the total retail reductions, then,

(a) Book inventory at retail = $115,200 − $98,400 = $16,800

and

(b) Book inventory at cost = $16,800 (100% − 45.4%) = $9,173

▪ Application Exercise

1. Given:

	Cost	Retail
Beginning inventory	$13,600	$24,800
Purchases	8,400	14,300
Freight	350	
Markdowns		4,500
Sales discounts		1,500
Net sales		23,600

Find (a) book inventory at retail and (b) book inventory at cost.

2. Given:

	Cost	Retail
Opening inventory	$32,600	$59,800
Net purchases	23,700	45,300
Transportation	1,800	
Operating expenses	25,246	
Markdowns		10,600
Markdown cancellations		3,800
Sales discounts		1,900
Net sales		73,800

Find (a) book inventory at retail, (b) book inventory at cost, (c) cost of merchandise sold, (d) gross margin, and (e) operating profit.

3. Given:

	Cost	Retail
BOM inventory	$23,800	$48,300
Gross purchases	18,600	35,200
Purchase returns	4,300	8,000
Freight charges	900	
Gross sales		53,500
Operating expenses	19,561	

	Cost	Retail
Customer returns		4,800
Markdowns		6,400
Markdown cancellations		3,300
Sales discounts		1,800

Find (a) book inventory at cost, (b) cost of merchandise sold, (c) gross margin, and (d) operating profit.

4. Given:

	Cost	Retail
Opening inventory	$47,600	$93,200
Gross purchases	26,700	52,500
Purchase returns	4,800	7,900
Transportation	2,300	
Operating expenses	39,653	
Markups		4,800
Gross sales		106,000
Customer returns		8,400
Markdowns		11,400
Markdown cancellations		5,800
Sales discounts		3,200

Find (a) total retail reductions, (b) book inventory at cost, (c) cost of merchandise sold, (d) gross margin, and (e) operating profit.

5. Given:

	Cost	Retail
BOM inventory	$96,400	$190,500
Gross purchases	37,800	75,600
Purchase returns	8,000	15,000
Transportation	2,300	
Operating expenses	81,122	
Markups		8,700
Markup cancellations		3,600
Gross sales		215,300
Customer returns		12,400
Markdowns		15,800
Markdown cancellations		7,500
Sales discounts		9,600
Ending physical inventory		33,600

Find (a) book inventory at retail, (b) inventory shortage, (c) physical inventory at cost, (d) cost of merchandise sold, (e) gross margin, and (f) operating profit.

▪ Solutions to the Application Exercises

Determination of the Ending Inventory at Both Cost and Retail (p. 340)

	Cost	Retail	Markon %
1. Opening inventory	$26,000	$43,600	40.4
Purchases to date	15,200	29,300	48.1
Total merchandise handled	$41,200	$72,900	43.5
Less net sales		53,900	
Book inventory	$10,735	$19,000	43.5

3. Opening inventory at retail = $8,300 ÷ (100% − 48%) = $15,962

    Cost of purchases = $5,800 (100% − 43.5%) = $3,277

	Cost	Retail	Markon %
Opening inventory	$ 8,300	$15,962	48.0
Purchases	3,277	5,800	43.5
Total merchandise handled	$11,577	$21,762	46.8
Less net sales		15,700	
Book inventory	$ 3,225	$ 6,062	46.8

5. Net sales = $83,200 − $1,300 = $81,900

    Cost of inventory 2/1 = $43,800 (100% − 42%) = $25,404

    Cost of purchases 2/1–7/31 = $72,100 (100% − 42%) = $41,818

	Cost	Retail	Markon %
Inventory 2/1	$25,404	$ 43,800	42
Purchases 2/1–7/31	41,818	72,100	42
Total merchandise handled	$67,222	$115,900	42
Less net sales		81,900	
Book inventory	$19,720	$ 34,000	42

Determination of the Cost of Merchandise Sold, Gross Margin, and Operating Profit (p. 342)

1. Average cost = $123,800 (100% − 40%) = $74,280

3. Net sales = $45,000 − $500 = $44,500

	Cost	Retail	Markon	Markon%
Inventory 7/1	$15,500	$30,200	$14,700	48.7
Purchases 7/31	23,800	45,500	21,700	47.7
Total merchandise handled	$39,300	$75,700	$36,400	48.1
Less net sales		44,500		
Less book inventory 7/31	16,193	$31,200		
Cost of merchandise sold	$23,107[a]			
Gross margin			$21,393[b]	
Less operating expenses	$18,800 ——————————————→		(18,800)	
Operating profit			$ 2,593[c]	

5. Cost of opening inventory = $327,000 (100% − 51.5%) = $158,595
   Cost of purchases = $278,600 (100% − 49.6%) = $140,414

	Cost	Retail	$Markon	Markon%
Opening inventory	$158,595	$327,000	$168,405	51.5
Purchases	140,414	278,600	138,186	49.6
Total merchandise handled	$299,009	$605,600	$306,591	50.6
Less net sales		432,000		
Less book inventory	85,758	$173,600		
Cost of merchandise sold	$213,251			
Gross margin			$218,749	
Less operating expenses	$184,032 ————————→		(184,032)	
Operating profit			$34,717	
Net other income			-0-	
Net profit			$34,717	

$$\text{Net profit \%} = \frac{\$34,717}{\$432,000} = 8\%$$

The Effect of Transportation Costs and Inventory Shortages on the Component Values of the Retail Method (p. 344)

	Cost	Retail	$Markon	Markon %
1. Beginning inventory	$32,800	$59,600	$26,800	45.0
Net purchases	18,600	35,400	16,800	47.5
Transportation	840		(840)	
Total merchandise handled	$52,240	$95,000	$42,760	45.0

	Cost	Retail	$Markon	Markon %
Less net sales		46,700		
Book inventory at retail		$48,300[(a)]		
Less ending physical inventory	$25,410[(c)]	46,200		
Stock shortages		$2,100[(b)]		
Cost of goods sold	$26,830[(d)]			

	Cost	Retail	$Markon	Markon %
3. Inventory 2/1	$26,235	$47,700	$21,465	45.0
Net purchases	12,400	23,600	11,200	47.5
Transportation	425		(425)	
Total merchandise handled	$39,060	$71,300	$32,240	45.2
Less net sales		53,600		
Book inventory		$17,700		
Less physical inventory 7/31	9,206	16,800		
Inventory shortage		$900[(a)]		
Cost of goods sold	$29,854[(b)]			

	Cost	Retail	$Markon	Markon %
5. BOM inventory	$83,600	$143,700	$60,100	41.8
Purchases	23,800	41,800	18,000	43.1
Transportation	500		(500)	
Total merchandise handled	$107,900	$185,500	$77,600	41.8
Less net sales		87,300		
Book inventory	$57,152	$98,200		
Less physical inventory		106,300		
Inventory overage[25]		$ (8,100)		
Cost of goods sold	$50,748			
Gross margin			$36,552	41.9

[25]While an inventory overage is theoretically possible, its genesis will always derive from some type of clerical error, either in the determination of the physical inventory or the calculation of the book inventory. Faced with an irreconcilable difference, the merchant should always choose the lower of the two figures, thus avoiding an understatement of the cost of goods sold and an overstatement of gross margin.

The Effect of Markup and Markup Cancellation on the Value of the Total Merchandise Handled and Cumulative Markon (p. 354)

	Cost	Retail	$Markon	Markon %
1. Opening inventory	$8,000	$14,300	$6,300	44.1
Purchases	7,600	13,900	6,300	45.3
Net markup		600	600	
Total merchandise handled	$15,600[b]	$28,800[a]	$13,200[c]	45.8[d]

	Cost	Retail	$Markon	Markon %
3. BOM inventory	$36,700	$48,900	$12,200	24.9
Net purchases	14,000	24,800	10,800	43.5
Freight in	1,400		(1,400)	
Net markup		2,500	2,500	
Total merchandise handled	$52,100	$76,200	$24,100	31.6
Less net sales		43,600		
Less book inventory	22,298	$32,600		
Cost of goods sold	$29,802			
Gross margin			$13,798[a]	31.6[b]

	Cost	Retail	$Markon	Markon %
5. Opening inventory	$18,444	$34,800	$16,356	47.0
Net purchases	15,300	29,331	14,031	47.8
Freight charges	650		(650)	
Markup cancellation		(1,500)[26]	(1,500)	
Total merchandise handled	$34,394	$62,631	$28,237	45.1
Less net sales		43,400		
Book inventory		$19,231		
Less physical inventory	9,827	17,900		
Shortage		$1,331		
Cost of merchandise sold	$24,567			
Gross margin			$18,833	43.4
Less operating expenses	$16,663		(16,663)	
Operating profit			$2,170	5.0

[26]Downward revisions in the original retail price to correct pricing errors are classified as markup cancellations, because only the retail value of the inventory is affected; cost values are left intact.

The Effect of Markdowns and Markdown Cancellations on the Retail Value of the Book Inventory (p. 357)

	Cost	Retail	$Markon	Markon %
1. Beginning inventory	$13,600	$24,800	$11,200	45.2
Purchases	8,400	14,300	5,900	41.3
Freight	350		(350)	
Total merchandise handled	$22,350	$39,100	$16,750	42.8
Net sales		23,600		
Markdowns		4,500		
Sales discounts		1,500		
Total retail reductions		$29,600		
Book inventory	$ 5,434[b]	$ 9,500[a]		

	Cost	Retail	$Markon	Markon %
3. BOM inventory	$23,800	$48,300	$24,500	50.7
Net purchases	14,300	27,200	12,900	47.4
Freight	900		(900)	
Total merchandise handled	$39,000	$75,500	$36,500	48.3
Net sales		48,700		
Net markdowns		3,100		
Sales discounts		1,800		
Total retail reductions		$53,600		
Less book inventory	11,322[a]	$21,900		
Cost of merchandise sold	$27,678[h]			
Gross margin			$21,022[c]	43.2
Less operating expenses	$19,561 ⟶		(19,561)	
Operating profit			$1,461[d]	3.0

	Cost	Retail	$Markon	Markon %
5. BOM inventory	$96,400	$190,500	$94,100	49.4
Net purchases	29,800	60,600	30,800	50.8
Transportation	2,300		(2,300)	
Net markup		5,100	5,100	
Total merchandise handled	$128,500	$256,200	$127,700	49.8

	Cost	Retail	$Markon	Markon%
Net sales		202,900		
Net markdowns		8,300		
Sales discounts		9,600		
Total retail reductions		$220,800		
Book inventory		35,400[(a)]		
Less physical inventory	16,867[(c)]	33,600		
Inventory shortage		1,800[(b)]		
Cost of merchandise sold	$111,633[(d)]			
Gross margin			$91,267[(e)]	45.0
Less operating expenses	$81,122 ⟶		(81,122)	
Operating profit			$10,145[(f)]	5.0

Topics for Discussion and Review

1. What are the two major deficiencies in the cost method of inventory valuation that preclude its general use by the modern retail merchant?
2. Explain the concept of the retail method of inventory.
3. What is the primary objective of the retail method? What advantages accrue to the merchant, assuming that this objective is achieved?
4. What is the underlying premise of the retail method?
5. Explain why the cost of the merchandise currently on hand, as defined by the retail method, theoretically represents the lower of original cost or market value.
6. Under the retail method, explain how an overage is theoretically possible and why, at the same time, it is actually impossible.
7. What type of structure supports the validity of the retail method?
8. What are the items of information needed for the accurate determination of gross margin, using the retail method?
9. Discuss the advantages and limitations of the retail method of inventory valuation.
10. Explain what happens when the merchant fails to achieve homogeneity in the markon. Why is this so?
11. What would you say is the greatest deficiency in the retail method? Explain your answer.

12. What is the cost of the merchandise sold entirely dependent upon? Why?

13. Discuss the effect of transportation charges on the cost of merchandise and the markon dollars.

14. Discuss the concept of retail price changes.

15. Explain the difference between a markon and a markup.

16. What is a markup cancellation? How does it differ from a markdown?

17. What is a markdown cancellation? How does it differ from a markup?

18. Explain the concepts of net markup and net markdown.

19. Explain how you would calculate the merchant's ending inventory (book), at both retail and cost.

20. Explain the effects of markups, markup cancellations, and net markups on the total merchandise handled and the cumulative markon.

21. How would you explain the effect of markdowns and markdown cancellations on the retail value of the book inventory?

22. Given an $1,800 shortage and a cumulative markon of 42.3%, explain the dollar effect of that shortage upon the cost of goods sold and the resulting gross margin.

23. What are transportation charges not included in operating expenses?

24. What is the effect of net markups on the total merchandise handled?

25. Why do net markdowns have no effect upon the cumulative markon?

Chapter 12
The Six-Month Merchandise Plan

Learning Objectives

- Explain the concept of the corporate operating budget.

- Explain the concept of the merchandise budget, including its immediate concerns.

- List the strategic goals forecast by the merchandise budget.

- Explain the concept of the retail accounting calendar.

- Define the six-month merchandise plan.

- Discuss the purposes and implied goals of the six-month merchandise plan.

- Identify eight tactical objectives of the six-month merchandise plan.

- List the components of the six-month merchandise plan.

- Explain the format and major characteristics of the six-month merchandise plan, including the essential elements of the plan.

- Explain how the historical seasonal data for the six-month merchandise plan are derived from the operating statements.

- Discuss the component parts of the body of the six-month merchandise plan, including a detailed explanation of "purchases at retail."

- Discuss the concept of sales planning in terms of historical data and impinging variables.

- Explain the top-down concept of sales planning.

- Predict a sales volume predicated upon the available square feet of selling space.

- Estimate net sales using planned inventory turnover and the average inventory.

- Plan a sales volume based upon the average dollar sale and the number of transactions.

- List six factors influencing the size of the average sale.

- Forecast net sales using the stock-to-sales ratio.

- Predict planned sales as a product of historical data and current trends.

- Explain how planned seasonal sales are distributed across six accounting periods.

- Discuss the three essential concepts in the dollar planning of a retail inventory.

- Explain the basic stock method of inventory planning, including the formulas for the BOM inventory and the basic stock.

- Discuss the limitations of the basic stock method.

- Calculate the BOM inventory for any given month using the basic stock method.

- Explain how the basic stock method is adapted to the retail accounting calendar.

- Discuss the percentage variation method of inventory planning as it relates to the basic stock method.

- Calculate the BOM stock for any given month using the percentage variation method.

- Explain the stock-to-sales method of inventory planning.

- Explain how stock-to-sales ratios relate to the concept of inventory turnover.

- Calculate the stock-to-sales ratio from historical data, and use it to forecast the BOM stock.

- Discuss the weeks supply method of inventory planning, including its limitations.

- Calculate the BOM stock using the weeks supply method.

- Compute the six-month merchandise plan in its entirety.

Key Merchandising Terms

Accounting Periods: Are analogous to months in the retail accounting calendar. They consist of discrete blocks of time commencing with a Sunday and running through a Saturday and are composed of either four or five weeks. Just as there are twelve months in the normal calendar year, so there are twelve periods in the retail accounting calendar; however, Period I corresponds to February, not January; thus, the numerical definition of a period is always one less than that definition as supplied by the Gregorian calendar. For example,

Month:	Jan.(1)	Feb.(2)	March(3)	April(4)	May(5)	June(6)
Period:	XII	I	II	III	IV	V
Month:	July(7)	Aug.(8)	Sept.(9)	Oct.(10)	Nov.(11)	Dec.(12)
Period:	VI	VII	VIII	IX	X	XI

Average Inventory: The average amount of inventory required to be on hand within a designated time frame in order to support a specific sales volume. Calculated by dividing the sum of the BOM inventories and the EOM inventory by the total number of inventories involved. (See Chapter 8 for a more detailed explanation.)

Average Sale: The dollar amount of net sales divided by the number of sales transactions.

BOM Inventory: The retail value of the inventory on hand at the beginning of each month or accounting period.

Basic Stock: An assortment of merchandise for which the demand is relatively heavy and consistent. Also defined as the minimum amount of inventory to be on hand, even in the slowest period of a season.

Basic Stock Method: A method of inventory planning whereby planned sales for each month are added to a basic stock, so as to determine the planned monthly BOM stock. (In this sense, basic stock may be defined as the minimum amount of inventory that should be maintained, even in the least active month.)

Cumulative Markon Percentage: The average percentage of initial markon taken over a period of time.

EOM Inventory: The retail value of the closing inventory at the end of each accounting period.

Fall Season: The last half of the fiscal year, commencing around the first of August and concluding approximately at the end of January. According to the retail accounting calendar, the fall season consists of periods VII through XII.

Gross Margin: The maintained markon, minus alteration costs, plus cash discounts earned.

Inventory Turnover: The number of times within a specific period of time (normally one year) that an inventory is sold and replaced.

Merchandise Strategy: The art of merchandise planning, directed towards the establishment of specific, profit-enhancing goals.

Merchandise Tactics: The techniques of securing the more immediate objectives designated by merchandising strategy.

Open-to-Buy: The amount of merchandise that the merchant may order during the balance of a given period. Open-to-buy is planned purchases, minus outstanding orders, plus merchandise received during the period.

Percentage Variation Method: A method of dollar BOM inventory planning, to be used where the annual stock turn is 6 or more or the seasonal turn is 3 or better.

Purchases at Cost: The merchant's cost, or the market value of the planned purchases at retail.

Purchases at Retail: The retail value of the merchandise to be purchased and received into inventory during any given period.

Retail Accounting Calendar: Also known as the 4–5–4 calendar. A fiscal accounting and control device used to facilitate an accurate comparison of current or planned data with relevant historical data. The retail accounting calendar reorganizes time, as defined by the Gregorian calendar, into a series of discrete and uniform weeks, periods, and seasons, all commencing on a Sunday and ending on a Saturday. The fiscal year is defined in terms of two seasons, twelve periods, and fifty-two 7-day weeks, or 364 days (52×7).

Retail Reductions: The total of markdowns, sales discounts, and estimated inventory shortages (shrinkage).

Retail Transaction: The sale, return, or exchange of merchandise between the retail merchant and the consumer.

Sales per Square Foot of Selling Space: The net sales derived from each square foot of selling space, often referred to as the "space-productivity ratio"; calculated by dividing the net sales by the number of square feet of selling space.

Six-Month Merchandise Plan: A seasonal dollar-control device designed for the periodic regulation of departmental inventories. It attempts to coordinate net sales, inventories, retail reductions, and purchases to maximize the achievement of gross margin.

Spring Season: The first half of the fiscal year, beginning around the first of February and terminating sometime near the end of July. More specifically, as defined by the retail accounting calendar, the spring season runs from Period I through Period VI.

Staple Stock: Merchandise that should be on hand at any given period of time.

Stock-to-Sales Ratio: The ratio between the BOM inventory and the sales for that month, computed by dividing the BOM inventory for any particular month or period by the net sales for that month or season. Thus,

$$\text{Stock-to-sales ratio} = \frac{\text{BOM inventory}}{\text{Net sales}}$$

This ratio is to be distinguished from turnover in that it is a ratio of inventory to sales on a periodic, or monthly, basis (the beginning or end of a month), rather than an average of stocks spread over a series of months.

Stockout: Merchandise not carried in sufficient quantity to satisfy customer demand.

Traffic: The number of potential customers who enter or pass by a retail store or a department within that store.

Vendor: An individual, firm, or corporation from which the merchant purchases merchandise; any source of merchandise for resale to the consumer.

12.1
Planning and the Retail Method of Inventory

The success of any retail merchandising operation ultimately derives from careful planning and control, coupled with prompt feedback and comparison of the achieved results with the projected performances. Formal planning is an integral part of the management and control of the merchant's inventory; indeed, true merchandise control may be defined as the regulation of action or the application of tactics within the parameters of a formalized plan. Thus, the achievements of merchandising activities can only be measured by the extent to which they conform to a predetermined plan. Planning clarifies thinking and provides the basis for an analysis of the current situation, future possibilities, and the potential means of bridging the perceived gap between what is and what could or should be.

The underlying premise of modern merchandise planning and control is that the retail method of inventory provides the most efficient and expedient means of defining accurate merchandise plans and the key standards for measuring the effectiveness of merchandising tactics. Merchandise planning is therefore normally established and maintained at the retail price level; where "cost" prices are required to measure and define specific levels of merchandising activities, they are always determined from the appropriate retail price by means of the complement of the cumulative markon percentage.

The Concept of Retail Store Budgeting

The genesis of profit is the establishment of corporate financial goals and the implementation of some type of planning and control device to guide and direct daily activities towards the achievement of those goals. These specific objectives, such as operating and net profit, sales volume, return on investment, and any other indicators of profitability, must be established so that relevant comparisons can subsequently be made between achieved results and forecasted probabilities.

Once put into place, these financial goals become the foundation and thus an integral part of the planning and budgeting process. In effect, the budget defines the more immediate objectives that will, at least theoretically, provide the sequence of activities necessary for the determination of the corporate financial goals.

The corporate budget may be viewed as a forecast of operating objectives for the entire retail store, encompassing all financial goals—from gross sales down through net profit. Such a budget is essentially the compilation of data in support of the two major objectives of any retail organization: an adequate gross margin and a realistic operating profit. Thus, the corporate operating budget must of necessity be subdivided into a merchandise budget and an expense budget. The merchandise budget incorporates the gross margin goal that is expected to be derived from the merchant's control and management of the retail inventory; the expense budget attempts to define all of the nonmerchandise-related store operating expenses within the parameters of gross margin and operating profit. Thus, the gross margin dollars derived from merchandising activities in effect translate into operating income, which serves to provide the necessary support system for merchandising activities[1] and still allows for a fair profit.

The Corporate Operating Budget

In order to put the merchandise budget into its proper perspective, it is necessary to first discuss the role of the corporate operating budget, for it is within this framework that all merchandising objectives must be established.

Sales
    Gross sales
    Less returns and allowances
                                    Net sales

Merchandise costs
    B O M inventory
    Net purchases
    Transportation

    Total merchandise handled
    Less E O M inventory

---

[1]For a detailed analysis of store operating expenses, see *Financial and Operating Results of Department and Specialty Stores* (New York: Financial Executives Division, National Retail Federation, Inc.). This is an annual publication.

Gross cost of merchandise sold
Less cash discounts
_____

Net cost of merchandise sold
Alteration costs
_____

Less total merchandise costs
_____
Gross margin
Less operating expenses
_____
Operating profit
Net other income
_____
Net profit

The corporate budget is a statement or financial definition of the retail image the store management desires to project; in this sense, it is a general appraisal of current conditions, predicated upon past performance and future potential. The corporate operating budget sets the parameters for all merchandising activity and by so doing construes the goals and directs the emphasis of the full spectrum of merchandising strategy. Thus, the operating budget is the primary instrument to be followed in the creation of departmental merchandising policies, goals, and limitations. The corporate operating budget is prepared in total rather than departmentally and illustrates the major objectives of corporate intention, with appropriate detail and by classification. The most desirable arrangement for the corporate operating budget is generally the same as that used for the reporting of previous operating results. This format was discussed in Chapter 2 and further amplified in Chapter 10; it is herewith reiterated solely to provide the context for a better understanding of the merchandise budget.

Once the corporate budget is established in the aggregate, its constituent elements are broken down by department and distributed across the six selling periods of the given season.[2]

---

[2]This process of budgeting is the "top-down" method, wherein top management establishes the individual components of the seasonal budget and then distributes those components across the various divisions and subdivisions of the retail store. An alternative method of budgeting is the "bottom-up" process, whereby the first line of unit managers, i.e., buyers, store managers, or operating managers, prepares budget estimates, which after revision are then consolidated at the various levels of store management. Bottom-up planning offers the advantage of the insight gained by those executives closest to the customer, while top-down planning commences with those executives best able to view the corporate structure as a whole and are thus in a position to more accurately define the availability of financial and other resources.

The Merchandise Budget

The merchandise budget is a subdivision of the operating budget and as such is concerned only with the following:

1. Net sales.

2. Cost of sales, including all impinging factors such as retail reductions, inventory valuation, additional purchases, earned discounts, and alteration costs.

3. Maintained markon and gross margin.

When finalized, the aggregates of the departmental merchandise budget, by period and in total for the season, are subsequently incorporated into the corporate operating budget.

Commencing with the inventory on hand at the beginning of the accounting period, the merchandise budget forecasts, or plans, the following strategic goals:

1. Net sales

2. Net purchases

3. Workroom costs

4. Price changes

5. Sales discounts

6. Inventory shortage

7. Value of the closing inventory

8. The rate of inventory turnover

9. The percentage of cumulative markon

10. Gross margin

11. Purchase discounts

12. Maintained markon

One of the most important features of the merchandise budget is the projected balancing of inventories in relationship to planned sales and the assistance this offers in the attainment of an adequate gross margin on those sales. Thus, the merchandise budget provides an effective control over purchases and tends to prevent an overstocked or understocked position. In effect, the merchandise budget[3] controls and manages the dollar value of the merchant's inventory, by

---

[3]Hereafter defined as the six-month merchandise plan.

detailing the components of the operating statement down through gross margin and by defining standards of performance by selling department and accounting period.

The Seasonal Nature of the Budget

Both the merchandise and expense components of the corporate retail budget are normally established to conform to two distinct selling seasons: spring–summer (roughly February through July) and fall–winter (approximately August through January). Each season is comparable with the like seasons of previous years, but the two seasons, spring and fall, are not directly comparable with each other.

The Retail Accounting Calendar

The retail accounting calendar, also known as the 4–5–4 calendar, was devised to facilitate the comparison of accounting data by avoiding the inherent complications of the Gregorian calendar—the lack of comparative selling weeks, months, and seasons.

As illustrated in Figure 12.1, the conventional calendar year is split into two 26-week seasons, spring and fall; spring commences with a Sunday in the latter part of January or early in February and ends with a Saturday around the end of July or the beginning of August; fall starts with the following Sunday and terminates with a Saturday sometime in late January or the first week of February. Each season is then divided into two quarters, each quarter originating with a Sunday and ending with a Saturday. Each of the resulting four quarters is subsequently separated into three time periods roughly equivalent to the standard calendar month, with the exception that each period once more starts with a Sunday and concludes with a Saturday. Each period or "month" is then broken down into a series of weeks, the first day of which is a Sunday and the last day a Saturday. The retail accounting calendar is so arranged that the first period of each quarter contains four weeks, the second period has five weeks, and the last, or third, period once more consists of four weeks. It is from this unique distribution of thirteen weeks across any given quarter that the concept of the 4–5–4 calendar is derived.

Figure 12.2 depicts the retail accounting calendar for the fiscal year of 1990 and 1991. Periods II, V, VIII, and XI (March, June, September, and December) consist of five 7-day weeks each; the remaining periods respectively contain four 7-day weeks. Thus, the fiscal year is composed of 364 days (52 weeks × 7 days), with the 365th day advanced to the following year for five or six years, depending upon the number of intervening leap years. In the fifth or sixth year, an additional week is added to Period XII (January), thus causing the last quarter to consist of one 4-week period (November) and two 5-week periods (December and January); in this manner, the fiscal calendar is brought into line with the Gregorian calendar.

		Fiscal Year February thru January Period I thru Period XII											
		Spring Season February thru July Period I thru Period VI						Fall Season August thru January Period VII thru Period XII					
		First Quarter February thru April Period I thru III			Second Quarter May thru July Period IV thru VI			Third Quarter August thru October Period VII thru IX			Fourth Quarter November thru January Period X thru XII		
		Period I Feb. 4 wks.	Period II March 5 wks.	Period III April 4 wks.	Period IV May 4 wks.	Period V June 5 wks.	Period VI July 4 wks.	Period VII August 4 wks.	Period VIII Sept. 5 wks.	Period IX Oct. 4 wks.	Period X Nov. 4 wks.	Period XI Dec. 5 wks.	Period XII Jan. 4 wks.
		Week 1 2 3 4	Week 1 2 3 4 5	Week 1 2 3 4	Week 1 2 3 4	Week 1 2 3 4 5	Week 1 2 3 4	Week 1 2 3 4	Week 1 2 3 4 5	Week 1 2 3 4	Week 1 2 3 4	Week 1 2 3 4 5	Week 1 2 3 4

Figure 12.1 The concept of the retail accounting calendar

Feb. 12 ......Lincoln's Birthday May 12 ....Mother's Day Nov. 5 ....Election Day
Feb. 14 ......Valentine's Day May 27 ....Memorial Day Nov. 11 ....Veteran's Day
Feb. 18 ......President's Day June 16 ....Father's Day Nov. 28 ....Thanksgiving
Feb. 22 ......Washington's Birthday July 4 ....Independence Day Dec. 25 ....Christmas Day
March 31 ......Easter Sunday Sept. 2 ....Labor Day Jan. 1 ....New Year's Day
                              Oct. 14 ....Columbus Day Jan. 20 ....M.L. King's Birthday

Fiscal 4-5-4
Calendar ⟨AMC⟩ **1991**
52 Weeks

FEBRUARY-4 WEEKS
WEEK SUN MON TUE WED THU FRI SAT
1 | 3 4 5 6 7 8 9
2 | 10 11 12 13 14 15 16
3 | 17 18 19 20 21 22 23
4 | 24 25 26 27 28 1 2

MARCH-5 WEEKS
WEEK SUN MON TUE WED THU FRI SAT
1 | 3 4 5 6 7 8 9
2 | 10 11 12 13 14 15 16
3 | 17 18 19 20 21 22 23
4 | 24 25 26 27 28 29 30
5 | 31 1 2 3 4 5 6

APRIL-4 WEEKS
WEEK SUN MON TUE WED THU FRI SAT
1 | 7 8 9 10 11 12 13
2 | 14 15 16 17 18 19 20
3 | 21 22 23 24 25 26 27
4 | 28 29 30 1 2 3 4

MAY-4 WEEKS
WEEK SUN MON TUE WED THU FRI SAT
1 | 5 6 7 8 9 10 11
2 | 12 13 14 15 16 17 18
3 | 19 20 21 22 23 24 25
4 | 26 27 28 29 30 31 1

JUNE-5 WEEKS
WEEK SUN MON TUE WED THU FRI SAT
1 | 2 3 4 5 6 7 8
2 | 9 10 11 12 13 14 15
3 | 16 17 18 19 20 21 22
4 | 23 24 25 26 27 28 29
5 | 30 1 2 3 4 5 6

JULY-4 WEEKS
WEEK SUN MON TUE WED THU FRI SAT
1 | 7 8 9 10 11 12 13
2 | 14 15 16 17 18 19 20
3 | 21 22 23 24 25 26 27
4 | 28 29 30 31 1 2 3

AUGUST-4 WEEKS
WEEK SUN MON TUE WED THU FRI SAT
1 | 4 5 6 7 8 9 10
2 | 11 12 13 14 15 16 17
3 | 18 19 20 21 22 23 24
4 | 25 26 27 28 29 30 31

SEPTEMBER-5 WEEKS
WEEK SUN MON TUE WED THU FRI SAT
1 | 1 2 3 4 5 6 7
2 | 8 9 10 11 12 13 14
3 | 15 16 17 18 19 20 21
4 | 22 23 24 25 26 27 28
5 | 29 30 1 2 3 4 5

OCTOBER-4 WEEKS
WEEK SUN MON TUE WED THU FRI SAT
1 | 6 7 8 9 10 11 12
2 | 13 14 15 16 17 18 19
3 | 20 21 22 23 24 25 26
4 | 27 28 29 30 31 1 2

NOVEMBER-4 WEEKS
WEEK SUN MON TUE WED THU FRI SAT
1 | 3 4 5 6 7 8 9
2 | 10 11 12 13 14 15 16
3 | 17 18 19 20 21 22 23
4 | 24 25 26 27 28 29 30

DECEMBER-5 WEEKS
WEEK SUN MON TUE WED THU FRI SAT
1 | 1 2 3 4 5 6 7
2 | 8 9 10 11 12 13 14
3 | 15 16 17 18 19 20 21
4 | 22 23 24 25 26 27 28
5 | 29 30 31 1 2 3 4

JANUARY-4 WEEKS
WEEK SUN MON TUE WED THU FRI SAT
1 | 5 6 7 8 9 10 11
2 | 12 13 14 15 16 17 18
3 | 19 20 21 22 23 24 25
4 | 26 27 28 29 30 31 1

Feb. 12 ......Lincoln's Birthday May 10 ....Mother's Day Nov. 3 ....Election Day
Feb. 14 ......Valentine's Day May 29 ....Memorial Day Nov. 11 ....Veteran's Day
Feb. 17 ......President's Day June 4 ....Father's Day Nov. 26 ....Thanksgiving
Feb. 22 ......Washington's Birthday July 4 ....Independence Day Dec. 25 ....Christmas Day
April 19 ......Easter Sunday Sept. 7 ....Labor Day Jan. 1 ....New Year's Day
                              Oct. 12 ....Columbus Day Jan. 18 ....M.L. King's Birthday

Fiscal 4-5-4
Calendar ⟨AMC⟩ **1992**
52 Weeks

FEBRUARY-4 WEEKS
WEEK SUN MON TUE WED THU FRI SAT
1 | 2 3 4 5 6 7 8
2 | 9 10 11 12 13 14 15
3 | 16 17 18 19 20 21 22
4 | 23 24 25 26 27 28 29

MARCH-5 WEEKS
WEEK SUN MON TUE WED THU FRI SAT
1 | 1 2 3 4 5 6 7
2 | 8 9 10 11 12 13 14
3 | 15 16 17 18 19 20 21
4 | 22 23 24 25 26 27 28
5 | 29 30 31 1 2 3 4

APRIL-4 WEEKS
WEEK SUN MON TUE WED THU FRI SAT
1 | 5 6 7 8 9 10 11
2 | 12 13 14 15 16 17 18
3 | 19 20 21 22 23 24 25
4 | 26 27 28 29 30 1 2

MAY-4 WEEKS
WEEK SUN MON TUE WED THU FRI SAT
1 | 3 4 5 6 7 8 9
2 | 10 11 12 13 14 15 16
3 | 17 18 19 20 21 22 23
4 | 24 25 26 27 28 29 30

JUNE-5 WEEKS
WEEK SUN MON TUE WED THU FRI SAT
1 | 31 1 2 3 4 5 6
2 | 7 8 9 10 11 12 13
3 | 14 15 16 17 18 19 20
4 | 21 22 23 24 25 26 27
5 | 28 29 30 1 2 3 4

JULY-4 WEEKS
WEEK SUN MON TUE WED THU FRI SAT
1 | 5 6 7 8 9 10 11
2 | 12 13 14 15 16 17 18
3 | 19 20 21 22 23 24 25
4 | 26 27 28 29 30 31 1

AUGUST-4 WEEKS
WEEK SUN MON TUE WED THU FRI SAT
1 | 2 3 4 5 6 7 8
2 | 9 10 11 12 13 14 15
3 | 16 17 18 19 20 21 22
4 | 23 24 25 26 27 28 29

SEPTEMBER-5 WEEKS
WEEK SUN MON TUE WED THU FRI SAT
1 | 30 31 1 2 3 4 5
2 | 6 7 8 9 10 11 12
3 | 13 14 15 16 17 18 19
4 | 20 21 22 23 24 25 26
5 | 27 28 29 30 1 2 3

OCTOBER-4 WEEKS
WEEK SUN MON TUE WED THU FRI SAT
1 | 4 5 6 7 8 9 10
2 | 11 12 13 14 15 16 17
3 | 18 19 20 21 22 23 24
4 | 25 26 27 28 29 30 31

NOVEMBER-4 WEEKS
WEEK SUN MON TUE WED THU FRI SAT
1 | 1 2 3 4 5 6 7
2 | 8 9 10 11 12 13 14
3 | 15 16 17 18 19 20 21
4 | 22 23 24 25 26 27 28

DECEMBER-5 WEEKS
WEEK SUN MON TUE WED THU FRI SAT
1 | 29 30 1 2 3 4 5
2 | 6 7 8 9 10 11 12
3 | 13 14 15 16 17 18 19
4 | 20 21 22 23 24 25 26
5 | 27 28 29 30 31 1 2

JANUARY-4 WEEKS
WEEK SUN MON TUE WED THU FRI SAT
1 | 3 4 5 6 7 8 9
2 | 10 11 12 13 14 15 16
3 | 17 18 19 20 21 22 23
4 | 24 25 26 27 28 29 30

Figure 12.2 The retail accounting (4–5–4) calendar (Courtesy of Associated Merchandising Corp.)

12.2

The Concept of the Six-Month Merchandise Plan

Profit is not an accidental phenomenon. Generally speaking, and not precluding some degree of good fortune, profit essentially is the product of a carefully planned course of action towards a definable and measurable financial goal. Thus, for the retail merchant, the idea of profit must be synonymous with sound planning and realistic objectives.

The Six-Month Merchandise Plan Defined

The six-month merchandise plan is the catalyst that translates profit objectives into dollar realities by astute planning and shrewd control; it is a profit-enhancing tool, more specifically defined as

> A seasonal dollar control device designed to regulate departmental inventories in accordance with preestablished financial objectives.

The essential goal for all merchandising activity is to minimize the use of capital and maximize the amount of achieved profit; the six-month merchandise plan is the fundamental means of supporting and directing this effort, in that it establishes financial objectives in terms of required merchandise dollars and provides a control method for the regulation of inventory levels.

Because financial objectives are rarely more than educated estimates, their degree of achievement will vary according to impinging unforeseen circumstances. Thus, the control element of the merchandise plan may be considered as its most valuable attribute, in that it not only regulates merchandising activity within the framework of a predetermined design of operating objectives but also provides the means for evaluating success in terms of achieved objectives versus projected goals.

The Strategic Goals of the Six-Month Merchandise Plan

As the basic dollar planning and control device available to the retail merchant, the six-month merchandise plan contains three distinct purposes, which in effect establish the strategic goals of any merchandising operation. These purposes and their implied goals are as follows:

1. *Purpose*:
   To provide a relatively sound estimate of the amount of capital required to be invested in a periodic inventory.
   a. *Strategic goal*:
      (1) The achievement of the correct ratio between inventory and net sales.

2. *Purpose*:

    To supply the merchant with a reliable basis for the estimation of periodic cash flow.

    a. *Strategic goal*:

        (1) To improve and facilitate the decision process with respect to capital and expense management and thus enhance profit ratios.

3. *Purpose*:

    To serve as an instrument of financial control.

    (a) *Strategic goals*:

        (1) The establishment of guidelines for the investment in inventory.

        (2) The creation of periodic tactical objectives as they relate to seasonal or strategic goals.

        (3) To provide a means of measuring achieved results against planned performance along with the implications for corrective action.

The Tactical Objectives of the Six-Month Merchandise Plan

Given the above strategic goals of the six-month merchandise plan, upon implementation the merchant may expect to achieve the following tactical objectives:

1. Reduced inventory investment.

2. Minimization of stockouts.

3. Reductions in, and better control over, markdowns.

4. Reduced carryover of previous-season merchandise.

5. Increased turnover.

6. Improved maintained markon and resulting gross margin.

7. Increased availability of the open-to-buy, so as to provide the means to take advantage of the vendors' offerings of off-price goods.

8. The maximization of classification profitability.

Components of the Six-Month Merchandise Plan

While there are many variants in the design of the six-month merchandise plan, due primarily to the size and scope of the merchandising activities to be controlled, it is generally agreed that the following elements, defined in terms of seasons, periods, departments, and classifications, constitute the essence of the plan,[4] regardless of the environment in which it is used:

1. Cumulative markon for the season.[5]

2. Net sales.

3. BOM inventories.

4. EOM inventories.

5. Stock-to-sales ratios.

6. Retail reductions.

7. Purchases at retail.

8. Purchases at cost.

9. Gross margin.

12.3

Procedure for Constructing the Six-Month Merchandise Plan

Frequency of Preparation

The six-month merchandise plan is normally prepared twice a year, each plan corresponding to the spring and fall season, the end of which usually finds inventories to be at their lowest levels. The preparation of each plan should begin approximately three to six months prior to the actual merchandising season, to enable the merchant to place vendor orders for specific delivery dates before and during the planned accounting period. The effectiveness of the plan is to a large extent dependent upon the merchant's receipt of orders prior to the expected selling date, including an allowance for sufficient time to complete the processing of the incoming merchandise.[6] Timing is a major consideration in maintaining the proper balance between inventory and sales; merchandise properly prepared and

---

[4]The essence of the plan is the control of inventory levels as they relate to net sales; thus, the bare essentials of any merchandise plan are the independently planned sales, beginning inventories, retail reductions, and cumulative markon percentage. All of the other elements—ie., EOM inventories, stock-to-sales ratios, purchases at retail, purchases at cost, and gross margin—are corollary features of the plan that serve only to enhance the control of inventories at levels previously determined. This concept will be developed in more detail as we progress into this chapter.

[5]The average of the initial, or purchase, markons.

[6]This includes, but is not limited to, the receiving, checking, marking, and distribution process.

available for sale "at the right time" is an asset; goods in transit, from whatever source, to the selling floor, are not accessible to the customer and thus are a liability.

Store Coverage

For a small specialty store, the merchandise plan may be prepared on a total-store basis.[7] However, for the larger retail store, where merchandising activities are conducted on a departmental and classification basis, the following procedure is to be followed.[8]

1. The six-month plan is prepared by classification and gathered into one departmental plan.

2. A merchandise plan for the entire store is then assembled from the accumulation of departmental plans.

3. If the retail organization consists of more than one store, a corporate six-month plan is developed by store, department, and classification.

Format and Content of a Typical Six-Month Merchandise Plan

As we have already noted, the format and content of the six-month merchandise plan may superficially vary from one retail organization to another; however, the essential ingredients and basic organizational structure remain intact wherever the concept of retail merchandise planning is applied.

Figure 12.3 illustrates a typical six-month merchandise plan employed by those merchants operating under the retail method;[9] the following major characteristics are intrinsic to all merchandise plans in which the retail method is employed:

1. The format is applicable to either the spring or fall season, depending upon which box is checked in the upper left-hand corner.

2. This same form is to be used, regardless of whether the merchant is planning by classification, department, store, or corporation; again, the specific activity is to be indicated by marking the appropriate box in the upper left-hand corner.

---

[7]This is not to deny the advantages of classification merchandising for even the smallest of stores.
[8]Regardless of whether the figures used are derived from a "top-down" or "bottom-up" planning process.
[9]Our study of the six-month merchandise plan is predicated upon the retail method.

☐ Corporation _____

☐ Store _____

☐ Department _____

☐ Classification _____

☐ Spring 19__

☐ Fall 19__

Seasonal Data

	Last Year	Planned	Actual
Cumulative markon %			
Markdown %			
Shortage %			
Sales discounts %			
Maintained markon %			
Operating expenses %			
Operating profit %			
Turnover			

	Feb. (I) Aug. (VII)		Mar. (II) Sept. (VIII)		Apr. (III) Oct. (IX)		May (IV) Nov. (X)		June (V) Dec. (XI)		July (VI) Jan. (XII)		Total
	$	%	$	%	$	%	$	%	$	%	$	%	$
Net sales Last year													
Plan													
Revised													
Actual													
BOM stock Last year													
Plan													
Revised													
Actual													
EOM stock Last year													
Plan													
Revised													
Actual													
Retail reductions Last year													
Plan													
Revised													
Actual													
Purchases at retail Last year													
Plan													
Revised													
Actual													
Purchases at cost Last year													
Plan													
Revised													
Actual													
Maintained markon Last year													
Plan													
Revised													
Actual													

Figure 12.3 Six-month merchandise plan

3. All dollar amounts are entered at retail (with the obvious exception of "purchases at cost").

4. All percentages, where entered, are percentages of retail sales, except planned net sales, which are indicated as a percentage of last year's actual sales.[10]

5. Pertinent seasonal data are indicated above the body of the plan; the entry of specific data is arbitrary, with the exception of the cumulative markon percentage or sufficient data from which to derive that percentage.[11]

6. The body of the form is apportioned according to the periods (corresponding to months) of the retail accounting calendar and the essential components of the merchandise plan.[12] These components are subsequently broken down into:
   Last year (actual)
   Plan (this year)
   Revised (this year)
   Actual (this year)

The construction of the six-month merchandise plan will focus upon the dollar control and management of a "short-sleeve, knit shirt" classification (51), under the umbrella of the men's furnishings department (514); the planning date is sometime in early September, in anticipation of the approaching spring season. We shall begin by assuming agreement on the historical data and anticipated seasonal projections as illustrated in Figure 12.4.

Determining the Numerical Components of the Six-Month Merchandise Plan

The six-month merchandise plan serves as a catalyst to bring together all of the merchandising tactics previously studied, and some yet to be studied, and directs them all towards the strategic objective of enhanced profit from the sale of merchandise. Essentially, this profit is defined as gross margin; in this instance, we shall use the term *maintained markon* because, for the sake of simplicity, earned

---

[10]For example, if last year's net sales were $94,000 and this year's planned sales were $106,000, the ratio of this year to last year would be 113% ($106,000 ÷ $94,000 = 113%).

[11]For example, if the cumulative (initial) markon percentage is not given, there must be sufficient data available, i.e., the percentage of operating expenses, net profit, and retail reductions, to permit its calculation. See Chapter 3 for the precise method of calculation.

[12]Again, the "essential components" consist of sales; BOM stock; markdowns, shortages, sales discounts; and the cumulative markon percentage. All other elements of the plan are simply deductions from these components.

☐ Corporation
☐ Store
☐ Department 514 (Men's Furn.)
☒ Classification 51 (S.S. Knits)
☒ Spring 19____
☐ Fall   19____

Seasonal Data

	Last Year	Planned	Actual
Cumulative markon %	47.2		
Markdown %	6.8		
Shortage %	3.0		
Sales discounts %	1.0		
Maintained markon %	41.5		
Operating expenses %	36.5		
Operating profit %	5.0		
Turnover	1.6		

	Feb. (I) Aug. (VII)		Mar. (II) Sept. (VIII)		Apr. (III) Oct. (IX)		May (IV) Nov. (X)		June (V) Dec. (XI)		July (VI) Jan. (XII)		Total
	$	%	$	%	$	%	$	%	$	%	$	%	$
Net sales													
Last year	16,300		17,500		18,600		19,700		21,300		21,000		114,400
Plan													
Revised													
Actual													
BOM stock													
Last year	78,240	4.8	78,750	4.5	74,400	4.0	70,920	3.6	70,290	3.3	63,000	3.0	435,600
Plan													
Revised													
Actual													
EOM stock													
Last year	78,750		74,400		70,920		70,290		63,000		60,000		417,360
Plan													
Revised													
Actual													
Retail reductions													
Last year	1,631	10.0	2,422	13.8	1,853	10.0	2,051	10.4	1,705	8.0	2,693	12.8	12,355
Plan													
Revised													
Actual													
Purchases at retail													
Last year	18,441		15,572		16,923		21,121		15,715		20,693		108,515
Plan													
Revised													
Actual													
Purchases at cost													
Last year	9,737		8,222		8,962		11,152		8,298		10,926		57,297
Plan													
Revised													
Actual													
Maintained markon													
Last year	6,830	41.9	6,983	39.9	7,793	41.9	8,215	41.7	9,159	43.0	8,484	40.4	47,464
Plan													
Revised													
Actual													

Figure 12.4 Six-month merchandise plan with last year's data added

cash discount and workroom costs have been eliminated.[13] With this in mind, let us briefly discuss the various components of the merchandise plan as illustrated by the historical, or "last-year," data shown in Figure 12.4. We will first consider the seasonal data above the body of the plan, then the components of the plan itself and their interrelationships.

Seasonal data derived from the operating statement

Before delving into the specifics of the merchandise plan, the following simplified operating statement from "last year" is presented, so as to provide a framework for a conceptual understanding of the seasonal data and the methods by which it is calculated.

	Cost	Retail	Markon %	% to Sales
B O M inventory	$231,810	$435,600	46.8	--
Purchases	55,008	107,615	48.9	--
Total merchandise handled	$286,818	$543,215	47.2	--
Cost of sales				
Net sales		$114,400		100.0
Markdowns		7,770		6.8
Sales discounts		1,145		1.0
Shortages		3,540		3.0
Total cost of sales	$ 66,979	$126,855		
Net sales		$114,400		
Less cost of sales		66,979		
Maintained markon		$ 47,421	41.5	
Less operating expenses		41,756		36.5
Operating profit		$ 5,665		5.0

Note the following:

$$\text{The cumulative markon} = \frac{\$543,215 - \$286,818}{\$543,215} = 47.2\%$$

Markdowns $= \$7,770 \div \$114,400 = 6.8\%$

Shortages $= \$3,540 \div \$114,400 = 3\%$

Sales discounts $= \$1,145 \div \$114,400 = 1\%$

---

[13]Recall from Chapters 7 and 8 that the concept of maintained markon is synonymous with the gross margin, when there are no cash discounts or workroom expenses.

The cost of sales (which does not show up on the merchandise plan) is derived as follows:

$$\$126,855 \times (100\% - 47.2\%) = \$66,979$$

The maintained markon % = $\$47,421 \div \$114,400 = 41.5\%$

Operating expenses = $\$41,756 \div \$114,400 = 36.5\%$

Operating profit = $\$5,665 \div \$114,400 = 5\%$

Seasonal data derived from the merchandise plan[14]

1. The *cumulative markon percentage*[15] is the maintained markon percentage plus the percentage of retail reductions:

   Retail reductions = $6.8\% + 1\% + 3\% = 10.8\%$

   Cumulative markon % = $\dfrac{41.5\% + 10.8\%}{100\% + 10.8\%} = 47.2\%$

2. The *maintained markon* equals the cumulative markon minus the cost of the retail reductions:

   Cost of reductions = $10.8\% \times (100\% - 47.2\%) = 5.7\%$
   Maintained markon = $47.2\% - 5.7\% = 41.5\%$
   Maintained markon also equals operating expenses plus operating profit:
   Maintained markon = $36.5\% + 5\% = 41.5\%$[16]

3. *Markdowns, shortages,* and *sales discounts* require little explanation, except to note that together they compose the concept of retail reductions, distributed across the body of the plan.

---

[14]Historical seasonal data are average figures derived from six months, or periods, of operating activity; specific periodic data (e.g., operating expenses for February) are not available. As we delve into the body of the plan from a "last-year" perspective (in the following section), periodic data in support of the monthly cumulative and maintained markons are missing and therefore must be assumed from the seasonal data. This is not to preclude the accuracy of the total seasonal data as illustrated in Figure 12.4.

[15]The cumulative markon, sometimes defined as the "purchase markon," is the average of many "initial" markons. In this instance, not only does the markon vary by purchases, but it will also vary by the period. The ultimate objective is always the cumulative markon for the season, as determined by a succession of variant initial markons.

[16]This figure can only be determined by this maneuver: Maintained markon percentage = Expenses + Profit on a seasonal basis, because the merchandise plan does not allow for a monthly distribution of operating expenses, operating profit, and cost of sales.

4. The *turnover* figure is a seasonal ratio derived from data illustrated in the body of the plan. Turnover is equal to net sales divided by the average stock for the season.

Net sales = $114,400

Average stock equals the sum of the BOM stocks ($435,600) plus the EOM stock for July ($60,000) divided by 7. Thus, the

$$\text{Average inventory} = \frac{\$435,600 + \$60,000}{7} = \$70,800$$

Therefore,

$$\text{Turnover} = \frac{\$114,400}{\$70,800} = 1.6$$

The body of the plan

1. *Net sales* represent last year's actual receipts (gross sales less returns and allowances) and provides the basis for the determination of this year's planned sales. The techniques of sales planning will be discussed in detail in the next section of this chapter.

2. The *BOM stock* represents the retail value of the inventory on hand at the beginning of each selling period. A detailed analysis of stock-planning methods is also presented further into this chapter; at this point, our only concern is with an understanding of the component parts of the six-month plan and their interrelationships. The *stock-to-sales ratio,* while not specifically defined as such on the six-month plan, is located to the right of the BOM stock figure in the percentage column. This ratio indicates the relationship between planned sales and the amount of inventory investment required to produce those planned sales. This concept, as an intrinsic part of stock planning, receives detailed consideration later in this chapter. For our purposes at this point, the following understanding, derived from February's figures, is sufficient:

$$\frac{\text{BOM inventory ($78,240$)}}{\text{Net sales ($16,300$)}} = (4.8) \text{ Stock-to-sales ratio}$$

Therefore, by transposition,

BOM inventory = Net sales × Stock-to-sales ratio

or, as indicated in Period I,

BOM stock = $16,300 × 4.8 = $78,240

3. The *EOM stock* defines the retail value of the closing inventory for each period of the season.[17] The EOM inventory is essentially not a matter of calculation[18] but simply an understanding of the concept that the dollar value of the opening inventory (BOM) must be the dollar value of the preceding closing (EOM) inventory.

4. *Retail reductions* consist of the sum of the markdowns, shortages, and sales discounts shown in the seasonal data. Along with sales, retail reductions serve to reduce the value of the merchant's inventory. Because the six-month merchandise plan is composed of dollars rather than units, retail purchases (discussed next) must include these reductions along with net sales, in order to restore the periodic value of the planned inventory. Should the retail reductions be omitted in the planning of retail purchases, the resulting inventory on hand would not suffice to meet the required monthly stock levels. In other words, the actual BOM inventory would be reduced by the amount of the "unplanned-for" retail reductions. It is to be noted that while the retail reductions represent 10.8% of the seasonal sales, it does not necessarily follow that they must be 10.8% of periodic sales; this is due primarily to the fluctuations in the monthly markdown percentages.

5. *Purchases at retail* refers to the retail value of the merchandise to be purchased and taken into the merchant's inventory within a specific accounting period. Essentially, the concept revolves around the difference between the retail dollar value of merchandise needs versus the immediate availability of merchandise to effectively complete the merchandise plan. In short, purchases at retail defines the difference between what the merchant has in inventory and should have in order to achieve the planned net sales. Thus purchases at retail may be conceptually defined as the difference between the periodic BOM inventory (what is available in inventory) and the collective requirements of net sales, the EOM stock, and the retail reductions (what the merchant needs to replenish the inventory so as to maintain a specific level of sales). Quantitatively stated, purchases at retail may be defined as follows:

$$\underbrace{\text{Net sales} + \text{EOM} + \text{stock Reductions}}_{\text{"Needs"}} - \underbrace{\text{BOM stock}}_{\text{"Has"}} = \text{Purchases at retail}$$

Or,

Purchases at retail = (Net sales + Retail reductions + EOM inventory) − BOM inventory

---

[17] Recall that the EOM inventory for any given period is the BOM inventory for the ensuing period. Thus, the EOM inventory in Figure 12.4 for February ($78,750) is the BOM inventory for March ($78,750).

[18] Except when the coming season, i.e., August, is unknown. Here a calculation is necessary, and it will be discussed as we progress.

Using the figures for February (Period I) in Figure 12.4 as an example, we find that the purchases at retail are

($16,300 + $1,630 + $78,750) − $78,240 = $18,440

6. *Purchases at cost* defines the market value of the "purchases at retail," or what the merchant may expect to pay for additional stock to replenish inventories. From a conceptual point of view, they simply represent purchases at retail reduced to cost by means of the complement of the cumulative markon percentage. Thus, assuming that the cumulative markon percentage for Period I was 47.2%,[19] the purchases at cost would have been:

$18,440 × (100% − 47.2%) = $9,736

7. *The periodic maintained markon*[20] may be derived from the merchandise plan as a percentage figure and then translated into dollars. The maintained markon is equal to the cumulative markon minus the cost of reductions. Thus, assuming a constant (although unrealistic) cumulative markon of 47.2%, the maintained markon for each month may be calculated by subtracting the cost of the retail reductions from that cumulative markon percentage and multiplying the result times the monthly sales. The maintained markon for February is calculated as follows:

Cost of reductions = 10% × (100% − 47.2%) = 5.3%

Maintained markon % = 47.2% − 5.3% = 41.9%

$Maintained markon = $16,300 × 41.9% = $6,830

This concludes our study of the six-month merchandise plan in terms of format and intrinsic concepts. However, before we proceed to develop an oper-

---

[19]The periodic percentage of cumulative markon cannot be derived from the merchandise plan because its emphasis is on seasonal rather than monthly data. These figures must be derived from an independent source. However, for the purpose of a simplistic illustration, all of the monthly "purchases at cost" were derived from the corresponding "purchases at retail" using the seasonal cumulative markon of 47.2%. While this concept is mathematically correct, it is hardly representative of a real-life situation, where there may be great fluctuations in the monthly cumulative markons.

[20]Although purchases at cost are the last figure called for in a typical six-month merchandise plan, a most important corollary feature of that plan is the resulting periodic and seasonal determination of gross margin. In this particular example, we define gross margin in terms of maintained markon. This is because, for the sake of simplicity, workroom costs and earned cash discounts have been excluded from the six-month merchandise plan; thus, for our purposes, the term *gross margin* is synonymous with *maintained markon*. See Chapters 7 and 8 for a discussion of maintained markon and gross margin.

ational plan for the coming season, two concepts, external but vital to the merchandise plan, must be further explored. These are the techniques of sales forecasting and stock planning.

Techniques of Sales Forecasting

The first numerical component of the six-month merchandise plan concerns a forecast of sales, either by period or month. This is the most critical of all merchandising decision, simply because, as we have seen, all other merchandising activities are planned in relation to net sales or are stated as a percentage of sales. Thus, if the sales forecast is inaccurate, all derived data will likewise be in error, with obviously disastrous results.

General Considerations

Because all other elements of the six-month merchandise plan are predicated upon net sales, this is the first item to be considered. While net sales are the fulcrum of all merchandising activity, they are at the same time the most subjective part of the planning process and therefore the most difficult and the least scientific. While there are many pragmatic approaches to the development of a retail sales plan, in the final analysis the essence of the accepted figures is a gut feeling, or an emotional response to the planner's understanding of contemporary environmental stimuli. Although the role of sales forecasting lies outside the realm of scientific activity, this is not to imply that it is simply a matter of "crystal ball gazing"; sales planning is an art, constantly to be perfected by means of practice and continuous education. The more educated the forecaster, the more precise and reliable will be the sales forecast.

The "education" of the retail merchant, as it relates to sales planning, commences with a thorough understanding of the determinants of last year's seasonal and periodic sales volumes; this stands as the fundamental guide for planning the sales volume for the anticipated selling season. However, previous sales figures serve only to advise the planner on future market activities and thus must be augmented by the consideration of the following impinging variables:

Planned storewide sales

Special events

Departmental promotions

Current business and storewide sales trends

Holidays

Fashion trends and the position of styles in their respective fashion cycles

Population shifts towards or away from the trading area in which the merchant is located

Shifts in the demographic characteristics of the population served by the retail merchant

The effect of new competitive elements

The consequences of inflation on price structures and the impact of unit sales

Changes in credit policies, including interest rates, third-party arrangements, and the impact of such changes on the retail image

Modification in parking facilities

Changes in store hours

Changes in the number of selling days in each month or period

Changes in selling space, either on a storewide or departmental basis

It should be fairly clear that a successful sales forecast depends upon three fundamental factors:

1. The accuracy of the utilized historical data.

2. The ability to interpret that data within the context of current events and to project it according to a realistic comprehension of future potentialities; this is, in effect, the exercise of sound judgment.

3. An understanding of the computations required to quantitatively evaluate those "future potentialities."

Historical data are simply a matter of record; sound judgment must of necessity derive from the marriage of innate intelligence with the continuous, practical application of learned techniques. In essence, the subjective interpretation of recorded data and the application of sound judgment define the nonscientific aspect of retail merchandising; in this sense, sales planning is an art, combining the exercise of intuitive faculties with the employment of empirical skills or merchandising tactics. Obviously, it is only the techniques, or tactics, of retail merchandising that can be appropriately conveyed through a textbook; therefore, of necessity, the main thrust of this section will be directed towards the computations required to enhance the art of retail sales forecasting.

Various techniques of sales planning are offered, none of which independently stand as the absolute authority in the determination of future sales activity. Each technique must be applied within the parameters of a unique planning situation, the determination of which reverts back to the "art" of retail merchandising.

Specific Techniques of Sales Forecasting

Forecasting Sales as a Result of Management Decree (Top-Down Planning)

Top-down planning occurs when senior-level executives establish corporate sales objectives for the entire retail operation. These objectives are in turn broken down by stores, merchandise divisions, and departments. Thus, buyers, store managers, and department managers have little or no input into their sales objectives, which are established for them by a higher authority.

∎ Study Problem

Given: Net sales last year were $50,000. Management has decreed a 10% increase in planned sales for this year.

Find: The dollar amount of the sales increase and the dollar amount of planned sales.

Solution:

Net sales increase = Last year's actual sales × The planned percentage of increase

Net sales increase = $50,000 × 10% = $5,000

Dollar amount of planned sales = Last year's actual sales + Dollar amount of planned increase

Dollar amount of planned sales = $50,000 + $5,000 = $55,000

Alternate Solution:

Dollar amount of planned sales = Last year's actual net sales × (100% + Planned percentage of increase)

Therefore,

Dollar amount of planned sales = $50,000 × 110% = $55,000

▪ Application Exercise

1. Net sales last year were $340,000. A 13% increase is planned for this year. What is the dollar value of the planned sales increase, and what is the new planned sales figure?

2. Sales last year for a classification of women's shoes was $75,500. Sales are planned to increase this year by 8.5%. What is the dollar amount of the planned increase and the projected sales volume?

3. If the projected sales volume is to be 112% of last year and last year's sales dollars were $83,600, what is the dollar volume of planned sales?

4. Following a definite fashion trend, sales for a classification of jeans are projected to decrease by 13.5% for next year. If net sales last year were $63,200, what is the new planned sales volume?

5. Net sales last year were $116,000. Sales for next year are realistically planned at 93.3% of last year's volume. What are the planned sales for next year?

Planning a Dollar Net Sales Volume Predicated upon the Available Square Feet of Selling Space

Sales per square foot[21] are an excellent indicator of profitability and therefore a sound basis upon which to establish a sales forecast. Published, typical figures, by store size and merchandise classifications, are readily available through trade associations such as the National Retail Federation, Inc.[22] and provide guidelines for a critical analysis of sales projections. The essence of the concept of sales per square foot is that sales volume is a result of the dollars achieved per square foot of selling space times the number of square feet of selling space available. Stated quantitatively,

$$\text{Sales per square foot} = \frac{\text{Net sales}}{\text{Number of square feet of selling space}}$$

Therefore,

$$\text{Net sales} = \text{Sales per square foot} \times \text{Number of square feet of selling space}$$

---

[21]Often referred to as the space-productivity ratio.
[22]*Department and Specialty Store Merchandising and Operating Results* (New York: Financial Executives Division, National Retail Federation, Inc.).

■ Study Problem

Given: A women's hosiery department occupies a selling area of 1,500 square feet. Net sales last year were $200 per square foot. This year, sales per square foot are planned at $205, with the same space allocation.

Find: (a) net sales for last year, (b) planned net sales this year, and (c) the percentage variation between planned sales and last year's actual sales.

Solution:

(a) Net sales last year = 1,500 (square feet) × $200 (sales per square foot) = $300,000

(b) Planned sales this year = 1,500 (square feet) × $205 (sales per square foot) = $307,500

(c) Percentage variation = $\dfrac{\$307,500 - \$300,000}{\$300,000}$ = 2.5%

■ Application Exercise

1. A small leather goods department occupied 300 square feet of selling space and last year produced $400 per square foot. Assuming that the amount of selling space remains constant and the space-productivity ratio is planned to increase by $6 per square foot, find (a) last year's actual sales, (b) this year's planned sales, and (c) the percentage of increase or decrease in the planned net sales over last year.

2. It was estimated that the sales per square foot of an infants' furniture department could be increased by 10% with the addition of two new merchandise classifications. The department currently occupies 2,000 square feet, with sales at $80 per square foot. Assuming no change in the size of the department, project the new sales volume should the two new merchandise classifications be introduced.

3. The owner of a chain of men's clothing stores is contemplating adding an additional store with approximately 3,000 square feet of selling space. Using historical data predicated upon the existing stores in the chain, sales per square foot for the potential addition are estimated at $320. What is the projected sales volume?

4. A dress department was laid out to cover 900 square feet of selling space. If net sales are projected to be $108,000, what is the required sales per square foot?

5. How many square feet of selling space are required by a fine jewelry department if the sales per square foot are $600 and net sales are planned at $1,200,000?

Estimating Net Sales Using the Planned Inventory Turnover and the Average Inventory

Another valid guideline for the estimation of net sales is the inventory turnover objective.[23] Turnover ratios may be derived from historical internal operating data (i.e., net sales and average inventories), or they may be obtained from sources external to the retail store, such as the previously noted *Merchandise and Operating Results,* published by the National Retail Federation. The essence of the turnover ratio as an indicator of sales volume derives from the turnover formula

$$\text{Turnover} = \frac{\text{Net sales}}{\text{Average inventory}}$$

Wherein,

$$\text{Net sales} = \text{Average inventory} \times \text{Turnover}$$

▪ Study Problem

Given: A cosmetics department had a turnover ratio of 3 for last year, with an average inventory of $125,000.

Find: Assuming that the turnover can be increased to 3.5 with the same average inventory, determine (a) net sales last year, (b) planned sales for this year, (c) the dollar increase this year, and (d) the percentage increase this year over last year.

Solution:

Average inventory × Turnover = Net sales

Therefore,

(a) Net sales last year = $125,000 × 3 = $375,000

(b) Planned sales this year = $125,000 × 3.5 = $437,500

(c) Dollar increase this year = $437,500 − $375,000 = $62,500

(d) Percentage increase this year = $62,500 ÷ $375,000 = 16.7%

---

[23]See Chapters 8 and 9 for a review of turnover and the average inventory.

▪ Application Exercise

1. A men's shoe department reported a stock turnover of 2.3 last year based upon an average inventory of $83,000. This year, the same average stock is planned; however, turnover is expected to increase to 2.5. What sales volume may be anticipated this year, and what is the percentage of increase over last year?

2. A classification of junior sportswear turned 2.8 times during the fall season last year, with an average inventory of $87,400. For the fall season, this year's turnover is planned at 3 with a 10% decrease in the average inventory. What are the planned sales this year and the percentage of increase or decrease over last year?

3. A gift shop experienced a turnover of 2.5 last year with an average inventory of $83,600. It is anticipated that by "narrowing and deepening" the merchandise assortment, the average stock can be reduced to $80,000 and the turnover can be increased to 3. What is the level of sales that should be planned for this year and the percentage variation from last year?

Planned Sales Based upon the Average Dollar Sale and the Number of Sales Transactions

In this instance, sales planning is predicated upon the relationship between the average sale and the number of retail transactions. The concept may be expressed as a formula, wherein,

Net sales[24] = Average dollar sale × Number of transactions

By transposition, the following two relationships may then be established:

$$\text{Average dollar sale} = \frac{\text{Net sales}}{\text{Number of transactions}}$$

$$\text{Number of transactions} = \frac{\text{Net sales}}{\text{Average dollar sale}}$$

This approach to sales planning recognizes that sales volume is a composite of the value of the average dollar sale and a specific number of retail transactions. To understand the probable change in each of these two components and then to bring them together into a single factor will provide a far more accurate forecast of consumer activity than if sales were to be treated as a single entity. This is due

---

[24]If the available data represent the gross sales and the gross (i.e., total) number of transactions, then the product is defined as the gross average sale. For our purposes, we shall use the concept of net sales.

to the fact that an established pattern of transactions tends to remain far more consistent and stable than does the sales volume, which responds with a greater degree of sensitivity to the impact of market variables such as inflation and deflation. It is, therefore, often easier to predict a volume of transactions than it is to project an amount of sales dollars.

This method of sales planning involves a detailed consideration of the relationship between sales, the number of transactions, and the resulting average sale. Consider the following data as an aid to sales planning:

Period I	Sales	% +/−	Transactions	% +/−	Average Sale	% +/−
4 years ago	$120,000		24,000		$5.00	
3 years ago	131,250	9.4	25,000	4.2	5.25	0.5
2 years ago	143,100	9.0	26,500	6.0	5.40	2.9
1 year ago	148,500	3.8	27,000	1.9	5.50	1.9
% change		23.8		12.5		10.0
% av. change		5.9		3.1		2.5

Assume that the merchant, after considering the above data and other relevant factors, decides that the planned average sale will increase by 2% to $5.61 and that transactions, as a result of in-store traffic, should be planned at 28,000. Automatically, the sales forecast, as a product of these two factors, will be $157,080, or 28,000 × $5.61. Concentration on the historical sales volume alone could well lead the merchant to project sales on the basis of last year's increase; in that case, the resulting forecast of $154,143 ($148,500 × 1.038) would not be as factually grounded as that based upon the average sale and transactions. Obviously, in both instances, the merchant is attempting to "read" the future, and such attempts are always subject to the vagaries of environmental influences. However, the degree to which the forecasted sales conform to the actual sales is, to a large extent, dependent upon the variety and accuracy of the data that form the genesis of that forecast. Past sales alone are not necessarily indicative of future sales, and the validity of the forecast can be greatly enhanced by the introduction of such extraneous data as the average sale and the number of anticipated transactions.

Factors influencing the size of the average sale

Assuming a relatively consistent transactional pattern, the major consideration in the aforementioned planning strategy is the determination of the size, or amount, of the average sale. Again, the size of the average sale is a predictive phenomenon subject to innumerable variables apart from those constituting its initial formation. Obviously, not all of these variables are subject to the merchant's control; however, strong consideration must be given to those factors that most immediately affect the size of the average sale. Consider the following:

1. Price changes on the wholesale, or vendor, level dictated primarily by
   a. The availability of credit and the supply of money.
   b. Consumer demand and the availability of specific goods and services.

2. Changes in the perceived quality level of the merchandise to be sold.

3. The position of a particular style in its cycle of fashion; changing consumer purchasing patterns.

4. The ability of salespeople to "build" the average sale by means of suggestive selling, thus changing the quantity of merchandise in the average transaction.

5. Changes in the relative demand for interrelated classifications of merchandise, particularly on the departmental level. This, in effect, modifies the merchandise "mix" of the average sale and thus directly influences the value of that average sale, in spite of the fact that the specific retail prices remain unchanged. Consider the following example of an "average sale" in the men's furnishings department, assuming consistent prices:

Historic Average Sale[25]		Current Average Sale	
No. Units	*Total $*	*No. Units*	*Total $*
1 $20 shirt	$20	2 $20 shirts	$40
2 $10 ties	20	1 $10 tie	10
Average sale	$40	Average sale	$50

Notice that in the historic sense the average sale consisted of one $20 shirt and two $10 ties, for a total value of $40. However, by modifying the mix of that sale to its current composition of two shirts and one tie, the average sale now amounts to $50, or an increase of 25%.

6. Fluctuations in the markon percentage can materially affect the average sale with no appreciable influence upon sales volume or the number of transactions.

▪ Study Problem

Given:

	Last Year	Planned
Average sale	$20	$22
Transactions	4,180	3,500

---

[25]Per transaction.

Find: (a) net sales last year, (b) planned sales, and (c) the percentage of sales variation this year over last year.

Solution:

(a) Net sales last year = $20 (the average sale last year) × 4,180 (transactions last year) = $83,600

(b) Planned sales = $22 (planned average sale) × 3,500 (planned transactions) = $77,000

(c) Percentage variation = $\frac{\$83,600 - \$77,000}{\$83,600} = -7.9\%$ [26]

▪ Application Exercise

1. The average sale for a hosiery department last year was $4, with 30,000 transactions. This year, the average sale is planned at $5 and transactions are anticipated to be 35,000. What are the planned sales this year and the percentage of increase or decrease over last year?

2. Last year's average sale was $18.50. This year, planned sales are $950,000, and transactions are estimated to be 50,000. What is the percentage variation between this year's average sale and last year's?

3. Last year's actual sales were $780,000 with an average sale of $12.35. This year, the average sale is planned at $12.50 with a 10% decrease in the amount of transactions over last year. What are this year's planned sales?

4. Plan the sales for a costume jewelry department given the following data:

Transactions last year	17,500
Net sales last year	$98,300
Average sale this year	8%
Transactions this year	-7.5%

5. Net sales and transactions are expected to decline from last year by 10% and 3%, respectively. What is the anticipated percentage of decline in the average dollar sale?

6. What percentage of increase might be expected in the number of transactions if dollar sales increase by 8% and the average dollar sale rises by 3%?

---

[26]This year's sales are planned to be 7.9% less than last year's, or 92.1% (100% − 7.9%) of last year's sales.

Planning Net Sales Using the Stock-to-Sales Ratio

The stock-to-sales ratio[27] provides a means of measuring a specific amount of inventory required to produce a predetermined volume of net sales. In this sense, it is a planning device for the control of inventory levels. However, because it is a function of both sales and inventory, the ratio may serve as a useful device to enhance the accuracy of sales forecasting, as the following formula indicates:

$$\text{Stock-to-sales ratio} = \frac{\text{BOM inventory}[28]}{\text{Net sales}}$$

Therefore,

$$\text{Net sales} = \frac{\text{BOM inventory}}{\text{Stock-to-sales ratio}}$$

∎ Study Problem

Given: The BOM inventory for Period VI last year was $60,000, with a stock-to-sales ratio of 2.5. This year, the opening inventory for the same period is $69,000 with a planned stock-to-sales ratio of 2.3.

Find: (a) net sales for last year, (b) net sales planned for this year, and (c) the percentage variation in net sales this year over last year.

Solution:

(a) Net sales last year = $60,000 ÷ 2.5 = $24,000

(b) Planned net sales = $69,000 ÷ 2.3 = $30,000

(c) Percentage variation = $\dfrac{\$30,000 - \$24,000}{\$24,000} = 25\%$

∎ Application Exercise

1. The BOM inventory for December of last year was $120,000 with a stock-to-sales ratio of 3.2. This year, December's BOM inventory is planned at $117,000

---

[27]This concept will be developed further in the section on stock planning.
[28]The BOM inventory is normally used in the determination of the stock-to-sales ratio. However, some merchants prefer to use the EOM figure, so as to ensure the availability of an adequate inventory on the first of the coming month. This has the effect of planning an inventory one month in advance, because the EOM for this month is the BOM for next month.

with a stock-to-sales ratio of 2.9. What are the planned sales this year and the percentage of increase or decrease over last year?

2. A children's boutique exhibited the following data for the month of April last year:
The BOM inventory was $98,600
The stock-to-sales ratio was 5.2.
For April this year, the same opening inventory is planned, with the stock-to-sales ratio reduced to 4.8. What are the projected planned sales for this year, and by what percentage will they deviate from last year?

3. Last year, a shoe department operated with a May stock-to-sales ratio of 5.8 and a BOM inventory of $206,000. This year, the BOM inventory for May is projected to be $210,000, with the same stock-to-sales ratio. What are the planned sales for May of this year, and what is the percentage of increase or decrease compared with last year?

Planned Sales as a Product of Historical Data and Current Trends

Here we speak of forecasting sales on the basis of current, prevalent trends in the consumer's purchasing activity. Again, the technique employed must be tempered with a certain amount of judgment and expertise.

▪ Study Problem

Given: A glassware department has the following sales data available for the first quarter of the spring season.

	Net Sales	
	Last Year	This Year
February	$23,000	$25,000
March	26,000	27,000
April	28,000	29,000
May	29,000	

Find: The probable sales for the month of May.

Solution: First, determine the trend increase for the first three months of the season this year over last year:

$$\text{February} = \frac{\$25,000 - \$23,000}{\$23,000} = \frac{\$2,000}{\$23,000} = 8.7\%$$

$$\text{March} = \frac{\$27{,}000 - \$26{,}000}{\$26{,}000} = \frac{\$1{,}000}{\$26{,}000} = 3.8\%$$

$$\text{April} = \frac{\$29{,}000 - \$28{,}000}{\$28{,}000} = \frac{\$1{,}000}{\$28{,}000} = 3.6\%$$

Although sales are currently running ahead of last year, there is a definite tendency for that increase to progressively decrease.

Second, consider the direction of the monthly sales this year as they progressively relate to each other:

$$\text{March-to-February} = \frac{\$27{,}000 - \$25{,}000}{\$25{,}000} = \frac{\$2{,}000}{\$25{,}000} = 8\%$$

$$\text{April-to-March} = \frac{\$29{,}000 - \$27{,}000}{\$27{,}000} = \frac{\$2{,}000}{\$27{,}000} = 7.4\%$$

Again, we see that while there is a progressive improvement in the consecutive monthly sales, there is some indication that this improvement may be declining.

Assessing the current monthly sales trend in conjunction with the established "this-year-to-last-year" relationship, we may logically conclude (although not without a great deal of subjective input) that sales for this May should conservatively lie somewhere between a 2.5% increase over last May and a 6% increase over the past April.

May sales based on last year = $29,000 × 102.5%[29] = $29,725

May sales predicated upon April = $29,000 × 106% = $30,740

Thus, we may arbitrarily forecast the sales for May to be $30,200, or the approximate average of $29,725 and $30,740.

▪ Application Exercise

Given the subjective nature of forecasting sales solely on the basis of historical data and current trends, the application exercises are limited to the generation of numerical data to support the approximation of a planned sales figure.

1. Given:

	Net Sales	
	Last Year	This Year
April	$18,000	$19,000
May	19,000	20,000

[29] 2.5% above last year.

	Net Sales	
	Last Year	*This Year*
June	21,000	21,500
July	23,000	

Find the approximate planned sales for July.

2. Determine the probable sales forecast for the month of November, given the following data:

	Net Sales	
	Last Year	*This Year*
August	$23,800	$24,600
September	25,900	25,300
October	25,000	24,200
November	23,800	

3. Plan the sales for the approaching August, given the following data:

	Net Sales	
	Last Year	*This Year*
April	$53,600	$52,700
May	54,200	53,500
June	52,100	53,000
July	48,700	52,000
August	46,300	

The Distribution of Seasonal Sales into Accounting Periods

The essence of the concept is the proportional allocation of a planned seasonal sales volume to the specific periods, or months, comprising that season. From a purely mechanical perspective, the process of allocation is relatively simple. While techniques are relatively easy to teach and learn, productive application of acquired skills requires an individual investment of time as well as practical experience. While both are obviously beyond the scope of any text, they are important variables to be considered in the periodic sales-planning process; accurate sales forecasting, however defined, will always be more of an art than a science.

The following procedure for the distribution of a planned seasonal net sales volume is generally applicable to all retail institutions, regardless of size or type, assuming, of course, that the retail method of accounting is to be employed. The underlying principle guiding the determination of any volume of sales, whether it be periodic or seasonal, is the establishment of reasonable objectives tempered by realistic expectations. With this in mind, let us consider the basic steps in the allocation of planned seasonal sales to specific months and periods.

1. Calculate last year's monthly sales as a percentage of last year's total seasonal sales. Last year's actual sales by month are illustrated in columns (1) and (2) in Figure 12.5. Column (3) defines each month as a percentage of the season's total sales. For example, February's sales represent 14.2% of last year's seasonal sales, calculated as follows:

$$\text{February sales} = \frac{\$16,300}{\$114,400} = 14.2\%$$

2. Determine the total sales volume for the coming fall season, using the pertinent factors and techniques previously discussed. Let us assume that, after due consideration, total sales for the coming spring season are to be planned at 10% above last year, or $125,840. This figure is shown as the total of column (6) in Figure 12.5.

3. After the total sales for next spring are estimated, they must be broken down, by a monthly percentage, as illustrated in column (4). The initial projected percentage of total sales will depend upon that month's historical performance; adjustments must then be made to account for the various mitigating factors previously discussed and the results totaled to 100%.

4. The periodic planned percentages from column (4) are now multiplied by the total projected sales volume for the approaching spring season, shown at the bottom of column (6), in order to achieve the monthly planned sales. These computations are illustrated in column (5) of Figure 12.5.

Because of the highly subjective nature of column (4), "planned % of sales next spring," and the simplistic mathematical computation involved in arriving at "monthly planned sales," column (6), an additional study problem and application

(1)	(2)	(3)	(4)	(5)	(6)
Month (Period)	Sales Last Spring	% of Sales Last Spring	Planned % of Sales Next Spring	Computation	Monthly Planned Sales
February I	$16,300	14.2	15.0	$125,840 × 15.0 =	$18,876
March II	17,500	15.3	14.6	$125,840 × 14.6 =	18,372
April III	18,600	16.3	16.5	$125,840 × 16.5 =	20,764
May IV	19,700	17.2	16.7	$125,840 × 16.7 =	21,015
June V	21,300	18.6	19.0	$125,840 × 19.0 =	23,910
July VI	21,000	18.4	18.2	$125,840 × 18.2 =	22,903
	$114,400	100%	100%		$125,840

Figure 12.5 Determination of monthly planned sales

exercise would appear to be unnecessary and even redundant. We will therefore proceed to analyze the concept of stock planning, which is the immediate derivative of the sales forecast.

12.5

Stock Planning

Some Basic Considerations

As we have seen in Chapter 11, a prime requisite for the achievement of a planned volume of sales is an adequate inventory or a dollar amount of stock attuned to a specific volume of sales. This, in effect, defines the concept of a balanced stock, which stands as the universal challenge to all retail merchants—that is, to maintain an inventory investment sufficient to meet customer demand at all times and yet small enough to ensure a realistic return on that inventory investment. Thus, there are two fundamental concepts to be considered in the dollar planning of a retail inventory:

1. Net sales (as a measure of the merchant's ability to predict and satisfy customer demand).

2. The rate of stock turnover (as an indicator of the profit to be derived from the merchant's investment in inventory).

This is not to imply that there should be a constant relationship between inventory and net sales. Indeed, just the opposite may be true, because peak selling periods normally require a greater investment in inventory than do those periods of reduced sales activity. Ideally, what the merchant seeks is a variable periodic ratio of inventory to sales that maximizes turnover within the confines of a specific merchandise assortment. This leads us to a third consideration inherent in the concept of stock planning. That is,

3. The planned periodic fluctuations in the value of the beginning inventory should be less than the corresponding fluctuations in the planned net sales.

This notion is predicated upon the fact that sound merchandising policy dictates the establishment of some form of a constant or basic stock that by definition should not appreciably vary with net sales. As a result, the inventory turnover should be expected to increase during periods of high sales volume and to decline in relation to reduced sales volume. In other words, the monthly fluctuations in stock levels will be above or below the seasonal average stock,[30] but that

---

[30]Sales for the season divided by the seasonal stock turnover.

percentage of variation should not be as great as the degree of change existing between the monthly, or periodic, fluctuations in planned sales volume. This concept will be developed further as we explore the three commonly accepted methods for the financial control of the merchant's inventory.

Because there is a causal relation between inventory and net sales, stocks are normally defined in terms of the beginning of the month (BOM) rather than the end of the month (EOM), even though the BOM stock for one month is equivalent to the EOM stock for the preceding month. The BOM inventory is established to produce sales for a given month; the resulting ending inventory bears no direct relationship to those sales, but in effect is in place to make possible the sales for the following period.

Stock-Planning Methods

Stock planning essentially involves two basic concepts:

1. The maintenance of adequate inventory assortments in terms of units.

2. The dollar control of inventories in relation to sales, so as to maintain a satisfactory turnover ratio.

For the purposes of this chapter, we shall concentrate on the latter consideration. Thus, four methods of stock planning are presented:

1. The basic-stock method

2. The percentage variation method

3. The stock-to-sales method

4. The weeks' supply method

The Basic-Stock Method

The essence of the concept is that the merchant should have on hand, at all times, a basic dollar amount of inventory and that this inventory should remain constant throughout the season, regardless of the monthly fluctuation in sales volume. Thus, the BOM inventory for any given month may be found by adding the sales for that month to a preestablished basic stock. Conceptually, we observe that:

BOM stock = Planned sales for the month + Basic stock

This method provides for a continual level of inventory (basic stock), even if sales should drop to a theoretical zero. Figure 12.6 illustrates the basic stock as the margin between planned sales for the month and the BOM inventory. Note that

1. The basic stock is the difference between the BOM inventory and planned sales.

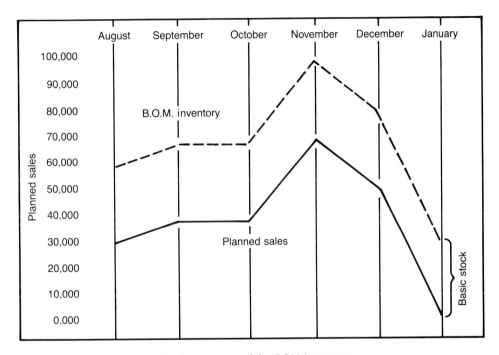

Figure 12.6 Basic stock as the determinant of the BOM inventory

2. The value of the basic stock remains intact, despite the fluctuations in planned sales.

3. Turnover in the busier months is higher than in the slower months.

Basic stock defined

Basic stock is the minimum amount of inventory to be maintained within a classification, department, or store, even in the least active month. It thus provides for a reserve stock, or a "cushion," against contingent stockouts, whether derived from an oversold condition or some failure on the part of the vendor to meet the merchant's immediate inventory demands. On the other hand, this reserve stock requires the merchant to maintain a relatively large investment in inventory, which not only increases the attendant carrying costs but also decreases the rate of stock turnover.

The basic stock may be defined as a reserve stock or a protection from contingent stockouts. Quantitatively speaking, a basic stock is equal to the average stock for the season[31] minus the average monthly sales.[32] Therefore,

---

[31]Average stock for the season $= \dfrac{\text{Net sales for season}}{\text{Stock turnover for season}}$

[32]Average monthly sales $= \dfrac{\text{Net sales for season}}{\text{Number of months in season}}$

$$\text{BOM stock} = \text{Planned sales for the month} + (\text{Average stock for the season} - \text{Average monthly sales})$$

Limitations of the basic-stock method

As long as the average monthly sales are less than the average monthly stock, this method will provide a basic stock that, when added to planned sales, will define a BOM inventory. In other words, the turnover ratio for the accounting period must always be less than the number of months in that accounting period; if such is not the case, the basic stock will be either zero or a negative value.

Determination of basic stock when the turnover is less than 6   As long as the stock turn is less than 6 times a season (i.e., as long as the average monthly sales are less than the average monthly stock), the basic-stock method produces a fixed inventory and thus yields a higher turnover in busy months than in the slower months.

▪ Study Problem

Given:

Planned sales for the fall season	$36,000
Planned seasonal stock turnover	3
Planned sales for October	$9,000

Find: The basic stock for October and the resulting BOM inventory.

Solution:

$$\text{Average stock for season} = \frac{\text{Seasonal sales}}{\text{Seasonal turnover}} =$$

$$\frac{\$36,000}{3 \text{ (times)}} = \$12,000$$

$$\text{Average monthly sales} = \frac{\text{Sales for season}}{\text{Months in season}} =$$

$$\frac{\$36,000}{6 \text{ (months)}} = \$6,000$$

Therefore,

Basic stock = $12,000 − $6,000 = $6,000

and

BOM inventory = Planned sales + Basic stock

or

$9,000 + $6,000 = $15,000

The average monthly sales are fixed for any given season, in the sense that they are simply the total sales divided by the number of months in that season. However, the average stock for the season is based on seasonal turnover, which will obviously vary by season and classification. The result is that as the turnover ratio approaches 6, the average stock decreases until, at the point of 6 turns, the average stock equates to the average monthly sales and the resulting basic stock is zero.

Determination of basic stock when the turnover is 6   When the stock turn is 6 times a season, the basic stock equates to zero and the formula obviously fails to produce satisfactory results.

▪ Study Problem

Given:

Planned sales for the fall season	$36,000
Planned seasonal stock turnover	6
Planned sales for October	9,000

Find: The basic stock for October and the resulting BOM inventory.

Solution:

$$\text{Average stock for the season} = \frac{\$36,000}{6 \text{ (times)}} = \$6,000$$

$$\text{Average monthly sales} = \frac{\$36,000}{6 \text{ (months)}} = \$6,000$$

Basic stock = $6,000 − $6,000 = $0

BOM inventory = $9,000 + $0 = $9,000

We may therefore conclude that the basic-stock method of inventory planning is invalid at the point of 6 turns per season, or 12 turns annually.[33] In fact, this method of stock planning is only recommended for use when the stock turn is less than 6 times per year or 3 times on a seasonal basis. Consequently, only those merchants who manage stores, departments, or classifications with relatively low turnover ratios are likely to find the basic-stock method suitable to their operations.

▪ Application Exercise

Using the previous examples as study problems, solve the following:

1. For the spring season, a china department is planning net sales of $90,000 with an estimated stock turnover of 1.2. What is the BOM inventory for April if April sales are planned at $18,000?

2. A girls' clothing department has planned the following data for the fall season:

Turnover	2.3
Net sales for the season	$200,000
Net sales for November	$35,000

   Determine the BOM inventory for November.

3. A classification of junior dresses was expected to achieve a turnover of 3 for the spring season. Net seasonal sales were planned at $350,000, and March sales were anticipated to be $65,000. What should the BOM inventory for March be?

4. A candy department's inventory turnover is projected to be 6 during the fall season. Seasonal sales were planned at $120,000, with November sales anticipated to be $25,000. Calculate the BOM inventory for November (using the basic-stock method as originally defined).

---

[33]However, the basic-stock formula may be modified to accommodate higher turnover ratios should the merchant so desire. This procedure requires that the BOM inventory be sufficient to cover the average weekly sales for the month and still have a "cushion" of basic stock. Here the basic stock is equal to the average stock for the season minus the average weekly sales for the season. The following equation expresses this concept for the purpose of illustration:

BOM stock = Average weekly sales for the month or accounting period
+ (Average stock for the season − Average weekly sales for the season)

The basic-stock method adapted to the retail accounting calendar

As we have previously noted, the retail accounting calendar divides the year into two 26-week seasons, each season consisting of six 4- or 5-week periods. Thus, for accounting purposes (the determination of the average "monthly" sales), there are 6.5 four-week periods in a season or 5.2 five-week periods. Quantitatively, this concept is expressed as follows:

$$\frac{26\text{-week season}}{4\text{-week accounting period}} = 6.5 \text{ (4-week periods)}$$

$$\frac{26\text{-week season}}{5\text{-week accounting period}} = 5.2 \text{ (5-week periods)}$$

Therefore, the number of weeks in a given period determines the number of corresponding periods within a season. For example, Period I (February) consists of 4 weeks, and a 26-week season would theoretically consist of 6.5 four-week periods (6.5 × 4 = 26 weeks); on the other hand, Period II (March) contains 5 weeks, thereby defining a 26-week season in terms of 5.2 five-week periods (5.2 × 5 = 26 weeks).[34]

While the above considerations do not change the basic concept of average monthly sales, the retail accounting calendar does require that the denominator of the formula be modified to reflect the number of periods in a season rather than the number of calendar months. Therefore,

$$\text{Average monthly sales} = \frac{\text{Net sales for season}}{\text{Periods in season (either 6.5 or 5.2)}}$$

▪ Study Problem

Given:

Planned sales in spring season	$90,000
Planned sales for March	$18,000
Planned stock turnover in spring season	1.5

Find: BOM inventory for March (Period II) in a notions department, using the retail accounting calendar.

---

[34]Refer to Figure 12.1 for a translation of calendar months into accounting periods and the number of weeks in each period.

Solution:

$$\text{Average seasonal stock} = \frac{\$90,000}{1.5} = \$60,000$$

$$\text{Average "monthly" sales} = \frac{\$90,000}{5.2} = \$17,308$$

$$\text{Basic stock} = \$60,000 - \$17,308 = \$42,692$$

$$\text{B.O.M. stock} = \$18,000 + \$42,692 = \$60,692$$

∎ Application Exercise

1. A major appliance department has planned sales to be $12,000 for the month of May, planned sales for the spring season at $52,000, and anticipates a stock turn of 2 for the season. Plan the BOM stock for May, based on the retail accounting calendar.

2. For the fall season, a bath shop is anticipating net sales of $125,000 and a stock turn of 2.7. Calculate the BOM inventory for September (based on the retail accounting calendar), assuming that planned sales are $21,500.

The Percentage Variation Method

This method is applicable to those situations where the stock turnover is anticipated to be 6 times or more on an annual basis, or 3 times or better per season. The percentage variation method gives recognition to the fact that higher turnover ratios, by definition, require levels of inventory that are more consistent with planned sales than those developed through the basic-stock method. The concept here is to correlate stock levels with actual variations in periodic, or monthly, sales. In order to achieve this optimum relationship between sales and inventory, the merchant obviously requires a minimum amount of stock; however, it does not follow that this minimum amount (i.e., basic stock) remains consistent throughout the season. In other words, the percentage variation method provides BOM stocks as a product of the variation in monthly sales, rather than a product of a predetermined basic stock. This method is based upon the premise that the BOM stock is increased or decreased from the planned average stock by half of the percentage that monthly sales fluctuate from the average monthly sale.[35] For

---

[35]That the BOM stock should vary by only half the percentage fluctuations in planned sales is purely an arbitrary determination. Obviously, the periodic variations in the BOM stock should be smaller than the fluctuations in sales, if for no other reason than that the BOM stock is in effect last month's EOM inventory. However, 50% does not necessarily define "smaller"; that precise definition is left to the intuitive judgment of the individual merchant and the unique requirements of specific situations.

example, if November's planned sales were 20% above the average monthly sales, the BOM stock would be planned at a level that was 10% higher than the average stock for the season.

The BOM stock, as a product of the percentage variation method, may be determined from the following formula:

$$\text{BOM stock} = \text{Average stock} \times 1/2 \left(1 + \frac{\text{Sales for month}}{\text{Average monthly sales}}\right)$$

When the seasonal stock turn is above 3, this percentage method will provide BOM inventories that fluctuate less from planned sales than do those inventories derived from the basic-stock method. When turnover is less than 3, the percentage method yields stocks that vary more from sales than do those stocks derived from the basic-stock method. At exactly 3 turns per season, the choice of methods makes no difference, because at this point both methods yield the same results. Figure 12.7 illustrates these concepts by generating different BOM stocks from the same seasonal and monthly planned sales, as a result of increasing the ratio of seasonal stock turn. Note the following:

The percentage variation method generates higher BOM inventories than does the basic-stock method when the turnover is below 3.

At 3 stock turns per season, the percentage variation method produces the same BOM stock as does the basic-stock method.

The percentage variation method provides for a far better correlation between the BOM stock and sales than does the basic-stock method when the stock turn exceeds 3. However, as turnover approaches 6 times per season, the average

			B.O.M. Stocks*	
Seasonal Stock Turn	Spring Season Sales	Monthly Sales	Percentage Variation Method	Basic Stock Method
1	$100,000	$20,000	$109,999	$103,333
2	100,000	20,000	54,999	53,333
3	100,000	20,000	36,666	36,666
4	100,000	20,000	27,500	28,333
5	100,000	20,000	22,000	23,333
6	100,000	20,000	18,333	20,000

Figure 12.7 BOM stocks planned according to the percentage variation and basic stock methods

*Verify the given BOM stocks by means of the application of the basic-stock and percentage variation formulas. This will serve as an additional application exercise using both concepts.

stock tends to equate with the average monthly sales; thus, neither method at this point provides an adequate BOM inventory, simply because monthly sales exceed, or equate with, the BOM stocks—an obvious impossibility.[36]

▪ Study Problem

Given: A department has planned sales for the fall season of $200,000 and anticipates a stock turnover of 5 for the six-month period.

Find: The BOM stock for October if the month's sales are planned at $35,000.

Solution:

Because the stock turnover is 5 times per season, the percentage variation method is to be used. As previously mentioned, the definition of the percentage variation method may be expressed by means of the following equation:

$$\text{B O M stock} = \text{Average stock} \times 1/2 \left(1 + \frac{\text{Monthly sales}}{\text{Average monthly sales}} \right)$$

$$\text{Average stock} = \frac{\$200,000}{5} = \$40,000$$

$$\text{Average monthly sales} = \frac{\$200,000}{6} = \$33,333$$

$$\text{October B O M stock} = \$40,000 \times 1/2 \left(1 + \frac{\$35,000}{\$33,333} \right)$$

$$= \$40,000 \times 1/2 \, (1 + 105\%)$$

$$= \$40,000 \times 1/2 \, (205\%)$$

$$= \$40,000 \times 102.5\%$$

$$= \$41,000$$

---

[36]Annual turnover ratios of less than 1 or more than 6 will rarely be encountered. A typical figure for a major general-merchandise department store will approximate 3.1 times, ranging somewhere between 2.7 and 3.4. For specialty stores, the typical figure may be expected to be somewhere around 3.9, with a range of roughly 2.7 to 4.

Proof:
The BOM stock is to be increased or decreased from the average monthly stock by half the variation in planned sales from the average monthly sales. Therefore, sales are planned to increase 5% over the average monthly sales, or

$$\frac{\$35,000 - \$33,333}{\$33,333} = 5\%$$

The BOM stock equals the average stock plus or minus half the percentage variation in planned sales from the average sale. Therefore,

Half the percentage variation $= \dfrac{5\%}{2} = 2.5\%$

$2.5\% \times \$40,000 = \$1,000$

BOM stock $= \$40,000 + \$1,000 = \$41,000$

▪ Application Exercise

1. A particular classification of women's blouses has planned sales of $120,000 and a planned stock turn of 5 for the fall season. What should the BOM stock be for November if sales for that month are expected to be $25,000?

2. A jewelry department planned sales for the spring season at $144,000, with an anticipated stock turnover of 4. The planned sales for March are $30,000. Calculate the BOM inventory for that month.

3. A toy department planned sales for the last quarter of the calendar year (October, November, and December) at $100,000, with a turnover of 4. Planned sales for November are $40,000; what should the November BOM stock be?

4. A gourmet food department had planned sales of $240,000 and a planned inventory turnover of 10 for the year. Define the BOM stock for September if planned sales for the month are $13,000.

The percentage variation method adapted to the retail accounting calendar

Recall that the retail accounting calendar is divided into either 4- or 5-week periods that roughly correspond to months, and that there are 6.5 (26 ÷ 4) 4-week periods or 5.2 (26 ÷ 4) 5-week periods in a 26-week season.[37] Therefore,

---

[37] See Figure 12.2.

as this concept relates to the percentage variation method, our concern lies with the translation of the "average monthly sales" into the "average periodic sales"; with this exception, the determination of the BOM inventory when the stock turn is 3 or above remains the same as previously discussed.

■ Study Problem

Given: A sportswear department has planned sales of $210,000 for the spring season and a planned stock turnover of 5.

Find: The BOM stock for Period IV if sales are planned at $35,000.

Solution:

$$\text{B O M stock} = \text{Average stock for season} \times 1/2 \left(1 + \frac{\text{Sales for period}}{\text{Average periodic sales}} \right)$$

$$\text{Average stock} = \frac{\text{Sales for period}}{\text{Stock turnover}} = \frac{\$210,000}{5} = \$42,000$$

$$\text{Average periodic sales} = \frac{\$210,000}{6.5} = \$32,308$$

$$\text{B O M stock} = \$42,000 \times 1/2 \left(1 + \frac{\$35,000}{\$32,308} \right)$$

$$= \$42,000 \times 1/2 \ (1 + 108\%)$$

$$= \$42,000 \times 1/2 \ (208\%)$$

$$= \$42,000 \times 104\%$$

$$= \$43,680$$

■ Application Exercise

1. A men's clothing department had planned sales of $165,000, with an inventory turnover of 4 for the spring season. Planned sales for June are $26,000. What should the BOM stock be for Period V?

2. Your department had planned sales of $187,200 and a planned stock turn of 4.5 for the fall season. Determine the BOM stock for October, Period IX, if the planned sales are $20,160.

The Stock-to-Sales Method

The stock-to-sales method of inventory planning requires that the merchant define a relationship between the BOM[38] stock for a given month and the planned sales for that month. Thus, we speak of the ratio between monthly net sales and the inventory required to produce those sales, or a stock-to-sales ratio, quantitatively defined as follows:

$$\text{Stock-to-sales ratio} = \frac{\text{BOM inventory}}{\text{Planned sales}}$$

Given the previous relationship, recall that

BOM stock = Planned sales × Stock-to-sales ratio

Stock-to-sales ratios are immediately available to the retail merchant, either from historical internal data (the past relationship of inventory to sales) or from published figures readily obtainable from trade sources such as the National Retail Merchants Federation, Menswear Retailers of America, or Dun and Bradstreet.

The merchant's acceptance of the stock-to-sales ratio as an inventory planning device assumes a predetermined balance between the BOM stock and the anticipated monthly sales. Thus, a stock-to-sales ratio of 4 indicates that the merchant planning sales of $25,000 for a particular month must have a beginning inventory of approximately $100,000. The term *approximately* is used to emphasize the fact that the stock-to-sales ratio is only a tool to facilitate the estimation of monthly stocks and not necessarily a decision in itself. Obviously, if sales were to double, this would not automatically imply a 100% increase in stock levels; sound merchandising management recognizes that inventories should not normally rise in the same proportion that sales increase. Indeed, the merchant should expect an inverse relationship between inventory and planned or actual sales. Thus, during the months when sales are relatively low, the stock-to-sales ratio would normally increase, simply because it is necessary to maintain an adequate level of merchandise, regardless of reduced sales volume.

Stock-to-sales ratios and their relationship to the concept of inventory turnover

Inventory turnover has been defined as sales divided by the average inventory, which in turn derives from the sum of the BOM stocks plus the EOM stock,

---

[38]While it is theoretically possible to use the EOM stock to express this ratio, the more commonly accepted method employs the BOM inventory, simply because there is a cause-and-effect relationship between the beginning inventory and the resulting volume of sales. In other words, the opening inventory is on hand to produce sales for a given month, whereas the ending inventory has no relationship to sales for that month but stands only as a factor to produce sales for the following period.

divided by the total number of stocks. Thus, the turnover ratio is an average figure, obtained from a series of BOM stocks over a given period of time (normally one year). The stock-to-sales ratio therefore relates to the rate of inventory turnover through the BOM inventory. In other words, the value of the BOM stocks determines the average inventory that, when divided into sales, accounts for the turnover ratio. We may therefore conclude that

1. Turnover is a product of the BOM stocks, averaged over a period of time.[39]

2. A predetermined turnover ratio may be used to validate a series of stock-to-sales ratios.

Figure 12.8 illustrates this relationship between inventory turnover and the stock-to-sales ratio. Assume that the turnover goal for the fall season is 2 and that the stock-to-sales ratio objectives and net sales have been planned for Periods VII through XII. The seasonal turnover ratio may then be calculated as follows:

$$\text{Average inventory} = \frac{\$90,300}{7} = \$12,900$$

$$\text{Seasonal turnover} = \frac{\$25,800}{\$12,900} = 2$$

Thus, the use of the BOM stock-to-sales ratios is supported or validated by the rate of inventory turnover produced for the fall season. In short, the seasonal turnover ratio is a manifestation of the monthly stock-to-sales ratios; should there not be a correlation between the two concepts, the stock plan must be reworked.

It should be noted that the stock-to-sales ratios differ from the turnover ratio in three respects:

1. Stock-to-sales ratios represent the relationship of inventory to sales for one month or period; turnover relates to a series of months, a season, or more commonly, the entire year.

2. The stock figure in the stock-to-sales ratio represents the actual inventory on hand at the beginning of the month, whereas the turnover ratio is defined by the average inventory maintained over a series of months.

[39]The BOM stock may not be derived from turnover, simply because the concept of turnover, quantitatively stated (sales divided by the average inventory) fails to recognize a BOM inventory. While the components of the turnover formula will yield an average inventory (average inventory = sales divided by turnover), it is of limited value to the merchant in the specific control of monthly stocks. However, because the average inventory is, in effect, an average of many stock-to-sales ratios, it does provide guidelines for the determination of unique stock-to-sales ratios within seasonal limitations.

Period	Planned Sales	×	B O M Stock-to-Sales Ratios	=	B O M Stock
VII	$3,100	×	3.4		$10,500
VIII	$3,500	×	3.2		11,200
IX	$4,300	×	3.6		15,500
X	$4,800	×	3.2		15,300
XI	$6,500	×	1.8		11,700
XII	$3,600	×	3.9		14,100
I	($3,000)*	×	4.0		12,000
Total	$25,800				$90,300

Figure 12.8 The relationship between turnover and the stock-to-sales ratio

*For the purposes of computing the average inventory, an estimation of the BOM stock for Period I (or the EOM stock for Period XII) must be determined and included in the calculation of the average inventory. However, the planned sales for Period I are not to be included in the fall season sales plan, because they obviously belong in the coming spring season.

3. The numerators and denominators are reversed in the two concepts:
   a. The stock-to-sales ratio represents the relationship of stock to sales; therefore, inventory is divided by sales.
   b. Turnover is just the opposite, or the ratio of sales to inventory; as a result sales are divided by inventory.

The major advantage of the stock-to-sales method of inventory planning, compared to the basic stock and the percentage variation methods, is that the stock-to-sales method provides an immediate response to sales for specific months or periods. The other two procedures rely upon an average of periodic sales for a given season, and averages, by definition, tend to mute, or negate, the effects of unusually high or low periods of sales volume. An average volume of sales implies an average stock, which may or may not meet the requirements for a specific periodic sales volume; again, from the perspective of inventory control, the averages are no substitute for specifics.

■ Study Problem

Given:

	Sales Last Year	B O M Last Year	Planned Sales
February	$ 8,300	$37,350	$ 8,700
March	8,900	33,820	9,300
April	10,200	32,640	10,700
May	12,800	35,840	13,400
June	9,700	35,890	10,200
July	8,600	41,280	9,000

Find:

The BOM stocks for the planned spring season. Assuming that the planned EOM stock for July is $39,400, what is the anticipated stock turn?

Solution:

Determine the stock-to-sales ratio for each month from last year's sales and BOM stock.

$$\text{Stock-to-sales ratio} = \frac{\text{BOM stock}}{\text{Sales}}$$

Thus,

$$\text{February stock-to-sales ratio} = \frac{\$37,350}{\$8,300} = 4.5$$

The stock-to-sales ratios for the season are summarized below:

February	4.5
March	3.8
April	3.2
May	2.8
June	3.7
July	4.8

Calculate the BOM stocks for the planned spring season.

BOM stock = Planned sales × Monthly stock-to-sales ratio

	Planned Sales	Stock-to-Sales Ratio	B.O.M. Stock
February	$ 8,700	4.5	$39,150
March	9,300	3.8	35,340
April	10,700	3.2	34,240
May	13,400	2.8	37,520
June	10,200	3.7	37,740
July	9,000	4.8	43,200

The anticipated stock turn will be:

Average inventory = Sum of the six B.O.M. stocks + July E.O.M. stock ÷

$$\text{Number of stocks} = \frac{\$227,190 + \$39,400}{7} = \frac{\$266,590}{7} = \$38,084$$

$$\text{Stock turn} = \text{Seasonal sales} \div \text{Average inventory} = \frac{\$61,300}{\$38,084} = 1.6$$

▪ Application Exercise

1. A shoe department had an October BOM stock of $12,000. Net sales totaled $4,800. What is the BOM stock-to-sales ratio?

2. A buyer had planned sales for Period III of $8,700. Assuming that the stock-to-sales ratio had been established at 5.7, what should be the BOM stock for Period III?

3. What should the planned sales be in a dress department for the month of April, given the following information?

Inventory as of 4/1	$11,500
Stock-to-sales ratio	2.5

4. A menswear specialty store planned the BOM stock-to-sales ratios for January and February at 8.1 and 10.3, respectively. Sales for January were planned at $40,000 and for February at $30,000. What is the turnover to be expected for January?

5. Determine the BOM stocks and the turnover ratio for the approaching fall season, given the following historical data and planned sales:

	Sales Last Year	*B.O.M. Last Year*	*Planned Sales*
August	$17,500	$131,250	$17,000
September	16,300	118,990	16,500
October	14,700	91,140	15,000
November	19,600	103,880	20,500
December	23,800	97,580	24,800
January	17,000	103,700	17,500
February	17,900	116,350	18,000

The Weeks' Supply Method

In this method, stocks are planned to ensure that a supply of inventory for a predetermined number of weeks is on hand, rather than a BOM inventory for a particular month or period. The required number of weeks' supply depends upon the turnover ratio, and the amount of inventory to be carried depends upon the average weekly sales. Conceptually, we may state the following relationships:

Planned stock = Average weekly sales × Number of weeks to be stocked

$$\text{Average weekly sales} = \frac{\text{Sales for the season}}{\text{Weeks in the season (26)}}$$

$$\text{Number of weeks to be stocked} = \frac{\text{Weeks in the season (26)}}{\text{Turnover ratio}}$$

The above relationships imply two distinct disadvantages:

1. Stocks will vary in direct proportion to the changes in sales. This in turn results in stocks being too high during peak selling periods and not high enough in the slack periods.

2. This method fails to provide for a basic stock and is thus generally unacceptable as a dollar control device for inventory planning. It is best used in systems of unit control involving staple merchandise, where a relatively active demand continually exists.

▪ Study Problem

Given: Departmental sales for the fall season are planned at $78,000 with a stock turn of 4 for the six-month period.

Find: How much stock should be carried in the department, according to the weeks' supply method.

Solution:

Planned stock = Average weekly sales × Number of weeks to be stocked

$$\text{Average weekly sales} = \frac{\$78,000}{26} = \$3,000$$

$$\text{Number of weeks to be stocked} = \frac{26}{4} = 6.5$$

Planned stock = $3,000 × 6.5 = $19,500

▪ Application Exercise

1. Given the following data for a classification of men's white dress shirts, determine the dollar amount of inventory to be carried.

   Spring season sales $46,800
   Turnover   6

2. A department of staple merchandise anticipates fall sales of $78,000 with a stock turn of 4. How much inventory should be on hand?

3. Plan the stock for a department with an annual turnover of 4.8 and average weekly sales of $7,800.

4. A classification of men's underwear is considered to be staple merchandise and is reordered by the weeks' supply method. Assuming that sales for the spring season are $52,000 and the rate of turnover is 3.6 times, what should the planned stock be?

5. Plan the stocks to be on hand for a classification of basic sweaters during the fall season. Sales are planned at $130,000, and turnover is anticipated to be 3.7.

12.6 Preparation of the Six-Month Merchandise Plan, the Determination and Control of Purchases at Cost, and Maintained Markon

At this point, you have been exposed to all of the various merchandising tactics required to implement sound merchandising strategy. Such strategy is defined as the six-month merchandise plan, a plan of action to define the amount of purchases or investment required by the merchant to achieve the planned sales forecast.

■ Study Problem

Given: Last year's figures and data pertinent to this year's merchandising objectives have been entered on Figure 12.9. In addition, sales are expected to increase over last year by 10%, with a planned monthly distribution, as follows:

	Last Year (%)	Planned (%)
February	14.2	14.0
March	15.3	16.3
April	16.3	15.2
May	17.2	17.6
June	18.6	18.4
July	18.4	18.5
	100%	100%

Employee discounts and inventory shortages are expected to remain the same; however, markdowns that were 6.8% last year are currently planned at 6%. The total retail reductions are to be distributed across the season as follows:

	Last Year (%)	Planned (%)
February	13.2	11.4
March	19.6	7.6
April	15.0	17.5

☐ Corporation
☐ Store
☒ Department 514 (Men's Furn.)
☒ Classification 51 (S.S. Knits)
☒ Spring 19____
☐ Fall   19____

Seasonal Data

	Last Year	Planned	Actual
Cumulative markon %	47.2		
Shortage %	6.8	6.0	
Shortage %	3.0	3.0	
Sales discounts %	1.0	1.0	
Maintained markon %	41.5		
Operating expenses %	36.5	36.5	
Operating profit %	5.0	5.5	
Turnover	1.6	2.0	

	Feb. (I) Aug. (VII)		Mar. (II) Sept. (VIII)		Apr. (III) Oct. (IX)		May (IV) Nov. (X)		June (V) Dec. (XI)		July (VI) Jan. (XII)		Total
	$	%	$	%	$	%	$	%	$	%	$	%	$
Net sales													
Last year	16,300		17,500		18,600		19,700		21,300		21,000		114,400
Plan													
Revised													
Actual													
BOM stock													
Last year	78,240	4.8	78,750	4.5	74,400	4.0	70,920	3.6	70,290	3.3	63,000	3.0	435,600
Plan													
Revised													
Actual													
EOM stock													
Last year	78,750		74,400		70,920		70,290		63,000		60,000		417,360
Plan													
Revised													
Actual													
Retail reductions													
Last year	1,631	10.0	2,422	13.8	1,853	10.0	2,051	10.4	1,705	8.0	2,693	12.8	12,355
Plan													
Revised													
Actual													
Purchases at retail													
Last year	18,441		15,572		16,973		21,121		15,715		20,693		108,515
Plan													
Revised													
Actual													
Purchases at cost													
Last year	9,737		8,222		8,962		11,152		8,298		10,926		57,297
Plan													
Revised													
Actual													
Maintained markon													
Last year	6,830	41.9	6,983	39.9	7,793	41.9	8,215	41.7	9,159	43.0	8,484	40.4	47,464
Plan													
Revised													
Actual													

Figure 12.9 Six-month merchandise plan for study problem

	Last Year (%)	*Planned (%)*
May	16.6	20.5
June	13.8	20.8
July	<u>21.8</u>	<u>22.2</u>
	100%	100%

Turnover is planned to increase from 1.6 to 2.

Find: In the merchandise plan, Figure 12.9:[40]

I. Under seasonal data:
  A. Planned maintained markon percentage.
  B. Planned cumulative markon percentage.
II. Within the body of the plan:
  A. Planned net sales dollars.
  B. Planned BOM stock dollars.
  C. Planned EOM stock dollars.
  D. Planned retail reduction dollars.
  E. Planned dollar purchases at retail.
  F. Planned dollar purchases at cost.
  G. Planned maintained markon dollars.

Solution:

I. Seasonal Data:

  A. Determine the percentage of maintained markon:

   Maintained markon = Operating expenses + Operating profit

   Maintained markon % = 36.5% + 5.5% = 42%

  B. Determine the percentage of cumulative markon:

   Cumulative markon = Maintained markon + Reductions

   $$\text{Cumulative markon \%} = \frac{42\% + 10\%}{100\% + 10\%} = \frac{52\%}{110\%} = 47.3\%$$

   Note that

   Maintained markon % = Cumulative markon % − Cost of reductions

---

[40]It is not always possible to obtain exact totals when the totals are the product of addition and/or multiplication percentages. However, minor discrepancies will not hinder the intent of this plan, that is, to minimize investment and maximize profit.

Cost of reductions $= 10\% \times (100\% - 47.3\%) = 5.3\%$

Maintained markon $\% = 47.3\% - 5.3\% = 42\%$

II. Now let us proceed with the body of the plan, taking each component in order:

A. *Net sales*

Sales are planned to increase by 10%; therefore,

Planned sales $= \$114,400 \times 110\% = \$125,840$

Planned sales are to be distributed as follows:

February sales	$=$	$14.2 \times$	$\$125,840$	$=$	$\$17,869$
March sales	$=$	$15.3 \times$	$125,840$	$=$	$19,254$
April sales	$=$	$16.3 \times$	$125,840$	$=$	$20,512$
May sales	$=$	$17.2 \times$	$125,840$	$=$	$21,644$
June sales	$=$	$18.6 \times$	$125,840$	$=$	$23,406$
July sales	$=$	$18.4 \times$	$125,840$	$=$	$23,155$

B. *BOM stock*

Since the planned turnover is less than 3 for the season, the BOM stocks may be planned according to the basic stock method:

BOM stock $=$ Monthly planned sales $+$ Basic stock

Basic stock $=$ Average stock for the season $-$ Average monthly sales

$$\text{Basic stock} = \frac{\$125,840}{2} - \frac{\$125,840}{6} = \$62,920 - \$20,973^{41} = \$41,947$$

Therefore,

February B O M stock	$= \$17,869$	$+ \$41,947$	$=$	$\$59,816$
March B O M stock	$= \$19,254$	$+ \$41,947$	$=$	$61,201$
April B O M stock	$= \$20,512$	$+ \$41,947$	$=$	$62,459$
May B O M stock	$= \$21,644$	$+ \$41,947$	$=$	$63,591$
June B O M stock	$= \$23,406$	$+ \$41,947$	$=$	$65,353$
July B O M stock	$= \$23,155$	$+ \$41,947$	$=$	$65,102$

The BOM stock-to-sales ratios (BOM stock $\div$ net sales) may now be calculated and entered.

---

[41]The average monthly sales are actually $20,973.33, resulting in a basic stock of $41,946.67. By rounding this number up to $41,947, we are inflating the total BOM stock for the season by approximately $2. While this is of no consequence at this point, it will affect the calculation of the EOM stock for July in the next section. The correction is therefore made by reducing the basic stock for February by $2.

C. *EOM stock*

The EOM stock for any given month is simply the BOM stock for the following month. For example, the EOM stock for February is the BOM stock for March. Thus,

February E O M	= March B.O.M.	= $61,201
March E O M	= April B.O.M.	= 62,459
April E O M	= May B.O.M.	= 63,591
May E O M	= June B.O.M.	= 65,353
June E O M	= July B.O.M.	= 65,102
July E O M	= August B.O.M.	= ?

However, because the BOM stock for August is unknown, we are unable to determine the EOM stock for July from the foregoing data. As a result, we must resort to a calculation that will show that the EOM stock for the last period of any season will be equal to the average stock for that season.[42]

$$\text{Average stock} = \frac{6 \text{ BOM stocks} + 1 \text{ EOM stock}}{7}$$

$$\text{Average stock} = \frac{\$377,520 + 1 \text{ E.O.M.}}{7}$$

The average stock has already been defined as

$$\frac{\$125,840}{2} = \$62,920$$

Therefore,

$$\$62,920 = \frac{\$377,520 + \text{July E.O.M.}}{7}$$

$$\$440,440 = \$377,520 + \text{July E.O.M.}$$

$$\text{July E.O.M.} = \$440,440 - \$377,520$$

July EOM = $62,920[43]

The EOM stock-to-sales ratio (EOM stock ÷ net sales) may now be calculated and entered. In the event that the merchant is working with stock-to-sales ratios and an unknown turnover, a similar procedure is used to determine the EOM stock and seasonal turnover:

[42]This is not to imply that the EOM stock for July must represent the average stock for the season. Indeed, it may be higher or lower, depending upon the judgment of the individual merchant.
[43]Because the average stock for the season equals the sum of the BOM stock plus the EOM stock for July divided by 7, then the average stock times 7 equals the total of the 6 BOM stocks plus the EOM stock.

$$\text{Average B O M stock} = \frac{\text{Total B.O.M. stock}}{6}$$

$$\text{Average B O M stock for August} = \text{July E O M stock}$$

$$\text{Average stock season} = \frac{\text{Total B O M stock} + \text{July E O M stock}}{7}$$

$$\text{Turnover} = \frac{\text{Sales for season}}{\text{Average stock}}$$

Therefore,

$$\text{Average B O M stock} = \frac{\$377,520}{6} = \$62,920$$

$$\text{July E O M stock} = \$62,920$$

$$\text{Average stock season} = \frac{\$377,520 + \$62,920}{7} = \$62,920$$

$$\text{Turnover} = \frac{\$125,840}{\$62,920} = 2$$

D. *Retail reductions*

Reductions are planned at 10% of this year's seasonal sales. Therefore,

Total reductions = $\$125,840 \times 10\% = \$12,584$

The seasonal dollar distribution of reductions, as previously defined in the problem, will be

February reductions	=	11.4%	×	$12,584	=	$1,435
March reductions	=	7.6	×	12,584	=	956
April reductions	=	17.5	×	12,584	=	2,202
May reductions	=	20.5	×	12,584	=	2,580
June reductions	=	20.8	×	12,584	=	2,617
July reductions	=	22.2	×	12,584	=	2,794

Retail reductions as a percentage of monthly planned sales are as follows:

February	=	$1,435 ÷	$17,869	=	8.0%
March	=	956 ÷	19,254	=	5.0
April	=	2,202 ÷	20,512	=	10.7
May	=	2,580 ÷	21,644	=	11.9
June	=	2,617 ÷	23,406	=	11.2
July	=	2,794 ÷	23,155	=	12.1

E. *Purchases at retail*

Purchases for any given period should be sufficient to supply inventory for those planned needs that are not already covered by the BOM stocks. What the merchant needs is defined as

1. An EOM inventory sufficient to maintain the business in the coming month.

2. The right amount of inventory on hand so as to meet the monthly planned sales.

3. Enough stock to cover the planned amount of retail reductions.

Each month has some stock on hand at the beginning of the period to cover a portion of these needs. As a result,

Planned purchases = (Sales + EOM stock + Reductions) − BOM stock

Therefore, purchases at retail are

February	= ($17,869 + $61,201 + $1,435) − $59,814	= $20,691
March	= ($19,254 + $62,459 + $ 956) − $61,201	= $21,468
April	= ($20,512 + $63,591 + $2,202) − $62,459	= $23,846
May	= ($21,644 + $65,353 + $2,580) − $63,591	= $25,986
June	= ($23,406 + $65,102 + $2,617) − $65,353	= $25,772
July	= ($23,155 + $62,920 + $2,794) − $65,102	= $23,767

F. *Purchases at cost*

Since the cumulative markon is planned at 47.3%, the cost of the purchases will be 52.7% of their retail value. Therefore, purchases at cost will be

February	=	$20,691 × 52.7%	=	$10,904
March	=	21,468 × 52.7	=	11,314
April	=	23,846 × 52.7	=	12,567
May	=	25,986 × 52.7	=	13,695
June	=	25,772 × 52.7	=	13,582
July	=	23,767 × 52.7	=	12,525

G. *Maintained markon*

The periodic maintained markon percentage is the cumulative markon percentage minus the cost of retail reductions. The maintained markon dollars are found by multiplying the maintained markon percentage times the planned sales for the period. Because the cumulative markon percentage is 47.3%, it will be assumed that the merchant will attempt to obtain that markon for each month. Therefore, the periodic maintained markon percentage will be

February	=	8.0%	× 52.7%	= 4.2%	47.3%	− 4.2%	= 43.1%
March	=	5.0	× 52.7	= 2.6	47.3	− 2.6	= 44.7
April	=	10.7	× 52.7	= 5.6	47.3	− 5.6	= 41.7
May	=	11.9	× 52.7	= 6.3	47.3	− 6.3	= 41.0
June	=	11.2	× 52.7	= 5.9	47.3	− 5.9	= 41.4
July	=	12.1	× 52.7	= 6.4	47.3	− 6.4	= 40.9

The completed merchandise plan is illustrated in Figure 12.10.

III. A question often arises concerning the accuracy of the mathematical calculations within the plan and thus the validity of the six-month plan itself. Simply put, how can we determine the soundness of the plan as a model for seasonal merchandising activities without the tedious process of recalculating each step? And even if we did so, the plan could be mathematically correct and still be invalid as a merchandising tool, simply because improper ratios properly determined are still improper. In the final analysis, our concern lies with the arrangement of the internal elements of the plan—i.e., sales, inventories, reductions, and purchases—that best contributes to the maximization of the maintained markon. A small amount of human error is to be expected and is tolerable, so long as that error is within the acceptable limits of the plan's strategic objectives defined in the heading.

With this in mind, the following method is offered as a check on the internal validity of the six-month merchandise plan.

The student will recall the relationship that exists between the cumulative markon, reductions, and the maintained markon:

Maintained markon = Cumulative markon − Cost of reductions

Thus, in the solution to the study problem,

$MMO = (47.3\% × \$125,840) − [(100\% − 47.3\%) × \$12,584]$

$MMO = \$59,522 − (52.7\% × \$12,584)$

$MMO = \$59,522 − \$6,632 = \$52,890$[44]

And

MMO% = \$52,890 ÷ \$125,840 = 42%

▪ Application Exercise

1. Last year's figures and agreed-upon data for this year have been entered on the merchandise plan shown in Figure 12.11. In addition, sales are expected to increase by 8% over last year, and the planned distribution is as follows:

---

[44]Close enough!

☐ Corporation
☐ Store
☒ Department 514 (Men's Furn.)
☒ Classification 51 (S.S. Knits)
☒ Spring 19___
☐ Fall 19___

Seasonal Data

	Last Year	Planned	Actual
Cumulative markon %	47.2	47.3	
Markdown %	6.8	6.0	
Shortage %	3.0	3.0	
Sales discounts %	1.0	1.0	
Maintained markon %	41.5	42.0	
Operating expenses %	36.5	36.5	
Operating profit %	5.0	5.5	
Turnover	1.6	2.0	

	Feb. (I) Aug. (VII)		Mar. (II) Sept. (VIII)		Apr. (III) Oct. (IX)		May (IV) Nov. (X)		June (V) Dec. (XI)		July (VI) Jan. (XII)		Total
	$	%	$	%	$	%	$	%	$	%	$	%	$
Net sales													
Last year	16,300		17,500		18,600		19,700		21,300		21,000		114,400
Plan	17,869		19,254		20,512		21,644		23,406		23,155		125,840
Revised													
Actual													
BOM stock													
Last year	78,240	4.8	78,750	4.5	74,400	4.0	70,920	3.6	70,290	3.3	63,000	3.0	435,600
Plan	59,814	3.3	61,201	3.2	62,459	3.0	63,591	2.9	65,353	2.8	65,102	2.8	377,520
Revised													
Actual													
EOM stock													
Last year	78,750		74,400		70,920		70,290		63,000		60,000		417,360
Plan	61,201		62,459		63,591		65,353		65,102		62,920		380,626
Revised													
Actual													
Retail reductions													
Last year	1,631	10.0	2,422	13.8	1,853	10.0	2,051	10.4	1,705	8.0	2,693	12.8	12,355
Plan	1,435	8.0	956	5.0	2,202	10.7	2,580	11.9	2,617	11.2	2,794	12.1	12,584
Revised													
Actual													
Purchases at retail													
Last year	18,441		15,572		16,973		21,121		15,715		20,693		108,515
Plan	20,691		21,468		23,846		25,986		25,772		23,767		141,530
Revised													
Actual													
Purchases at cost													
Last year	9,737		8,222		8,962		11,152		8,298		10,926		57,297
Plan	10,904		11,314		12,567		13,695		13,582		12,525		74,587
Revised													
Actual													
Maintained markon													
Last year	6,830	41.9	6,983	39.9	7,793	41.9	8,215	41.7	9,159	43.0	8,484	40.4	47,464
Plan	7,702	43.1	8,607	44.7	8,554	41.7	8,874	41.0	9,690	41.4	9,470	40.9	52,897
Revised													
Actual													

Figure 12.10 Solution to study problem

☐ Corporation _____

☐ Store _____

☐ Department _____

☐ Classification _____

☒ Spring 19____

☐ Fall 19____

Seasonal Data

	Last Year	Planned	Actual
Cumulative markon %	51.5		
Markdown %	10.0	8.0	
Shortage %	2.0	2.0	
Sales discounts %	1.5	1.5	
Maintained markon %	45.0		
Operating expenses %	40.0	39.0	
Operating profit %	5.0	6.0	
Turnover	2.0	2.4	

	Feb. (I) Aug. (VII)		Mar. (II) Sept. (VIII)		Apr. (III) Oct. (IX)		May (IV) Nov. (X)		June (V) Dec. (XI)		July (VI) Jan. (XII)		Total
	$	%	$	%	$	%	$	%	$	%	$	%	$
Net sales													
Last year	18,400		21,200		25,400		28,800		26,300		24,500		144,600
Plan													
Revised													
Actual													
BOM stock													
Last year	66,600	3.6	69,400	3.3	73,600	2.9	77,000	2.7	74,500	2.8	72,700	3.0	433,800
Plan													
Revised													
Actual													
EOM stock													
Last year	69,400		73,600		77,000		74,500		72,700		72,300		439,500
Plan													
Revised													
Actual													
Retail reductions													
Last year	1,952	10.6	1,308	6.2	4,256	16.8	4,802	16.7	2,479	9.4	4,724	19.3	19,521
Plan													
Revised													
Actual													
Purchases at retail													
Last year	23,152		26,708		33,056		31,102		26,979		28,824		169,821
Plan													
Revised													
Actual													
Purchases at cost													
Last year	11,229		12,953		16,032		15,084		13,085		13,980		82,363
Plan													
Revised													
Actual													
Maintained markon													
Last year	8,538	46.4	10,282	48.5	11,024	43.4	12,499	43.4	12,335	46.9	10,315	42.1	64,993
Plan													
Revised													
Actual													

Figure 12.11 Six-month merchandise plan for application exercise 1

February	10%
March	18%
April	22%
May	20%
June	20%
July	10%

Markdowns are expected to decrease by 2%, while sales discounts and inventory shortages are planned at last year's level. The seasonal distribution of reductions is anticipated to be

February	10%
March	5%
April	20%
May	25%
June	15%
July	25%

Using the basic stock method of inventory planning, complete Figure 12.11.

2. Using the planned stock-to-sales ratios and their distribution as developed in application exercise 1 (see Figure 12.11), complete the six-month merchandise plan as presented in Figure 12.12. The following data are also available:
   a. Sales are planned to increase by 10% and are to be distributed as follows:

February	8%
March	12%
April	16%
May	24%
June	22%
July	18%

   b. Sales discounts are planned at 2% and markdowns at 8%, and stock shortages are anticipated to be 2%. The distribution of reductions will be

February	10%
March	4%
April	6%
May	15%
June	30%
July	35%

3. Complete the merchandise plan illustrated in Figure 12.13, using the percentage variation method of stock planning and the following data:
   a. The average sale last year was $15 and is planned at $16 for this year. Last year's transactions amounted to 12,500, and transactions are expected to reach 13,000 this year.

☐ Corporation

☐ Store

☐ Department

☒ Classification

☒ Spring 19___

☐ Fall   19___

Seasonal Data

	Last Year	Planned	Actual
Cumulative markon %	48.6		
Markdown %	10.0	8.0	
Shortage %	3.0	2.0	
Sales discounts %	2.0	2.0	
Maintained markon %	40.9		
Operating expenses %	34.9	34.0	
Operating profit %	6.0	7.0	
Turnover	1.8		

	Feb. (I) Aug. (VII)		Mar. (II) Sept. (VIII)		Apr. (III) Oct. (IX)		May (IV) Nov. (X)		June (V) Dec. (XI)		July (VI) Jan. (XII)		Total
	$	%	$	%	$	%	$	%	$	%	$	%	$
Net sales													
Last year	18,000		23,400		30,600		32,400		45,000		30,600		180,000
Plan													
Revised													
Actual													
BOM stock													
Last year	97,600	5.4	101,200	4.3	99,400	3.2	104,800	3.2	97,600	2.2	99,400	3.2	600,000
Plan													
Revised													
Actual													
EOM stock													
Last year	101,200		99,400		104,800		97,600		99,400		100,000		602,400
Plan													
Revised													
Actual													
Retail reductions													
Last year	2,700	15.0	1,350	5.8	1,350	4.4	5,400	16.7	6,750	15.0	9,450	30.9	27,000
Plan													
Revised													
Actual													
Purchases at retail													
Last year	24,300		22,950		37,350		30,600		53,550		40,650		209,400
Plan													
Revised													
Actual													
Purchases at cost													
Last year	12,490		11,796		19,198		15,728		27,525		20,894		107,631
Plan													
Revised													
Actual													
Maintained markon													
Last year	7,362	40.9	10,670	45.6	14,168	46.3	12,960	40.0	18,405	40.9	10,006	32.7	73,571
Plan													
Revised													
Actual													

Figure 12.12 Six-month merchandise plan for application exercise 2

☐ Corporation _____

☐ Store _____

☐ Department _____

☒ Classification _____

☒ Spring 19___

☐ Fall 19___

Seasonal Data

	Last Year	Planned	Actual
Cumulative markon %	48.9		
Markdown %	10.0	10.0	
Shortage %	2.5	2.0	
Sales discounts %	1.0	1.0	
Maintained markon %	42.0		
Operating expenses %	37.0	38.0	
Operating profit %	5.0	5.0	
Turnover	4.0	5.0	

	Feb. (I) Aug. (VII)		Mar. (II) Sept. (VIII)		Apr. (III) Oct. (IX)		May (IV) Nov. (X)		June (V) Dec. (XI)		July (VI) Jan. (XII)		Total
	$	%	$	%	$	%	$	%	$	%	$	%	$
Net sales													
Last year	9,375		28,125		46,875		37,500		37,500		28,125		187,500
Plan													
Revised													
Actual													
BOM stock													
Last year	30,469	3.3	44,531	1.6	58,594	1.3	51,563	1.4	51,563	1.4	44,531	1.6	281,251
Plan													
Revised													
Actual													
EOM stock													
Last year	44,531		58,594		51,563		51,563		44,531		46,875		297,657
Plan													
Revised													
Actual													
Retail reductions													
Last year	2,531	27.0	1,266	4.5	1,266	2.7	3,788	10.1	7,613	20.3	8,859	31.5	25,323
Plan													
Revised													
Actual													
Purchases at retail													
Last year	25,968		43,454		41,110		41,288		38,081		39,328		229,229
Plan													
Revised													
Actual													
Purchases at cost													
Last year	13,270		22,205		21,007		21,098		19,450		20,097		117,136
Plan													
Revised													
Actual													
Maintained markon													
Last year	3,291	35.1	13,106	46.6	22,266	47.5	16,388	43.7	14,438	38.5	9,225	32.8	78,714
Plan													
Revised													
Actual													

Figure 12.13 Six-month merchandise plan for application exercise 3

b. The seasonal distribution of sales and reductions is planned as follows:

	Sales	Reductions
August	8%	12%
September	12%	6%
October	20%	8%
November	25%	14%
December	23%	25%
January	12%	35%

▪ Solutions to the Application Exercises

Forecasting Sales as a Result of Management Decree (Top-Down Planning) (p. 393)

1. $340,000 × 13% = $44,200

   $340,000 + $44,200 = $384,200

   or,

   $340,000 × 113% = $384,200

3. $83,600 × 112% = $93,632

5. $116,000 × 93.3% = $108,228

Planning a Dollar Net Sales Volume Predicated upon the Available Square Feet of Selling Space (p. 394)

1. a. 300 × $400 = $120,000

   b. 300 × $406 = $121,800

   c. $\dfrac{\$121,800 - \$120,000}{\$120,000} = 1.5\%$

3. Potential sales volume = 3,000 × $320 = $960,000

5. $1,200,000 ÷ 600 = 2,000 square feet

Estimating Net Sales Using the Planned Inventory Turnover and the Average Inventory (p. 396)

1. Sales volume this year = 2.5 × $83,000 = $207,500

   Sales volume last year = 2.3 × $83,000 = $190,900

$$\text{Percentage of increase} = \frac{\$207,500 - \$190,900}{\$190,900} = 8.7\%$$

3. Net sales last year = $83,600 × 2.5 = $209,000

   Planned sales this year = $80,000 × 3 = $240,000

   $$\text{Percentage variation} = \frac{\$240,000 - \$209,000}{\$209,000} = 14.8\%$$

Planned Sales Based upon the Average Dollar Sale and the Number of Sales Transactions (p. 399)

1. Sales last year = $4 × 30,000 = $120,000

   Planned sales = $5 × 35,000 = $175,000

   This year's planned sales as a percentage of last year's sales

   $$= \frac{\$175,000 - \$120,000}{\$120,000} = 45.8\%$$

3. Transactions last year = $780,000 ÷ $12.35 = 63,158

   Transactions this year = 63,158 × 90% = 56,842

   Planned sales = $12.50 × 56,842 = $710,525

5. $$\text{Average dollar sale} = \frac{\text{Planned sales}}{\text{Number of transactions}}$$

   Therefore,

   $$\text{Average dollar sale} = \frac{100\% - 10\%}{100\% - 3\%} = \frac{90\%}{97\%} = 92.8\%$$

   or a decline of 7.2% (100% − 92.8%)

Planning Net Sales Using the Stock-to-Sales Ratio (p. 400)

1. Planned sales this year = $117,000 ÷ 2.9 = $40,345

   Sales last year = $120,000 ÷ 3.2 = $37,500

   $$\text{Percentage of increase} = \frac{\$40,345 - \$37,500}{\$37,500} = 7.6\%$$

3. Sales last May = $206,000 ÷ 5.8 = $35,517

   Planned sales this May = $210,000 ÷ 5.8 = $36,207

$$\text{Percentage of increase} = \frac{\$36,207 - \$35,517}{\$35,517} = 1.9\%$$

Planned Sales as a Product of Historical Data and Current Trends (p. 402)

1. Trend increase for this year over last year:

$$\text{April} = \frac{\$19,000 - \$18,000}{\$18,000} = \frac{\$1,000}{\$18,000} = 5.6\%$$

$$\text{May} = \frac{\$20,000 - \$19,000}{\$19,000} = \frac{\$1,000}{\$19,000} = 5.3\%$$

$$\text{June} = \frac{\$21,500 - \$21,000}{\$21,000} = \frac{\$500}{\$21,500} = 2.4\%$$

Monthly sales as a percentage of the previous month this year:

$$\text{April-to-May} = \frac{\$20,000 - \$19,000}{\$19,000} = \frac{\$1,000}{\$19,000} = 5.3\%$$

$$\text{May-to-June} = \frac{\$21,500 - \$20,000}{\$20,000} = \frac{\$1,500}{\$20,000} = 7.5\%$$

Planned sales for July may be somewhere between:

$21,500 (June this year) × 109.0% = $23,435

$23,000 (July last year) × 102% = $23,460

or approximately

$$\frac{\$23,435 + \$23,460}{2} = \$23,448$$

3. Establish the trend this year over last year:

$$\text{April} = \frac{\$53,600 - \$52,700}{\$53,600} = -1.7\%$$

$$\text{May} = \frac{\$54,200 - \$53,500}{\$54,200} = -1.3\%$$

$$\text{June} = \frac{\$53,000 - \$52,100}{\$52,100} = 1.7\%$$

$$\text{July} = \frac{\$52,000 - \$48,700}{\$48,700} = 6.8\%$$

Establish the current trend this year:

$$\text{April-to-May} = \frac{\$53,500 - \$52,700}{\$52,700} = 1.5\%$$

$$\text{May-to-June} = \frac{\$53,500 - \$53,000}{\$53,500} = -0.9\%$$

$$\text{June-to-July} = \frac{\$53,000 - \$52,000}{\$53,000} = -1.9\%$$

It would appear that the trend of sales this year over last year would imply that August sales would increase by at least 6% or rise to about $49,078 ($46,300 × 106%). However, this must be tempered with an obvious decline in the current sales pattern of approximately 2%, which would place August sales close to 98% of July's sales, or $50,960 ($52,000 × 98%). Thus, we would approximate sales for August to be

$$\frac{\$50,960 + \$49,078}{2} = \$50,019$$

The Basic Stock Method (p. 410)

1. $\text{Average stock for season} = \dfrac{\$90,000}{1.2} = \$75,000$

   $\text{Average monthly sales} = \dfrac{\$90,000}{6} = \$15,000$

   $\text{Basic stock} = \$75,000 - \$15,000 = \$60,000$

   $\text{B O M inventory} = \$18,000 + \$60,000 = \$78,000$

3. $\text{Average stock for the season} = \dfrac{\$350,000}{3} = \$116,667$

   $\text{Average monthly sales} = \dfrac{\$350,000}{6} = \$58,333$

   March B O M inventory $= \$65,000 + (\$116,667 - \$58,333)$
   $= \$65,000 + \$58,334$
   $= \$123,334$

The Basic Stock Method Adapted to the Retail Accounting Calendar (p. 412)

1. $\text{Average seasonal stock} = \dfrac{\$52,000}{2} = \$26,000$

   $\text{Average "monthly" sales} = \dfrac{\$52,000}{6.5} = \$8,000$

   May B O M inventory $= \$12,000 + (\$26,000 - \$8,000) = \$30,000$

The Percentage Variation Method (p. 415)

1. November B O M stock $= \$24,000 \times 1/2 \left(1 + \dfrac{\$25,000}{\$20,000}\right)$

$$= \$24,000 \times 1/2 \ (225\%)$$
$$= \$24,000 \times 112.5\%$$
$$= \$27,000$$

3. November B O M stock $= \$25,000 \times 1/2 \left(1 + \dfrac{\$40,000}{\$33,333}\right)$

$$= \$25,000 \times 1/2 \ (220\%)$$
$$= \$25,000 \times 110\%$$
$$= \$27,500$$

The Percentage Variation Method Adapted to the Retail Accounting Calendar (p. 416)

1. Average stock for season $= \dfrac{\$165,000}{4} = \$41,250$

   Average periodic sales $= \dfrac{\$165,000}{5.2} = \$31,731$

   B O M stock $= \$41,250 \times 1/2 \left(1 + \dfrac{\$26,000}{\$31,731}\right)$

   B O M stock $= \$41,250 \times 1/2 \ (1 + \ 82\%)$

   $$= \$41,250 \times 91\%$$

   $$= \$37,538$$

The Stock-to-Sales Method (p. 421)

1. B O M stock $= \dfrac{\$12,000}{\$4,800} = 2.5$

3. Planned sales $= \dfrac{\$11,500}{2.5} = \$4,600$

	Planned Sales	Stock-to-Sales Ratio	Planned B.O.M. Stock
5. August	$17,000	7.5	$127,500
September	16,500	7.3	120,450
October	15,000	6.2	93,000
November	20,500	5.3	108,650

	Planned Sales	Stock-to-Sales Ratio	Planned B O M Stock
December	24,800	4.1	101,680
January	17,500	6.1	106,750
February	18,000	6.5	117,000

Average inventory $= \dfrac{\$775,030}{7} = \$110,719$

Turnover $= \dfrac{\$111,300}{\$110,719} = 1$

The Weeks' Supply Method (p. 422)

1. Average weekly sales $= \$46,800 \div 26 = \$1,800$

   Number of weeks $= 26 \div 6 = 4.3$

   Planned stock $= \$1,800 \times 4.3 = \$7,740$

3. Average weekly sales $= \$7,800$

   Number of weeks $= 52 \div 4.8 = 10.8$

   Planned stock $= \$7,800 \times 10.8 = \$84,240$

5. Average weekly sales $= \$130,000 \div 26 = \$5,000$

   Number of weeks $= 26 \div 3.7 = 7$

   Planned stock $= \$5,000 \times 7 = \$35,000$

Preparation of the Six-Month Merchandise Plan (p. 430)

1. The completed six-month merchandise plan is exhibited in Figure 12.14.

3. The completed six-month merchandise plan is illustrated in Figure 12.15.

Topics for Discussion and Review

1. Explain the immediate objectives of the merchandise budget and the operating budget. How do they relate to each other, and what objectives do they share in common?

2. What strategic objectives does the six-month plan specifically attempt to define?

3. Explain the concept and construction of the retail accounting calendar.

4. Define the six-month merchandise plan. What is its essential goal?

☐ Corporation _____

☐ Store _____

☐ Department _____

☒ Classification _____

☒ Spring 19____

☐ Fall 19____

Seasonal Data

	Last Year	Planned	Actual
Cumulative markon %	51.5	50.7	
Markdown %	10.0	8.0	
Shortage %	2.0	2.0	
Sales discounts %	1.5	1.5	
Maintained markon %	45.0	45.0	
Operating expenses %	40.0	39.0	
Operating profit %	5.0	6.0	
Turnover	2.0	2.4	

	Feb. (I) Aug. (VII) $	%	Mar. (II) Sept. (VIII) $	%	Apr. (III) Oct. (IX) $	%	May (IV) Nov. (X) $	%	June (V) Dec. (XI) $	%	July (VI) Jan. (XII) $	%	Total $
Net sales													
Last year	18,400		21,200		25,400		28,800		26,300		24,500		144,600
Plan	15,617		28,110		34,357		31,234		31,233		15,617		156,168
Revised													
Actual													
BOM stock													
Last year	66,600	2.8	69,400	3.3	73,600	2.9	77,000	2.7	74,500	2.8	72,700	3.0	433,800
Plan	55,659	3.5	67,152	2.4	73,399	2.1	70,276	2.2	70,275	2.3	54,659	3.5	390,420
Revised													
Actual													
EOM stock													
Last year	69,400		73,600		77,000		74,500		72,700		72,300		439,500
Plan	67,152		73,399		70,276		70,275		54,659		65,070		400,831
Revised													
Actual													
Retail reductions													
Last year	1,952	10.6	1,308	6.2	4,256	16.8	4,802	16.7	2,479	9.4	4,724	19.3	19,521
Plan	1,796	11.5	898	3.2	3,592	10.5	4,490	14.4	2,694	8.6	4,490	28.8	17,959
Revised													
Actual													
Purchases at retail													
Last year	23,152		26,708		33,056		31,102		26,979		28,824		169,821
Plan	29,906		35,255		34,826		35,723		18,311		30,518		184,538
Revised													
Actual													
Purchases at cost													
Last year	11,229		12,953		16,032		15,084		13,085		13,980		82,363
Plan	14,744		17,381		17,169		17,611		9,027		15,045		90,977
Revised													
Actual													
Maintained markon													
Last year	8,538	46.4	10,282	48.5	11,024	43.4	12,499	43.4	12,335	46.9	10,315	42.1	64,993
Plan	7,028	45.0	13,802	49.1	15,632	45.5	13,618	43.6	14,523	46.5	5,700	36.5	70,303
Revised													
Actual													

Figure 12.14 Completed six-month merchandise plan for application exercise 1

☐ Corporation _____

☐ Store _____

☐ Department _____

☐ Classification _____

☐ Spring 19___

☒ Fall 19___

Seasonal Data

	Last Year	Planned	Actual
Cumulative markon %	48.9	49.6	
Markdown %	10.0	10.0	
Shortage %	2.5	2.0	
Sales discounts %	1.0	1.0	
Maintained markon %	42.0	43.0	
Operating expenses %	37.0	38.0	
Operating profit %	5.0	5.0	
Turnover	4.0	5.0	

	Feb. (I) Aug. (VII)		Mar. (II) Sept. (VIII)		Apr. (III) Oct. (IX)		May (IV) Nov. (X)		June (V) Dec. (XI)		July (VI) Jan. (XII)		Total
	$	%	$	%	$	%	$	%	$	%	$	%	$
Net sales													
Last year	9,375		28,125		46,875		37,500		37,500		28,125		187,500
Plan	16,640		24,960		41,600		52,000		47,840		24,960		208,000
Revised													
Actual													
BOM stock													
Last year	30,469	3.3	44,531	1.6	58,594	1.3	51,563	1.4	51,563	1.4	44,531	1.6	281,251
Plan	30,784	1.9	35,776	1.4	45,760	1.1	52,000	1.0	49,504	1.0	35,776	1.4	249,600
Revised													
Actual													
EOM stock													
Last year	44,531		58,594		51,563		51,563		44,531		46,875		297,657
Plan	35,776		45,760		52,000		49,504		35,776		41,600		260,416
Revised													
Actual													
Retail reductions													
Last year	2,531	27.0	1,266	4.5	1,226	2.7	3,788	10.1	7,613	20.3	8,859	31.5	25,323
Plan	3,245	19.5	1,622	6.5	2,163	5.2	3,786	7.3	6,760	14.1	9,464	37.9	27,040
Revised													
Actual													
Purchases at retail													
Last year	25,968		43,454		41,110		41,288		38,081		39,328		229,229
Plan	24,877		36,566		50,003		53,290		40,872		40,248		245,856
Revised													
Actual													
Purchases at cost													
Last year	13,270		22,205		21,007		21,098		19,450		20,097		117,136
Plan	13,538		18,429		25,202		26,858		20,599		20,285		123,911
Revised													
Actual													
Maintained markon													
Last year	3,291	35.1	13,106	46.6	22,266	47.5	16,388	43.7	14,438	38.5	9,225	32.8	78,714
Plan	6,623	39.8	11,556	46.3	19,552	47.0	23,868	45.9	20,332	42.5	7,613	30.5	89,544
Revised													
Actual													

Figure 12.15 Completed six-month merchandise plan for application exercise 3

5. Give three reasons for the establishment of the six-month merchandise plan, and relate those reasons to strategic objectives.

6. What results may be expected from the implementation of a six-month merchandise plan?

7. What are generally considered to be the constituent elements of the six-month merchandise plan?

8. Describe the format of a typical six-month merchandise plan.

9. Explain the concept of retail reductions as they relate to the six-month plan.

10. Explain the concept of purchases at retail. How are they derived? What do they consist of?

11. What is the most crucial element of the six-month plan? Why?

12. What three fundamental factors underlie a sound sales forecast?

13. What is meant by sales per square foot, and how is the concept applied to sales forecasting?

14. How would you explain turnover as a predictor of sales volume?

15. What is the relationship between the average sale and the number of retail transactions? How is this concept applied to sales planning? What advantages does it provide?

16. Discuss the factors that influence the size of the average sale.

17. What is a stock-to-sales ratio? Explain its function as an indicator of net sales.

18. Explain how a seasonal planned sales figure might be distributed across six periods or months.

19. Why is turnover expected to increase with a rising sales volume and to decrease as sales volume falls?

20. Explain the essence of the basic-stock method. What is a basic stock, and how does it relate to sales? Why must the turnover always be less than the number of months in the accounting period?

21. When using the retail accounting calendar, how and why are the number of months in a season translated into accounting periods?

22. Upon what premise is the percentage variation method of inventory predicated? What makes it so different from the basic-stock method?

23. What does a stock-to-sales ratio of 5.7 mean? How does the stock-to-sales ratio contribute to stock planning? How does the stock-to-sales ratio relate to turnover?

24. Explain how the merchant arrives at the dollar value of purchases at retail. Why must the retail value be converted to cost?

25. Explain how you would prove the internal validity of the six-month merchandise plan without recalculating each individual step.

Chapter 13
Planning Dollar Open-to-Buy

Learning Objectives

- Explain the concept of open-to-buy.

- Explain the function of open-to-buy in terms of a planning and control device and as a diagnostic tool.

- Discuss the results of an overbought condition.

- Identify the methods of increasing the open-to-buy.

- Determine the open-to-buy as of the first of the month.

- Calculate the open-to-buy as of a specific date when the stock on hand is known.

- Calculate the open-to-buy as of a specific date when the stock on hand is not known.

Key Terms

Automatic Cancellation Date: The date specified by the merchant on the purchase order as the latest acceptable shipment date.

Merchandise Available: Beginning-of-the-month inventory.

Merchandise in Transit: Any goods legally owned by the merchant but not yet charged to a retail selling department.

Merchandise Received: Legally owned merchandise taken into the retail store and charged against a specific selling department.

Merchandise Required: The sum of markdowns, shortages, sales discounts, the EOM inventory, and net sales.

Off-Price Merchandise: Items of merchandise offered by the vendor at a lower price than the normally established price.

Open-to-Buy: The amount of merchandise that may be purchased for delivery during the balance of a given control period, if the planned EOM stock is to be achieved.

Outstanding Order: The dollar amount of merchandise on order, but not yet received, from a vendor for the balance of any given accounting period.

Overbought: A situation where the merchant has become committed to purchases in excess of a planned purchase allotment for a given merchandising period.

Planned Purchases: The value of the merchandise that may be charged against a selling department during a given accounting period. Planned purchases are normally expressed in terms of retail dollars, but must be converted to cost dollars when an actual purchase is under consideration. Obviously, the merchant does not spend retail dollars, only cost dollars.

Purchase Order: The legally binding record of a sales agreement between the merchant and the vendor, stipulating the cost of the goods purchased, discount terms, method of shipment, and delivery date.

Underbought: A situation where the total merchandise available is insufficient to meet the merchant's needs, in terms of sales, reductions, and the EOM stock.

Unit Control: The control of inventory in terms of merchandise units, rather than retail dollars. These "units" are normally defined as stock-keeping units, or the lowest level of merchandise identification, usually size and color within a unique style.

13.1

Open-to-Buy Derived from Monthly Planned Purchases

In Chapter 1, it was pointed out that retail merchandising is a "management system of strategic planning and tactical control." Chapter 12 identified the six-month merchandising plan as the culmination of the merchant's strategic planning activity. Dollar open-to-buy is now presented as the primary factor in the administration and control of that planning effort.

The primary thrust of the merchandise plan was to establish a dollar amount for the purchases to be made each month. The essence of the planned-purchase concept was defined as the dollars required to supply inventory for those planned monthly requirements not already provided for by the BOM stock. Thus, from the merchant's perspective, the planned-purchase figure defines the value of the goods that may be purchased as of the first of each month and for the duration of that month or accounting period.

However, simply because the monthly planned purchases are neatly defined on the merchandise plan, that is not to imply that the merchant has license to actually spend that amount for the given period. Planned purchases must be modified to accommodate two basic impinging factors:

1. Outstanding orders, or commitments to vendors, to purchase merchandise not yet received. The value of these orders will reduce the planned purchases for the months in which the merchandise is scheduled for delivery, not for the month in which the order was placed.

2. Not all of the required monthly stock is purchased at the beginning of the period. Purchase decisions must be distributed across the accounting period:
   a. to take advantage of new merchandise lines or items introduced during the month.
   b. to reorder unexpectedly fast-selling items.
   c. to acquire off-price merchandise, thus increasing promotional activity, markon, or both.

As a result, the merchant must be able to calculate, on a specific date during the month, the amount of merchandise to be purchased during the balance of that month. These remaining purchases are defined as open-to-buy, and the system that controls this flow of merchandise into the periodic inventories is known as the open-to-buy (OTB) control. Open-to-buy may be determined in either dollars or units. However, our immediate concern lies with dollars, simply because dollars ultimately define units, regardless of the type or amount of units planned for.

The Concept of Open-to-Buy

Open-to-buy may be conceptually defined as simply the difference between the planned purchases at retail for a given accounting period, as shown on the six-month merchandise plan, and the value of the goods already owned by the merchant.[1] The underlying concept of open-to-buy is the same as that which defines purchases at retail, that is,

Merchandise required for the period[2]
Less merchandise available for the period
Planned purchases for the period

---

[1] Open-to-buy is always calculated at retail unless otherwise stated.
[2] Recall from the six-month merchandise plan that

Merchandise required = Sales + Reductions + EOM inventory
Merchandise available = BOM inventory

However, the concept of open-to-buy requires a redefinition of merchandise available for the period, so as to include, along with the BOM stock, merchandise received during the period and the outstanding purchase orders. Thus, we have the following quantitative formula:

$Planned sales	$BOM stock
$EOM stock	$Merchandise received
$Retail reductions	$Outstanding purchases
$Merchandise required —	$Merchandise available = Open-to-buy

The total "merchandise available" to the merchant at any given time within the accounting period derives from the three following sources, only one of which, the BOM inventory, is from the six-month merchandise plan:

1. The BOM stock, as illustrated in the six-month plan.

2. Merchandise received during the accounting period.

3. Funds committed during prior accounting periods or before a specific planning date within the current accounting period—merchandise in transit and the outstanding purchases.

In effect, we may now state the concept of open-to-buy as follows:

Merchandise required for the period
Less merchandise available for the period
Planned purchases for the period
Less out standing purchases
Less merchandise received during the period
Open-to-buy

The Function of Open-to-Buy

The open-to-buy concept serves the merchant in two significant ways, first as a planning and control device and second as a diagnostic tool in the evaluation of merchandising activities.

Open-to-Buy as a Planning and Control Device

Achieving merchandise control, as indicated throughout this text, requires a balanced relationship between inventory and net sales. We have specifically seen this relationship in our study of gross margin, turnover, and stock planning methods, all of which culminated in the six-month merchandise plan, and in the determination of monthly purchases, at both retail and cost. However, this monthly or periodic purchase figure is valid as a control device only if the three following conditions are met:

1. It is the first of the month or the beginning of a period.

2. Prior orders have not been placed for delivery in the month under consideration.

3. The BOM inventory will be exactly as planned—that is, the EOM inventory for the previous month has met its planned expectations in terms of net sales, inventory, retail reductions, and actual purchases.

Obviously, the above three conditions will rarely, if ever, be met at the same time; therefore, the initial periodic purchase figure is subject to modification as it is distributed across the given accounting period.

Open-to-buy control is instituted to ensure (to the extent possible) that incremental purchasing within a defined accounting period conforms with the total purchases allowed for that period. By specifically defining the relationship between the merchandise required and the merchandise available at any given date within an accounting period, the open-to-buy figure performs a control function, in that it

1. Regulates the balance between inventory and sales, thus limiting an overbought or underbought situation.

2. Prevents loss of sales due to an out-of-stock position.

3. Maintains purchases within the financial limitations of the periodic merchandise budget.

4. Reduces markdowns, increases sales, and thus enhances both turnover and gross margin.

5. Allows the merchant to conserve or hold back purchase dollars so as to
   a. Reorder fast-selling items and replenish staple stock.
   b. Take advantage of off-price merchandise offerings by the vendor.
   c. Sample new vendor lines or items.

Open-to-Buy as a Diagnostic Tool

The open-to-buy figure may serve as a diagnostic tool in the analysis and evaluation of overbought and underbought situations. For example, if the open-to-buy dollars appear to be less than what the merchant seems to need, the situation is defined as overbought and may be indicative of any one, or combination, of the following factors:

1. Planning errors, such as an inaccurate sales forecast.

2. Buying errors, such as failure to recognize fashion trends.

3. Promotional errors or the lack of promotional efforts.

4. Timing errors, normally the receipt of merchandise either too late or too early in the season.

On the other hand, if the open-to-buy indicates that more merchandise is required than can be ordered and processed during the remaining portion of the period, the merchant is said to be underbought. This condition may also be the result of the above-mentioned errors; however, more specifically we would look for

1. An unexpected success in the achievement of sales volume or in the promotional efforts that produced that amount of sales.
2. The failure to place orders with vendors in time to meet the planned merchandise requirements.

Open-to-Buy as a Guide to Merchandising Activity

The concept of open-to-buy as an immutable dollar figure is certainly not justified. The function of open-to-buy is to guide the merchant in the balancing of inventory to sales, not to rigidly dictate the exact terms of that balance. Obviously, because of the volatile nature of merchandising activities, the amount budgeted for open-to-buy does not preclude additional purchases, should customer demand so indicate. A department may well be overbought but still in need of fast-selling staple goods, and to refuse the merchant additional purchase dollars would only serve to intensify the problem rather than solve it. For example, if the men's furnishings stock is overbought due to an excess of sweaters, to attempt to remedy the condition by running short of white dress shirts would be ridiculous.

The results of an overbought condition

When the open-to-buy figure is determined to be unsatisfactory, generally speaking the merchant will be in an overbought position; indeed, it is not uncommon for the outstanding orders to exceed the planned purchases for the balance of the accounting period. When this condition exists, it means that the merchant's inventory carries an excess of unwanted items, which is symptomatic of the following historic buying errors:

1. Inferior merchandise was purchased, whether defined in terms of quality, fashion level, price, size range, color, or whatever.
2. Purchase orders were initiated too late to capitalize on the selling period.
3. All of the open-to-buy dollars were spent in advance of the current selling period, with no funds available for reorders.
4. Major opportunities were missed to exploit potentially profitable items.

5. The merchant missed the ideal price points where the major volume of sales could be achieved.

To the degree that the merchant fails to correct any of the foregoing buying errors, the following immediate results may be expected:

1. Unplanned markdowns will increase.
2. Maintained markon and gross margin will decrease.
3. Average stock will increase, thus decreasing the turnover ratio.
4. Open-to-buy for the succeeding periods will decrease.
5. Operating profit will certainly decrease.

Methods of increasing the open-to-buy

The following activities are suggested to correct the overbought condition or to increase the open-to-buy:

1. Explore the realistic possibilities of increased sales for the balance of the period.
2. Reduce the value of the inventory on hand by one or more of the following methods:
   a. Increase the markdowns for the remaining portion of the month. This will not only decrease the value of the current stock but will also enhance the rate of stock turn. While this method obviously entails some risk, a reduced gross margin as a result of a price decrease is far better than zero gross margin from higher-priced merchandise still sitting on the merchant's shelves.
   b. Attempt to return some overstocked merchandise to the vendor. This practice is not always unethical, especially where good vendor relationships exist and the vendor has a ready market in which to dispose of the merchant's excess goods. Remember that, theoretically at least, the merchant and the vendor are linked in partnership and that what benefits one is also good for the other.
   c. Transfer the oversupply of goods to another selling unit of the retail organization. If the receiving unit is to offer the merchandise at a reduced price, the sending unit must take the markdown prior to initiating the merchandise transfer. Where applicable, this markdown is an additional plus factor in increasing the open-to-buy dollars.
   d. Again, depending upon the quality of the merchant's relationship with the vendor, it is entirely possible to postpone outstanding orders for current delivery to a later period, when conditions for receipt might be more favorable.

    e. Cancel outstanding orders where they are overdue. This is perfectly legit-
imate, assuming that the purchase order, which is a legally binding document, contains an automatic cancellation date that the vendor, for whatever
reason, has chosen to ignore.

    f. Another possibility is to increase the value of the ending inventory. This will
increase the merchant's "required merchandise" in relation to the BOM
stock or the available merchandise, thus proportionally increasing the open-
to-buy. While this may be a measure of last resort, it is justifiable given the
following conditions:

    (1) The original stock plan has proven to be inaccurate.

    (2) Sales for the coming period appear to be underestimated.

    (3) The immediate merchandise requirements outweigh the more distant
need for a strict control of inventory.

13.2

Calculation of Open-to-Buy, Given Specific Merchandising Considerations

Determination of Open-to-Buy as of the First of the Month or the Beginning of an Accounting Period

The following study problem illustrates the effects of previous purchase commitments and reductions on open-to-buy as of the first of the month.

▪ Study Problem

Given: The following data for the month of June:

B O M stock	$23,000
E O M stock	25,000
Planned sales	12,000
Reductions	1,000
Stock on order for June delivery	5,000

Find: The merchant's open-to-buy as of June 1.

Solution:

Merchandise required 6/1 through 6/30

EOM stock	$25,000
Sales	12,000
Reductions	1,000
Total required	$38,000

Merchandise available as of 6/1

BOM stock	$23,000
Stock on order 6/1[3]	5,000
Total available	$28,000
Total merchandise required	$38,000
Less total merchandise available	28,000
Open-to-buy, 6/1	$10,000

▪ Application Exercise

1. A merchant had a retail stock of $10,500 on April 1 and a planned stock figure of $13,800 for May 1. Sales for April were planned at $6,000, with retail reductions of 8%. If $2,500 worth of merchandise was on order for April receipt, determine the open-to-buy for April.

2. Given the following data, determine the June 1 open-to-buy for a sporting goods department:

B O M stock	$23,800
E O M stock	21,500
Planned sales	11,000
Stock on order	5,800
Markdowns	600
Shortages	100

3. Given the following information derived from the six-month merchandising plan, determine the open-to-buy at retail and cost for a classification of housewares during Period VI.

B O M stock	$10,700
E O M stock	8,500
Planned sales	5,000
Stock on order	2,300
Retail reductions	5%
Cumulative markon	30%

4. A merchant had a BOM stock of $43,800 at retail. The following figures for the month were planned: EOM stock $35,600, net sales $19,900, initial markon 48.5%, and markdowns 8.5%. What was the open-to-buy at retail and at cost?

5. A toy department planned sales at $21,000 for October, with a BOM stock of $36,300. The initial markon was 42.8%, with subsequent markdowns planned

---

[3]Stock on order expected to arrive at the store within the accounting period must be considered as available and is thus an addition to the BOM inventory.

at 4.7%. Assuming that the outstanding orders for October receipt were $8,300 and the anticipated BOM stock for November was $48,700, find
a. Open-to-buy at retail.
b. Open-to-buy at cost.
c. Purchases at retail.
d. Purchases at cost.

Calculation of the Open-to-Buy for the Balance of the Accounting Period

In order to ensure that purchase dollars are always available for merchandise reorders, or the trial and testing of new items, it is necessary to be able to determine the open-to-buy as of a specific date. Normally, the stock on hand for the determination of open-to-buy would be available. However, in smaller or less sophisticated retail stores, where the book inventory as of a specific date is unobtainable or stock counts are not feasible, the merchant must of necessity determine the open-to-buy without knowledge of the stock on hand. Given these two considerations, it becomes necessary for the merchant to be able to calculate open-to-buy when the stock on hand is either known or unknown.

Determination of Open-to-Buy as of a Specific Date When the Stock on Hand Is Known

The concept is essentially the same as in previous examples, with the exception that our concern now is with a partial rather than a full month or period.

▪ Study Problem

Given:

Cumulative markon	47%
Stock on hand, March 12	$12,500
Planned E O M stock	13,700
Total March planned sales	7,300
Actual sales as of March 12	3,000
Total March reductions	400
Actual reductions as of March 12	200
Outstanding orders as of March 12	2,500

Find: The open-to-buy for a classification of men's pajamas, as of March 12, at both retail and at cost.

Solution:

Open-to-buy as of 3/12 = Merchandise required (3/12–3/31) − Merchandise available (3/12–3/31)

Merchandise required 3/12–3/31

E O M stock, 3/31		$13,700	
Planned sales, 3/1–3/31	$7,300		
Less actual sales, 3/1–3/12	3,000		
Balance of sales, 3/12–3/31		4,300	
Planned reductions, 3/1–3/31	400		
Less actual reductions, 3/1–3/12	200		
Balance of reductions, 3/12–3/31		200	
Total merchandise required, 3/12–3/31			$18,200

Merchandise available as of 3/12

Stock on hand	$12,500	
Outstanding orders	2,500	
Less total merchandise available		15,000
Open-to-buy, 3/12, retail		$3,200
Open-to-buy, 3/12, cost ($3,200 × 53%)		$1,696

▪ Application Exercise

1. Determine the retail open-to-buy as of October 14, based upon these data:

October planned sales	$12,200
Actual sales as of 10/14	6,000
Stock on hand, 10/14	18,500
Planned E O M stock	23,800
Reductions, 10/1–10/31	1,200
Reductions as of 10/14	600
Outstanding orders, 10/14	8,500

2. Given the following departmental information, calculate the open-to-buy as of November 20:

Total planned sales, 11/1–11/30	$53,600
Sales, 11/1–11/20	36,000
Stock on hand, 11/20	80,500
Planned E O M stock	100,000
Reductions, 11/1–11/30	8%
Reductions, 11/1-11/20	2,800
Outstanding orders, 11/20	7,300

3. A children's shoe buyer wishes to try a new line of attractive sneakers, assuming that the open-to-buy on June 18 is sufficient to cover a purchase order of $2,800 at retail. After considering the following information, determine the status of the merchant's open-to-buy as of June 18 as a guide to the purchase decision.[4]

Stock on hand, 6/18	$12,200
Outstanding orders, 6/18	1,200
Planned sales for June	7,150
Planned E O M stock for June	13,600
Planned markdowns for June	300
Actual sales, 6/1–6/18	4,500
Actual markdowns, 6/1–6/18	100

4. As a result of an abnormally cold fall season, on October 19 a coat buyer suddenly realizes that the department is seriously understocked. An immediate stock count indicates that a replenishment order of $12,800 is required to meet the current level of customer demand for merchandise. The merchant's records indicate the following merchandise activity for the month to date:

Planned sales, 10/1–10/31	$30,500
E O M stock, 10/31	63,700
Reductions, 10/1–10/31	2,500
Sales, 10/1–10/19	23,400
Reductions, 10/1–10/19	800
Merchandise on hand, 10/19	48,600
Merchandise on order, 10/19	5,800

Determine the available amount of open-to-buy and the amount remaining should the replenishment order be placed.

5. A sweater buyer is anxious to try a new line of imported merchandise. It is estimated that the minimum assortment, in terms of styles, color, and size, for an adequate distribution to all selling locations will cost $6,700. The date of the purchase decision is September 9. Using the following data, calculate the buyer's open-to-buy as of 9/9 and advise the buyer as to a course of action.

---

[4]Open-to-buy is not designed to dictate the merchant's purchase decisions but only to guide that decision. While the merchant may be overbought, that does not necessarily imply an overstocked position.

Cumulative markon	48%
September planned sales	$30,000
September E O M stock	65,500
September reductions	3,500
Sales to date	8,700
Reductions to date	800
Merchandise on hand, 9/9	86,700
Merchandise on order, 9/9	9,400

Calculation of Open-to-Buy as of a Specific Date When the Stock on Hand is Not Known

The method for the determination of the merchandise required for the balance of the season is the same as in the previous exercises. However, because the dollar value of the stock on hand is unknown, this amount must be computed by adding the receipts to date to the BOM inventory and then subtracting the sum of the sales and retail reductions. Thus,

> Stock on hand = BOM stock + Receipts to date − (Retail reductions to date + Sales to date)

▪ Study Problem

Given: The following data for the month of March:

B O M stock	$19,600
Orders received, 3/1–3/8	3,500
Outstanding orders, 3/8	2,700
Planned sales, 3/1–3/31	10,000
Actual sales, 3/1–3/8	2,600
Planned reductions, 3/1–3/31	1,000
Actual reductions, 3/1–3/8	200
Planned E.O.M. stock	17,300

Find: The open-to-buy for a classification of men's slacks as of March 8.

Solution:

Merchandise needed, 3/8–3/31

Planned E O M stock		$17,300
Planned sales, 3/1–3/31	$10,000	
Less actual sales, 3/1–3/8	2,600	

Balance of sales, 3/8–3/31		7,400	
Planned reductions, 3/1–3/31	$1,000		
Less actual reductions, 3/1–3/8	200		
Balance of reductions, 3/8–3/31		800	
Total merchandise needed, 3/8–3/31			$25,500

Merchandise available, 3/8–3/31

B O M stock	$19,600		
Receipts, 3/1–3/8	3,500		
Total merchandise handled, 3/1–3/8		23,100	
Sales, 3/1–3/8	2,600		
Reductions, 3/1–3/8	200		
Total inventory reductions, 3/1–3/8		(2,800)	
Stock on hand, 3/8		$20,300	
Stock on order, 3/8		2,700	
Total merchandise available, 3/8			(23,000)
Open-to-buy, 3/8			$2,500

▪ Application Exercise

1. Given the following information, determine the open-to-buy for a gift shop as of May 12:

B O M stock	$18,600
Orders received, 5/1–5/12	1,300
Outstanding orders, 5/12–5/31	5,200
Planned sales, 5/1–5/31	10,000
Actual sales, 5/1–5/12	3,900
Planned reductions, 5/1–5/31	500
Actual reductions, 5/1–5/12	100
Planned E.O.M. stock	20,300

2. A hosiery buyer is considering a $3,000 purchase but is unable to reach a decision due to the inability to determine the open-to-buy as of April 23. Given the following data, calculate the open-to-buy for this buyer and give advice concerning the purchase decision.

Cumulative markon	51%
B O M stock	$20,700
Orders received, 4/1–4/23	7,400

Outstanding orders, 4/23–4/30	3,700
Planned sales, 4/1–4/30	12,800
Actual sales, 4/1–4/23	9,500
Planned reductions, 4/1–4/30	600
Actual reductions, 4/1–4/23	600
Planned E O M inventory	18,400

3. A jewelry buyer wishes to determine the open-to-buy as of July 15. The BOM inventory was $36,000 and the planned EOM stock was $31,300. Purchases received to date were $4,800, and additional merchandise on order totals, $6,300. Planned sales for the month are $16,700, and actual sales to date are $10,500. Total reductions are planned at 7.3%, the buyer having consumed 60% of that amount as of the 15th. The cumulative markon for the period is 46.5%. What is the buyer's open-to-buy at both retail and at cost?

4. On June 18, a women's sportswear buyer is presented with an exceptional offering of off-price, name-brand sweaters to be retailed during the coming fall season. The buyer knows that the current stock is in an overbought condition, but by just how much is unknown. Given the following information, determine the amount that the buyer is overbought and suggest six methods of increasing the open-to-buy so as to permit the purchase of the sweaters.

E O M stock	$43,800
June planned sales	20,600
Actual June sales to date	12,600
Planned reductions for June	1,650
Actual June reductions to date	900
Merchandise received to date	13,700
Outstanding orders as of 6/18	12,300
B O M stock	40,300
Cumulative markon	42.8%

5. An unexpected increase in sales volume has prompted a toy buyer to consider additional purchases for the balance of the Christmas season. As of December 12, the buyer reviewed the following merchandise activity to date, in contrast with the original plans for December:

Planned activity, 12/1–12/31

Net sales	$300,000
B O M stock	650,000
E O M stock	430,500
Retail reductions	12.3%
Cumulative markon	42.5%

Merchandise activity, 12/1–12/12

Actual sales	$180,500
Actual reductions	10,800

Merchandise received	18,700
Outstanding orders	33,800

Define the amount of the merchant's open-to-buy if any, as of 12/12, in terms of both retail and cost dollars.

▪ Solutions to the Application Exercises

Determination of Open-to-Buy as of the First of the Month or the Beginning of an Accounting Period (p. 453)

1. Merchandise required 4/1 through 4/30

E O M stock	$13,800
Sales	6,000
Retail reductions	480
Total required	$20,280

Merchandise available as of 4/1

B O M stock	$10,500
Stock on order	2,500
Total available	$13,000

O T B = $20,280 − $13,000 = $7,280

3. Merchandise required for period VI

E O M stock	$ 8,500
Planned sales	5,000
Retail reductions	250
Total required	$13,750

Merchandise available for Period VI

B O M stock	$10,700
Stock on order	2,300
Total available	$13,000

O T B at retail = $13,750 − $13,000 = $750

O T B at cost = $750 × 70% = $525

5. Merchandise required for October

E O M stock	$48,700
Planned sales	21,000
Markdowns	987
Total required	$70,687

Merchandise available for October

B O M stock	$36,300
Outstanding orders	8,300
Total available	$44,600

a. O T B at retail = $70,687 − $44,600 = $26,087

b. O T B at cost = $26,087 × 57.2% = $14,922

c. Purchases at retail = $70,687 − $36,300 = $34,387[5]

d. Purchases at cost = $19,669

Determination of Open-to-Buy as of a Specific Date When the Stock on Hand Is Known (p. 455)

1. Merchandise required, 10/14–10/31

E O M stock		$23,800
Planned sales, 10/1–10/31	$12,200	
Less actual sales, 10/1–10/14	6,000	
Balance of sales, 10/14–10/31		6,200
Planned reductions, 10/1–10/31	1,200	
Less actual reductions, 10/1–10/14	600	
Balance of reductions, 10/14–10/31		600
Total merchandise required, 10/14–10/31		$30,600

Merchandise available as of 10/14

Stock on hand	$18,500	
Outstanding orders	8,500	
Total merchandise available		(27,000)
Open-to-buy as of 10/14		$3,600

---

[5]Merchandise required	$70,687
Less BOM stock	36,300
Planned purchases	34,387
Less outstanding orders	8,300
Open-to-Buy	$26,087

3. Merchandise required, 6/18–6/30

E O M stock		$13,600	
Planned sales, 6/1–6/30	$7,150		
Less actual sales, 6/1–6/18	4,500		
Balance of sales, 6/18–6/30		2,650	
Planned markdowns, 6/1–6/30	300		
Less actual markdowns, 6/1–6/18	100		
Balance of markdowns, 6/18–6/30		200	
Total merchandise required, 6/18–6/30			$16,450
Merchandise available, 6/18			
Stock on hand		$12,600	
Outstanding orders		1,200	
Total merchandise available			(13,800)
Open-to-buy			$2,650

5. Merchandise needed, 9/9–9/30

E.O.M. stock		$65,500	
Planned sales, 9/1–9/30	$30,000		
Less actual sales, 9/1–9/9	8,700		
Balance of sales, 9/9–9/30		21,300	
Planned reductions, 9/1–9/30	3,500		
Less actual reductions, 9/1–9/9	800		
Balance of reductions, 9/9–9/30		2,700	
Total merchandise needed, 9/9–9/30			$89,500
Merchandise available, 9/9			
Stock on hand, 9/9		$86,700	
Outstanding orders, 9/9		9,400	
Total merchandise available, 9/9			(96,100)
Open-to-buy, 9/9			($6,600)

Advice: Don't buy; you are already overbought by $6,600.

Calculation of Open-to-Buy as of a Specific Date When the Stock on Hand Is Not Known: (p. 458)

1. Merchandise needed, 5/12–5/31

Planned E O M stock		$20,300
Planned May sales	$10,000	
Less actual sales, 5/1–5/12	3,900	

Planned sales, 5/12–5/31		6,100	
Planned May reductions	500		
Less actual reductions, 5/1–5/12	100		
Planned reductions, 5/12–5/31		400	
Total merchandise needed, 5/12–5/31			$26,800

Merchandise available, 5/12–5/31

B O M stock	$18,600		
Receipts, 5/1–5/12	1,300		
Total merchandise handled, 5/1–5/12		$19,900	
Sales, 5/1–5/12	3,900		
Reductions, 5/1–5/12	100		
Total inventory reductions, 5/1–5/12		(4,000)	
Stock on hand, 5/12		$15,900	
Stock on order, 5/12		5,200	
Total merchandise available, 5/12–5/31			(21,100)
Open-to-buy, 5/12			$5,700

3. Merchandise needed, 7/15–7/31

Planned E O M stock		$31,300	
Planned July sales	$16,700		
Less actual sales, 7/1–7/15	10,500		
Planned sales, 7/15–7/31		6,200	
Planned July reductions	1,219		
Less actual reductions, 7/1–7/15	731		
Planned reductions, 7/15–7/31		488	
Total merchandise needed, 7/15–7/31			$37,988

Merchandise available, 7/15–7/31

B O M stock	$36,000		
Receipts, 7/1–7/15	4,800		
Total merchandise handled, 7/1–7/15		$40,800	
Sales, 7/1–7/15	10,500		

Reductions, 7/1–7/15	731		
Total inventory reductions, 7/1–7/15		(11,231)	
Stock on hand, 7/15			$29,569
Stock on order, 7/15–7/31			6,300
Total merchandise available, 7/15–7/31			(35,869)
Open-to-buy at retail, 7/15			$2,119
Open-to-buy at cost, 7/15			$1,134

5. Merchandise needed, 12/12–12/31

Planned E O M stock			$430,500
Planned sales, 12/1–12/31	$300,000		
Less actual sales, 12/1–12/12	180,500		
Planned sales, 12/12–12/31		119,500	
Planned reductions, 12/1–12/31	36,900		
Less actual reductions, 12/1–12/12	10,800		
Planned reductions, 12/12–12/31		26,100	
Total merchandise needed, 12/12–12/31			$576,100

Merchandise available, 12/12–12/31

B O M stock	$650,000		
Receipts, 12/1–12/12	18,700		
Total merchandise handled, 12/1–12/12		$668,700	
Sales, 12/1–12/12	180,500		
Reductions, 12/1–12/12	10,800		
Total inventory reductions, 12/1–12/12		(191,300)	

Stock on hand, 12/12	$477,400
Stock on order, 12/12–12/31	33,800
Total merchandise available, 12/12–12/31	(511,200)
Open-to-buy at retail, 12/12	$64,900
Open-to-buy at cost, 12/12	$37,318

Topics for Discussion and Review

1. Explain the concept of open-to-buy.

2. Describe the objectives of open-to-buy. How are these objectives achieved?

3. Describe the causes of an overbought condition and the merchandising problems it creates.

4. What means would you explore to alleviate an overbought situation?

5. Why is an open-to-buy plan necessary when the merchant already has a six-month merchandise plan?

6. What element of the six-month merchandise plan forms the basis of the open-to-buy concept?

7. Essentially, open-to-buy is the difference between what the merchant needs and that which is available. What does the merchant "need," and what is "available"?

8. What are the functions of open-to-buy?

9. What is merchandise control, and how is it achieved?

10. How does open-to-buy perform the control function?

11. What is meant by "overbought"?

12. What is meant by "underbought"?

13. What are the consequences of an overbought situation?

14. When is merchandise "on order" considered to be "merchandise available"?

15. Given the necessary data, explain how you would determine the open-to-buy as of the first of an accounting period.

16. How would you calculate the open-to-buy as of a specific date when the inventory on-hand is unknown?

17. How do markdowns reduce the open-to-buy?

18. What effect will markups have on the open-to-buy?

19. A buyer requests that a shipment of merchandise be postponed until the next accounting period. What will be the effect on the open-to-buy for the current period?

20. Assuming that a markdown must be taken on an interstore transfer, when should the markdown be effected?

21. When the merchant adds the BOM stock to receipts and deducts sales and reductions, the results are a substitute for what?

22. How do you account for stock on order for a given period that has not yet been received?

23. When the average stock increases as the result of an overbought condition, what results may be expected?

24. What effect should a department's overbought position have on its replenishment of basic stock?

25. What is an automatic cancellation date, and what effect could it have on the merchant's open-to-buy?

Chapter 14
Planning Merchandise Assortments

Learning Objectives

- Explain the difference between fashion merchandise and staple merchandise.
- Define a model stock.
- Define the two forms of a model stock.
- Identify the objectives of merchandise assortment planning.
- Identify and explain the variables in unit assortment planning.
- Provide examples of various types of selection parameters.
- Explain the concepts breadth and depth in a merchandise assortment.
- Explain the function of a unit control system.
- Explain two methods for the determination of the status of a unit stock.
- Define the basic elements of a model stock plan.
- Explain the concept of a model stock plan for fashion merchandise.
- Calculate the number of units within a subclassification for a model stock plan.
- Determine the value of the model stock at retail and cost.
- Explain how a unit open-to-buy for fashion merchandise is developed from a model stock plan.
- Explain the concept of a basic stock list.

- Define the components of the minimum stock in terms of weeks and units.

- Explain the components of the maximum stock in terms of weeks and units.

- List the components of unit open-to-buy for staple merchandise.

- Calculate unit turnover.

- Explain the concept of the average unit stock.

- Define net sales in units.

- Explain the maximum system, for the periodic replenishment of staple stock (unit open-to-buy).

- Conceptually explain the following terms: minimum stock, delivery period, maximum stock, reserve stock, rate of sale, reorder period, unit open-to-buy, on hand, net sales, on order.

Key Terms

Assortment: The range of choices offered to the customer within a particular classification of merchandise, planned to various depths of inventory to meet customer demand.

Average Unit Stock on Hand: The reserve stock in units plus half the normal reorder amount in units.

BOM Stock: The stock on hand at the beginning of the month or other accounting period.

Basic Stock List: A description of the basic (staple) stock carried by the store and the minimum number of units for each classification that will provide adequate selection of merchandise at any time of the year.

Book Inventory: The amount of retail stock that is shown to be on hand in a perpetual-inventory system.

Breadth of Assortment: The range of choices within a classification's selection parameters.

Buying Plan: The breakdown of the dollar open-to-buy into the number of units to purchase within classifications and subclassifications.

Classification: All merchandise of a given type or use, regardless of style, size, color, model, or price, e.g., women's shoes.

Delivery Period: The number of time periods (weeks) between the placement of an order and the receipt of goods.

Depth: The number of units of each element in the range of choice of a selection parameter.

Fashion Basics: Fashion merchandise that has a selling life of several plan periods, or seasons.

Fashion Cycle: The rise, culmination, and decline of the popular acceptance of a particular style.

Fashion Merchandise: New goods that have a relatively short life cycle and are in high demand by a majority of a store's customers.

In Transit: Merchandise that has actually left the vendor's premises and is en route to its destination but is not yet on the selling floor.

Intermediate Reorder Amount: One half of the total unit reorder amount.

Maximum Stock: The upper limit of a unit assortment of merchandise; the greatest number of units that ever needs to be on hand at any given time.

Maximum System of Stock Control (Order-up-to-Level): The system of setting, for each item of basic (staple) merchandise carried, an amount large enough to satisfy customer demand at any given time. This amount is defined as the "maximum." Reordering of merchandise is based upon the difference between this maximum and the merchandise on hand as indicated by a periodic stock count.

Merchandise Mix: The different items stocked by a merchandise department.

Minimum Stock: The lower limit of a unit assortment of merchandise; the specific number of units that should be on hand at all times so as to avoid stockouts.

Model Stock Plan: An outline of the composition of an ideal stock in terms of general characteristics or assortment factors, usually with optimum quantities related to planned sales; generally associated with, but not limited to, fashion merchandise.

On-Hand Units: The number of units on hand that are available for resale.

On-Order Units: The number of units on order, in transit, or in receiving, checking and marking; units purchased but not yet available for resale.

Periodic Reorder Form: Essentially, that part of the basic stock list that determines when, and in what quantities, merchandise must be reordered to maintain a maximum level of inventory.

Perpetual Inventory: A running inventory, based upon the retail method of accounting. It consists of a beginning inventory plus periodic additions (purchases, markups, transfers in, etc.) less daily reductions (net sales, sales discounts, markdowns, etc.).

Physical Inventory: The actual count of each item on hand at the end of an accounting period.

Price Line: Retail prices set by store policy to give a range for customer choice within a department.

Purchase Order: A record of agreement made with the vendor that includes merchandise cost, discount terms, and method of shipping. (From the buyers point of view, a sales invoice.)

Rate of Sale: The quantity of units anticipated to sell during a particular period of time; normally expressed as the number of units sold on a weekly basis.

Reorder Period: The length of time between periodic inventory counts; normally expressed in weeks.

Reserve Stock: A safety factor in terms of time periods (weeks), or units, to offset an unexpected sales increase, delivery problems, or any unplanned contingencies.

Sales Analysis: That part of sales audit that provides totals of sales by salespeople, departments, classifications, colors, sizes, etc.

Season: A selling period of the year, generally spring (February through July) and fall (August through January).

Selection Parameters: Merchandise characteristics, or descriptors, that permit the reclassification of merchandise into style, color, fabric, price, size, pattern, brand, etc.

Staple Merchandise: Merchandise that the average customer expects to be in stock at all times and that is generally reorderable over relatively long periods of time. (Also defined as basic stock.)

Stock-Keeping Unit (SKU): The lowest level of identification of merchandise for inventory management. Within a particular style, this usually refers to the identification of a unique size within a particular color.

Stockout: A lack of stock, or inventory, to meet customer demand.

Subclassification: A division of groups of items within a major classification. Such items must be similar in nature, because most reports are geared to subclassification data.

Total Merchandise Available: The total of the merchandise on hand plus purchases for a given period; the sum of the dollar commitment for an accounting period.

Turnover: The number of times, in a given period of time, that an average inventory is sold and replaced; may be calculated in either dollars or units.

Unit Control: The control of stock in terms of merchandise units, rather than retail or cost dollars.

Unit Open-to-Buy: The number of units required to bring an inventory up to its maximum level.

Unit Planning: A combination of merchandise mix and quantity that will meet customer demand at a given time.

Variety: The number of classifications or product lines carried by a store or department.

Vendor: Any individual or company from which purchases are made.

Weekly Rate of Sale: The average number of units sold per week.

Weeks Supply: The number of weeks that a unit assortment of merchandise can be expected to satisfy customer demand.

14.1

Merchandise Assortment Concepts

Because customers purchase units and not dollars, all dollar-planning concepts must eventually translate into some form of unit assortment. A unit assortment is not simply a random collection of merchandise. It is a systematic organization of items, balanced to customer needs and bound by the financial constraints of the six-month merchandise plan and dollar open-to-buy.

Model Stocks

This "systematic organization of items" is defined as a "model stock," the function of which is to obtain a maximum volume of sales from a minimum investment in inventory. Thus, all unit assortment planning results in some form of a model stock, the specific format being dependent upon the type of merchandise being assembled.

For buying purposes, merchandise units are generally classified into two broad types of merchandise assortments: fashion merchandise and staple merchandise. Fashion merchandise refers to those goods that have a high demand over a relatively short period of time, normally a season, whereas staple merchandise defines those items that are consistently in demand over long periods of time, i.e., multiple seasons or years. While customers expect staple merchandise to be in stock at all times, fashion merchandise may be out of stock due to excessive customer demand, vendor shortages, or the decline of a fashion cycle.

As a result of the characteristics that differentiate these two types of merchandise assortments, two forms of model stock planning are employed by the merchant. For staple stocks, a periodic reorder form (often referred to as a basic stock list) is used; for fashion merchandise, a model stock plan is employed. While the titles and procedures for building the two types of merchandise assortments may differ, they both fall under the generic heading of model stock planning. Thus, in effect what we have is a model stock for basics, and a model stock for fashion merchandise.

This is not to suggest that all fashion items must be purchased exclusively through a model stock plan and that all staple goods must be relegated to a basic stock list. Indeed, some fashion items, defined as "fashion basics" sell well for multiple seasons and thus may be treated as staple merchandise within a model stock plan. Likewise, it is entirely reasonable to have a model stock plan for some classifications of staple merchandise.[1]

The Objectives of Merchandise Assortment Planning

While different in methodology and in concept, the objectives of the basic stock list and the model stock plan remain the same: to obtain the ideal combination of merchandise mix and quantity that will satisfy customer demand as it changes over a period, season or year. In essence, the objective of all merchandise assortment planning is the profitable satisfaction of customer needs at any given time.

Unit Planning Variables: Variety and Assortment

The degree of success in assembling and maintaining any merchandise assortment is dependent upon the astuteness with which the merchant handles two variables, variety and assortment, within the constraints of a dollar investment in inventory. Variety defines the number of different classifications, or product lines, carried by the store or department. Assortment refers to the breadth and depth of merchandise within a classification or subclassification. The breadth of a merchandise assortment defines a range of choice of a classification's selection parameters as illustrated below:

	Range of Choice
Size:	38, 40, 42, 44, etc.
Color:	black, brown, blue, etc.
Selection Price:	$150, $175, $200, etc.
Parameters[2] Fabric:	wool, linen, silk, etc.
Pattern:	solid, striped, plaid, etc.
Brand:	A, B, C, D, etc.
Style:	101, 201, 301, etc.

---

[1]The precise definitions of "fashion" and "staple" are beyond textbook definition. In reality, they are based on the merchant's judgment concerning a store's unique characteristics and the customer's perception of those characteristics in terms of store image.

[2]The list is arbitrary and may include more or fewer selection parameters, at the discretion of the merchant. Also, the selection parameters are not mutually exclusive, that is, a man's suit may be size 40, brown, of wool fabric, and be priced at $175.

"Depth" indicates the number of units of each element within the range of choice of a selection parameter. For example, at the $200 price point, the merchant may offer the following depth in size and color:

> Size: 3 units in size 32, 6 units in size 40, 3 units in size 42, and 2 units in size 44
>
> Color:[3] 3 units in black, 6 units in brown, and 5 units in blue

When depth and breath are integrated, the merchandise assortment plan for a $200 item will appear as follows:

	Size	Quantity	Black	Brown	Blue	Total
				Color		
Depth	38	3	1	1	1	3
Number	40	6	2	3	1	6
of Units	42	3	0	1	2	3
	44	2	0	1	1	2
		14	3	6	5	14

Breadth (Range of Choice)

It becomes readily apparent that any merchandise assortment plan—model stock or basic stock—is simply a unique grouping of merchandise units within a classification or subclassification, derived from dollar open-to-buy and balanced to customer demand.

Unit Control Systems

Because the types of unit control systems vary so greatly, not only from store to store but also between the various kinds of merchandise assortments, any detailed discussion of the subject is beyond the scope of this chapter. However, a basic knowledge of unit control concepts is essential to a complete understanding of merchandise assortment planning.

Once the unit assortment has been defined and established, it becomes necessary to institute some form of unit control system. The function of any unit control system is to provide the merchant with current data on the number of units on hand, on order, received, and sold. Thus, the specific purposes of unit control are to regulate buying so that units will be stocked in proportion to sales and to manage selling so that the proper promotional emphasis can be given to each type of unit in proportion to its rate of sale and quantity on hand. Depending

---

[3]Color is further broken down into size by color.

upon its level of detail, a unit control system can inform the merchant as to the rate at which each classification, brand, price line, style, model, size, color, pattern, etc., is moving into and out of stock. It thereby aids the merchant in deciding which units of stock to increase, eliminate, or reprice, as well as the most opportune time at which to do so.

Determination of Unit Stock Status

There are two basic methods for the determination of the status of the unit stock. The first is the physical inventory system, where a stock count is taken on a periodic basis (weekly, monthly, etc.) and the unit sales are derived from the following formula:

Net Sales = Previous physical inventory + Subsequent net merchandise receipts − New physical inventory.

The second method is the sales analysis system, whereby records are kept of each day's unit sales in terms of classification, price, resource, color, size, and style, and then incorporated into a perpetual book inventory. Conceptually,

The current book inventory = the previous book inventory + subsequent merchandise receipts − net sales.

14.2

The Model Stock Plan for Fashion Merchandise[4]

A model stock plan is a proposed unit assortment of merchandise, within dollar limitations, that best satisfies customer demand over a specific period of time. Initially, it is broken down by subclassification and price lines and then further regrouped into those selection parameters deemed appropriate by the merchant. The ultimate objective of all merchandising strategy is to maximize the sales and profits derived from an investment in inventory. The model stock plan is essentially a tool developed to further this end; its functions are to balance the inventory in terms of dollars and units against planned sales, thus achieving both minimal stockouts and a planned turnover ratio.

A model stock plan is normally constructed on a monthly or period[5] basis, utilizing the beginning-of-the-month stock figures developed in the six-month merchandise plan and converting those dollars into units. However, it is also

---

[4]While we are dealing here with fashion merchandise, the concepts, apart from the implementation stage, are equally applicable to basic stocks.
[5]Refer to the retail accounting calendar in Chapter 12.

possible to work backward from units to dollars. In addition, the model stock plan is not limited to months; or accounting periods; model stocks may be developed for a season or a unique selling period, such as Christmas, "Back-to-School," Easter, etc.

Furthermore, the model stock plan need not be rigidly followed during the course of the planned selling season. Rather, the plan should serve as a guide, because the demand by classification, price, style, color, etc., may vary considerably as the season progresses. As the term indicates, it is a model plan, not an absolute plan.

The importance of the model stock concept cannot be overemphasized. Not only does it force the merchant into planning the merchandise assortment for a particular period of time, but it provides the basis for the establishment of unit open-to-buy by subclassification, price line, and whatever other selection parameters are decided upon.

Planning Fashion Inventories

Model stock planning involves making decisions on the number of items to have on hand in terms of predetermined selection factors—e.g, price, color, size, fabric—within a subclassification. Normally, the model stock plan for fashion merchandise is set up according to price lines within a subclassification, thus facilitating the calculation of unit open-to-buy for each price line.

The construction of a model stock plan will vary considerably from store to store; however, all formats will generally include (but are not limited to) the following concepts:

1. The division of classifications into subclassifications.

2. The division of subclassifications into selection parameters:
   a. unit price
   b. color
   c. size
   d. style

3. The number of units within a selection parameter.

4. The retail value of the model stock.

5. A specific time frame.

Figure 14.1 illustrates the concept of a departmental model stock with two merchandise classifications. Each classification is divided into subclassifications, which in turn are further broken down into price, color, and size. As Figure 14.1 indicates, the lowest level of identification of merchandise for inventory management is a unique size within a unique color; this is known as a stock-keeping unit (SKU).

Department X

	Classification A								Classification B							
	Subclass A (1)				Subclass A (2)				Subclass B (1)				Subclass B (2)			
	Price (Low)		Price (High)		Price (Low)		Price (High)		Price (Low)		Price (High)		Price (Low)		Price (High)	
	Color (Red)	Color (Blue)	Color (Red)	Color (Blue)	Color (Red)	Color (Blue)	Color (Red)	Color (Blue)	Color (White)	Color (Green)	Color (White)	Color (Green)	Color (White)	Color (Green)	Color (White)	Color (Green)
Size	8	8	8	8	8	8	8	8	10	10	10	10	10	10	10	10
	9	9	9	9	9	9	9	9	12	12	12	12	12	12	12	12

Figure 14.1 Model stock concept

Figure 14.2 illustrates a generic type of model stock format, utilizing all of the concepts illustrated in Figure 14.1.

▪ Study Problem

Given: Assume that the six-month merchandise plan for a men's furnishings department projects a beginning-of-the-month stock of $110,000 for period I, which includes $10,000 of leftover stock from the preceding period. A model stock plan for the $100,000 of new stock is to be prepared.

The department consists of five classifications of merchandise, with sales distributed as follows:

Classification	% of Period I Sales
Sweaters	37.5
Underwear	17.5
Hosiery	15.0
Shirts	25.0
Neckwear	5.0
	100.0%

It is the buyer's intention to first plan a model stock for the sweater classification, which consists of three price lines: $35, $55, and $75. It is anticipated that the $35 price line will account for 30% of sweater sales; the $55 price line, 50%; and the $75 price line, 20%. The merchandise distribution by price line and subclassification, along with the anticipated percent of price line sales, is illustrated below:

$35 Price Line

Subclassification	$ Price Line Sales
Crew neck	40.5%
V-neck	35.5%
Turtle neck	24.0%

$55 Price Line

Subclassification	$ Price Line Sales
Crew neck	43.6%
V-neck	33.4%
Turtle neck	23.0%

$75 Price Line

Subclassification	$ Price Line Sales
Crew neck	48.7%
V-neck	30.8%
Turtle neck	20.5%

Model Stock Plan

Department: _____
Dept. No.: _____
Season: Fall/Spring _____
Period: _____

Classification: _____
Retail Price: _____
Buyer: _____

Sub-classification (Style)		Size	Quantity for Model Stock		Color									Model Stock at Retail		
%	Units		%	Units	%	Units	%	Units	%	Units	%	Units	%	%	Units	$
$_____		Total														
$_____		Total														
$_____		Total														
100		Grand Total														

Figure 14.2 Model stock plan format

The percentage distribution of the number of units required, in terms of size and color, has been carefully researched by the buyer and has been entered on the model stock plan for $35 sweaters (see Figure 14.3).

Find:

1. For the $35 price line, the number of units in each subclassification.

2. The number of units by size in each subclassification.

3. The number of units by color within each size.

4. The retail value of the model stock by size and color, by subclassification, and in total.

Solution:

1. Determine the retail value of the entire sweater classification:

Classification	% of Sales	×	Total Sales	=	Stock at Retail
Sweaters	37.5	×	$100,000	=	$37,500

2. Find the retail value of the $35 price line:

Price Line	% of Sales	×	Total Sales	=	Stock at Retail
$35	30.0%	×	$37,500	=	$11,250

3. Break down the model stock at retail ($11,250) into its three subclassifications:

Subclassification	% of Sales	×	Total Sales	=	Stock at Retail
Crew neck	40.5%	×	$11,250	=	$4,556
V-neck	35.5%	×	$11,250	=	3,994
Turtle neck	24.0%	×	$11,250	=	2,700
Total	100%				$11,250

4. Determine the number of units within each subclassification by dividing the dollars in each subclassification by the $35 price per unit:

Crew neck	$4,556	÷	$35	=	130 units[6]
V-neck	3,994	÷	$35	=	114 units
Turtle neck	$2,700	÷	$35	=	77 units
Total					321 units[7]

---

[6]In the determination of units, all figures are to be rounded to the nearest whole unit because it is impossible to purchase a percentage of an item.
[7]The student will notice that 32 units × $35 equals $11,235, not the $11,250 shown in step 3. This is because mathematically we have 321.42 units (321.42 × $35 = $11,250) and we cannot purchase 42% of a unit. Therefore, the total must be rounded to the nearest whole unit, or 321.

Model Stock Plan

Department:	Men's Furnishings
Dept. No.:	3021
Season: Fall/Spring	Spring
Period:	I (February)

Classification:	Sweaters
Retail Price:	$35
Buyer:	Marjorie Pratt

Sub-classification (Style) %	Units	Size	Quantity for Model Stock %	Units	Red %	Units	White %	Units	Blue %	Units	%	Model Stock at Retail Units	$
		Crew Neck											
		Small	10		25		50		25		100		
		Medium	50		30		50		20		100		
		Large	25		20		40		40		100		
		X-Large	15		15		60		25		100		
45.5	$	Total	100										
		V-Neck											
		Small	15		15		45		40		100		
		Medium	40		20		60		20		100		
		Large	30		25		35		40		100		
		X-Large	15		30		40		30		100		
35.5	$	Total	100										
		Turtle Neck											
		Small	5		33		50		17		100		
		Medium	30		28		47		25		100		
		Large	35		35		53		12		100		
		X-Large	30		30		50		20		100		
24.0	$	Total	100										
100		Grand Total											

Figure 14.3 Model stock plan: study problem

480

5. Calculate the number of units by size for each subclassification, for example, for crew necks:

10%	× 130 =	13	small
50%	× 130 =	65	medium
25%	× 130 =	33	large
15%	× 130 =	19[8]	extra-large
100%		130	

The remaining subclassifications are completed in like manner.

6. Allocate the units by size, to colors, according to the predetermined percentages. For example, the color distribution for small crew neck sweaters will be

13 (small units)	×	25.0% (red)	=	3	small red
13 (small units)	×	50.0% (white)	=	7	small white
13 (small units)	×	25.0% (blue)	=	3	small blue
		100.0%	=	13 (small units)	

The same procedure is followed for the remaining subclassifications.

7. Determine the model stock at retail. Adding across, the percentage in colors must equal 100%, the total number of units in color must equal the number of units in the designated size, and for that portion of the model stock, the retail value is the number of units times the retail price ($35).

8. Determine the accuracy of the model stock plan. The sum total of the model stock at retail in units must equal the number of units originally planned for (321); the dollar value of the model stock at retail (321 units × $35 = $11,235) must closely approximate the planned retail value of the $35 price line as developed in Step 2 (30% × $37,500 = $11,250). The completed model stock for the $35 price line is shown in Figure 14.4.

■ Application Exercise

1. Utilizing the data supplied in the study problem, complete the model stock plan for $55 sweaters, as shown in Figure 14.5.

2. Utilizing the data supplied in the study problem, complete the model stock plan for $75 sweaters, as shown in Figure 14.6.

---

[8]Because the calculation of the number of units for the large and extra-large sizes resulted in the figures 32.5 and 19.5, respectively, it was arbitrarily decided to delete the unit from the extra-large size in order to maintain the 130 units for the subclassification. This is always a problem in model stock planning, and its resolution is left to the buyer's judgment. The point is, that if 130 units were initially planned, then the buyer must end up with 130 units; otherwise, the dollar value of the plan will be distorted.

Model Stock Plan

Department: Men's Furnishings
Dept. No.: 3021
Season: Fall/Spring — Spring
Period: I (February)

Classification: Sweaters
Retail Price: $35
Buyer: Marjorie Pratt

Sub-classification (Style) %	Sub-classification (Style) Units	Style	Size	Quantity for Model Stock %	Quantity for Model Stock Units	Color — Red %	Red Units	White %	White Units	Blue %	Blue Units	Color — %	Units	Model Stock at Retail %	Units	$
		Crew Neck	Small	10	13	25	3	50	7	25	3			100	13	455
			Medium	50	65	30	20	50	32	20	13			100	65	2,275
			Large	25	33	20	7	40	13	40	13			100	33	1,155
			X-Large	15	19	15	3	60	11	25	5			100	19	665
45.5	130	$4,556	Total	100	130		33		63		34			100	130	4,550
		V-Neck	Small	15	17	15	3	45	7	40	7			100	17	595
			Medium	40	46	20	9	60	28	20	9			100	46	1,610
			Large	30	34	25	9	35	12	40	13			100	34	1,190
			X-Large	15	17	30	5	40	7	30	5			100	17	595
35.5	114	$3,994	Total	100	114		26		54		34			100	114	3,990
		Turtle Neck	Small	5	4	33	1	50	2	17	1			100	4	140
			Medium	30	23	28	6	47	11	25	6			100	23	805
			Large	35	27	35	9	53	14	12	4			100	27	945
			X-Large	30	23	30	7	50	12	20	4			100	23	805
24.0	77	$2,700	Total	100	77		23		39		15			100	77	2,695
100	321		Grand Total	100	321		82		156		83			100	321	11,235

Figure 14.4 Completed model stock for the $35 price line: solution to study problem

Model Stock Plan

Department: Men's Furnishings
Dept. No.: 3021
Season: Fall/Spring — Spring
Period: 1 (February)

Classification: Sweaters
Retail Price: $55
Buyer: Marjorie Pratt

Sub-classification (Style)	Size	Quantity for Model Stock %	Units	Red %	Units	White %	Units	Blue %	Units	%	Units	Model Stock at Retail Units	$
Crew Neck	Small	23		26		38		36		100			
	Medium	36		31		53		16		100			
	Large	21		25		50		25		100			
	X-Large	20		38		40		22		100			
% ___ $ ___													
43.6	Total	100											
V-Neck	Small	18		15		40		45		100			
	Medium	37		23		48		29		100			
	Large	30		28		42		30		100			
	X-Large	15		25		40		35		100			
% ___ $ ___													
33.4	Total	100											
Turtle Neck	Small	26		23		40		37		100			
	Medium	21		28		36		36		100			
	Large	32		32		48		20		100			
	X-Large	21		30		50		20		100			
% ___ $ ___													
23.0	Total	100											
100	Grand Total												

Figure 14.5 Model stock plan: application exercise 1

Model Stock Plan

Department: Men's Furnishings
Dept. No.: 3021
Season: Fall/Spring — Spring
Period: I (February)

Classification: Sweaters
Retail Price: $75
Buyer: Marjorie Pratt

Subclassification (Style)		Size	Quantity for Model Stock		Color — Red		Color — White		Color — Blue		Model Stock at Retail	
%	Units		%	Units	%	Units	%	Units	%	Units	Units	$
Crew Neck		Small	18		20		60		20			
		Medium	36		30		50		20			
		Large	20		25		50		25			
		X-Large	26		30		35		35			
48.7 $___		Total	100									
V-Neck		Small	23		26		40		34			100
		Medium	30		33		34		33			100
		Large	25		10		70		20			100
		X-Large	22		38		53		9			100
30.8 $___		Total	100									
Turtle Neck		Small	20		30		48		22			100
		Medium	40		27		53		20			100
		Large	30		33		48		19			100
		X-Large	10		23		57		20			100
20.5 $___		Total	100									100
100		Grand Total	100									100

Figure 14.6 Model stock plan: application exercise 2

3. A women's shoe department is planning sales for period IX of $83,500. The six-month merchandise plan indicates that the BOM stock for the period is $125,250. The buyer's immediate concern is to plan a model stock for the "leather pump" classification, which accounts for 43% of departmental sales. Leather pumps come in three styles, flat (1-inch heel), mid heel (2-inch heel), and high heel (2⅝-inch heel), with sales planned as follows:

Flat heel   28%
Mid-heel   58%
High-heel 14%

The percentage distribution across size and color is believed to represent an excellent assortment for this department's customers. Complete the model stock plan as shown in Figure 14.7.

4. A women's sportswear buyer is planning a model stock in bathing suits for period IV. Departmental sales are planned for $106,000, with swimwear accounting for 35%. The BOM stock for the period is $137,800. Three styles are offered, scoop-necked, bikini, and high-necked tank, with a sales distribution of 23%, 48%, and 29%, respectively. Size and color percentages have been allocated to maximize customer satisfaction. Complete the model stock plan in Figure 14.8.

5. A men's shoe buyer is assembling a model stock for casual leather footwear. Departmental sales for period X are planned at $93,800, with a BOM stock of $140,700. "Casual leathers," which are expected to produce 43% of departmental sales, consist of the following three styles, with their anticipated percentages of the classification sales:

Half boots   28.5%
Loafers   33.5%
Boat shoes   38.0%

Four colors are available: black, brown, mahogany, and putty, within a size range from 8D to 12D.

As the assistant buyer, you are asked to estimate the percentages in size and color and complete the model stock plan shown in Figure 14.9.[9]

6. A men's clothing department is planning sales of $250,000, based upon a B.O.M. inventory of $375,000. The sport coat classification is expected to produce 28.5% of net sales from three basic styles: two-button, three-button, and

---

[9]The point here, and in application exercise 6, is to encourage the student's individualism and expertise in model stock planning. While obviously the percentages and resulting units in size and color will vary, all students should arrive at the same model stock at retail in terms of percentage units and dollars. This will emphasize the freedom of unit planning, within dollar constraints.

Model Stock Plan

Department: Women's Shoes
Dept. No.: 4511
Season: Fall/Spring — Fall
Period: IX (October)

Classification: Leather Pumps
Retail Price: $45
Buyer: Mary Zingler

Sub-classification (Style) %	Units	Size	Quantity for Model Stock %	Units	Color Pink %	Units	White %	Units	Black %	Units	Bone %	Units	%	Model Stock at Retail Units	$
Flat Heel		5½B	15		15		20		25		40		100		
		6B	18		20		25		25		30		100		
		6½B	23		23		28		21		28		100		
		7B	25		18		32		28		22		100		
		7½B	10		13		35		30		22		100		
		8B	9		21		25		33		21		100		
$															
28.0		Total	100												
Mid Heel		5½B	18		13		18		36		33		100		
		6B	20		20		25		25		30		100		
		6½B	25		18		30		24		28		100		
		7B	17		23		27		30		20		100		
		7½B	12		25		28		21		26		100		
		8B	8		22		30		32		16		100		
$															
58.0		TOTAL	100												
High Heel		5½B	13		28		30		25		17		100		
		6B	20		25		33		28		14		100		
		6½B	28		18		29		23		30		100		
		7B	18		25		28		21		26		100		
		7½B	14		19		31		27		23		100		
		8B	7		20		32		26		22		100		
$															
14.0		Total	100												
100		Grand Total											100		

Figure 14.7 Model stock plan: application exercise 3

486

Model Stock Plan

Department: Women's Sportwear
Dept. No.: 1041
Season: Fall/Spring — Spring
Period: IV (May)

Classification: Swimwear
Retail Price: $38
Buyer: Hank Lindborg

Sub-classification (Style)	%	Units	Size	Quantity for Model Stock %	Units	Aqua Green %	Units	Light Coral %	Units	Light Blue %	Units	Black %	Units	Total %	Model Stock at Retail Units	$
Scoop-neck			5-6	16		30		23		28		19		100		
			7-8	18		27		30		25		18		100		
			9-10	25		25		28		30		17		100		
			11-12	30		20		30		23		27		100		
			13-14	11		28		35		29		8		100		
$____	23.0		Total	100												
Bikini			5-6	17		32		28		19		21		100		
			7-8	9		28		33		25		14		100		
			9-10	23		26		28		32		14		100		
			11-12	26		20		35		28		17		100		
			13-14	15		18		23		33		26		100		
$____	48.0		Total	100												
High-Neck Tank			5-6	15		33		27		23		17		100		
			7-8	20		28		25		31		16		100		
			9-10	25		30		33		24		13		100		
			11-12	30		27		31		22		20		100		
			13-14	10		31		28		31		10		100		
$____	29.0		Total	100												
	100		Grand Total													

Figure 14.8 Model stock plan: Application exercise 4

Model Stock Plan

Department: Men's Shoes   **Classification:** Casual Leathers
Dept. No.: 4521   **Retail Price:** $50
Season: Fall/Spring   Fall   **Buyer:** Ed Henry
Period: X (November)

Sub-classification (Style)		Size	Quantity for Model Stock		Color								Model Stock at Retail		
					Black		Brown		Mahogany		Putty				
%	Units		%	Units	%	Units	%	Units	%	Units	%	Units	%	Units	$
Half-Boots		8D													
		9D													
		10D													
		11D													
		12D													
$_____		Total													
28.5															
Loafers		8D													
		9D													
		10D													
		11D													
		12D													
$_____		Total													
33.5															
Boat Shoe		8D													
		9D													
		10D													
		11D													
		12D													
$_____		Total													
38.0		Grand Total													
100															

Figure 14.9 Model stock plan: application exercise 5

double-breasted. These three styles are to be distributed across three colors, black, brown and grey, within a size range from 38 to 42.

Exercise your own judgment in the percentage distribution of units by style, size, and color, and complete the model stock plan illustrated in Figure 14.10.

14.3

The Control of Fashion Stocks

While planning and control are the essential determinants of profit in both fashion and staple stocks, the types of control required differ in at least two respects: First, due to their volatile nature, fashion goods must be monitored more frequently than staple goods; fashion merchandise is normally reviewed on a weekly basis, whereas staple stocks do not require such frequent attention. Second, the control of fashion reorders is based upon heterogeneous units—i.e., sizes within colors and colors within price lines and styles—whereas each different unit within the staple assortment may require a unique type of control.

The model stock provides the basis for an order control system, or buying plan, that attempts to balance the merchandise assortment to planned sales.

The Buying Plan and Unit Open-to-Buy

The buying plan is an organized attempt by the merchant to procure and maintain a fashion merchandise assortment conforming to the guidelines set forth by the model stock plan. In this sense, it is a plan of action for the implementation of the model stock plan, designed to provide a unit open-to-buy on a periodic or monthly basis.

The buying plan is based upon a recapitulation of the model stock plan, in terms of subclassification, price point, and the unit quantity desired for the period.[10] Conceptually, the buying plan is developed by adding to the model stock (the BOM stock for a given period) the sales for a preceding buying period and subtracting any purchases that carry over into the current planning period. It can be reduced to this formula:

Unit open-to-buy = Model stock + Sales for the previous period − (Units on hand first of previous period + Units on order first of previous period[11])

---

[10]The initial buying plan will produce an open-to-buy in terms of the number of units of a subclassification at a specific price point; these units are later distributed across size and color by the predetermined percentages found in the model stock plan. Space limitations preclude this extension of the buying plan.
[11]Units on order for the previous month are outstanding orders for delivery *prior* to the first of the current planning period.

Model Stock Plan

Department: _____ Men's Clothing   **Classification:** _____ Sportcoats
Dept. No.: _____ 3041   **Retail Price:** _____ $120
Season: Fall/Spring _____ Spring   **Buyer:** _____ Ronnie Campopiano
Period: _____ III (April)

Sub-classification (Style)		Size	Quantity for Model Stock		Color								Model Stock at Retail	
					Black		Brown		Mahogany		Putty			
%	Units		%	Units	%	Units	%	Units	%	Units	%	Units	Units	$
$ ___														
___		Total												
$ ___														
___		Total												
$ ___														
___		Total												
		Grand Total												

Figure 14.10 Model stock plan: application exercise 6

Essentially, the unit open-to-buy is the difference between what is "needed" and what is "available" to complete the planned model stock for a given period. Thus,

Unit model stock (period covered)
Unit sales (previous period)

Units "needed"

Less units on hand (previous period)
Less units on order (previous period)

Less units "available"
Unit open-to-buy

Figure 14.11 illustrates a format for a class-price buying plan. The manner in which it is completed is as follows:

Assume that the period covered by the plan is February. Assume that the planning date is January 3.

Column 1. Unit sales for 13 months prior to the planning date (January) are the sales for December a year ago.

Column 2. Unit sales for one month prior to the planning date (January) are the unit sales for the past December.

Column 3. Unit sales for twelve months prior to the planning date (January) are the sales for January last year.

Column 4. Sales for one month prior to the period covered (February) are planned sales for January of this year. These sales are calculated in the following manner:

(1) $\dfrac{\text{Column 1} - \text{Column 2}}{\text{Column 1}} = \%$ increase or decrease

(2) Column 3 × (100% + % of increase/decrease) = planned sales for January

Column 5. The BOM stock for the period covered (February) is the total number of units in the model stock by subclassification and price.

Column 6. On hand one month prior to period covered (February) is the amount of units on hand as of January 1.

Column 7. On order one month prior to the period covered (February) is the outstanding orders for delivery *prior* to February 1.

Column 8. OTB units = (Column 4 + Column 5) − (Column 5 + Column 6).

Column 9. $OTB = Column 8 × the unit retail price.

Column 10. $OTB cost = Column 9 × (100% − the markon percent).

Buying Plan (Unit Open-to-Buy)

Department _____ Classification _____

Department Number _____ Markon _____

Period Covered _____ Buyer _____

Preparation Date _____

Subclassification / Unit Price	(1) Sales 13 Mos Prior to Prep Date	(2) Sales 1 Mo Prior to Prep Date	(3) Sales 12 Mos Prior to Prep Date	(4) Sales 1 Mo Prior to Period Covered	(5) BOM Stock for Period Covered	(6) On Hand 1 Mo Prior to Period Covered	(7) On Order 1 Mo Prior to Period Covered	(8) OTB Units	(9) $OTB Retail	(10) $OTB Cost

Figure 14.11 Buying plan (unit open-to-buy)

■ Study Problem

Given: On January 8, Marjorie Pratt, the sweater buyer for men's furnishings, completed her period-I model stock for $35 crew neck sweaters (see Figure 14.4). She now wants to complete a buying plan in order to implement the model stock plan. The following other information is available to her:

1. December sales one year ago (13 months): 200 units

2. December sales past December (1 month): 210 units

3. January sales last year: 120 units

4. Currently on hand: 90 units

5. Currently on order: 24 units

Find: The open-to-buy for February, in units, retail dollars, and cost dollars.

Solution:

1. Enter the following given data in the appropriate columns on the buying plan illustrated in Figure 14.12:
   a. December sales one year ago, 200 units (column 1).
   b. December sales past December, 210 units (column 2).
   c. January sales last year, 120 units (column 3).
   d. The BOM stock for the period covered (February) is taken from the $35 crew neck sweater subclassification shown in Figure 14.4 and entered in column 5.
   e. The 90 units currently on hand (in January, the planning month) are entered in column 6.
   f. The 24 units currently on order (for delivery in January) are entered in column 7.

2. Calculate the planned sales for January (column 4).
   a. Unit sales for December, 13 months ago (column 1) = 200.
   b. Unit sales for December, 1 month ago (column 2) = 210.
   c. Percent of increase = 210 − 200/200 = 5%.
   d. Planned sales for January (column 4) = 120 (column 3) × 105% = 126 units.

3. Determine the open-to-buy for February (column 8):
   OTB = sales (column 4) + BOM stock (column 5) − on hand (column 6) − on order (column 7)
   O.T.B. = 126 + 130 − 90 − 24 = 142

Buying Plan (Unit Open-to-Buy)

Department __Men's Furnishings__   Classification __Sweaters__

Department Number __3021__   Markon __48.0%__

Period Covered __1 (February)__   Buyer __Marjorie Pratt__

Preparation Date __January 9__

Subclassification / Unit Price	(1) Sales 13 Mos Prior to Prep Date	(2) Sales 1 Mo Prior to Prep Date	(3) Sales 12 Mos Prior to Prep Date	(4) Sales 1 Mo Prior to Period Covered	(5) BOM Stock for Period Covered	(6) On Hand 1 Mo Prior to Period Covered	(7) On Order 1 Mo Prior to Period Covered	(8) OTB Units	(9) $OTB Retail	(10) $OTB Cost
Crew Neck Sweaters $35	200	210	120	126	130	90	24	142	$4970	$2584

Figure 14.12 Buying plan: solution to study problem

4. Determine the open-to-buy at retail:
   $OTB retail = 142 × $35 = $4970

5. Determine the open-to-buy at cost:
   $OTB cost = $4970 × 52% − $2584

■ Application Exercise

1. Given the following information, complete the buying plan shown in Figure 14.13.
   a. The subclassification is V-neck sweaters, found in Figure 14.4.
   b. Assume that the period to be covered is April.[12]
   c. The planning date is March 15.
   d. Sales for February a year ago = 120 units.
   e. Sales for last February = 130 units.
   f. Sales for March last year = 153 units.
   g. Units on hand March 1 = 119.
   h. Units on order March 1 = 36.

2. Given the following information, complete the buying plan shown in Figure 14.14.
   a. The subclassification is turtleneck sweaters, found in Figure 14.4.
   b. Assume that the period to be covered is October.
   c. The planning date is September 1.
   d. Sales for August a year ago = 48 units.
   e. Sales for past August = 59 units.
   f. Sales for last September = 63 units.
   g. On hand, September 1 = 37 units.
   h. On order, September 1 = 48 units.

3. A women's athletic-shoe buyer is planning an open-to-buy for a line of $48 tennis shoes for the month of September. The planning date is August 8. Currently, there are 128 units on hand, with 36 more on order. Sales for this past July were 116 units, and for July a year ago, 136 units were sold. Sales for August one year ago were 149 units. The model stock plan indicates that there should be 144 units on hand September 1. Complete the buying plan shown in Figure 14.15.

4. On April 3, a furniture buyer has 103 $200 sofas on hand and 149 more on order. In anticipation of the annual "celebration sale" during the month of May, the buyer is planning a May 1 inventory of 200 units. Sales for last April were

---

[12]Obviously, a February model stock plan cannot be used to develop an April buying plan. Figure 14.4 is simply used as an expedient means of illustrating the fact that the BOM stock in the buying plan derives from the model stock plan.

Buying Plan (Unit Open-to-Buy)

Department _____ Men's Furnishings

Department Number _____ 3021

Period Covered _____ III (April)

Preparation Date _____ March 15

Classification _____ Sweaters

Markon _____ 46.5%

Buyer _____ Marjorie Pratt

Subclassification	(1) Sales 13 Mos Prior to Prep Date	(2) Sales 1 Mo Prior to Prep Date	(3) Sales 12 Mos Prior to Prep Date	(4) Sales 1 Mo Prior to Period Covered	(5) BOM Stock for Period Covered	(6) On Hand 1 Mo Prior to Period Covered	(7) On Order 1 Mo Prior to Period Covered	(8) OTB Units	(9) $OTB Retail	(10) $OTB Cost
Unit Price										

Figure 14.13 Buying plan: application exercise 1

Buying Plan (Unit Open-to-Buy)

Department ___Men's Furnishings___   Classification ___Sweaters___

Department Number ___3021___   Markon ___52.9%___

Period Covered ___IX (October)___   Buyer ___Marjorie Pratt___

Preparation Date ___September 1___

Subclassification Unit Price	(1) Sales 13 Mos Prior to Prep Date	(2) Sales 1 Mo Prior to Prep Date	(3) Sales 12 Mos Prior to Prep Date	(4) Sales 1 Mo Prior to Period Covered	(5) BOM Stock for Period Covered	(6) On Hand 1 Mo Prior to Period Covered	(7) On Order 1 Mo Prior to Period Covered	(8) OTB Units	(9) $OTB Retail	(10) $OTB Cost

Figure 14.14 Buying plan: application exercise 2

Buying Plan (Unit Open-to-Buy)

Department _____ Women's Shoes
Department Number _____ 4511
Period Covered _____ VIII (September)
Preparation Date _____ August 8

Classification _____ Athletic Shoes
Markon _____ 46.7%
Buyer _____ Student

Subclassification / Unit Price	(1) Sales 13 Mos Prior to Prep Date	(2) Sales 1 Mo Prior to Prep Date	(3) Sales 12 Mos Prior to Prep Date	(4) Sales 1 Mo Prior to Period Covered	(5) BOM Stock for Period Covered	(6) On Hand 1 Mo Prior to Period Covered	(7) On Order 1 Mo Prior to Period Covered	(8) OTB Units	(9) $OTB Retail	(10) $OTB Cost

Figure 14.15 Buying plan: application exercise 3

230 units. Sales for the past March were 93 units, and for a year ago March, 72 units. As the assistant buyer, you are asked to develop the May 1 open-to-buy for the sofa subclassification, utilizing Figure 14.16.

5. A model stock for a hosiery department indicates that there should be 400 pairs of $4.50 ribbed, crew socks in the BOM inventory as of June 1. Sales for May last year were 385 units, and sales for the preceding April and for April a year ago were 279 and 323 units, respectively. As of May 3, there were 315 units on order and 293 units on hand. Complete the buying plan as shown in Figure 14.17.

6. On February 1, a men's furnishings buyer took a stock count and found that there were 55 $26 Madras shirts in stock and another 60 on order. An opening inventory of 250 shirts is planned for March 1. Sales for the past January were 78 units, and for January a year ago, 57 units. Sales for last March were 83 units. Calculate the buyer's open-to-buy as of February 1; use the buying plan illustrated in Figure 14.18 for your calculations.

14.4

The Model Stock Plan for Staple Merchandise

The model stock plan for staple merchandise is defined as the "periodic reorder form" or the "basic stock list." It is based upon the concept that a relatively constant level of maximum stock, in terms of units, is maintained at all times. Thus, the maintenance of the model stock is dependent upon a system of periodic reordering of its constituent units. This system of periodic reordering is, in effect, a method of planning unit open-to-buy, which needs to be understood as a prerequisite for implementing the periodic reorder form (basic stock list).

Unit Open-to-Buy

The concept of unit open-to-buy flows logically from dollar open-to-buy as discussed in Chapter 13; it is simply the translation of open-to-buy dollars into units, or the number of pieces to be purchased to complete a merchandise assortment. While the concept of unit open-to-buy is applicable to both fashion and staple merchandise, it is best utilized to control the upper and lower limits of a merchandise assortment that is in continuous demand by customers, i.e., staple stock and/or fashion basics. The upper limit of the assortment is defined as the maximum stock, and the lower limit indicates the minimum stock.

The calculation of unit open-to-buy is based upon several important considerations.

Minimum Stock

"Minimum stock" refers to the lower limit of a merchandise assortment. It defines the specific number of units that should be in stock at all times so as to avoid

Buying Plan (Unit Open-to-Buy)

Department	Furniture		Classification	Upholstered Goods
Department Number	7011		Markon	38.7%
Period Covered	IV (May)		Buyer	Student
Preparation Date	April 3			

Subclassification / Unit Price	(1) Sales 13 Mos Prior to Prep Date	(2) Sales 1 Mo Prior to Prep Date	(3) Sales 12 Mos Prior to Prep Date	(4) Sales 1 Mo Prior to Period Covered	(5) BOM Stock for Period Covered	(6) On Hand 1 Mo Prior to Period Covered	(7) On Order 1 Mo Prior to Period Covered	(8) OTB Units	(9) $OTB Retail	(10) $OTB Cost

Figure 14.16 Buying plan: application exercise 4

500

Buying Plan (Unit Open-to-Buy)

Department _____ Hosiery _____   Classification _____ Socks
Department Number _____ 2015 _____   Markon _____ 43.8%
Period Covered _____ V (June) _____   Buyer _____ Student
Preparation Date _____ May 3 _____

Subclassification	(1) Sales 13 Mos Prior to Prep Date	(2) Sales 1 Mo Prior to Prep Date	(3) Sales 12 Mos Prior to Prep Date	(4) Sales 1 Mo Prior to Period Covered	(5) BOM Stock for Period Covered	(6) On Hand 1 Mo Prior to Period Covered	(7) On Order 1 Mo Prior to Period Covered	(8) OTB Units	(9) $OTB Retail	(10) $OTB Cost
Unit Price										

Figure 14.17 Buying plan: application exercise 5

Buying Plan (Unit Open-to-Buy)

Department ___ Men's Furnishings ___ Classification ___ Shirts ___
Department Number ___ 3021 ___ Markon ___ 49.0% ___
Period Covered ___ II (March) ___ Buyer ___ Student ___
Preparation Date ___ February 1 ___

	(1) Sales 13 Mos Prior to Prep Date	(2) Sales 1 Mo Prior to Prep Date	(3) Sales 12 Mos Prior to Prep Date	(4) Sales 1 Mo Prior to Period Covered	(5) BOM Stock for Period Covered	(6) On Hand 1 Mo Prior to Period Covered	(7) On Order 1 Mo Prior to Period Covered	(8) OTB Units	(9) $OTB Retail	(10) $OTB Cost
Subclassification Unit Price										

Figure 14.18 Buying plan: application exercise 6

stockouts between delivery periods. Theoretically, it is the number of units that should be on hand at the time a purchase order is written. Therefore, the minimum stock defines the merchant's reorder point and must be equal to a reserve, or a safety factor, in terms of

1. The number of weeks supply of the item necessary to maintain an assortment of merchandise that matches the customers expectations and
2. The number of weeks supply of the item that could be sold during the period of time that it reasonably takes for a delivery to arrive.

Expressed as an equation, we see that the:

Minimum stock (MN) in weeks = Reserve stock (RS) in weeks + Delivery period (DP) in weeks

The minimum stock can also be expressed as a specific quantity in terms of the number of items required to maintain an adequate unit assortment. This can be accomplished simply by multiplying the minimum stock in weeks times the weekly rate of sale,[13] or the number of units sold per week. Thus, the

Minimum stock (MN) in units = (Reserve stock (RS) in weeks + Delivery period (DP) in weeks) × Weekly rate of sale (R)

It is important to note that in the above formula both the reserve stock and the delivery period are given in weeks. Thus, both must be multiplied by the rate of sale to determine the minimum number of units. However, if the reserve stock were given in units and the delivery period in weeks, only the delivery period would have to be converted into units. Thus, the basic formula would have to be modified as follows:

Minimum stock (MN) in units = Reserve stock (RS) in units + (Delivery period in weeks (DP) × Rate of sale (R))

The point is that all elements in the formula must be the same, either weeks or units, for the calculation to take place. The same concept applies to the maximum stock.

Maximum Stock

The maximum stock defines the upper limit of the merchandise assortment in terms of weeks supply, or a specific number of units. It also determines the merchant's frequency of reorder. The maximum stock must be equal to

[13]The weekly rate of sale is used to convert time periods (weeks) into units. For example, if the delivery period is 2.5 weeks and the rate of sale is 30 units per week, then the number of units required for selling purposes is 2.5 × 30 = 75.

1. The minimum stock available at all times, and

2. The amount of stock that will be sold during the period of time up to the next reorder date.

The maximum stock, in terms of weeks supply, may be expressed through the following formula:

Maximum stock (MX) in weeks[14] = Minimum stock (MN) in weeks + Reorder period (RP) in weeks

The maximum stock in units is found by multiplying the maximum stock in weeks by the weekly rate of sale, as follows:

Maximum stock (MX) in units[15] = (Minimum stock (MN) in weeks + Reorder period (RP) in weeks) × Weekly rate of sale (R)

Calculation of Unit Open-to-Buy

Unit open-to-buy is the difference between the maximum stock in units and the total merchandise available, in terms of what the merchant has in inventory (on hand) and what has been purchased but is not yet available for sale (on order).[16] Thus, the formula for unit open-to-buy is

Open-to-buy (OTB) in units = Maximum stock (MX) in units − (Stock on hand (OH) + Stock on order (OO))

Unit Turnover

While not necessarily a component of unit open-to-buy, unit turnover is an important concept in planning unit merchandise assortments. You will recall from Chapter 9 that dollar turnover was the product of net sales divided by the average inventory at retail, and that it defined the number of times that a dollar inventory was sold and replaced. The same concept is applicable to units, where our concern lies with the number of times a unit assortment is sold and replaced. The formula for unit turnover is expressed as follows:

---

[14]Also, Maximum (MX) in weeks = Reserve stock (RS) in weeks + Delivery period (DP) in weeks + Reorder period (RP) in weeks.

[15]Also, Maximum stock (MX) in units = (Reserve stock (RS) in weeks + Delivery period (DP) in weeks + Reorder period in weeks) × Weekly rate of sale (R).

[16]Reasons vary, but they could include merchandise in transit, merchandise lost in transit, delayed shipping date, and such in-house problems as receiving, checking, and marking. The point is that there has been a legal commitment to purchase, but the merchandise is unavailable for resale to the customer.

$$\text{Unit turnover (T)} = \frac{\text{Unit net sales (NS)}}{\text{Average unit stock (AS)}}$$

Average Unit Stock

The amount of unit stock that is on hand at any given time is equal to the reserve stock plus the unsold portion of the last reorder. Thus, the number of units on hand will fluctuate between a "high" of the reserve stock plus a full reorder and a "low" of the reserve stock of itself.[17] Thus, the average unit stock on hand is equal to the reserve stock plus the intermediate amount between "no reorder" and "full reorder."

Figure 14.19 illustrates the concept of the average unit stock.

The concept of the average unit stock must be expressed in terms of weeks or units, utilizing one of the three following formulas:

1. Average stock (AS) in weeks = Reserve stock (RS) in weeks + ½ Reorder period (RP) in weeks.

2. Average stock (AS) in units = Reserve stock (RS) in units + ½ Reorder period (RP) in units.

3. Average stock (AS) in units = (Reserve stock (RS) in weeks + ½ Reorder period (RP) in weeks) × Weekly rate of sale (R).[18]

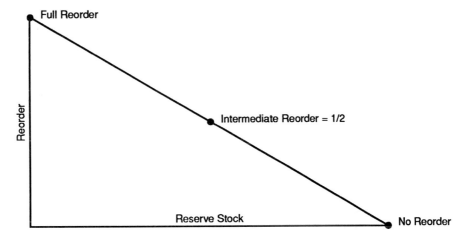

Figure 14.19 Average unit stock

---

[17]This is theoretically the point at which the last unit of the previous reorder has been sold with the current reorder not yet being on hand.
[18]Weeks may be converted into units simply by multiplying the number of weeks times the weekly rate of sale.

Net Sales

Net sales are normally calculated on an annual basis (52 weeks). However, any block of time appropriate to a given situation may be used, such as a season (26 weeks), a quarter (13 weeks), or a period (4 or 5 weeks). The following formula expresses annual net sales in units:

$$\text{Net sales (NS)} = \text{Weekly rate of sale (R)} \times 52$$

The following summarizes the components and formulas for determining unit open-to-buy and turnover for a classification or a subclassification:

Unit Open-to-Buy Components

MN	= Minimum Stock	RS	= Reserve Stock
DP	= Delivery Period	R	= Rate of Sale
MX	= Maximum Stock	RP	= Reorder Period
OTB	= Open-to-Buy	NS	= Net Sales
OH	= On Hand	OO	= On Order

Unit Open-to-Buy Formulas

$$\text{MN (weeks)} = \text{RS} + \text{DP}$$
$$\text{MN (units)} = (\text{RS} + \text{DP}) \times \text{R}$$
$$\text{MX (weeks)} = \text{MN} + \text{RP}$$
$$\text{MX (units)} = (\text{MN} + \text{RP}) \times \text{R}$$
$$\text{OTB (units)} = \text{MX} - (\text{OH} + \text{OO})$$

Unit Turnover Components

T	= Unit Turnover	NS	= Net Sales
AS	= Average Stock	RP	= Reorder Period
	RS	= Reserve Stock	

Unit Turnover Formulas

$$\text{T} = \text{NS} \div \text{AS}$$
$$\text{AS} = \text{RS} + \tfrac{1}{2}\,\text{RP}$$
$$\text{NS} = \text{R} \times 52$$

Determination of Unit Open-to-Buy for a Price Line or a Subclassification[19]

The basic concepts of unit open-to-buy and unit turnover are illustrated in the following study problem.

[19]Units are normally planned by subclassification, and dollars are planned by classification.

▪ Study Problem

Given: A men's-shirt buyer estimates that a reserve of 40 shirts in a $22 price line is required to satisfy customer demand. Reorders are planned on a two-week basis, with a one-week delivery period upon placement of the order. There are 25 shirts in stock and a dozen on order. Sales are planned at 30 shirts per week.

Find:

1. The minimum stock

2. The maximum stock

3. The unit open-to-buy

4. The unit turnover

Solution:

1. Determine the minimum stock:
   $MN = RS + (DP \times R)$[20]
   $MN = 40 + (1 \times 30)$
   $MN = 40 + 30$
   $MN = 70$ shirts

2. Determine the maximum stock:
   $MX = MN + (RP \times R)$[21]
   $MX = 70 + (2 \times 30)$
   $MX = 70 + 60$
   $MX = 130$ shirts

3. Determine the unit open-to-buy
   $O.T.B. = MX - (OH + OO)$
   $O.T.B. = 130 - (25 + 12)$
   $O.T.B. = 130 - 37$
   $O.T.B. = 93$ shirts

---

[20]Because the reserve stock is given in units and the delivery period in weeks, it becomes necessary to convert the delivery period into units. Obviously, weeks and units cannot be added. Thus, the basic formula, $MN = (RS - DP) \times R$, must be modified to $MN = RS + (DP \times R)$ to convert DP in weeks to DP in units.

[21]As in the above, the reorder period must be converted into units.

4. Determine the unit turnover

$NS = R \times 52$
$NS = 30 \times 52$
$NS = 1560$

$AS = RS + \frac{1}{2} (RP \times R)$
$AS = 40 + \frac{1}{2} (2 \times 30)$
$AS = 40 + 30$
$AS = 70$

$T = NS \div AS$
$T = 1560 \div 70$
$T - 22.3$[22]

▪ Application Exercise

1. A fine-jewelry buyer has 200 watches in the $130 price line and 75 on order. Sales are estimated at 40 per week, and a reserve of 50 watches is considered sufficient. The reorder period is 3 weeks, with a delivery period of 4 weeks. Determine the unit open-to-buy and the annual unit turnover.

2. The rate of sale for a $50 food processor is 28 units per week. The reserve stock is planned at 35 units, with a 2-week reorder period and a 4-week delivery period. Currently, there are 23 units in stock and 30 units on order. Calculate the unit open-to-buy and the turnover for the fall season.

3. A particular style of men's suit sells at a rate of 43 units per week. A recent stock count indicates that there are 87 units on hand and 24 more on order. The delivery period is 5 weeks, and the reorder period is 6 weeks. A reserve of 50 units is planned. Find the unit open-to-buy and the annual unit turnover rate.

4. A men's furnishings buyer had 6 dozen ties on hand with 4 dozen on order. The rate of sale is 48 ties per week, with a reorder period of 2 weeks and a delivery period of 3 weeks. The reserve is estimated to be 6 dozen ties. Determine the unit open-to-buy in dozens and the annual unit turnover.

5. A hardware buyer had 80 hammers on hand and 36 on order. The reserve stock was 50 hammers. The reorder period was every 2 weeks, and the delivery period was 1 week. The rate of sale was 20 hammers per week. Determine the buyer's unit open-to-buy and annual unit stock turnover.

6. A paint buyer sells 63 gallons of a particular brand of paint per week. Reserve stock was estimated at 100 cans. The reorder period was 1 week, and the

---

[22]The average unit stock will be sold and replaced 22.3 times within a year.

delivery period was 3 weeks. Currently, the buyer has 150 gallons on hand, with another 50 gallons on order. What is the buyer's unit open-to-buy and annual unit turnover?

Periodic Replenishment of Staple Stocks: Basic Stock List

By definition, staple goods are those items of merchandise that the customer expects to find in good assortment throughout the year or within a season. Staple items range from fashion basics, such as cardigan sweaters, to items totally devoid of fashion interest, such as white cotton socks or lightbulbs. To qualify as staple stock (basics), merchandise needs only the element of continuing, consistent, customer demand.

Essentially, staple stock will exhibit the following four characteristics:

1. A relatively long life cycle, with infrequent changes in product characteristics.

2. A predictable pattern of sales.

3. A relatively short delivery period.

4. A regular and frequent reorder period.

Basic Stock List for Staple Merchandise

Basic stock lists differ in composition from store to store as a result of the different types of basic unit assortments that they represent. However, conceptually they all strive to achieve the same results: to facilitate the ordering of correct types and quantities of staple merchandise to meet consistent customer demand over predetermined periods of time. Essentially, the basic stock list is a two-part, one-page document, in a series of documents, describing the basic stock for a given department. The first part of the document (normally the top) lists all the data pertinent to the basic item, such as department identification, classification, subclassification, item description, vendor, style number, material, unit cost and retail, etc. This portion may also contain the maximum and minimum number of units required to be on hand at all times.

The second portion of the basic stock list incorporates a format for some type of unit control system most appropriate to the merchandise assortment. Figure 14.20 illustrates one format for a basic stock list, utilizing a form of the physical inventory system previously discussed. This method is known as the "order-up-to-level" or "maximum system" of unit control.

Maximum System of Unit Control

The maximum system for the periodic replenishment of staple stocks is based upon the difference between a predetermined maximum stock and the number

Basic Stock List

Department No. —————————— Classification —————————— Style No. ——————————
                                Subclassification ——————————
Supplier ——————————   Address ——————————
Unit Cost $ —————————— Unit Retail $ —————————— Terms ——————————

Unit Description	Max. Stock	Date ————				Date ————				Date ————				Date ————				Date ————			
		OH*	OO	R	S	OH	OO	R	S	OH	OO	R	S	OH	OO	R	S	OH	OO	R	S

Figure 14.20 Basic stock list

*OH = On Hand
OO = On Order
R = Receipts
S = Sales

of units on hand. This difference represents the number of units on order, or the open-to-buy. Initially, the number of units on hand is determined by a physical stock count, thereafter by the following formula:

Units on hand for the planned period = Units on hand for the previous period + Receipts during the previous period − Planned sales for the previous period

For the purpose of uniform calculation, assume that the units on order will be received into the inventory on the last day of the delivery period. Thus, merchandise with a 2-week delivery period will be received at the end of the second week, merchandise with a 1-week delivery period, at the end of the first week, etc.

Also, the student is asked to recall the formula for the maximum stock:

Maximum stock = (Reserve stock in weeks + Delivery period in weeks + Reorder period in weeks) × Weekly rate of sale

The general layout of the unit control portion of the basic stock list is designed to conform with the retail accounting calendar; thus, it will accommodate either 4- or 5-week periods.

■ Study Problem

Given: As the buyer for women's polo shirts, the following information is available to you:

	Small	Medium	Large	X-Large
Rate of Sale	30	45	36	23
Delivery Period (weeks)	2	2	2	2
Reorder Period (weeks)	3	3	3	3
Reserve (weeks)	1	1	1	1

Find: Complete the basic stock list as shown in Figure 14.21.[23]

Solution:

1. Determine the weekly maximum stock:
   MX = (RS + DP + RP) × R
   Thus,

---

[23]The on-hand figures are the product of a physical inventory, or a stock count. The sales are projected and are assumed to be achieved.

Basic Stock List

Department No. _____ 1041   **Classification** _____ Women's Sportswear

                                 Subclassification _____ White Polo Shirts   **Style No.** _T–31_

Supplier _____ ABC Company

Address _____ New York, NY

Unit Cost $ _7.79_   **Unit Retail** $ _14.99_   **Terms** _____ 2/10/net 30

Unit Description	Max. Stock	Date 4/1				Date 4/8				Date 4/15				Date 4/22				Date ___			
		OH	OO	R	S	OH	OO	R	S	OH	OO	R	S	OH	OO	R	S	OH	OO	R	S
Small		150			73				53				83				103				
Medium		175			87				93				203				197				
Large		180			93				91				138				83				
X-Large		97			36				48				97				79				

Figure 14.21 Basic stock list: study problem

Small	MX = (1 + 2 + 3) × 30 = 180
Medium	MX = (1 + 2 + 3) × 45 = 270
Large	MX = (1 + 2 + 3) × 36 = 216
X-Large	MX = (1 + 2 + 3) × 23 = 138

2. Determine the stock on order (Unit − Open-to-buy) as of 4/1:
OO 4/1 = MX − OH 4/1
Thus,

Small	OO = 180 − 150 = 30
Medium	OO = 270 − 175 = 95
Large	OO = 216 − 180 = 36
X-Large	OO = 138 − 97 = 41

3. Assuming that there was no merchandise previously on order, enter 0 in the receipt column. (The stock currently on order will not arrive until the end of week 4/8.)

4. Determine the stock on hand for the week of 4/8:
OH 4/8 = OH 4/1 + R 4/1 − S 4/1
Thus,

Small	OH = 150 − 73 = 77
Medium	OH = 175 − 87 = 88
Large	OH = 180 − 93 = 87
X-Large	OH = 97 − 36 = 61

5. Calculate the stock on order (unit open-to-buy) for the week of 4/8:
OO 4/8 = MX − OH 4/8
Thus,

Small	OO = 180 − 77 = 103
Medium	OO = 270 − 88 = 182
Large	OO = 216 − 87 = 129
X-Large	OO = 138 − 61 = 77

6. The on-order units from 4/1 have now been perceived (the end of the second week); enter these figures as receipts for the week of 4/8.

7. Find the stock on hand for the week of 4/15:
OH 4/15 = OH 4/8 + R 4/8 − S 4/8
Thus,

Small	OH = 77 + 30 − 53 = 54
Medium	OH = 88 + 95 − 93 = 90
Large	OH = 87 + 36 − 91 = 32
X-Large	OH = 61 + 41 − 48 = 54

8. Calculate the units on order for week 4/15:
OO 4/15 = MX − OH 4/15
Thus,

Small	OO = 180 − 54 = 126
Medium	OO = 270 − 90 = 180
Large	OO = 216 − 32 = 184
X-Large	OO = 138 − 54 = 84

9. Enter the units on order from week 4/8 under week 4/15 in the receipt column.

10. Determine the on-hand units for week 4/22:
OH 4/22 = OH 4/15 + R 4/15 − S 4/15
Thus,

Small	OH = 54 + 103 − 83 = 74
Medium	OH = 90 + 182 − 203 = 69
Large	OH = 32 + 129 − 138 = 23
X-Large	OH = 54 + 77 − 97 = 34

11. Calculate the stock on order for the week 4/22:
OO 4/22 = MX − OH 4/22
Thus,

Small	OO = 180 − 74 = 106
Medium	OO = 270 − 69 = 201
Large	OO = 216 − 23 = 193
X-Large	OO = 138 − 34 = 104

12. Enter the receipts from the on-order column in week 4/15.

The completed basic stock list is shown in Figure 14.22.

■ Application Exercise[24]

The following eight application exercises are based upon this scenario: A china buyer is planning the unit open-to-buy for the 5 weeks of period V. The subclassification is "Mikasa®, five-piece place settings," which contain eight patterns. These patterns and their control data are listed below:

	R	DP	RS	RP
1. Moonbeams	3	1	2	3
2. Ultrastone Blue	5	2	2	3

---

[24]In all problems, assume that the units on order are received on the last day of the delivery period.

Basic Stock List

Department No. ___1041___ Classification ___Women's Sportswear___

Subclassification ___White Polo Shirts___ Style No. ___T–31___

Supplier ___ABC Company___ Address ___New York, NY___

Unit Cost $ ___7.79___ Unit Retail $ ___14.99___ Terms ___2/10/net 30___

Unit Description	Max. Stock	Date 4/1				Date 4/8				Date 4/15				Date 4/22				Date ___			
		OH	OO	R	S	OH	OO	R	S	OH	OO	R	S	OH	OO	R	S	OH	OO	R	S
Small	180	150	30	0	73	77	103	30	53	54	126	103	83	74	106	126	103				
Medium	270	175	95	0	87	88	182	95	93	90	180	182	203	69	201	180	197				
Large	216	180	36	0	93	87	129	36	91	32	184	129	138	23	193	184	83				
X-Large	138	97	41	0	36	61	77	41	48	54	84	77	97	34	104	84	79				

Figure 14.22 Basic stock list: solution to study problem

3. Arabella	7	1	2	3
4. Wedding Band	6	2	2	3
5. Tracings	8	1	2	3
6. Sheraton	2	2	2	3
7. Silk Flowers	4	1	2	3
8. Star Dust	3	2	2	3

Complete the eight sections of the basic stock list for the "Mikasa®, five-piece settings," as shown in Figure 14.23 (page 517).

▪ Solutions to Application Exercises

Planning Fashion Inventories (p. 481)

1. Figure 14.24.

3. Figure 14.25.

5. Figure 14.26.

The Buying Plan and Unit Open-to-Buy (page 495)

1. Figure 14.27.

3. Figure 14.28.

5. Figure 14.29.

Determination of Unit Open-to-Buy for a Specific Price Line (p. 508)

1. $MN = RS + (DP \times R)$
   $MN = 50 + (4 \times 40) = 50 + 160 = 210$

   $MX = MN + (RP \times R)$
   $MX = 210 + (3 \times 40) = 210 + 120 = 330$

   $OTB = MX - (OH + OO)$
   $OTB = 330 - (200 + 75) = 330 - 275 = 55$

   $T = NS \div AS$
   $T = (40 \times 52) \div [50 + \frac{1}{2}(3 \times 40)]$
   $T = 2{,}080 \div 110 = 18.9$

3. $MN = RS + (DP \times R)$
   $MN = 50 + (5 \times 43) = 50 + 215 = 265$

Basic Stock List

Department No. ___7021___ Classification ___China, Open Stock___ Style No. ___2379___

Subclassification ___Mikasa® Five-Piece Setting___

Supplier ___China Imports___ **Address** ___Philadelphia, PA___

Unit Cost $ ___24.50___ **Unit Retail $** ___35.00___ **Terms** ___2/10/net 30___

Unit Description	Max. Stock	Date 7/1 OH	OO	R	S	Date 7/8 OH	OO	R	S	Date 7/15 OH	OO	R	S	Date 7/22 OH	OO	R	S	Date 7/29 OH	OO	R	S
1. Moonbeams		6			10				15				12				14				12
2. Ultrastone Blue		27			20				12				15				23				31
3. Arabella		38			27				36				29				31				28
4. Wedding Band		31			15				18				23				28				21
5. Tracings		40			31				39				33				31				28
6. Sheraton		12			8				3				6				8				10
7. Silk Flowers		16			18				13				18				16				14
8. Star Dust		18			12				7				10				15				16

Figure 14.23 Basic stock list: application exercises 1–8

Model Stock Plan

Department: Men's Furnishings
Dept. No.: 3021
Season: Fall/Spring — Spring
Period: 1 (February)

Classification: Sweaters
Retail Price: $55
Buyer: Marjorie Pratt

Sub-Class. %	Sub-Class. Units	Style / $	Size	Qty %	Qty Units	Red %	Red Units	White %	White Units	Blue %	Blue Units	(color) %	(color) Units	MSR %	MSR Units	MSR $
		Crew Neck	Small	23	34	26	9	38	13	36	12			100	34	1,870
			Medium	36	54	31	17	53	28	16	9			100	54	2,970
			Large	21	31	25	8	50	15	25	8			100	31	1,705
			X-Large	20	30	38	11	40	12	22	7			100	30	1,650
43.6	149	$8,175	Total	100	149		45		68		36				149	8,195
		V-Neck	Small	18	21	15	4	40	8	45	9			100	21	1,155
			Medium	37	42	23	10	48	20	29	12			100	42	2,310
			Large	30	34	28	10	42	14	30	10			100	34	1,870
			X-Large	15	17	25	4	40	7	35	6			100	17	935
33.4	114	$6,263	Total	100	114		28		49		37				114	6,270
		Turtle Neck	Small	26	20	23	5	40	8	37	7			100	20	1,100
			Medium	21	17	28	5	36	6	36	6			100	17	935
			Large	32	25	32	8	48	12	20	5			100	25	1,375
			X-Large	21	16	30	5	50	8	20	3			100	16	880
23.0	78	$4,313	Total	100	78		23		34		21				78	4,290
100	341		Grand Total		341		96		151		94				341	18,755

Figure 14.24 Model stock plan: solution for application exercise 1

Model Stock Plan

Department: Women's Shoes
Dept. No.: 4511
Season: Fall/Spring — Fall
Period: IX (October)

Classification: Leather Pumps
Retail Price: $45
Buyer: Mary Zingler

Sub-Classification (Style) %	Units	$	Size	Qty for Model Stock %	Units	Pink %	Units	White %	Units	Black %	Units	Bone %	Units	%	Units	Model Stock at Retail Units	$
			5½B	15	50	15	8	20	10	25	12	40	20	100	50	50	2,250
			6B	18	60	20	12	25	15	25	15	30	18	100	60	60	2,700
Flat Heel			6½B	23	77	23	18	28	21	21	16	28	22	100	77	77	3,465
			7B	25	84	18	15	32	27	28	24	22	18	100	84	84	3,780
			7½B	10	34	13	4	35	12	30	10	22	8	100	34	34	1,530
		$15,080	8B	9	30	21	6	25	8	33	10	21	6	100	30	30	1,350
28.0	335		Total	100	335		63		93		87		92	100	335	335	15,075
			5½B	18	125	13	16	18	23	36	45	33	41	100	125	125	5,625
			6B	20	139	20	28	25	34	25	35	30	42	100	139	139	6,255
Mid Heel			6½B	25	174	18	31	30	52	24	42	28	49	100	174	174	7,830
			7B	17	118	23	27	27	32	30	35	20	24	100	118	118	5,310
			7½B	12	83	25	21	28	23	21	17	26	22	100	83	83	3,735
		$31,238	8B	8	55	22	12	30	17	32	17	16	9	100	55	55	2,475
58.0	694		Total	100	694		135		181		191		187	100	694	694	31,230
			5½B	13	22	28	6	30	7	25	5	17	4	100	22	22	990
			6B	20	33	25	8	33	11	28	9	14	5	100	33	33	1,485
High Heel			6½B	28	47	18	8	29	14	23	11	30	14	100	47	47	2,115
			7B	18	30	25	8	28	8	21	6	26	8	100	30	30	1,350
			7½B	14	24	19	5	31	7	27	6	23	6	100	24	24	1,080
		$7,540	8B	7	12	20	2	32	4	26	3	22	3	100	12	12	540
			Total	100	168		37		51		40		40	100	168	168	7,560
14.0	168		Total	100	168		37		51		40		40	100	168	168	7,560
100	1,197		Grand Total	100	1,197		235		325		318		319	100	1,197	1,197	53,865

Figure 14.25 Model stock plan: solution for application exercise 3

Model Stock Plan

Department: Men's Shoes
Dept. No.: 4521
Season: Fall/Spring — Fall
Period: X (November)
Classification: Casual Leathers
Retail Price: $50
Buyer: Ed Henry

Sub-Classification (Style)		Size	Quantity for Model Stock		Color								Model Stock at Retail		
					Black		Brown		Mahogany		Putty				
%	Units		%	Units	%	Units	%	Units	%	Units	%	Units	%	Units	$
		8D	10	35	20	7	25	9	30	10	25	9	100	35	1,750
		9D	15	52	15	8	30	16	35	18	20	10	100	52	2,600
	Half-Boots	10D	30	103	18	19	28	29	37	38	17	17	100	103	5,150
		11D	20	69	21	14	26	18	40	28	13	9	100	69	3,450
		12D	25	86	19	16	27	23	38	33	16	14	100	86	4,300
28.5	345	Total	100	345		64		95		127		59	100	345	17,250
$ 17,243															
		8D	15	61	15	10	25	15	30	18	30	18	100	61	3,050
		9D	15	61	18	11	23	14	33	20	26	16	100	61	3,050
	Loafers	10D	20	81	20	17	24	19	31	25	25	20	100	81	4,050
		11D	30	121	25	31	30	36	34	41	11	13	100	121	6,050
		12D	20	81	23	19	32	26	29	23	16	13	100	81	4,050
	405	Total	100	405		88		110		127		80	100	405	20,250
$ 20,268															
		8D	10	46	13	6	23	11	31	14	33	15	100	46	2,300
		9D	20	92	15	14	27	24	30	28	28	26	100	92	4,600
	Boat Shoe	10D	30	138	18	25	28	39	32	44	22	30	100	138	6,900
		11D	30	138	20	28	32	44	20	28	28	38	100	138	6,900
		12D	10	46	21	10	31	14	27	12	21	10	100	46	2,300
33.5	405	Total	100	460		83		132		126		119	100	460	23,000
$ 22,990															
38.0	460	Total	100	460		235		337		380		258	100	460	23,000
100	1210	Grand Total		1210		235		337		380		258	100	1,210	60,500

Figure 14.26 Model stock plan: solution for application exercise 5

Buying Plan (Unit Open-to-Buy)

Department ___ Men's Furnishings
Department Number ___ 3021
Period Covered ___ III (April)
Preparation Date ___ March 15

Classification ___ Sweaters
Markon ___ 46.5%
Buyer ___ Marjorie Pratt

Subclassification / Unit Price	(1) Sales 13 Mos Prior to Prep Date	(2) Sales 1 Mo Prior to Prep Date	(3) Sales 12 Mos Prior to Prep Date	(4) Sales 1 Mo Prior to Period Covered	(5) BOM Stock for Period Covered	(6) On Hand 1 Mo Prior to Period Covered	(7) On Order 1 Mo Prior to Period Covered	(8) OTB Units	(9) $OTB Retail	(10) $OTB Cost
V-Neck Sweaters $35	120	130	153	166	114	119	36	125	$4375	$2341

Figure 14.27 Buying plan: solution to application exercise 1

Buying Plan (Unit Open-to-Buy)

Department: Women's Shoes
Department Number: 4511
Period Covered: VIII (September)
Preparation Date: August 8

Classification: Athletic Shoes
Markon: 46.7%
Buyer: Student

Subclassification / Unit Price	(1) Sales 13 Mos Prior to Prep Date	(2) Sales 1 Mo Prior to Prep Date	(3) Sales 12 Mos Prior to Prep Date	(4) Sales 1 Mo Prior to Period Covered	(5) BOM Stock for Period Covered	(6) On Hand 1 Mo Prior to Period Covered	(7) On Order 1 Mo Prior to Period Covered	(8) OTB Units	(9) $OTB Retail	(10) $OTB Cost
Tennis Shoes $48	136	116	149	127	144	128	36	107	$5136	$2737

Figure 14.28 Buying plan: solution to application exercise 3

Buying Plan (Unit Open-to-Buy)

Department _____ Hosiery _____ Classification _____ Socks _____
Department Number _____ 2015 _____ Markon _____ 43.8% _____
Period Covered _____ V (June) _____ Buyer _____ Student _____
Preparation Date _____ May 3 _____

Subclassification / Unit Price	(1) Sales 13 Mos Prior to Prep Date	(2) Sales 1 Mo Prior to Prep Date	(3) Sales 12 Mos Prior to Prep Date	(4) Sales 1 Mo Prior to Period Covered	(5) BOM Stock for Period Covered	(6) On Hand 1 Mo Prior to Period Covered	(7) On Order 1 Mo Prior to Period Covered	(8) OTB Units	(9) $OTB Retail	(10) $OTB Cost
Ribbed Crew $4.50	323	279	385	333	400	293	315	125	$563	$316

Figure 14.29 Buying plan: solution to application exercise 5

$$MX = MN + (RP \times R)$$
$$MX = 265 + (6 \times 43) = 265 + 258 = 523$$

$$OTB = MX - (OH + OO)$$
$$OTB = 523 - (87 + 24) = 523 - 111 = 412$$

$$T = NS \div AS$$
$$T = (43 \times 52) \div [50 + \frac{1}{2}(6 \times 43)]$$
$$T = 2,236 \div 179 = 12.5$$

5. $MN = RS + (DP \times R)$
$$MN = 50 + (1 \times 20) = 50 + 20 = 70$$

$$MX = MN + (RP \times R)$$
$$MX = 70 + (2 \times 20) = 70 + 40 = 110$$

$$OTB = MX - (OH + OO)$$
$$OTB = 110 - (80 + 36) = 110 - 116 = -6^{25}$$

$$T = NS \div AS$$
$$T = (20 \times 52) \div [50 + \frac{1}{2}(2 \times 20)]$$
$$T = 1,040 \div 70 = 14.9$$

The Maximum System of Unit Control (p. 514)

1. Figure 14.30.
3. Figure 14.30.
5. Figure 14.30.
7. Figure 14.30.

▪ ━━━━━━━━━━━━━━━━━━━━━━━━━━━━━━━━━━━━━

Topics for Discussion and Review

1. Explain the concept of unit assortments.
2. What is meant by variety and assortment?
3. Discuss the concept of selection parameters.
4. What is the difference between a merchandise assortment and a unit control system?

---

[25]The buyer is overbought by six hammers and therefore has no open-to-buy.

Basic Stock List

Department No. 7021	Classification China, Open-Stock		
	Subclassification Mikasa® Five-Piece Setting	Style No. 2379	
Supplier China Imports	Address Philadelphia		
Unit Cost $ 24.50 Unit Retail $ 35	Terms 2/10/net 30		

Unit Description	Max. Stock	Date 7/1				Date 7/8				Date 7/15				Date 7/22				Date 7/29			
		OH	OO	R	S	OH	OO	R	S	OH	OO	R	S	OH	OO	R	S	OH	OO	R	S
1. Moonbeams	18	6	12	12	10	8	10	10	15	3	15	15	12	6	12	12	14	4	14	14	12
2. Ultrastone Blue																					
3. Arabella	42	38	4	4	27	15	27	27	36	6	36	36	29	13	29	29	31	11	31	31	28
4. Wedding Band																					
5. Tracings	48	40	8	8	31	17	31	31	39	9	39	39	33	15	33	33	31	17	31	31	28
6. Sheraton																					
7. Silk Flowers	24	16	8	8	18	6	18	18	13	11	13	13	18	6	18	18	16	8	16	16	14
8. Star Dust																					

Figure 14.30 Basic stock list: solutions to study problems 1, 3, 5, 7

525

5. How would you answer the following statement? "Model stocks are only useful for the planning and control of fashion merchandise."

6. What is meant when we speak of the breadth and depth of a merchandise assortment?

7. How would you explain the concept of variety in a merchandise assortment?

8. Discuss the function of a unit control system.

9. Discuss two ways to determine the status of a unit merchandise assortment.

10. What is the ultimate objective of the model stock plan?

11. Why is the model stock never "cast in stone"?

12. Explain the relationship between the model stock plan and unit open-to-buy.

13. What is an S.K.U., and what is its function?

14. How does the six-month merchandise plan relate to model stocks?

15. What concepts are inherent in any model stock plan?

16. Why is a classification normally planned in dollars and a subclassification planned in units?

17. What is the essential nature of fashion stocks, and how do they differ from staple stocks?

18. What is a buying plan, and how does it relate to the model stock plan for fashion merchandise?

19. Explain the concept of unit open-to-buy.

20. What is a basic stock list, and what concepts does it embrace?

21. Explain the concept of a minimum stock.

22. What is the factor that converts weeks of supply into units?

23. Explain the function of the maximum stock and its components.

24. Discuss the concept of unit turnover and how it is calculated.

25. How does the maximum system of unit control work?

Chapter 15
Quantitative Vendor Relations: The Structure of the Quoted Wholesale Price

Learning Objectives

- Discuss the underlying structure of the wholesale price.
- Identify the factors that constitute the terms of the sale.
- Explain the concept of immediate dating.
- Explain the concept of future dating.
- Illustrate the concept of ordinary dating with a specific example of a dated invoice and terms of the sale.
- Explain the concept of E.O.M. dating, using a specific example.
- Explain the concept of R.O.G. dating, using a specific example.
- Explain the concepts of advanced and extra dating, using specific examples of each.
- Explain the concept of cash discounts.
- Explain the function of the cash discount.
- Explain the significance of the cash discount in terms of the annual interest rate.
- Translate the cash discount into an annual interest rate.

- Discuss the concept of cash discount loading, including a specific example.

- Discuss the concept of anticipation, including its two functions.

- Explain the calculation of anticipation.

- Explain the function of the trade discount.

- Calculate the single-discount equivalent of a chain discount and explain why the single discount is not an average of the series.

- Explain the two forms of a quantity discount.

- Explain why quantity discounts directly affect purchases at cost and do not necessarily affect purchases at retail.

- List the order of calculation when the quantity discount is involved with the trade and cash discount.

- Discuss the two factors of inconvenience that arise when the merchant purchases goods at any point beyond the stores receiving docks.

- Define and explain the following concepts:
  1. F.O.B. factory, freight collect.
  2. F.O.B. factory, freight prepaid.
  3. F.O.B. factory, freight prepaid and charged back.
  4. F.O.B. store, freight collect.
  5. F.O.B. store, freight prepaid.
  6. F.O.B. store, freight collect and allowed.

Key Terms

Advanced or Post Dating: The dating of the invoice sometime after the merchandise has actually been shipped. Seasonal dating is another way of defining advanced, or post, dating.

Anticipation: An additional discount based upon the number of days remaining in the cash discount period after the invoice has been paid.

Billed Cost Price: The merchant's cost price as stated upon the vendor's invoice before the deduction of cash discounts and after the subtraction of any trade or quantity discounts.

Cash Dating: Immediate dating that embraces the concept of cash on delivery, cash with order, and cash before delivery.

Cash Discount A reduction in the vendor's billed cost price for paying the invoice before the expiration of the cash discount period.

Cash Discount Date: The last date for the payment of an invoice before the expiration of the cash discount period.

Cash Discount Period: The time frame within which the merchant may take advantage of discounts offered by the vendor.

C.B.D.: Cash before delivery.

Chain, or Series, Discount: Two or more trade discounts quoted in a series form, e.g., 30%–20%–10%. Each discount in the chain is deducted from the previous discount.

C.O.D.: Cash on delivery.

Cumulative Quantity Discount: A reduction in billed cost based upon the amount of merchandise purchased over a predetermined period of time; expressed as a percentage of net sales.

C.W.O.: Cash with order.

Dating: The time at which payment for the merchandise is due to the vendor.

D.O.I.: Date of the invoice.

End of the Month (E.O.M.) Dating: Terms of the sale under which the cash discount and net credit periods are calculated from the end of the month in which the invoice is dated, rather than the date of the invoice itself.

Extra Dating: The extension of the cash discount period by the addition of a specific amount of "extra" days; a form of deferred dating.

F.O.B.: A shipping term that stands for "free on board." Any agreed-upon destination to which the transportation charges are paid for by the vendor. Title to the merchandise transfers to the merchant at the point of destination.

Future Dating: The designation of specific future dates defining the cash discount period and the last day of payment for the total billed cost; refers to the time element of the terms of the sale.

Invoice: An itemized statement from the vendor that defines the cost of merchandise. The vendor's invoice should always agree with the merchant's purchase order.

Invoice Loading: Increasing the gross invoice price of merchandise and crediting cash discounts with the amount of the increase, or load. This is normally the practice when the vendor insists on the quoted price, and, at the same time, the merchant must show a greater cash discount.

List Price: The theoretical retail price suggested by a manufacturer for the resale of its goods to the ultimate consumer. This suggested retail price is not legally binding on the merchant, since legal resale price maintenance came to an end in March of 1976, with the repeal of the Fair Trade laws.

Markdown Money: Money given by the vendor to the merchant so as to enable the merchant to reduce prices on the vendor's lines of merchandise that are slow sellers.

Net Payment Date: The final date for the payment of an invoice after the expiration of the cash discount period. Payment after this date subjects the merchant to interest penalties.

Net Price: The merchant's cost after the deduction of the trade discount.

"On" Percentage: A single percentage that, when multiplied by the list price, will obtain the net price. It is the complement of the single-discount equivalent and is often used as a short-cut method when a chain, or series, discount is to be deducted.

Ordinary Dating: Terms of the sale under which the cash discount and net credit periods begin with the date of the invoice. If the invoice is paid within the cash discount period, the specified discount may be deducted from the payment; otherwise, the full amount is due at the end of the net credit period, normally 30 days. Ordinary dating is also referred to as regular, or date of the invoice (D.O.I.), dating.

Price Level: The visible, or numerical, aspects of the originally quoted wholesale price.

Price Structure: The time and convenience dimensions inherent in the quoted wholesale price, quantitatively defined as discounts, dating, and transportation arrangements.

Prime Bank Rate: The interest rate that commercial banks charge their best customers.

Quantity Discount: A reduction in the cost of merchandise based upon the size of the merchant's order; deducted prior to the trade discount.

Receipt of Goods (R.O.G.) Dating: Terms of the sale in which the cash discount period starts with the merchant's receipt of the goods, rather than the date of the invoice.

Single-Discount Equivalent: One trade discount percentage equivalent to a chain, or series, discount. This value is not equal to the sum of the series discount.

Trade Discount: A discount from a vendor's list price, expressed as a percentage or a series of percentages, to determine the merchant's cost; always deducted prior to the cash discount.

15.1

The Underlying Structure of the Wholesale Price: Time and Convenience

The concept of the wholesale price is substantially more than a number expressed in terms of dollars and cents. While it is obviously true that the wholesale price quoted to the merchant is a numerical statement of a level of value for a particular item, e.g., $23.80, the perception of that price may be altered by its underlying structure of time and convenience. From the merchant's perspective, the time component of the cost price defines specific dates and amounts to be paid to the vendor, and the convenience dimension relates to the location, or geographical point, at which the title to the merchandise transfers from the vendor to the merchant. Because the merchant, when in the wholesale market, is more immediately concerned with buying than selling, the awareness of wholesale costs tends to focus upon the more obvious price level, rather than on the more subtle, but nevertheless extremely important, price structures. Indeed, where market prices are relatively homogeneous, competition among vendors for the merchant's dollar is of necessity predicated upon the structural dimensions of the wholesale cost, rather than on the observable level of those costs. It is therefore incumbent upon the merchant to thoroughly understand the structural components of the vendor's quoted price, because it is those elements that ultimately determine the merchant's total cost of merchandise sold and the resulting gross margin.

Terms of the Sale

The structural dimensions of the quoted wholesale price (i.e., time and convenience), in the reality of the marketplace, are known as the *terms of the sale*. This concept embraces factors other than the apparent cost price that must be negotiated in order to determine the merchant's final cost. Although there are many negotiable variables influencing the purchase decision,[1] those factors directly influencing gross margin are of our most immediate concern. Thus, within this context, we define the terms of the sale to consist of three distinct yet interrelated concepts that serve as an "umbrella" definition for the more specific elements of

---

[1] Other factors may include storage of merchandise until needed by the merchant; guarantees of quality and quantity; return privileges; preticketing of the merchandise by the vendor; packing for shipment and packaging for resale; price guarantees on reorders and reorder availability; promotional aids and allowances; changes in the product itself, including size and color assortments; advertising allowances; and guarantees of markdown money.

quantitative vendor relations. These concepts are *discounts, dating,* and *transportation arrangements.* While transportation arrangements obviously bear upon earned discounts and the concept of dating, they tend to stand as a separate entity and are therefore treated as such in the following sections of this chapter. However, discounts and dating, while indeed separate concepts, are inextricably combined and thus lend themselves to a less precise means of classification. As you will soon realize, the amount of discount earned depends upon the merchant's compliance with the terms dictated by the dating concept, and mutually agreed-upon dates evolve from the discount amount to be earned by the merchant. Thus, we have a "chicken and egg" phenomenon, and to define which comes first, or which is of greater importance, is a futile exercise. As a result, dating is presented as an integral function of earned discounts, the emphasis being placed upon the concept of dating and its impact on gross margin. In the following section, the specific types of discounts alluded to here will be discussed in detail.

15.2

Terms of the Sale: Dating[2]

Aside from the transportation arrangements, the terms of the sale, as negotiated between the merchant and the vendor, consist of three elements:

1. The cash discount, or a percentage reduction in the billed cost of the merchandise, earned by the merchant for payment of the invoice within a specific period of time.[3]

2. The last date on which the invoice must be paid in order for the merchant to earn the discount; this is defined as the cash discount date.

3. The final date for payment of the entire billed cost of the merchandise. This date follows that expiration of the cash discount period and thus precludes the merchant from taking advantage of the cash discount. This is the net payment date.

Thus, if we momentarily remove, for the sake of analysis, the cash discount from the terms of the sale, we are left with the concept of *dating,* or the time at which payment for the merchandise is due to the vendor.

Essentially, there are only two time frames that serve as reference points for the merchant's financial obligations to the vendor: the present or the future.

---

[2]Represents the time component of the price structure; the amount to be paid depends on the remittance date.

[3]Cash discounts, along with other forms of discounts, will be discussed in the following section.

Immediate Dating

Immediate dating, sometimes referred to as *cash dating,* technically calls for the merchant to make payment for the goods either upon receipt of the order or prior to its shipment. While immediate dating is relatively rare, it is imposed by the vendor upon those merchants who are in poor financial condition or who lack a satisfactory credit history. Three self-explanatory terms generally cover the concept of immediate, or cash, dating:

1. C.O.D.: cash on delivery.

2. C.W.O.: cash with order.

3. C.B.D.: cash before delivery.

   When the terms of the sale call for some type of immediate dating, this obviously precludes the calculation of payment dates and the various forms of earned discounts. Thus, we will proceed immediately to the concept of delayed, or future, dating.

Future Dating

Future dating specifies some point in time, after the merchant's receipt of goods, that defines the cash discount period and the final date for the payment of the total billed cost of the merchandise. Frequently, but not always, future dating is subject to negotiation, because the merchant wants as long a discount and net term period as possible and the vendor would like to be paid immediately. Future dating is preferred by most merchants, especially the smaller ones, simply because the more time gained between purchase and payment to the vendor, the more merchandise that can be sold and turned into cash. Obviously, this additional income may significantly reduce the merchant's burden of repayment and contribute to the enhancement of turnover and gross margin.

Ordinary Dating, or Date of the Invoice (D.O.I.)

Ordinary dating, so called because the merchant's repayment obligations commence with the date of the invoice,[4] is the most common form of dating. It contains all three of the elements mentioned earlier and is defined as follows:

2/10/net 30

"2" represents the percentage of the billed cost that may be deducted from the vendor's invoice if it is paid within the cash discount period.

---

[4]Normally corresponds with the date of shipment.

"10" defines the cash discount period, that is, the number of days from the date of the invoice within which the merchant is allowed to pay for the goods and take advantage of the 2% cash discount.

Ordinary dating requires that the full amount of the invoice be paid thirty days from the vendor's date of invoice. Therefore, "net 30" states that the full amount of invoice, without allowance for the cash discount, is due 30 days from the invoice date. Upon expiration of this 30-day period, the merchant is subject to interest penalties.

In effect, 2/10/net 30 states that the merchant may take a 2% discount, if the invoice is paid within 10 days from the date of the invoice; however, the total amount is due within 30 days.

Ordinary dating is not necessarily the best terms that the merchant can negotiate because it tends to allow the vendor too much discretion in establishing the date of the invoice. For example, if the vendor is slow in shipping the merchant's order, payment may actually be due prior to the arrival of the merchandise. Thus, the merchant must consider alternate forms of dating if the gross-margin objectives are to remain viable. These other methods will be explored as we progress.

∎ Study Problem

Given: A merchant receives an invoice dated 7/23. Terms of the sale are 3/12/net 30.

Find:

1. The last day to pay the vendor and still take advantage of the cash discount (cash discount date).

2. The last day to pay the vendor without any cash discount (net payment date).

Solution:

1. The last day to pay the vendor and take the discount is:

Date of the invoice	July	23
Days allowed to take the discount		12
		35
Less number of days in July		31
Cash discount date, on or before	August	4

2. Date of the invoice	July	23	
Net terms (number of days)		30	
		53	
Less number of days in July		31	
Net payment date, on or before	August	22	

■ Application Exercise

1. An invoice is dated 10/13, with terms of 3/10/net 30.
   a. What is the cash discount date?
   b. What is the net payment date?

2. Determine the cash discount date and the net payment date for an invoice dated 5/23 with terms of 3/15/net 30.

3. A merchant purchased a quantity of goods on December 12, with terms of 3/18/net 30. The merchandise was received on March 6 and was followed by the invoice dated March 5. What were the cash discount date and the net payment date?

4. Find the cash discount date and the net payment date, given the following data:

Date of receipt	6/22
Purchase order date	5/18
Shipment date	6/18
Date of invoice	6/20
Terms of the sale	4/14/net 30

5. A merchant placed a $2,000 order on July 16 for delivery during the first week in September. The merchandise arrived on September 4, followed by the invoice dated September 3. What was the last date to take the cash discount and the final date for the payment of the invoice, if the terms of the sale were 2/20/net 30?

End-of-the-Month (E.O.M.) Dating

E.O.M. dating means that the cash discount period and the net payment date are always computed from the end of the month in which the invoice is dated, rather than the date of the invoice itself. For example, an invoice dated 6/12 with terms of 6/10/E.O.M. means that the merchant will receive a 6% discount on the billed cost of the merchandise if the invoice is paid on or before the tenth day of the following month. Thus, the effective date of the invoice is not 6/12 but the end of the month, or 6/30, resulting in a cash discount period that begins on 7/1 and runs through 7/10.

Although not implicitly stated in the terms, the 30-day net payment period is implied in the concept of E.O.M. dating. This means that the net payment date will always be 30 days from the end of the month in which the invoice was dated, or, in this instance, 7/30.

The essential idea behind E.O.M. dating is that both the cash discount period and the 30-day terms commence on the first day of the month following the month in which the invoice was dated. Thus, given the terms 6/10/E.O.M. on the invoice dated 6/12, the cash discount date must of necessity be next month (July) plus 10 days, or 7/10; likewise, the net payment date is July plus 30 days, or 7/30.

Normally, under E.O.M. terms, an invoice dated on or after the 25th of the month may be considered as dated the first of the following month. Thus, an invoice dated 6/26, with terms of 6/10/E.O.M., states that

1. The date of the invoice is to be considered 7/1.

2. Dating is to commence as of 7/31.

3. The cash discount period runs from 8/1 through 8/10.

4. The net amount of the invoice is due 8/30.

■ Study Problem

Given: The terms are 6/10/E.O.M., and the invoice is dated 7/14.

Find:

1. The cash discount date.

2. The net payment date.

Solution:

1. End-of-the-month[5]	July	31
Ten days		10
		41
Less days in July		31
Cash discount date	August	10
2. End-of-the-month	July	31
Thirty days		30
		61

---

[5]In which the invoice was written.

Less days in July		31
Net payment date	August	30

▪ Study Problem

Given: The terms are 6/10/E.O.M., and the invoice is dated 7/25.

Find:

1. The cash discount date.

2. The net payment date.

Solution: 7/25 implies 8/1, and the E.O.M. concept translates 8/1 into 8/31. Thus,

1. End-of-month	August	31
Ten days		10
		41
Less days in August		31
Cash discount date	September	10
2. End-of-month	August	31
Thirty days		30
		61
Less days in August		31
Net payment date	September	30

▪ Application Exercise

1. The terms are 8/10/E.O.M. on an invoice dated November 12. Find:
   a. The cash discount date.
   b. The net payment date.

2. What is the last day to pay an invoice dated October 26 in order to take advantage of the cash discount offered in the terms 6/15/E.O.M.?

3. An invoice is dated 3/2 with terms of 6/12/E.O.M. What is the last date to pay the vendor without incurring any interest penalties?

4. A shoe buyer received a $2,500 invoice dated 7/25 with terms of 3/20/E.O.M. What is the last day to pay the invoice and take the cash discount?

5. On 5/20, the owner of a small boutique received an invoice dated 5/18 for merchandise purchased on February 16. Terms were 4/16/E.O.M. On or before what date should this invoice be paid if the discount is to be taken?

Receipt of Goods (R.O.G.) Dating

R.O.G. dating defines the cash discount and net payment periods as commencing with the merchant's receipt of the goods ordered, as evidenced by the delivery date on the freight bill, rather than from the date of the invoice.

The concept behind R.O.G. dating is to equalize the time and distance variables existing between competing vendors and their retail customers. Certain suppliers are more distant from the merchant than others, thus creating competitive disadvantages in terms of the length of delivery times. In other instances, a resource may be unable to say exactly when the merchant's order will be delivered. In either case, R.O.G. terms may be added to ordinary or E.O.M. dating, to enhance the vendor's competitive edge by creating a form of time equality for its various retail customers.

■ Study Problem

Given:

Terms of sale	2/10/net 30–R.O.G.
Invoice date	6/30
Date of receipt	7/3

Find:

1. The cash discount date.

2. The net payment date.

Solution:

Since the terms are R.O.G., we use the date of receipt, rather than the date of the invoice, to determine the cash discount date and the net payment date.

1. Date of receipt	July	3
Ten days		10
Cash discount date	July	13

2. Date of receipt	July	3
Thirty days		30
		33
Less days in July		31
Net payment date	August	2

■ Study Problem

Given: A merchant receives an invoice dated 4/18 with terms of 3/15/E.O.M.–R.O.G. On 5/18, the merchandise arrives in the store.

Find:

1. The last day to take the cash discount.

2. The final date on which the full amount of the invoice is due.

Solution:

Since the terms are R.O.G., we use 5/18, the date of receipt, as the base date to work the problem. Thus,

1. E.O.M. date	May	31
Fifteen days		15
		46
Less days in May		31
Cash discount date	June	15

2. E.O.M. date	May	31
Thirty days		30
		61
Less days in May		31
Net payment date	June	30

■ Application Exercise

1. A candy buyer received a shipment of Easter eggs on April 3. The invoice, previously received, was dated February 18, with terms 2/10/net 30–R.O.G. On what date should the invoice be paid in order to take advantage of the cash discount?

2. A buyer purchased merchandise on 6/18. Shortly thereafter, the invoice was received, dated 6/27 with terms of 3/18/E.O.M.–R.O.G. On August 23, the order was received. Determine the last date to pay the invoice and still take advantage of the 3% cash discount.

3. A jewelry buyer ordered some custom-made goods on 1/18. The invoice was received on 1/27, dated 1/25, with terms of 5/15/E.O.M.–R.O.G. The finished goods were finally received on 4/25. What was the last day to pay the invoice and take the cash discount?

4. The owner of a small-children's boutique received an invoice dated 7/23 with terms of 4/10/net 30–R.O.G. When the merchandise arrived on 8/17, the owner was short of cash and decided to pay the full amount of the invoice on the latest possible date. What was that date?

5. Given the following data, calculate the cash discount date and the net payment date:

Terms of the sale	3/12/E.O.M.–R.O.G.
Date of invoice	5/26
Date of purchase	5/18
Date of receipt	7/26

Advanced (Post) Dating

Advanced dating, sometimes called post or seasonal dating, refers to the dating of the invoice sometime in the future, after the actual shipment of the goods to the merchant has taken place. The reason for this action is normally prompted by the vendor's desire to reduce inventory to make room for new production. Thus, as an inducement to convince the merchant to buy, the vendor offers more time to make payment and still take advantage of the cash discount.

The following study problems are only offered as a means of demonstration of the concept of advanced dating. The mathematical computations to arrive at the cash discount and net payment dates are the same as in previous examples; thus, another application exercise would be redundant.

▪ Study Problem

Given: A coat buyer purchased $3,000 worth of fur-lined jackets on June 8 for delivery on September 15. The vendor agreed to date the purchase order November 1, with terms of 3/12/net 30.

Find:

1. The cash discount date.

2. The net payment date.

Solution:

1. Date of the invoice   November   1

   <u>12 days</u>   <u>12</u>

   Cash discount date   November   13

2. Date of the invoice   November   1

   <u>Thirty days</u>   <u>30</u>

                                          31

   <u>Less days in November</u>   <u>30</u>

   Net payment date   December   1

■ Study Problem

Given: As an inducement to purchase early and receive merchandise prior to the season, a sportswear buyer was offered an assortment of bathing suits for delivery on November 15, with the invoice to be dated May 1. Terms of the sale were to be 6/10/E.O.M.

Find: What would be the last date to pay the vendor and take the cash discount?

Solution:

E.O.M. date   May   31

<u>Ten days</u>   <u>10</u>

                               41

<u>Less days in May</u>   <u>31</u>

Cash discount date   June   10

Extra Dating

Extra dating means that the cash discount period is extended for a specific number of extra days. The effect is to allow the merchant more time to pay for purchases without the loss of the cash discount. This is simply another form of advanced dating, which either encourages the merchant to purchase goods out of season or serves as a means of extending the cash discount period to those merchants experiencing temporary cash flow difficulties. For example, if the vendor's terms are 2/10/net 30,[6] and by agreement, 60 days are added to the 10-day cash discount period, the terms are changed to read 2/10–60x. This means that

---

[6]Extra dating is predicated upon the concept of ordinary dating.

1. The merchant is granted the regular 10-day cash discount period plus 60 days extra, or a total of 70 days from the date of the invoice, to pay the vendor and still take the cash discount.

2. The net payment date requires that the full amount of the invoice is due 90 days from the date of the invoice, or 30 days plus the number of extra days granted.[7]

▪ Study Problem

Given: The vendor's terms are 2/10/net 30. The merchant has requested that the cash discount period be extended by 60 days. The vendor has agreed to the request and changed the terms to 2/10–60x on an invoice dated May 16.

Find:

1. The last day to pay the invoice and take advantage of the cash discount.

2. The last day to make payment on the billed cost of the merchandise.

Solution:

1. Since the total number of days in which to take the cash discount is 70 days (10 + 60), the last day of the discount period must be 70 days from the date of the invoice (5/16). Therefore,

Total discount days	70
Less discount days in May (5/31–5/16)	15
	55
Less days in June	30
Cash discount date	July 25

2. The net payment date is 30 days from the date of the invoice plus 60 extra days, or a total time period of 90 days. Thus,

Total net payment days	90
Less days remaining in May (5/31–5/16)	15
	75
Less days in June	30
	45
Less days in July	31
Net payment date	August 14

---

[7]Since net 30 is implied but not stated in extra dating, the net payment date may also be defined as 20 days after expiration of the 70-day cash discount period.

Alternate Solution:

Since extra dating is essentially a variation of ordinary dating, the merchant is allowed 20 days after the expiration of the cash discount date (7/25) in which to make full payment. Therefore, a shorter way in which to determine the net payment date is as follows:

Days remaining in net payment period (30 − 10)	20
Less days remaining in July (7/31−7/25)	6
Net payment date	August 14

▪ Application Exercise

1. An invoice dated 3/16 carried terms of 3/10−60x. Find
   a. The cash discount date.
   b. The net payment date.

2. What is the cash discount date and net payment date for an invoice dated August 12 with terms of 3/10−30x?

3. Determine the cash discount date and the net payment date for an invoice dated 5/16 with terms of 3/10−60x.

4. An invoice is dated 6/28 with terms of 3/10−40x. Find the cash discount date and the net payment date.

5. Terms of the sale are 6/15−90x. The invoice is dated April 18. What is the cash discount date and the net payment date?

15.3

Terms of the Sale: Merchandise Discounts

Generally speaking, a merchandise discount may be defined as a percentage reduction in the vendor's quoted, or gross, wholesale price. The function of a merchandise discount is to reduce the cost of merchandise and thereby increase the gross margin dollars.

Discounts do not automatically accrue to the merchant; they are offered by the vendor in return for the merchant's ability and willingness to perform some service for that vendor. In this sense, all discounts must be earned by the merchant, and it is these services sought by the vendor that underlie the concept of all merchandise discounts. The following are the most prevalent reasons why the merchant may be offered discounts:

1. To induce the merchant to pay the invoice prior to the normal due date.

2. To encourage the merchant to make an early purchase decision.

3. To persuade the merchant to purchase larger quantities of goods than would be normally expected.

4. To prompt the merchant to carry and sell a greater amount of specific vendor's goods.

While discount practices and schedules vary greatly between producers, vendors, and merchandise classifications, there are only three basic types of discounts with which the merchant is generally concerned. These are the cash discount, which includes cash discount loading and anticipation; the quantity discount; and trade discounts. It is now appropriate that we integrate these concepts into our previous study of dating, so as to complete our understanding of the structural component of time as it affects the terms of the sale and ultimately the true cost of the merchant's inventory.

Cash Discounts

The history of the cash discount dates back many years to when vendors would allow merchants a percentage reduction in the billed cost of the merchandise if the invoice was paid promptly. Thus, the term *cash discount* evolved from the payment of the vendor's invoice within a specific time frame and, as a result, has no direct relation to interest rates or their degree of fluctuation.[8]

Originally, the cash discount that the merchant was able to achieve was a product of individual negotiation between buyer and seller, each transaction resulting in its own unique terms of the sale. Gradually, over a period of many years of haggling between the merchant and the vendor, the amount of the discount and the time allowed for its deduction stabilized and became relatively standard throughout the various trades and industries. Thus, custom has established the prevailing rates of cash discount and the time frames to which they relate. As a result, and this is the major point to be made, the vendor is well aware of prevailing market rates and simply figures the discount into the merchant's cost of the goods and the quoted wholesale price. It naturally follows that if the cash discount is not taken advantage of, the merchant pays a penalty; and, when the discount is deducted from the billed cost, the vendor is only returning to the merchant the extra dollars built into the cost for the very purpose of returning them to the merchant.

---

[8]The one exception to this is the anticipation discount, which does relate to the prime interest rate.

Functions of the Cash Discount

Cash discounts as a profit cushion

Recall from our study of gross margin in Chapter 8 that the full use of the cash discount concept is an approach to decreasing the total cost of merchandise sold with no corresponding decrease in net sales. Because the markon is calculated on the billed cost of the merchandise rather than its net cost (billed cost less cash discount), a natural profit cushion is built into the merchant's price structure. For example, assume that an item planned to retail at $8 cost $4 with a 4% cash discount. The markon percentage, normally computed from billed cost, would be

$$\frac{\$8 - \$4}{\$8} = 50\%$$

However, the actual markon, assuming that the cash discount has been taken, is as follows:

Net cost of merchandise = $4 × 4% = $.16
$4 − $.16 = $3.84

$$\text{Markon \%} = \frac{\$8 - \$3.84}{\$8} = 52\%$$

Notice that while the cash discount represents 4% of the cost of the merchandise ($.16 ÷ $4), it represents only 2% of net sales ($.16 ÷ $8); nevertheless, considering that the profit derived from merchandising operations is generally less than 5%, 2% may well turn the merchant's loss into a small operating profit.

This obviously answers the question as to why the merchant should not deduct the cash discount prior to the calculation of the markon. However, a more basic concept underlies why this should not be done, and that goes back to the original reason for taking the cash discount. The cash discount is an incentive to encourage the merchant to pay the invoice promptly, and thus, in this sense, it must be "earned." If the merchant fails to pay the bill within a specific period of time, the discount is forfeited, and the gross amount (billed cost) stands as the cost of the merchandise. In other words, the discount does not belong to the merchant until the invoice is paid within a specified period of time. Because the selling department has no capital of its own and does not manage the store's money, the cash discount is not really a reduction in the cost of merchandise but a contribution to corporate profits resulting from management's provision of the necessary funds to pay for the merchant's immediate obligations.[9] Our study of

---

[9]This concept is literally true in the operation of a large retail corporation and is still theoretically true in a small store, even a sole proprietorship.

gross margin and the retail method stand in support of this position; it will be remembered that the dollar amount of the cash discount did not reduce the cost of the merchandise but was credited to the "gross cost of merchandise sold" under the heading, "earned cash discounts."

Significance of the cash discount: annual interest rate

The concept of the cash discount is not to be taken lightly by the merchant. While a 2% discount may appear insignificant, especially when translated into dollars (2% of $100 is "only" $2), its tremendous impact upon merchandising profitability deserves further exploration. Consider a 2% discount within the context of 2/10/net 30, which states that the merchant may deduct 2% if the invoice is paid within 10 days of the date of the invoice and the total amount is due within 30 days. By paying the invoice 20 days early, the merchant, in effect, is lending the vendor the billed amount of the invoice for 20 days and then deducting 2% as interest on the "loan."

The question often arises as to whether it is advisable for the merchant to tie up relatively large amounts of capital in return for what may be perceived as an insignificant amount of interest. The answer becomes obvious when the terms of the sale are translated into their equivalent annual rates of interest. If the terms of the sale are 2/10/net 30 and the invoice is paid on the cash discount date, the merchant receives a 2% discount for a payment that is actually 20 days early (net 30 minus 10 days). Thus, the merchant receives 2% interest for 20 days, or 0.1% (one-tenth of 1%) per day (2% ÷ 20 days). On an annual basis, this equates to 36%, or 0.1% × 360 days.[10] This concept may be stated, quantitatively, as follows:

Annual interest rate =

$$\frac{360 \text{ days}}{\text{Net payment date} - \text{Cash discount date}} \times \text{Cash discount \%}$$

Accordingly, the annual interest rate for terms of 2/10/net 30 may be derived from the previous formula:

$$\frac{360 \text{ (Days)}}{20 \text{ (Days)}} = 18 \text{ (20-day periods)} \times 2\% = 36\%$$

When one considers terms of 8/10/net 30, not uncommon in the apparel industry, the annual rate of interest is an unbelievable 144%. It becomes clear, then, that the merchant should always take advantage of the cash discount, even if it means borrowing the necessary funds at the prevailing rates of interest. Consider some of the trades that have traditionally offered a relatively standard discount percentage and that percentage as it translates into the annual interest rate; assume that

---

[10]The number of days used for computing interest is based on the business year, or 360 days.

the invoice is paid 20 days early, as in 2/10/net 30. Thus, the annual rate is the product of 360 days divided by 20 days times the cash discount.

	Approximate Discount	Annual Rate
Cosmetics	1%	18%
Home furnishings	2%	36%
Handbags	3%	54%
Gloves	6%	108%
Millinery	7%	126%
Women's apparel	8%	144%

▪ Application Exercise

Using the formula for the annual interest rate, calculate the annual interest rates as derived from the following terms of the sale. (A reminder: The number of days that the annual rate is predicated upon is derived by subtracting the number of days in the cash discount period from the total number of days in the net payment period. Thus, 2/10/net 30 equates to 20 days, or 30 days less 10 days; 3/12/net 60 allows for 48 days, or 60 days minus 12 days, etc.)

  a. 3/15/net 30
  b. 4/10/net 30
  c. 8/12/net 30
  d. 2/10/net 60
  e. 2/30/net 60
  f. 3/10/net 120

The Cash Discount Applied to the Concept of Dating

Once the concept of dating has been mastered, the calculation of the actual cash discount and its effect upon the billed cost is a relatively simple matter. It needs little explanation, other than to say that the cash discount represents a percentage reduction in the dollar value of the vendor's invoice, if that invoice is paid within a specific period of time. However, its simplicity of calculation does not preclude the fact that the cash discount is but one type of discount among other forms of discounts and thus must be discussed within that context. Also, the cash discount has ramifications in discount loading and anticipation, concepts to be discussed shortly.

▪ Study Problem

Given: A buyer received an invoice dated 9/6 in the amount of $2,000. The terms of the sale were 3/15/net 30.

Find:

1. The last day to take the cash discount.
2. The amount of the cash discount.
3. The dollar amount to be remitted to the vendor if the cash discount is obtained.
4. The last day to pay the invoice.
5. The amount to be paid.

Solution:

1. The last day to take the cash discount is 9/21 (9/6 + 15 days).
2. The amount of the discount is $60 ($2,000 × 3%).
3. The dollar amount to be remitted to the vendor if the cash discount is obtained is $1,940 ($2,000 − $60).
4. The last day to pay the invoice is 10/6.
5. The billed cost, $2,000, is due (the discount is lost).

▪ Application Exercise

1. Given the following information, determine (a) the dollar amount of the cash discount, (b) the amount to be paid to the vendor if the cash discount is obtained, and (c) the cash discount date.

Date of the invoice	6/15
Amount of the invoice	$3,800
Terms of the sale	3/10/net 30

2. A merchant purchased 200 sweaters at a total cost of $4,000. The merchandise was shipped on 8/14 and received in the store on 8/17. The invoice arrived on 8/18, dated 8/15 with terms of 4/15/E.O.M. Assuming that the cash discount will be taken, on what date must the invoice be paid and in what amount?

3. Given:
   An invoice in the amount of $3,240.
   Date of the invoice 8/20.
   Terms of the sale 2/10–60x.
   Find:
   a. The amount to be paid if the cash discount is to be taken.
   b. The cash discount period.

4. A merchant received an invoice for $1,200, dated 5/25 with terms of 3/12/EOM. The bill was paid on 7/12. What amount should have been remitted to the vendor?

5. An invoice in the amount of $1,640 is dated 10/14, with terms of 2/12/EOM– R.O.G. The merchandise was shipped on 10/15 and received by the merchant on 11/5. When should the merchant pay the bill, and what should the amount of the remittance be?

Cash Discount Loading

Cash discount loading is the practice established by top management of intentionally increasing the billed cost of the invoice to allow a theoretical greater percentage of cash discount. In other words, the vendor will agree to a higher percentage of cash discount if the merchant will consent to a correspondingly higher billed-cost price. Thus, the billed-cost price is increased in proportion to the inflated cash discount; the net amount paid to the vendor remains the same.

The essential objective of cash discount loading is to establish a standardized cash discount percentage, which in turn permits the merchant to

1. Establish a larger reserve of cash discounts.

2. Seek a higher percentage of cash discount in the marketplace.

3. Facilitate the computation of the store's net merchandise indebtedness.

4. Analyze net cost prices quoted by several vendors on similar merchandise offerings. (As you will observe in the following study problem, it is not sufficient to just compare various quoted wholesale prices alone. The underlying structure of cash discounts must be taken into consideration, and the loaded discount, by equalizing the various cash discounts, facilitates that comparison.)

■ Study Problem

Given: A merchant is considering the purchase of 100 dozen women's blouses to be retailed at $30 each and subject to a loaded cash discount of 8%. The following quotations from three vendors, offering similar merchandise in terms of style and quality, have been received:

	Vendor A	Vendor B	Vendor C
Cost per dozen	$195	$198	$201
Terms of the sale	2/10/net 30	5/10/net 30	8/10/net 30

Find: The actual net cost, the loaded net cost, and the adjusted cost per dozen for each of the three vendors' quotations.

Solution:

$$\text{Loaded cost} = \frac{\text{Net cost}}{100\% - \text{Loaded discount \%}}$$

	Vendor A	Vendor B	Vendor C
Total billed cost	$19,500	$19,800	$20,100
Less cash discount	(2%) 390	(5%) 990	(8%) 1,608
Net cost	$19,110	$18,810	$18,492
Loaded discount reciprocal (100% − 8%)	92%	92%	92%
Loaded net cost	$20,772	$20,446	$20,100
Adjusted cost per dozen	$207.72	$204.46	$201.00

The lowest net cost is offered by vendor C, in spite of the fact that the quoted cost is the highest of the three vendors.

Another important concept to note is that the loaded net cost, when reduced by the loaded cash discount, equals the original net cost. Vendor A originally offered a net cost of $19,110, which is the same as the loaded net cost of $20,772 minus the loaded 8% cash discount: $20,772 × 92% = $19,110. Thus, we see that while the net amount actually paid to the vendor remains unchanged, that is, $19,110, the merchant records the net cost as $20,772 to reflect the loaded 8% cash discount. Notice the relationship between the two "net" costs:

$$\frac{\$20,772 - \$19,110}{\$20,772} = \frac{\$1,662}{\$20,772} = 8\%$$

The practice of cash discount loading, besides increasing the book cost of the inventory, also affects the merchant's markon. For instance, if the retail price had been predetermined on the basis of customer demand, the higher loaded cost would obviously reduce the percentage of markon. On the other hand, if the retail price is arbitrarily determined by applying a fixed markon percentage to the billed cost, the higher loaded cost would result in a higher retail price, with its attendant effect upon the salability of the merchandise.

▪ Application Exercise

1. A vendor quotes the price of a handbag at $40, with terms of 3/10/net 30. However, the merchant is seeking a cash discount of 8%. What will the net cost of the handbag be when loaded for the 8% cash discount? Prove your answer.

2. A merchant has placed a $500 order with a vendor whose terms of sale were 3/15/net 30. The vendor is asked to load the invoice so as to reflect a 7% cash discount. What is the loaded net cost?

3. A cosmetics buyer is contemplating placing an $8,300 order with a vendor whose established terms are 4/10/net 30. Under pressure from the merchandise manager, the buyer requests terms of 9/10/net 30 and suggests that the invoice be loaded accordingly. What is the loaded net cost that the buyer will be expected to pay?

4. As an assistant buyer, you are asked to evaluate similar items of merchandise from two different vendors, in terms of true, or actual, net cost and loaded net cost with an arbitrary 6% cash discount. Given the following data, with which vendor would you suggest that your buyer place an order and why?

	Vendor A	Vendor B
Cost per item	$123	$132
Terms of the sale	4/10/net 30	6/10/net 30

5. From the following three vendors, each offering similar types of merchandise, select the best price based upon an arbitrary 7% loaded cash discount.

	Vendor A	Vendor B	Vendor C
Quoted wholesale price	$308.50	$297.20	$310.80
Terms of the sale	4/10/net 30	2/10/net 30	6/10/net 30

Anticipation

Anticipation is an extra discount that, when permitted or requested by the vendor, is usually determined by the prevailing prime rate of interest. Although seldom used in periods of high inflation and tight money, anticipation represents an additional cash discount taken by the merchant for the payment of an invoice prior to the end of the cash discount period. Essentially, an anticipation discount serves two purposes:

1. To further reduce the net cost of the merchant's inventory.

2. To provide a ready source of funds for a vendor hard-pressed for cash. In this sense, the merchant regards the early payment of the invoice as a "loan" to the vendor and anticipation as the "interest" earned on that loan.

While not all vendors permit an additional anticipation discount, alert merchants, if allowed, deduct it, unless a notification on the vendor's invoice expressly forbids it. The dollar amount of the anticipation discount is based upon the number of days remaining between the actual date that the invoice is paid and the last day of the cash discount period. Therefore, the amount of anticipation is deducted from the net amount of the invoice, that is, after the cash discount has been deducted. In effect, anticipation rewards the merchant for paying the discounted invoice prior to the expiration of the cash discount period. The merchant has fulfilled the vendor's requirements and taken the cash discount at some time prior to the cash discount date. Thus, the merchant obtains the extra discount (anticipation), based upon the net amount due the vendor at that point within the cash discount period, plus an additional "bonus," predicated upon the number of days remaining within that cash discount period.

For purposes of illustration, consider 12% as the annual prime interest rate. This would be equivalent to 1% per month, which when applied to the net invoice cost ("net" of cash discounts) and multiplied by the remaining days in the cash discount period (expressed as a percentage of 360 days) would finally result in the amount of anticipation allowed. The following formula more precisely defines the concept of anticipation:

$$\text{Anticipation} = \text{Net cost} \times \text{Prime rate} \times \frac{\text{Unused discount days}}{360}$$

▪ Study Problem

Given:

Billed cost of the invoice	$1,000
Date of the invoice	6/8
Terms of the sale	5/10/net 30, anticipation allowed
Prime rate	12%
Invoice paid	6/13

Find: The net amount paid to the vendor on 6/13.

Solution:

Net cost = $1,000 × 5% = $50
$1,000 − $50 = $950

The last day to take the cash discount would be 6/18 (6/8 + 10 days). Because the invoice was paid on 6/13, it was anticipated by 5 days (6/18 − 6/13), or 1.4% (5 ÷ 360) of the business year.

Anticipation = $950 × 12% = $114
= $114 × 1.4% = $1.60

Therefore:

Billed cost of the invoice		$1,000
Less cash discount	$50.00	
Anticipation	1.60	
Less total amount of discount		51.60
Net amount paid to vendor on 6/13		$948.40

▪ Application Exercise

1. Given:

Billed cost of the invoice	$1,000
Date of the invoice	6/10
Terms of the sale	5/30/net 60, anticipation allowed
Prime rate	12%
Invoice paid	6/20

Find the net amount paid to the vendor.

2. Given:

Billed cost of the invoice	$600
Date of the invoice	7/20
Terms of the sale	6/10–30x, anticipation allowed
Prime rate	6%
Invoice paid	8/14

Find the net amount paid to the vendor.

3. An invoice in the amount of $850 dated 3/6 carries terms of 8/20/E.O.M., anticipation allowed. The prime rate is established at 9%, and the invoice is paid on 3/10. What is the amount of remittance to the vendor?

4. An invoice for $7,845 dated 7/25 is received. The terms are 6/10/E.O.M., with anticipation allowed. The prime rate is 10%. If the invoice is paid on 8/10, how much should be remitted to the vendor?

5. A shipment of merchandise was received 8/25. It was preceded by an invoice in the amount of $3,745 dated 6/3, with terms of 8/12/E.O.M.–R.O.G., anticipation allowed. If the prime rate was 11.5% and the invoice was paid 9/15, how much was paid to the vendor?

Trade Discounts

Trade discounts, often referred to as *functional discounts,* are a reduction from the manufacturer's list price offered to both wholesalers and the retail merchant for the performance of certain marketing functions, such as storage, quantity purchases, and the dissemination of product information. Trade discounts are expressed as a percentage, or a series of percentages, off the manufacturer's quoted catalog prices. Thus, they are to be distinguished from all other forms of discounts, in that the trade discount is not a reduction in cost but a reduction in retail in order to determine cost. In effect, the trade discount attempts to dictate the merchant's initial markon, insofar as the selling price reflects the manufacturer's list, or suggested retail, price. This type of discount is rarely if ever found in the apparel trades; however, it is quite common among vendors of toys, cosmetics, photo equipment, hardware, auto accessories, and various classifications of vendor-marked merchandise.

Essentially, the function of the trade discount is to establish the merchant's billed cost, defined within this context as the net price. This being the case, the trade discount is always deducted prior to the cash discount. The date of payment has no effect upon the trade discount. The trade discount simply defines the cost value of the merchandise and thus is not earned in the sense that the cash discount is.

Besides establishing cost prices and attempting to influence the merchant's retail price, the trade discount also acts as a device to facilitate price changes. Because it is costly to publish and distribute new catalogs to reflect constantly changing prices, trade discounts are printed independently of the catalog and thus permit a change in cost simply by adding or subtracting discounts for a preexisting series of discounts. For example, given a trade discount of 30% − 10% − 5%, it is a relatively simple matter to increase its value by subtracting one or more discounts. Thus, the merchant may be notified of a price change at a minimum of cost, without the vendor incurring the expense of new catalog publication and distribution.

A trade discount may be quoted as a single discount off the list price or a series of discounts, often referred to as a chain discount. To determine the merchant's cost with a single discount is simply a case of multiplying the vendor's list price by the complement of the trade discount. However, where there is a series of discounts, each is treated as a percentage of the previous balance and not of the original price. The individual discounts in a series may not be added together so as to total a single discount because the sum of the discounts will always be greater than the single discount actually achieved.

▪ Study Problem

Given: A camera lists at $25 with trade discounts of 20% − 10% − 5%.

Find:

1. The net price of the camera (billed cost).
2. The single-discount equivalent.

Solution: Any one of the following three methods may be used to determine the net retail, or billed, cost price and the single-discount equivalent.
a. Direct method:

List price		$25.00
Less 20%	($25 × 20%)	5.00
First net		20.00
Less 10%	($20 × 10%)	2.00

Second net		18.00
Less 5%	($18 × 5%)	.90
1. Net price (billed cost)		$17.10

2. Single-discount equivalent $= \dfrac{\$25 - \$17.10}{\$25} = 31.6\%$

31.6% is the one discount equivalent to the chain discount of 20% − 10% − 5%. It not only represents the true value of the discount (as opposed to the sum of the discounts, that is, 20% + 10% + 5% = 35%), but also the merchant's initial markon. Another method of obtaining this single discount is as follows:

Retail = 100%

Then, 100% × 80% × 90% × 95% = 68.4%

and,

100% − 68.4% = 31.6%

Therefore, the billed cost price is

(100% − 31.6%) × $25 = $17.10

b. The cost complement method:

This method is essentially the same as that discussed in Chapter 3 as a means of converting retail to cost, using the cost complement of the markon. In this instance, we simply have a chain of markon complements that when multiplied by the retail price (manufacturer's list) result in the cost price. Thus,

Net retail price = $25 × 80% = $20 × 90% = $18 × 95% = $17.10

The single-discount equivalent $= \dfrac{\$25 - \$17.10}{\$25} = 31.6\%$

c. The "on" percentage method:

The "on" percentage represents the complement of the single-discount equivalent, or it may be calculated by multiplying the complements of the individual trade discounts together. The resulting percentage will then serve to reduce the list (retail) price to the net price, or the merchant's billed cost. Thus,

80% × 90% × 95% = 68.4%

$25 × 68.4% = $17.10

The single-discount equivalent is therefore the product of:

100% − 68.4% = 31.6%

$\dfrac{\$25 - \$17.10}{\$25} = 31.6\%$

∎ Application Exercise

1. Given 6 dozen watches listing at $50 each and billed at a trade discount of 35% − 10% − 5%, find
   a. The net price of the watches.
   b. The single-discount equivalent.

2. A manufacturer offers terms of 20% − 8% − 4% on an automobile tire that lists at $50. Find
   a. The merchant's billed cost.
   b. The merchant's initial markon.

3. A bottle of perfume is offered with a list price of $40 and a trade discount of 40% − 12% − 6%. Determine
   a. The "on" percentage.
   b. The merchant's net price.
   c. The percentage of initial markon.

4. A buyer purchased 8 dozen batteries that listed at $1.50 per dozen with a trade discount of 35% − 20% − 12%. When the invoice arrived, it was dated 6/8 with terms of 2/12/net 30. Find
   a. The buyer's percentage of initial markon.
   b. The amount remitted to the vendor, assuming that the invoice was paid on or before 6/20.

5. A quantity of watches was purchased by the owner of an independent drug store. The invoice was billed at $830 less a trade discount of 23% − 18% − 11% − 7%. Terms of the sale on the invoice dated 8/25 were 3/10/E.O.M. Find
   a. The cash discount date.
   b. The percentage of initial markon.
   c. The amount remitted to the vendor.

Quantity Discounts

A *quantity discount* is a percentage reduction in the cost of merchandise based upon the amount of the purchase. The essential concept is that the larger the quantity purchased, the lower the cost is likely to be. The economic justification for this assumption is that large orders tend to result in lower unit operating costs for the vendor. To the extent that operating costs are reduced, the merchant may be offered a quantity discount, but the magnitude of that discount is limited, by law,[11] to no more than the provable savings incurred by the vendor.

---

[11]The amount of the discount must be justified by a reduction in the vendor's cost associated with the handling of a larger quantity of merchandise—i.e., the expense incurred by the cost of manufacture, sale, and delivery—if the merchant is to avoid prosecution under the Robinson-Patman Act of 1936.

While the concept of quantity discounts is relatively simple to comprehend, a number of points need to be emphasized:

1. Quantity discounts take two essential forms:
   a. Direct reductions in the cost of merchandise based upon the amount purchased.
   b. "Free" merchandise—for example, one free item with the purchase of a specified number of items. The effect is to reduce the price per unit, based upon the amount of the purchase; thus, free merchandise qualifies as a quantity discount.

2. There are two classifications of quantity discounts in which the merchant's cost is directly reduced:
   a. Noncumulative quantity discounts, based upon the amount of goods purchased at a single time, are offered to encourage the merchant to increase the size of the order.
   b. Cumulative quantity discounts apply to several orders placed with the vendor over an extended period of time, normally one year. This type of quantity discount will increase as the accumulated orders increase. Cumulative quantity discounts, also known as patronage discounts, encourage return trade by reducing the cost of merchandise on subsequent orders.

3. Because quantity discounts do not necessarily affect the retail value of the merchant's inventory, they should always be recorded as reductions of purchases at cost. Should the merchant wish to make a downward revision of the retail price as a result of quantity discounts, the proper technique is to employ a markup cancellation.

4. In the event that quantity discounts are involved with cash and trade discounts, the proper mathematical procedure for arriving at the merchant's net cost is as follows:

Gross amount of the order
Less quantity discount (first discount)
Result
Less trade discount (second discount)
Result
Less cash discount (third discount)
Net cost of the order

▪ Application Exercise

1. A merchant is offered a quantity discount of 10% if 500 or more $1 screwdrivers are ordered. The trade discount is 20% − 10% − 5%, with terms of

2/10/net 30. Assuming that 500 screwdrivers are purchased and that the invoice is paid within the cash discount period, what is the net cost of the screwdrivers?

2. A trade discount was offered on a single toaster of 25% − 18% − 8%, with terms of 3/12/E.O.M. Also, a quantity discount of 4% was offered if the merchant purchased 12 or more units. Assuming that the terms of the sale were met, what would the net cost of a dozen toasters be if a single unit was quoted at $14.80?

3. Given:

Trade discount	15% − 15% − 6%
Terms of the sale	4/12/E.O.M.
Quantity discount	5%, on 15 or more items
Quoted wholesale cost per item	$8.64

What was the amount of remittance to the vendor, assuming that the merchant purchased twenty-one items and paid the invoice dated 6/26 on 8/18?

4. A merchant purchased fourteen blenders quoted at $23.85, with a trade discount of 15% − 12% − 5%. Terms of the sale were 5/15/net 30, and a quantity discount of 6% was available on orders of twelve or more units. The invoice dated 6/5 was paid on 6/20. Find:
   a. The net amount paid to the vendor.
   b. The amount of initial markon achieved by the merchant (assuming that the list price remains intact).

5. A men's furnishings buyer was offered a dozen "free" pairs of athletic socks if an order for 12 dozen was placed with the manufacturer. If the list price was $4.50 per unit with trade discounts of 30% − 15% − 10%, what was the effective percentage of quantity discount?

15.4

Transportation Arrangements

In the introductory portion of this chapter, we noted that the merchant's perception, or understanding, of the quoted market price can be altered by the underlying structures of time and convenience. We have seen, up to this point, that time not only defines when the invoice is due but also the amount of the merchant's legal indebtedness to the vendor. Thus, time, in effect, is the catalyst that transforms the quoted wholesale price into the reality of the vendor's actual price, obviously two different concepts. There is, however, yet another factor that impinges upon the merchant's true cost of the merchandise, and that is the manner and location in which the title to the purchase transfers from the vendor to the merchant. It is in this sense that we speak of convenience as a structural element of the cost price; for a New York merchant to take possession of merchandise in New York is far more convenient than possession acquired in, say, Chicago. When the retail merchant acquires title to the goods purchased at any point beyond the store's receiving docks, two factors of inconvenience arise:

1. The cost of transportation.
2. The filing of a claim, in the event of damage, loss, or nondelivery of the merchandise.

Thus, insofar as these two concepts are included in the terms of the sale, not only has the merchant's cost level been altered by the addition of transportation charges (freight inward),[12] but the structure of that cost has been materially modified by the added inconvenience of claim processing. We therefore need to examine some of the more common transportation arrangements as they pertain to the terms of the sale.

The origin of the most common shipping terms is the concept of *free on board,* simply designed as F.O.B., which has to do with the point up to which the vendor will pay the freight costs and that geographical location where title to the goods transfers from the merchant to the vendor. Thus, F.O.B. is always followed by a point of destination and the terms of the transportation arrangements. In negotiating these cost factors with the vendor, the merchant must give consideration to the following four issues:

1. Does the merchant or the vendor ultimately bear the cost of transportation?
2. Who initially will pay the freight cost?
3. At what geographic point will the title change hand?
4. Who has title liability and is thus responsible for the filing of any claims?

As Figure 15.1 indicates, the party who initially pays the transportation cost is not necessarily the one with that ultimate responsibility. For example, either the vendor or the merchant, whoever can obtain the best terms or ship most efficiently, may initially pay the freight cost and then charge the other party back, by means of a deduction from or an addition to the purchase invoice.

Probably of greater consideration than who pays the freight charges is the question of where (at what geographic point) does the title to the goods transfer. If this exchange should occur at the vendor's point of shipment (F.O.B. factory), the merchant legally owns the goods at that location and is thus responsible not only for freight charges but also for the cost of any insurance in excess of the carrier's liability. Also, and even more important, the merchant is now responsible

---

[12]It has been estimated that freight charges increase the average cost of merchandise in a department store by 1.5% to 2%. In some departments, such as housewares, where bulk and weight are high relative to price, this 2% figure may be extremely conservative.

Transportation Terms	Title Transfers at	Pays Freight	Bears Freight	Owns Good in Transit	Files Claim
F.O.B. factory freight collect	F	M	M	M	M
F.O.B. factory, freight prepaid	F	V	V	M	M
F.O.B. factory, freight prepaid and charged back	F	V	M*	M	M
F.O.B. store, freight collect	S	M	M	V	V
F.O.B. store, freight prepaid	S	V	V	V	V
F.O.B. store, freight collect and allowed	S	M	V†	V	V

Figure 15.1 The effects of transportation arrangements on merchant and vendor

Key: S = Store; F = Factory; M = Merchant; V = Vendor.
*Freight charges are added to the invoice.
†Freight charges are deducted from the amount of the invoice.

for filing and collecting on claims against the carrier for merchandise lost or damaged in transit. Not only can this be a costly and time-consuming process, but it also negatively impacts on the merchant's inventory assortment.

▪ Solutions to the Application Exercises

Ordinary Dating, or Date of the Invoice (D.O.I.) (p. 535)

1.	a.	Date of the invoice	October	13
		Days to take discounts		10
		Cash discount date	October	23
	b.	Date of invoice	October	13
		Net terms		30
				43
		Less days in October		31
		Net payment date	November	12
3.		Date of invoice	March	5
		Days to take discount		18
		Cash discount date	March	23

Date of invoice	March	5
Net terms		30
		35
Less days in March		31
Net payment date	April	4
5. Date of invoice	September	3
Days to take discount		20
Last date to take cash discount	September	23
Date of invoice	September	3
Net terms		30
		33
Less days in September		30
Final date for payment of invoice	October	3

End-of-the-Month (E.O.M.) Dating (p. 537)

1. a. End-of-the-month	November	30
Ten days		10
		40
Less days in November		30
Cash discount date	December	10
b. End-of-the-month	November	30
Thirty days		30
		60
Less days in November		30
Net payment date	December	30
3. End-of-the-month	March	31
Thirty days		30
		61
Less days in March		31
Net payment date	April	30
5. End-of-the-month	May	31
Sixteen days		16
		47
Less days in May		31
Cash discount date	June	16

Receipt of Goods (R.O.G.) Dating (p. 539)

1. Date of receipt	April	3
Ten days		10
Cash discount date	April	13
3. E.O.M. date	May	31
Fifteen days		15
		46
Less days in May		31
Cash discount date	June	15
5. E.O.M. date	August	31
Twelve days		12
		43
Less days in August		31
Cash discount date	September	12
E.O.M. date	August	31
Thirty days		30
		61
Less days in August		31
Net payment date	September	30

Extra Dating (p. 543)

1. a. Total discount days		70
Less discount days in March (3/31–3/16)		15
		55
Less days in April		30
Cash discount date	May	25
b. Total net payment days		20
Less days remaining in May (5/31–5/25)		6
Net payment date	June	14
3. Total discount days		70
Less discount days in May (5/31–5/16)		15
		55
Less days in June		30
Cash discount date	July	25

Total net payment days		20
Less days in July (7/31–7/25)		6
Net payment date	August	14

5. Total discount days 105

Less discount days in April (4/30–4/18)		12
		93
Less days in May		31
		62
Less days in June		30
		32
Less days in July		31
Cash discount date	August	1
Total net payment days		15
Days in August		1
Net payment date	August	16

Significance of the Cash Discount: Annual Interest Rate (p. 547)

1. a. $\dfrac{360}{15} = 24 \times 3\% = 72\%$

   b. $\dfrac{360}{20} = 18 \times 4\% = 72\%$

   c. $\dfrac{360}{18} = 20 \times 8\% = 160\%$

   d. $\dfrac{360}{50} = 7.2 \times 2\% = 14.4\%$

   e. $\dfrac{360}{30} = 12 \times 2\% = 24\%$

   f. $\dfrac{360}{110} = 3.3 \times 3\% = 9.9\%$

The Cash Discount Applied to the Concept of Dating (p. 548)

1. a. $\$3,800 \times 3\% = \$114$

   b. $\$3,800 - \$114 = \$3,686$

   c. $6/15 + 10 \text{ days} = 6/25$

3. a. The amount to be paid if the cash discount is to be taken:

$3,240 × 2% = $64.80

$3,240 − $64.80 = $3,175.20

  b. The cash discount period runs from 8/20 through 10/29.

Total cash discount days (60 + 10)		70
Less days remaining in August (8/31–8/20)		11
		59
Less days in September		30
Cash discount date	October	29

5. Base date is date of receipt, 11/5.

E.O.M. is	November	30
Twelve days		12
		42
Less days in November		30
Bill should be paid by	December	12

The amount of remittance should be:

$1,640 × 2% = $32.80

$1,640 − $32.80 = $1,607.20

Cash Discount Loading (p. 550)

1. Net cost = $40 × 3% = $1.20

$40 − $1.20 = $38.80

Loaded net cost = $38.80 ÷ 92% = $42.17

Proof:

$42.17 × 8% = $3.37

$42.17 − $3.37 = $38.80

3. Net cost = $8,300 × 4% = $332

$8,300 − $332 = $7,968

Loaded net cost = $7,968 ÷ 91% = $8,756

	Vendor A	*Vendor B*	*Vendor C*
5. Quoted wholesale price	$308.50	$297.20	$310.80
Less cash discount	12.34	5.94	18.65
Net cost	$296.16	$291.26	$292.15
100% – 7%	93%	93%	93%
Loaded net cost	$318.45	$313.18	$314.14

Vendor B offers the best price.

Anticipation (p. 553)

1. Net cost = $1,000 × 95% = $950

   Last day to take cash discount:

Date of invoice	June	10
Days to take discount		30
		40
Less days in June		30
Cash discount date	July	10

   Dollar amount of anticipation: When the invoice was paid on 6/20, it was anticipated by 20 days (10 days in June + 10 days in July) or 5.6% (20 ÷ 360) of the business year. Thus:

   Anticipation = $950 × 12% = $114
   $114 × 5.6% = $6.38

   Net amount paid to vendor:

Billed cost		$1,000
Less cash discount	$50	
Anticipation	6.38	
Less total amount of discount		56.38
Net amount paid to vendor		$943.62

3. The net amount of the invoice = $850 − $68 = $782

   Last day to take discount:

E.O.M.	March	31
Twenty days		20
		51
Less days in March		31
Cash discount date	April	20

Dollar amount of anticipation:

Number of days anticipated = 21 (March) + 20 (April) = 41

41 ÷ 360 = 11.4% of business year

Anticipation = $782 × 9% = $70.38

$$= \$70.38 \times 11.4\% = \$8.02$$

Net amount paid = $850 − ($68 + $8.02) = $773.98

5. Net amount of the invoice = $3,745 × 92% = $3,445.40

Last day to take the cash discount (since the terms are R.O.G., the base date is 8/25):

E.O.M. date	September	30
Twelve days		12
Cash discount date	October	12

Dollar amount of anticipation:

Number of days anticipated = 15 (September) + 12 (October) = 27

27 ÷ 360 = 7.5% of the business year

Anticipation = $3,445.40 × 11.5% = $396.22

$$= \$396.22 \quad \times \quad 7.5\% = \$29.72$$

Amount paid to vendor = $3,745 − ($299.60 + $29.72) = $3,415.68

Trade Discounts (p. 556)

1. Total list = 6 × 12 × $50 = $3,600

   a. Net price = $3,600 × (65% × 90% × 95%)

   $$= \$3,600 \times 55.6\%$$

   $$= \$2,001.60^{13}$$

   b. Single-discount equivalent $= \dfrac{\$3,600 - \$2,001.60}{\$3,600} = \dfrac{\$1,598.40}{\$3,600} = 44.4\%$

   or,

   65% × 90% × 95% = 55.6%

   100% − 55.6% = 44.4%

---

[13]The direct, or complement, method will yield an answer of $2,000.70. The discrepancy is due to rounding the on-percentage figure from .55575 to .556.

3. a. "On" percentage = 60% × 88% × 94% = 49.6%

   b. Net price = $40 × 49.6% = $19.84

   c. Markon % = 100% − 49.6% = 50.4%

   or,

   $$\frac{\$40 - \$19.84}{\$40} = 50.4\%$$

5. a. Cash discount date = 8/25 − 9/1 − 9/30 − 9/10

   Net price = $830 × (77% × 82% × 89% × 93%)

   = $830 × 52.3%

   = $434.09

   b. Markon% = $\dfrac{\$830 - \$434.09}{\$830} = \dfrac{\$395.91}{\$830} = 47.7\%$

   c. Amount remitted = $434.09 × 97% = $421.07

Quantity Discounts (p. 557)

1. 500 × $1 = $500 × 90% = $450

   $450 × (80% × 90% × 95%) = $307.80

   Net cost = $307.80 × 98% = $301.64

3. 21 × $8.64 = $181.44 × 95% = $172.37

   $172.37 × (85% × 85% × 94%) = $117.07

   Cash discount disallowed, because cash discount period was over as of 8/12. Therefore, the amount of remittance was $117.07.

5. $4.50 × 144 = $648

   $648 × (70% × 85% × 90%) = $347

   12 dozen unit cost = $347 ÷ 144 = $2.41 (each)

   13 dozen unit cost = $347 ÷ 156 = $2.22 (each)

   Quantity discount = $\dfrac{\$2.41 - \$2.22}{\$2.41} = \dfrac{\$.19}{\$2.41} = 7.9\%$

■ ━━━

Topics for Discussion and Review

1. Explain the underlying structure of the merchant's cost price. How does this structure influence the cost of the merchandise, gross margin, and operating profit?

2. Why is the concept of future dating so important to the retail merchant?

3. What is the most common type of dating? Describe how it works.

4. What is meant by the concept of E.O.M. dating? Explain how it works, especially when the invoice is dated on or after the 25th of the month.

5. Explain the concept of R.O.G. dating. What effect does it have on the merchant's payment schedule when combined with E.O.M. terms?

6. How would you explain the advantages and disadvantages of advanced dating? How does advanced dating tie in with the concept of extra dating?

7. Why do we say that all discounts must be earned? What must the merchant do to earn them?

8. Why has it been said that the merchant's failure to take advantage of the cash discount results in a penalty?

9. Explain the functions of the cash discount from the merchant's point of view.

10. Explain the significance of the cash discount to the retail merchant.

11. Explain, with specific illustrations, the concept of cash discount loading. What are its effects on the retail price and the merchant's profit structure?

12. Anticipation is an extra discount. What does this mean, and how is it calculated?

13. What makes the trade discount unique among the forms of discounts? What is the function of the trade discount?

14. Using the trade discount concept, describe three methods of arriving at the billed cost price.

15. Explain the concept of a quantity discount. How does it affect the retail price, and how does it relate to markup cancellations?

16. How do quantity discounts relate to trade discounts and cash discounts?

17. Explain how free merchandise qualifies as a quantity discount.

18. What is meant by the convenience factor as a structure underlying the merchant's cost of goods?

19. Explain the concept of F.O.B. What factors must be considered when negotiating transportation arrangements?

20. Explain the following transportation terms:
  a. F.O.B. factory, freight collect
  b. F.O.B. factory, freight prepaid
  c. F.O.B. factory, freight prepaid and charged back
  d. F.O.B. store, freight collect
  e. F.O.B. store, freight prepaid
  f. F.O.B. store, freight collect and allowed

21. Explain the concept of ordinary dating.

22. What is meant by extra dating?

23. Explain how you would translate a cash discount into its annual interest rate?

24. What is a single-discount equivalent?

25. Distinguish between immediate dating and future dating.

Index